MORE RECIPES WITH A JUG OF WINE

Other books by

MORRISON WOOD

WITH A JUG OF WINE—1949

FISHERMAN'S WHARF COOKBOOK—1955

More Recipes

With

A JUG OF WINE

By Morrison Wood

FARRAR, STRAUS & CUDAHY · NEW YORK

Library of Congress catalog card number 56-11636

Fourth Printing, January, 1960
Fifth Printing, February, 1961

The author acknowledges permission to reprint one recipe from each of the following books: *Cook at Home in Chinese,* by Henry Low (The Macmillan Co.); *The New Fannie Farmer Boston Cooking-School Cookbook,* edited by Wilma Lord Perkins (Little, Brown & Co.,); *Wonderful Ways to Cook,* by Edith Key Haines. Copyright 1937, 1951 by Edith Key Haines. Reprinted by permission of Rinehart & Co., Inc. The chapter on wines appeared in somewhat different form in *House & Garden,* copyright 1955, The Condé Nast Publications, Inc.

Published simultaneously in Canada by

Ambassador Books, Ltd., Toronto

Manufactured in the United States of America
American Book–Stratford Press, Inc., New York

To

BEATRICE

My Wife

Who has tolerated me through the
writing of three cookbooks (though
I'll never know how!), and who is
still an ardent champion of my culinary exploits and adventures

CONTENTS

FOREWORD

PROLOGUE

Once upon a TIME there was a CHAIRMAN of the Board by the name of Horatio.

The big SHOTS in his industrial EMPIRE called him "MR. A."

HIS beginnings were HUMBLE, and he never FORGOT them.

He CAME up the hard WAY; no pull, no BACKERS, no INFLUENCE.

He operated his BUSINESS on the same principles.

His tastes WERE simple.

WHENEVER the subject of FOOD was brought up, he LOUDLY proclaimed himself a "MEAT and potatoes GUY."

ACT I.

Due to UNFORESEEN circumstances, the OFFICE of President of Mr. A's ENTERPRISES became vacant.

There were two EAGER Beavers who aspired to THE job.

Mr. B.

AND Mr. C.

The less SAID about them the better.

They ARE only minor characters, ALBEIT smart.

INDIVIDUALLY and separately, they DECIDED to BUTTER up the BOSS by inviting him, AND his wife, to their HOMES for dinner.

ACT II.

MRS. B. whipped up a well-thought-out DINNER for Mr. and Mrs. A.

Warned by HER husband, she kept the DINNER simple.

TOMATO juice, out of a CAN, was served in the LIVING room.

The APPETIZER was chunks of CANNED fruit in a COMPOTE.

The soup course was CREAM of tomato—out of a CAN.

The entree was BROILED chicken, done to a TURN, savory and BROWN.

The ACCOMPANIMENTS were mashed potatoes, SMOOTH and creamy, and peas, WHICH had come out of THE freezer.

The salad WAS canned pear halves on LETTUCE, with a MAYONNAISE dressing.

The dessert was ice CREAM and cake. The first came FROM the drug store, and THE cake came from the NEIGHBORHOOD bakery.

BUT don't JUMP to conclusions!

The whole DINNER was delicious and PERFECTLY cooked.

Mr. A. BEAMED.

There had not been enough LEFT on his plate to FEED a dieting GNAT.

He MADE a mental note that Mr. B. was a PEARL of great PRICE.

The host AND hostess looked like the CAT who had swallowed the CANARY.

ACT III.

By a STRANGE coincidence, Mrs. C.'s dinner closely followed that OF Mrs. B.

She, TOO, had been WARNED.

But she was a SMART cookie.

TOMATO juice, out of a can, was SERVED in the living room.

It was DELICATELY spiked with vodka and LEA & Perrins.

After the second one, Mr. C.'s BON mots were getting BELLY laughs from Mrs. A.

The APPETIZER was chunks of CANNED fruits.

But chopped mint LEAVES, lemon JUICE, a touch of GIN, and MARASCHINO cherries had been ADDED.

THE soup came out of CANS too.

Tomato soup and PEA soup. But ADDED starters were cream, BOILED shrimps, and a jigger of LIGHT rum.

By the time the ENTREE was served, Mrs. A.'s taste BUDS were beginning to do NIP-ups!

BROILED chicken was the ENTREE. But what BROILED chicken!

It would have made EVEN a life-loving FOWL lay its HEAD on the chopping BLOCK, just to be EATEN.

Rubbed WITH garlic, the chicken was basted, WHILE broiling, with a white WINE sauce.

The accompaniments were MASHED potatoes, and PEAS from the FREEZER.

BUT the potatoes had been FLAVORED with rosemary butter, and BROILED mushrooms had been MIXED with the peas.

The dessert was ICE cream. It came from the DRUG store.

But CANNED Bing cherries had been MARINATED in brandy, COINTREAU, and kirsch, then SET alight, and ladled OVER the ice cream.

Mrs. A.'s spoon was at the READY even before she was SERVED.

When dinner was over, Mr. A. WANTED to get to the card table.

But Mrs. A. LINGERED.

She raved over DINNER, and wanted RECIPES.

Mr. A. thought THAT was a waste OF time.

His PRIVATE opinion was that the C.'s had LOUSED up a perfectly good DINNER.

EPILOGUE

The following WEEK the trade papers ANNOUNCED in headlines:
"Mr. C. made President of ALGER Enterprises."

The MORAL?

There are a NUMBER.

For INSTANCE:

The Spirit of ADVENTURE is akin to the SPIRIT of '76.

BUT I like this ONE best:

To HELL with the Boss; CATER to his WIFE!

LOCUS POENITENTIAE

In the *Apologia* of my first cookbook, *With a Jug of Wine,* I wrote: "I might as well be brazen right at the start. I think this is a damn good cookbook."

Just as I was finishing the first draft of this book, over six years later, I received a letter from a man who had apparently recently bought *With a Jug of Wine.* I am reproducing it here in full, without comment.

Dear Mr. Wood:

I, also, might as well be brazen. You are completely correct. . . . *Jug of Wine* IS a damned good cookbook.

After a lifetime . . . well, nearly a lifetime, of eating "real good" midwestern food, such as boiled sirloin steaks, French-fried garden hose, etc., it has been with purest animal delight that we have eaten EVERY dish tried thus far from your damned good cookbook.

The strange part: we have been successful each and every time . . . absolutely NO failures. This is not the usual result with cookbooks.

If you write another damned good cookbook, put us on your list.

Until then, thank you very much for some real fine cooking and eating adventures!

With delighted regards,
John Boyle

Thank you very, very much, Mr. John Boyle.

Well, here I am, brazen again. I believe this is another damn good cookbook. Many of the recipes contained herein have appeared in my weekly syndicated newspaper column, "For Men Only!" Others have come from gourmet friends, and from inspired chefs across the country who labor lovingly at the altar of Gastronomy. I don't believe any of the recipes are beyond the average man or woman who cooks, either frequently or only occasionally. As always, I try to be specific in my directions and ingredients, and I try to keep the recipes as simple as possible. Sometimes they will take time and work, but, if I may coin a phrase, "Rome was not built in a day."

One of the most frequent exhortations to amateur chefs is to experiment. Some writers even go so far as to advise the neophyte to disregard specific directions right at the start, and to improvise. That's all very well for cooking enthusiasts who have a sound, basic knowledge of flavors, ingredients, and what goes well with what. But my advice to beginners is to follow new recipes exactly the first time you try them. Then, as more skill is acquired, as well as knowledge, experiment a little. Not enough to ruin a dish and have to throw it away, because that is waste. But occasionally add something here, or substitute something there, or try this and that combination, and presto! you come up with a delectable and unusual dish.

During the years I have happily been working with food, I have come across people who deplore the so-called gourmet cooking, with its use of wines and herbs and sauces. Actually, I have heard one man say that gourmets were the product of a decadent civilization!

Traditionally, we Americans are apt to look upon wine as a luxury. Yet the humblest European peasants (the thriftiest people in the world) use wine as matter-of-factly as we use butter or sugar. Of course, they use what they call the wine of the country, or *vin ordinaire,* which is very cheap. Very well, so can Americans use the wine of their country, which, with a few exceptions, equals or surpasses the ordinary wines of European countries.

Flavor is called the soul of food. It is flavor that makes all dishes, hot or cold, sweet or sour, enjoyable. And wine adds an indefinable flavor to a great many foods. As a matter of fact, wine and food are sweethearts!

Once again I would like to correct the erroneous impression that wine or liquor is employed in cooking for its alcoholic content. With the few exceptions where spirits are used as a last-minute flavoring, the alcohol contained in the bottled ingredients will have evaporated long before the dish is served. For instance, it is perfectly safe to serve fruits cooked or baked in wine to children, or to Aunt Mehitabel, president of the local W.C.T.U. What little alcohol there was will all be gone, but a heavenly flavor will have permeated an otherwise dull fruit. The same thing applies to meat or fish or game cooked with wine or spirits; or, for that matter, to a Soufflé Grand Marnier. If little Johnny, or teenaged Mary Lou are allowed to have a bit of that soufflé, the Grand Marnier flavor won't hurt them any more than would the customary few drops of vanilla extract—

which, by the way, contains a fairly large percentage of alcohol.

Spices, sauces, dressings, and other stimulants are used in culinary combinations of food not merely to impart their own flavor, but to excite our taste buds to a keener appreciation of the flavor of soups, fish, meat, poultry, game, vegetables, etc., in which they are present. The art of making memorable culinary combinations lies in producing a happy blending in which the elementary flavors are all lost and indistinguishable in a new union created by their combined effect upon the palate.

And now, as to gourmets.

Webster defines a gourmet as a "connoisseur [one competent to act as a critical judge] in eating and drinking."

Here's another definition that I like: "A gourmet is a gourmet because of his special qualities of taste and intelligence. He may sit down to a perfectly appointed table, with a butler to serve him dishes so delectable that their preparation requires the skill of a lifetime of practice; or he may seat his work-weary body at a rude table in a peasant hut and scoop up his nourishment from a blackened pot. In either case, if he realizes that the food set before him is not only meat for his bones, but also pleasure for his taste, and appreciates its subtle nuances of flavor, then he is a gourmet."

It has been said that the whole of nature is a conjugation of the verb to eat, in the active or the passive. The true gourmet realizes this truth instinctively, and takes advantage of the tremendous variety of food possibilities that nature offers, and in the pursuit of new combinations and more thrilling flavors he finds an exciting interest that adds zest to the other pleasures of living.

In these times we should all become gourmets, in the sense that we should try to make health-giving foods pleasing to the palate, with as little strain as possible upon the purse. It means that we should make sure that what we buy is appetizingly prepared, and it means that we should buy with intelligence and economy.

The great French gourmet, Brillat-Savarin, sums up the art of eating very succinctly. He wrote: "Gastronomy [the art of eating] is a science which sustains us from the cradle to the grave; which enhances the pleasures of love and the intimacy of friendship; which disarms hatred, renders business more easy, and offers us, in the short journey of life, the only recreation which, not followed by fatigue, makes us yet find relief from all others."

Amen!

There is one little matter I would like to bring to the attention of readers of this book. Frequently, throughout the recipes, I make mention of specific brand names, such as Ac'cent, Spice Island products (herbs and spices), Uncle Ben's Converted Rice, Old Monk products, etc. I name such names only because I have found them to be of great excellence, and I use them in my own preparation of food. I do not mean to imply that other products are not just as good. And, furthermore, the naming of brands is not in payment for supplies gratuitously received. In no sense of the word is this a "subsidized" cookbook. Thank God I am beholden to no firm, manufacturer, or trade association.

Some years ago, when I was handling a radio program in Chicago called the "Answer Man," a listener, who signed herself as a "Bride Living in Peoria, Illinois," wrote in to the program with a question.

"In your collection of verses do you have one that will inspire me to like cooking? I'm new and dumb at cooking—and I suppose that's why I hate it."

The Answer Man had a delightful reply. It was a gay little anonymous verse that went this way:

Serve a laugh with meat loaf,
Serve a smile with steak,
Serve a grin with gingerbread,
And chuckles with a cake.
Whistle with the waffles,
Sing a song with salad,
Hum a tune while kneading dough,
Don't you know a ballad?
Beat time with a rolling pin,
Tap dance while you fry,
There's kitchen fun for everyone
Who'll make it—why not try?

MORRISON WOOD

San Mateo
California

MORE RECIPES WITH A JUG OF WINE

(1) WINE

> God made Man, frail as a bubble
> God made Love, Love made Trouble
> God made the Vine; was it a sin
> That Man made Wine to drown Trouble in?
>
> Oliver Herford

Wine is a simple, natural, and delightful thing. As the Psalmist said, "it maketh glad the heart of man." And long before, Plato, the great Greek philosopher, wrote: "Nothing more excellent or valuable than wines was ever granted by the gods to man."

In this chapter I should like to tell you very simply about wine, how to select it, how to serve it, and how to enjoy it. And I'm going to talk about American wines, not only because they are excellent and enjoyable and reasonably priced, but because they avoid many of the complexities of European wines.

Getting acquainted with wine does not involve an extensive knowledge of viticulture and grapes, nor a strict adherence to the rituals of tasting and serving. Which wine goes best with what food is easily and quickly learned, and you can forget most of the dogmatic statements you have heard or read about. You can also dismiss, but quickly, all the snobbery and semantics with which a few so-called sophisticates and phony connoisseurs have surrounded the whole subject of buying, serving, and drinking of wine.

The two most important things to know about wine are the *classes* and *types* of wine. Virtually all wines fit into five classes: appetizer wines, red table wines, white table wines, sweet dessert wines, and sparkling wines.

APPETIZER WINES:

These are so-called because they are favored for before-meal or cocktail use, and in America largely consist of sherry and vermouth. They both range from dry (not in the sense of sour, but rather in the sense of the opposite of sweet), to semi-sweet.

Sherry is characterized by its "nutty" flavor, and ranges in color from pale to dark amber. It may be dry (so labeled), or (sometimes labeled "cocktail sherry"), medium, or sweet (sometimes labeled "cream sherry"). The alcoholic content of sherries is around 20 per cent. Sherry may or may not be served chilled.

Vermouth is wine flavored with herbs and other aromatic substances. There are two types of vermouth—dry (French type) and sweet (Italian type). Their alcoholic content runs between 15 per cent and 20 per cent. Vermouth, according to the taste of many, is at its best when served chilled, or "on the rocks."

RED TABLE WINES:

These are usually dry, and accompany main-course dishes. There are two types, Burgundy and claret, and they both rarely exceed an alcoholic content of 12 per cent. They should be served at room temperature, or slightly below. It is often a good idea to draw the cork from the bottle about one half hour before serving, to allow the wine a chance to breathe.

Burgundy-type table wines should be completely dry, full-bodied, rich in flavor and aroma, and deep red in color.

Claret-type table wines should be completely dry, light- or medium-bodied, with a fruity taste and aroma.

Rather a newcomer in America is a third type of red wine called Rosé. This is literally a rose-colored wine, with a delicate grape sweetness without being sweet. It is light-bodied, fragrant, and fruity, and goes pleasantly with any food with which wine can be drunk. It should be served chilled.

WHITE TABLE WINES:

These vary from extremely dry and rather tart to sweet and full-bodied, and their delicate flavor blends best with white meats, fowl, and seafood. Their colors range from pale straw to gold. They should always be served chilled. Their alcoholic content is the same as red table wines. There are three types of white table wines: sauterne, Rhine, and white Burgundy.

While true French sauternes are white wines on the sweet side only, in America there are three kinds of sauterne; dry, medium, and sweet. The latter may be labeled "Haute" or "Château" sauterne. Sweet sauternes go best with desserts.

German white table wines vary from sweet to dry. But in America, Rhine wines are thoroughly dry, rather tart, and light-bodied, and of pale gold color.

The American white Burgundy table wines are similar to the white Burgundy wines of France. They are delicate, straw-colored, and less tart than the Rhine wines, with a more fruity flavor and heavier body.

DESSERT WINES:

These are sweet, full-bodied wines served with desserts, and as refreshments in the afternoon and evening. Their alcoholic content is usually around 20 per cent. The four types are port, white port, muscatel, and Tokay, with some other variations.

SPARKLING WINES:

The two most popular types are champagne and sparkling Burgundy, both of which are effervescent.

Champagne may be either straw-colored, pink, or red. It ranges from completely dry (usually labeled "Brut"), semi-dry (labeled "Extra Dry," "Dry," or "Sec"), and sweet (usually labeled "Doux"). Champagne may be served before dinner, with or without appetizers; with almost any dinner entree; and with dessert, always chilled.

Sparkling Burgundy is red, full-bodied, and moderately dry. It goes best with red meats and game, and is always chilled.

Wine type names are of two origins. Names like Burgundy, claret (the British names for red Bordeaux table wines), sauterne, Rhine, Chablis and champagne came into use centuries ago as the names of the wines of the Old World viticultural districts which were famous for those particular types of wines. As the wine types became known all over the world, the same names were applied to all wines, wherever grown, which had similar type characteristics. Such names are called *generic* names of geographical origin.

The other wine type name is *varietal,* and a wine is called a varietal wine when the wine type is named for the principal grape variety from which the wine is made. Such names as Cabernet, Pinot Noir, Gamay, Riesling, Semillon, Pinot Blanc, and Traminer are varietal names.

However, most of the varietal wines fall within one of the generic categories mentioned before. Thus, Cabernet and Zinfandel are both claret types, but with the special flavors and aromas of the cabernet and zinfandel grapes. Johannisberg Riesling, Grey Riesling, Sylvaner, and Traminer are really Rhine wines, broadly speaking. Pinot Blanc, Pinot Chardonay and Folle Blanche are white Burgundy types. Semillon and Sauvignon Blanc are sauterne types.

In the eastern United States there are a number of varietal wines named after native American grapes, such as Isabella, Ives, and Norton (red wines), and Diamond, Diana, Dutchess, and Iona (white wines).

It is generally conceded that the best American wines have varietal names, an important buying point.

At this point it is possible, particularly if you are a novice, that you are slightly confused by the discussion of generic and varietal names. So, for clarity's sake, the following is a list of the principal red and white American table wines, and will indicate what wine name they have, from which locality they come, and their general characteristics. Copy this list if you will, and when you go shopping for wine, take the list with you and refer to it. You'll have as good, and possibly a better knowledge of American wines than the average dealer. Incidentally, the wine names preceded by an asterisk are, in my opinion, the very best American wines.

RED TABLE WINES

BARBERA: Italian type. Varietal. California. Full-bodied, robust, and fruity. Excellent with Italian food.

BURGUNDY: Burgundy type. Generic. California, Ohio, and New York. Quality varies. Better select a varietal type of Burgundy, such as a Pinot Noir. Goes with red meats, game, and cheese.

*CABERNET, or CABERNET SAUVIGNON: Claret type. Varietal. California. A superior quality wine, medium-bodied, rich, and fruity, with a soft fragrance. For red and white meats and fowl.

CHARBONO: Italian type. Varietal. California. Similar to Barbera, but inferior. Goes with Italian meals.

CHIANTI: Italian type. Generic. California and East. Pleasant, but not made from the same grapes as Italian Chianti. Medium-bodied, dry, fruity, and slightly tart. Goes with Italian foods.

CLARET: Claret (or Bordeaux) type. Generic. California and

New York. Medium-bodied, soft, and fruity. Not as good as a Cabernet or Cabernet Sauvignon. Goes with red meats and fowl.

*GAMAY: Burgundy type. Varietal. California. Full-bodied and soft, with a fragrant bouquet. Excellent with red meats and cheese.

GAMAY ROSÉ: Rosé type. Varietal. California. Light rose wine made from Gamay grapes. For all foods. Serve chilled.

*GRENACHE ROSÉ: Rosé type. Varietal. California. This wine is made from the Grenache grapes, which give it a superiority over the Gamay Rosé. Has a fruity fragrance. For all foods. Serve chilled.

GRIGNOLINO: Italian type. Varietal. California. Less robust than Barbera, but more tart. A pleasant wine with red meats and Italian food.

MOURESTAL: Claret type. Varietal. California. A wine with medium body, but on the thin side. Soft, with fruity aroma. Goes with red meats or fowl.

*PINOT NOIR: Burgundy type. Varietal. California. The finest of American Burgundy-type wines. Full-bodied, robust, with a fine bouquet and flavor. Serve with red meats, game and cheese.

RED PINOT: (See Pinot Noir.)

ROSÉ: Rosé type. California. A rose-colored wine, light-bodied and fruity. Goes with any food. Serve chilled.

VIN ROSÉ: (See Rosé, Gamay Rosé, and Grenache Rosé.)

*ZINFANDEL: Claret type. Varietal. California. A fairly light-bodied, tart, aromatic wine, with a fruity bouquet. A delightful luncheon or dinner wine. In this wine, look for the locality in California in which it is produced. The best comes from Sonoma and Napa counties, and the Santa Cruz Mountains. Serve with red meats and fowl.

WHITE TABLE WINES

CHABLIS: White Burgundy type. Generic. California and New York. A light, clean wine, with a somewhat flinty taste and fruity flavor. Pale amber color. Seldom a great wine outside France. Choose rather a varietal white Burgundy type, such as a Pinot Blanc or a Pinot Chardonnay. Serve chilled with seafoods, white meats, and fowl. Particularly good with oysters.

*DELAWARE: Rhine wine type. Varietal. New York and Ohio. Clean, fresh, and fruity, with a spicy bouquet. New York wines of this type are drier, resembling a German Moselle. Serve chilled with seafood and fowl.

*DIANA: Rhine wine type. Varietal. New York and Ohio. A very dry clean wine on the astringent side, with a fresh and pleasing bouquet. Excellent with fish. Chill.

*DUTCHESS: Rhine wine type. Varietal. New York. Very dry and light, and slightly tart. Serve chilled with seafood and fowl.

DRY SAUTERNE: Sauterne type. Generic. California, Ohio, and New York. Great French sauternes are never dry, they vary only in sweetness. Most American "dry sauternes" are merely a white table wine with little character. Choose rather a dry Semillon or a Sauvignon Blanc.

*DRY SEMILLON: Sauterne type. Varietal. California. Along with Sauvignon Blanc, the very best of the "dry" sauternes. Fruity and medium full-bodied. An ideal main dinner wine with chicken, seafood, and white meats, chill.

FOLLE BLANCHE: White Burgundy type. Varietal. California. A delicate, dry, straw-colored wine, very refreshing. It is rather thin-bodied, with a slight acidity and flinty taste, similar to a French Chablis. Serve chilled with seafood and fowl.

*GEWURZTRAMINER: Rhine or Alsatian type. Varietal. California. Fragrant, distinctly aromatic with a spicy scent and flavor. So far, the outstanding Gewurztraminer is produced by Louis Martini. Serve chilled.

*GREY RIESLING: Rhine wine type. Varietal. California. This is not a true Riesling wine, but it is soft, mild, and refreshing, light in body and sprightly in character. Serve chilled with seafood, fowl, and light entrees.

HAUTE SAUTERNE: Sauterne type. Generic. California, Ohio, and New York. This name is usually applied to American sauternes which are sweeter than dry sauternes. A dessert wine.

*JOHANNISBERG RIESLING: Rhine wine type. Varietal. California. One of the finest white wines of California. Sprightly, brilliant, fragrant, and fruity. It is excellent with all kinds of seafood and fowl. The best comes from the northern counties of California —Napa, Sonoma, and Santa Clara. Serve chilled.

MOSELLE: Rhine wine type. Generic. California. These are, as a rule, indifferent wines, and bear not the slightest resemblance to the German Moselles. Serve chilled with seafood and fowl.

*PINOT BLANC: White Burgundy type. Varietal. California. A

superior wine, fresh, fragrant, quite lively in taste, and dry. Best with seafood and chicken, chilled.

*PINOT CHARDONNAY: White Burgundy type. Varietal. California. Another of the finest California wines, but scarce. Delicately fragrant, aromatic, rich in body. Excellent, chilled, with seafood and chicken.

RHINE: Rhine wine type. Generic. California, New York, and Ohio. Usually undistinguished in America, and often made from table grapes. For those wanting a wine comparable to the fine German Rhine wines, or Alsatian wines, a Johannisberg Riesling, a Sylvaner, a Traminer, or a Gewurztraminer should be selected.

RIESLING: Rhine wine type. Generic. California, New York, and Ohio. A dry, fresh, clean wine, very good if made from the Riesling grape. But little of it really is. Better buy the Grey Riesling or Johannisberg Riesling. Serve chilled with seafood and fowl.

SAUTERNE: Sauterne type. Generic. California, Ohio, and New York. Wines so labeled can be made from almost any grape. Ohio, however, produces a delicate, semi-sweet sauterne labeled "Isle St. George," which is delightful. Serve chilled.

*SAUVIGNON BLANC: Sauterne type. Varietal. California. A fruity wine of extreme dryness, full-bodied, and of superb quality. Excellent with almost any meal, but best with shellfish and fowl. There is also a semi-sweet Sauvignon Blanc. The semi-sweet goes with chicken, and the sweet with desserts. Serve chilled.

*SWEET SEMILLON: Sauterne type. Varietal. California. A rich, full-bodied sauterne, fairly sweet. It is a wine to serve chilled, with desserts, and is wonderful in punches and cups.

SYLVANER: Rhine wine type. Varietal. California. This is more of an Alsatian wine than a Rhine. It is light, fresh, soft, and a little tart. Goes particularly well with seafood. Serve chilled.

*TRAMINER: Rhine (or Alsatian) type. Varietal. California. A fine dry wine of fragrant bouquet and flowery flavor. Some experts have called the Charles Krug Traminer California's finest white wine. Serve chilled with chicken, seafoods, and veal.

WHITE PINOT: White Burgundy type. Varietal. California. This name is sometimes used instead of Pinot Blanc, but in California the White Pinot wine is generally made from the Chenin Blanc grape, and should not be confused with the Pinot Blanc. It is pleasing, dry, light, and fruity. Serve chilled with seafood and fowl and light meats.

The prices of the foregoing varietal wines may run anywhere from a little more than a dollar a bottle (fifth) to two dollars a bottle, with two or three running up to nearly three dollars a bottle. I would say that the average would be about $1.45 per fifth. The generic wines are priced below the varietal wines, and in many cases may be purchased well under a dollar per fifth, and even cheaper if bought by the half gallon or gallon.

A new type of wine has recently made its appearance on the market. It comes from California, and is called an old-fashioned table wine. It is on the dry side, "mellow," as one vintner puts it. They are in no sense premium-quality wines, and connoisseurs would wrinkle their noses in disdain at them. But they are very pleasant, especially for everyday drinking, and their price puts them within the reach of almost everyone. They sell for from ninety-six to ninety-nine cents a half gallon. I believe there are twenty-three California wine producers who bottle these wines, such as the Gallo Wine Company, under the label "Vino Paisano," the Petri Wine Company under the label "Marca Petri," and the Wine Growers Guild under the label "Vino da Tavola." For budget-wise families who enjoy wine with their meals, these wines are decidedly worth a trial.

There are a number of large wine companies which bottle wines which sell for around fifty to seventy-five cents a fifth. These are almost exclusively generic wines, and they are just ordinary. Some of these large companies also bottle premium wines, notably Cresta Blanca and Italian Swiss Colony.

Champagnes are bottled in many sections of the country, but in my opinion, and in the opinion of many others, the finest American champagnes have come from New York State. They are excellent, and have been superior to all but the great French champagnes. The two leading New York brands are Gold Seal, bottled by the Urbana Wine Company, of Hammondsport, New York, and Great Western, bottled by the Pleasant Valley Wine Company of Rheims, New York.

In the past year or so, however, a new group have taken over the F. Korbel & Brothers winery in northern California, which produces only sparkling wines. For many years Korbel champagne was probably the leading California champagne, but it did not come up to the New York State champagne. But since the Hecks have taken over, Korbel champagne now ranks as one of America's finest champagnes. I had some undosaged (unsweetened) Korbel champagne in September at the winery, and it was one of the finest champagnes I have ever drunk.

Another excellent California champagne, which is unique, is the Paul Masson Triple Red Champagne. This is not a pink champagne, nor a sparkling Burgundy, but a true champagne, with a red color.

In the field of vermouths, I must confess that I cannot enthuse over American dry vermouths. Many people consider Tribuno dry vermouth the best. But for a straight dry vermouth, or for a dry vermouth in mixing martinis, pay a dollar or so more and get Noilly Prat. On the other hand, I have tasted some excellent American sweet vermouths, both by themselves, chilled, and in cocktails. Tribuno also makes an excellent sweet vermouth.

I guess there is hardly a vintner in America who does not produce and bottle sherries. They range from excellent to pretty bad, and in price from around fifty cents a fifth to nearly $3.75 a fifth. I would say that the average price of an American premium-quality sherry would be about $1.50 a fifth.

Like sherry, scores of vintners throughout the United States produce and bottle dessert wines. And they too range from excellent to pretty dreadful. There are a number of fine American ports, notably those bottled by H. T. Dewey and Sons, of Egg Harbor, New Jersey, and the ports of Ficklin Vineyard, in California. Premium-quality ports average about the same price as sherries.

Most of the American muscatels and Tokays are very ordinary. The so-called Tokay wines in America do not even remotely resemble the Hungarian Tokays. However, there is a muscatel wine produced and bottled by Beaulieu Vineyards in California that is a fine, delicate after-dinner wine. It is labeled Muscat de Frontignan.

In buying American wines, there are three things to look for on a bottle's label: the varietal or generic name of the wine, the district in which the wine is made, and the vintner's name.

There are three principal districts in the United States which produce fine wines: California, Ohio, and New York State. In California, there are three localities which lie close to San Francisco that have a cool climate, which is favorable to slow-ripening grapes, and so produce the best red and white table wines. They are the Sonoma and Napa valleys, the Livermore-Contra Costa area, and the Santa Clara-Santa Cruz district. The San Joaquin Valley produces the finest dessert wines. Southern California, in the area northeast of Los Angeles, largely produces sweet wines.

In Ohio, the best wine-producing area is the Sandusky-Lake Erie Islands in the northern part of the state.

The Finger Lakes region in west-central New York State is considered to be the most important wine-producing area in the United States outside of California.

I wouldn't hazard a guess as to the number of wine producers there are in the United States. The following list is by no means complete. There are many wineries which produce and bottle fine wines, but who do not have sufficient gallonage to warrant national distribution, and the sale of their wines is indigenous to their location. The vintners and companies I am listing, however, are sound and reliable. Most of them have fairly wide distribution, and their name on a bottle of wine is indicative of premium quality.

CALIFORNIA

Almaden Vineyards
Beaulieu Vineyards
Beringer Brothers
Buena Vista Vineyards
Christian Brothers
Concannon Vineyard
Cresta Blanca Wine Company
Ficklin Vineyards (notably port)
Inglenook Vineyard Company
Italian Swiss Colony (Asti Brand)
F. Korbel & Brothers (Champagne)
Charles Krug Winery
Los Amigos Vineyards
Paul Masson, Inc.
Louis M. Martini Winery
Novitiate of Los Gatos
Wente Brothers

NEW JERSEY

H. T. Dewey & Sons (notably port)

NEW YORK

Pleasant Valley Wine Company
Taylor Wine Company
Urbana Wine Company
Widmer's Wine Cellars

OHIO

Meier's Wine Cellars

Opinions on which wine should accompany each particular dish range from the sublime to the ridiculous. The purist will say that white wine should never be served with red meats or game, and that red wines should never be served with seafood. He believes that Chablis is the only wine that should be served with oysters. He will tell you, if you are going to serve wine, to abjure all dishes cooked in red wine, all rich, brown gravies, all sauces that contain wine or a preponderance of spices and herbs, and he will warn you that wine does not go well with eggs, tomatoes, carrots, and so on, ad infinitum.

On the other hand there are those who say with great gusto, "Forget any hard and fast rules. If you like a wine, drink it with anything." But the matter isn't quite that simple, and such advice is just as deadly as that of the purist. You would neither enjoy the wine or the food if you drank a sweet sauterne with a steak, or a heavy Burgundy with a filet of sole. A good dish can easily be spoiled by drinking the wrong wine with it, just as an excellent wine can be disappointing when served with the wrong dish.

In general, the heavier-bodied red table wines go best with red meats, game, and cheese. The lighter red table wines can be served with fowl, and some of the more robust seafoods, as well as with red meats. Dry white table wines go best with white meats, fowl, and seafood, but also go well with lamb, veal, ham, and some of the variety meats. This is particularly true of the heavier-bodied dry white wines, such as the white Burgundy types. Sweet white wines should accompany desserts. Rosé wines can go with almost any food, as can champagne. And remember, white table wines, Rosé wines, champagne, and sparkling Burgundy should be served chilled. Red table wines should be served at room temperature, or a little below. *Apéritif* wines may be served at room temperature, or chilled. Dessert wines (outside of the sweet white wines) should be served at room temperature.

Forget all the nonsense about each type of wine needing its special glass. Your *apéritif* wines, sherry and vermouth, can be served in cocktail glasses, or, if served "on the rocks," in old-fashioned glasses. Table wines are usually served in five- to six-ounce stemmed glasses, about 5¾ inches high, and about 2¾ inches wide, tulip-shaped. You can get nice-looking, serviceable wine-glasses in many liquor stores for about forty cents each. Of course, lovely crystal glassware adds eye appeal to the wine, and if you have such, use it by all means. Oh yes, when serving wine, only fill the glasses about two-thirds full.

Wines keep best in dry, dark places, free from vibration, and at a temperature of 55 to 60 degrees Fahrenheit. If you have a basement, wonderful. If you live in an apartment, a closet will do very nicely, if it remains cool. You can make your own wine racks, or you can buy metal ones very reasonably, each holding twelve bottles. Of course, bottles should be stored on their sides, so that the corks will be kept moist, and no air will get in the bottle. In storing wine, keep white wines and champagne on the lowest levels, and red wines above them. Appetizer and dessert wines can be stored upright.

Finally, don't forget that, although wine is usually served without mixing, it is equally versatile in mixed cold drinks for summer, hot drinks for winter, punches and cups for parties all the year around, and cocktails anytime.

(2) HORS D'OEUVRES

I have always been under the impression that appetizers, or hors d'oeuvres, originated in the north countries, such as Scandinavia and Russia, where appetites are lusty, and liquor is, to put it mildly, potent. But recent delving into early times has proven me wrong.

I have been completely fascinated of late, reading one of the oldest cookery books known, *The Deipnosophists,* by Athenaeus. The English translation of this title is "The Sophists at Dinner."

In seven small volumes, it is an immense storehouse of miscellaneous information, chiefly on matters connected with the table. But it also contains remarks on music, songs, dances, games, and courtesans. Much of it will leave you breathless in wonder at the eating and drinking habits of early Greeks and Romans. Brother, when they sat (or reclined) at the dining table, they didn't fool around with food and wine (although they did with the dancing girls!).

Throughout the books almost every comestible known to the ancient and modern world is discussed. And I found that one of the most important parts of any and all dinners was the appetizers. Athenaeus says: "A moderate quantity of food should be eaten before the drinking, and chiefly the dishes which form the ordinary courses at the beginnings of a feast."

The ancients employed many foods and dishes to whet the appetite, such as olives in brine (Aristophanes asks, "Do you, Master, love the ladies who are over-ripe, or the virginal ones with bodies firm as olives steeped in brine?"), many vegetables accompanied with condiments, snails, pickled fish, shellfish, and salads with sour dressings. Such things, Athenaeus writes, "most speedily arouse the sensory organs of men . . . and make them glad to eat."

So you see that hors d'oeuvres are not a gastronomic Johnny-come-lately. Now, as in ancient times, appetizers are practically indispensable to dining, and they seem to be growing in popularity every year.

I think that this is due to two things. In the first place, a very definite change in dining habits has taken place. Prior to World War I dinner parties were quite formal. Before-dinner libations were more or less limited to champagne or champagne cocktails, or such *apéritifs* as dry white wine, sherry, vermouth, and Dubonnet. Caviar was almost a "must" with champagne, and unsalted crackers spread with *pâté de foie gras* were served with the others. But hors d'oeuvres were usually served as a first course at the table. These usually consisted of shellfish cocktails, or savory trifles, such as *Quiche Lorraine*.

Then along came the war, and a curtailment of formal dinner parties. And closely following, prohibition. And that did it! Only those who were born prior to 1913 can know the horror of cocktails during prohibition. They'd eat the lining right out of your stomach unles you mixed them with some sort of food. And so tidbits became not only desirable, but an absolute necessity. Thank God prohibition cocktails are no longer with us, but, alas, the battalions of gooey and sickening canapés and hors d'oeuvres still march through living rooms from border to border and coast to coast. But don't get me wrong, I am very fond of unusual and taste-teasing appetizers in their proper place.

It has long been my considered opinion that the serving of hors d'oeuvres (or canapés or appetizers) indelibly stamps a host or hostess as discriminating or inept. If I were to paraphrase the great French epicure, Brillat-Savarin, I'd say, "Show me what hors d'oeuvres you serve, and I'll tell you the caliber of your dinner."

Not long ago I was talking with a group of women who have enviable reputations as hostesses in their homes. The subject of hors d'oeuvres came up, and one of the women said rather plaintively, "I'm just about at the end of my rope as far as hors d'oeuvres are concerned. I'd be so happy to discover some that are new and unusual and yet would not take the edge off one's appetite." And I immediately made a mental note: "There is a discriminating hostess."

It seems to me there are three approaches to the hors d'oeuvres question. Are you going to serve appetite whets with cocktails or other libations in the living room? Or are you going to serve hors d'oeuvres as a first course at dinner? Or are you serving appetizers and/or canapés at a cocktail party? The answer to any one of those three questions can well determine what sort of hors d'oeuvres are best to serve.

As appetite whets, hors d'oeuvres should be extremely simple, few in number, and should stimulate the appetite rather than satiate it. And they should not be served as blotters for a flock of hard liquor.

If they are served as a first course at the dinner table, they should again not be too heavy or filling, or of great amount. They should still put a hungry edge on appetite, and that can be accomplished by making them not only appealing to the taste, but also to the eye.

At a cocktail party, where dinner is not indicated, you can go to town as far as hors d'oeuvres are concerned. The only limit you need consider is your purse.

One appetizer that all of my guests have absolutely raved over every time we have served them is what I have called a Torpedo Onion Canapé. It is at its succulent best when torpedo onions are used, because they are so delicate and sweet. However, I have never come across torpedo onions outside of California, so if you can't get them, you can use slices of sweet Bermuda or Spanish onions instead.

TORPEDO ONION CANAPÉ

Small English muffins	*Slices of sweet onion*
Butter	*McLaren's Imperial sharp*
Lemon juice	*Cheddar cheese*
	Paprika

I order from my bakery English muffins made the size of a silver dollar (in diameter, not thickness). I cut each one in half, and spread the halves with butter, and sprinkle over a little lemon juice. Then I place a slice of torpedo onion, cut about ¼ inch thick, on each muffin half. If you can't get the torpedo onions, pare slices of sweet Bermuda or Spanish onions to fit the muffin halves. Then cover the onion slices with a layer of McLaren's Imperial sharp Cheddar cheese. Sprinkle a little paprika over the top, and place the prepared muffin halves on a cookie sheet under the broiler flame. Watch it, and when the cheese begins to bubble, serve immediately. Figure on serving only two halves to each guest, and when they beg for more, be firm!

Dips and dunks have gained tremendously in popularity during the past few years. One reason, I suppose, is that they are very easy to prepare, and can be made ahead of time and refrigerated until an hour or so before serving.

If you're like I am, you get pretty tired of encountering the same old bowl of mayonnaise or cocktail sauce with shrimps hung around the edge. But here's a dip for shrimps, or lobster chunks, that will make everything disappear like magic, for the flavor is truly magical.

SHRIMP OR LOBSTER DIP

1 *pint mayonnaise*	½ *tsp. caraway seeds*
1 *cup cottage cheese*	½ *tsp. celery seed*
¾ *cup finely chopped onion*	½ *tbsp. dry mustard*
1 *tsp. garlic salt*	1½ *tbsp. Worcestershire sauce*
½ *tsp. salt*	1 *tsp. dry sherry*
½ *tsp. black pepper*	1 *tsp. chili sauce*

¼ *tsp. Tabasco sauce*

Mix together thoroughly the mayonnaise, cottage cheese, and the chopped onion. Then add the remaining ingredients, and blend everything well. Allow the mixture to stand in a cool place (not the refrigerator) for at least 6 hours. This makes about 1 quart of dip.

To serve, place the dip in a bowl, and set the bowl on a plate. Hang around the edge of the bowl cleaned and cooked shrimps (jumbo size, if possible), and/or surround the bowl with diced cooked lobster in bite-size chunks impaled on toothpicks.

Clam Dip has become a rather commonplace appetite whet, and you are apt to run into it frequently. So I experimented with it, and came up with one that has a most unusual flavor. So I've called it Clam Dip Supreme.

CLAM DIP SUPREME

2 *3-oz. pkgs. cream cheese*	¼ *tsp. salt*
¾ *cup mayonnaise*	¼ *tsp. freshly ground pepper*
¼ *tsp. Lawry's garlic spread*	½ *tsp. paprika*
1 *7-oz. can minced clams*	1 *tsp. Worcestershire sauce*

Small pinch ground cardamom

Cream the cream cheese, mayonnaise, and garlic spread together until perfectly smooth. Then add the minced clams, drained, the salt, freshly ground pepper, the paprika, Worcestershire sauce, and the ground cardamom seed (this condiment is put out in small glass jars by the Spice Islands Company, who manufacture, to my way of thinking, the finest herbs and spices I have ever found). Blend everything well, and chill before serving. Try this dip with the fairly new barbecued potato chips, or pumpernickel crackers. This will make about 2 cups of dip.

Another dip that has become tremendously popular is made by combining Lipton's Prepared Onion Soup Mix with sour cream and various condiments. It does have a most unusual flavor, and I am very fond of it. After making it a few times, I got an idea for another dip, and I experimented.

Lawry's Products, Incorporated, is an outgrowth of the famous Lawry's Prime Rib Restaurant in Beverly Hills, California, which is patterned after Simpson's, in London. In Lawry's restaurant great prime ribs of beef are wheeled to your table on a mobile cart, and you are served roast beef as it should be served, along with perfect Yorkshire pudding. One of the features of Lawry's has been a marvelous seasoned salt, which you sprinkled on your roast beef, Yorkshire pudding, baked potato, and salad. It proved to be so popular that a company was organized to manufacture and sell the salt to the general public through grocery outlets. It was so successful that a short time later Lawry's Products began selling the famous Lawry salad dressings, and a garlic spread.

A year or so ago Lawry's conceived the idea of producing a spaghetti sauce mix, and it was placed on the market. Again, the product rang the bell. The mix makes a very decent spaghetti sauce with a minimum of time and effort. All you do is to put 1½ cups of boiling water in a saucepan, pour in the contents of a package of spaghetti sauce mix, simmer for 15 minutes, add 1 8-ounce can of tomato sauce and 2 or 3 tablespoons of olive or cooking oil, and simmer for 10 minutes more.

This mix has another virtue—it can be combined with other comestibles to make gourmet dishes, such as Chicken Supreme, the recipe for which appears in the chapter on poultry. And with it I developed a very swell appetizer dip. I'm going to call it simply Lawry's Dip. Who knows—after they read this recipe and try it, maybe they'll put me on their payroll! (Well, I can dream, can't I?)

LAWRY'S DIP

1 *pkg. Lawry's Spaghetti Sauce Mix*	1 *tsp. Worcestershire sauce*
½ *pint commercial sour cream*	½ *tsp. garlic salt*
	Paprika

Mix the spaghetti sauce mix and the sour cream, and blend thoroughly. Then add the Worcestershire sauce and the garlic salt, and again blend thoroughly. Refrigerate about an hour before serving. It is even better if it is refrigerated for 24 hours. This is more of a dip than the onion soup mix, because it is of thinner consistency. Before serving, sprinkle with paprika, and use potato chips or crackers with it.

Are you a pizza fan? An amazingly large number of people seem to be. All over the country, particularly in Italian sections, there are restaurants springing up which make a specialty of pizzas, and the good ones are jammed from the dinner hour on to the wee sma' hours of the morning. (Incidentally, pizzas seem to have a very salubrious effect after a prolonged bout with libations!)

I love pizzas, and some time ago I had an idea for individual pizzas as appetizers for a cocktail party. Then the Lawry people developed a recipe for individual pizzas. So I have sort of combined their easy-to-make spaghetti sauce with an idea or two of my own, and the result is very zestful. This will get an outdoor barbecue party off to a mighty good start.

INDIVIDUAL PIZZAS

1 *pkg. Lawry's Spaghetti Sauce Mix*	*Mozzarella cheese*
	Flat filets anchovies
1 *#2 can tomatoes*	*Dried oregano*
1 *clove garlic*	*Olive oil*
2 *tbsp. olive oil*	*Grated Parmesan cheese*
	English muffins

In a saucepan place the contents of the package of the spaghetti sauce mix, the can of tomatoes, the minced clove of garlic, and 2 tablespoons of olive oil. Stir thoroughly, bring to a boil, cover, and simmer 20 minutes.

Split either the large or small English muffins in half and toast until lightly browned. Cover each slice with a layer of Mozzarella cheese. Then place about 2 tablespoons of the sauce over the cheese, lay a couple of flat filets of anchovy on top of the sauce, sprinkle a little of the dried oregano on, drizzle a little olive oil over, and sprinkle liberally with the grated Parmesan cheese.

Place the prepared muffin halves on a cookie sheet and put under the broiler. When the cheese begins to bubble, take out and serve.

If small English muffins are used, allow a half one to each serving. The larger muffin halves can be cut in wedges for individual servings. The above recipe makes about 12 servings, depending, of course, on the size of the servings.

Some years ago, when I was living in Chicago, I belonged to a club-within-a-club at the South Shore Country Club. This inner club was called the Salty Dogs. On dance nights, or special occasions, our group was wont to gather in our own clubrooms for nightcaps and midnight snacks. The "Court Jester" of the crowd, Gordon Glaescher, delighted in ordering a Cannibal Sandwich (ground raw beef on a slice of bread, and topped with a raw egg). When it was set before him, it always elicited mild shrieks of horror from the Silly Cats (the feminine auxiliary of the Salty Dogs). While Gordon loved the dish, I think he got a greater kick out of shocking the girls than he did in eating his sandwich.

It was from the Cannibal Sandwich that I developed my Tartare Canapés, the recipe for which is in my *With a Jug of Wine*. However, in that recipe, I did not give any definite measures or amounts of ingredients, believing that people could vary it according to their tastes. But I had so many requests for a recipe giving specific amounts that I published one in my syndicated newspaper column, "For Men Only!" And here it is, with a few improvements.

TARTARE CANAPÉS

2½ *lbs. ground round steak*
1 *lime, juice of*
4 *tbsp. dry red wine*
3 *cloves garlic, minced*
¾ *tsp. Tabasco sauce*
2 *tsp. dry mustard*

1 *tsp. salt*
2 *tbsp. Worcestershire sauce*
1 *tsp. hickory smoked salt*
1 *tsp. curry powder*
1 *tsp. Escoffier Sauce Diable*
Drained capers

Put, or have your butcher put, the raw, lean round steak through the meat grinder twice. Then, in a large bowl, add the remaining ingredients, except the capers. Blend the mixture thoroughly, using the hand and fingers to squeeze, and then turn out onto a large plate or platter, making a round mound. Refrigerate for a couple of hours before serving.

To serve, have a bowl of drained capers beside the platter of seasoned ground meat, and a basket of icebox rye bread, cut silver-dollar thin. The guests spread the beef on the bread, and sprinkle a few capers over the top.

How many will this serve? Possibly 20, but I have seen guests eat 5 or 6 apiece in rapid succession. My wife, who was one of the leading shudderers at Gordon Glaescher's Cannibal Sandwiches, now eats Tartare Canapés with great gusto, and loves 'em!

A delectable hot snack is spiced tiny meatballs, which can be prepared ahead of time, and sautéed quickly at serving time.

TINY SPICED MEATBALLS

½ lb. ground lean beef
4 tbsp. fine breadcrumbs
½ tsp. salt
¼ tsp. pepper
½ tsp. caraway seeds
⅛ tsp. grated nutmeg

1½ tsp. minced onion
¼ tsp. horseradish
1 tbsp. mayonnaise
1 dash Tabasco sauce
2 tbsp. bacon drippings
Grated Parmesan cheese

Combine all the ingredients except the bacon drippings and the grated Parmesan cheese in a mixing bowl. Mix and blend well, and then shape the mixture into 24 tiny balls.

Sauté the balls in the bacon drippings until all sides are thoroughly browned, about 4 minutes. Drain briefly on paper toweling, then roll each ball in the grated Parmesan cheese. Insert a toothpick in each ball, and serve hot.

I think the most unusual appetizer I have ever had was served at the Golden Era Dinner of the American Spice Trade Association in New York some years ago. This was a very formal dinner, which I shall speak of later. With the predinner champagne two appetizers were served, one of which was called Oyster-Turkey Balls. The flavor was out of this world, and some sort of a medal should be pinned on the chef who dreamed it up. And, amazingly enough, it is not at all difficult to prepare in your own home, as are so many of the creations of master chefs, who have so many ingredients at their fingertips, and complete facilities for making almost anything.

OYSTER-TURKEY BALLS

½ cup cooked turkey meat
¼ cup oysters, poached
½ tsp. mace
¼ tsp. pepper
¼ tsp. celery salt
1 tbsp. dry white wine

2 tbsp. heavy cream
2 egg yolks, slightly beaten
¼ cup blanched almonds,
    chopped fine
¼ cup fine breadcrumbs
Deep fat for frying

Grind the turkey meat and the drained, lightly poached oysters together through the fine blade of a meat grinder. Add the mace, pepper, celery salt, dry white wine, heavy cream, and egg yolks. Stir until well blended. Pack into a jar and store in the refrigerator for 24 hours.

When ready to serve, form the turkey-oyster mixture into small balls about the size of a large marble, and roll the balls in the combined almond and breadcrumb mixture. Fry in deep fat until golden brown. Serve on toothpicks. This recipe makes 30 to 35 balls.

The other appetizer was smoked salmon canapés, which was also delicious, especially with champagne.

SMOKED SALMON CANAPÉS

1 pkg. cream cheese
3 tbsp. heavy cream
¾ tsp. curry powder
¼ tsp. onion salt

4 thin slices smoked salmon
24 rounds of toast, or crackers
24 thin slices cucumber
24 slices stuffed olives

Combine the first 4 ingredients, and blend well. Spread the mixture carefully on the slices of smoked salmon, being careful to carry the mixture to the edge of each slice. Then roll up as for a jelly roll, and chill for 6 to 8 hours.

On the rounds of toast, or crackers, place a thin slice of scored, unpeeled cucumber. Slice the salmon rolls into thin slices and place 1 slice on top of each slice of cucumber. Top each canapé with a slice of stuffed olive. This makes 24 canapés.

Pâté de foie gras, like caviar, is strictly a rich man's dish. It is superlatively good, but also superlatively expensive. A tiny earthenware crock containing hardly enough *pâté de foie gras* to put in your eye costs around $3.65 a copy!

I am very fond of *pâté de foie gras,* not only as an appetizer spread on unsalted crackers, but as a cooking ingredient. One of my pet dishes is Tournedos of Beef Rossini, which is broiled filet mignon placed on a slice of toast spread with *pâté de foie gras,* and a rich mushroom gravy poured over. This recipe is in my *With a Jug of Wine.*

However, not having the income of a Las Vegas night club star, it is damn seldom that I serve the Tournedos. So I decided to experiment. And, to my delight, the experiment was a success. The result is what I call a "Poor Man's *Pâté de Foie Gras,*" and I not only use it now in preparing Tournedos of Beef Rossini, but I serve it as an appetizer on unsalted crackers. All except those with a very discriminating palate will never know the difference, and (but don't let this get noised around) I've even fooled some gourmets!

POOR MAN'S PÂTÉ DE FOIE GRAS

½ *lb. liverwurst sausage*	1 *tbsp. Worcestershire sauce*
1 3-*oz. pkg. cream cheese*	1 *tbsp. dry sherry wine*
4 *tbsp. mayonnaise*	¼ *tsp. each salt and pepper*
⅓ *cup cream*	½ *tsp. curry powder*
1 *tbsp. melted butter*	*Tiny pinch cayenne pepper*

Tiny pinch grated nutmeg

With a fork mash and blend the sausage, cream cheese, mayonnaise, and cream. Then add the remaining ingredients, blending everything thoroughly (an Osterizer electric blender does the job perfectly). Let chill in the refrigerator before serving.

I might say, due to the difference in curry powders, that you should start with ¼ teaspoon of curry powder, and taste. If necessary, add a little more, pinch by pinch, until you have the right effect. The curry powder should not be discernible, as such.

In the opinion of many gourmets, particularly authorities on Chinese food, Otto G. Graf, Associate Professor of German at the University of Michigan (he may be a full professor by now), is one of the best Oriental chefs in America. A fellow faculty member of his, Karl Litzenberg (a professor of English and an authority on Victorian literature), is a long-time correspondent of mine. In one of his letters to me he sent one of Otto Graf's menus (and recipes) for a Mandarin dinner. He said, in part, "What Otto Graf can do with both Japanese and Mandarin food is beyond description." Starting off the menu was an hors d'oeuvre, Chinese Cold Roast Pork.

CHINESE COLD ROAST PORK

Small boned pork rib   1 cup soy sauce
2 tsp. salt   2 large cloves garlic
4 tbsp. sugar   1 tbsp. ground cinnamon

Get a boned pork rib, or, better yet, a boned pork shoulder, known as a Boston Butt.

Mix together the salt, sugar, soy sauce, the cloves of garlic, finely chopped, and the cinnamon. Marinate the pork roast for 4 hours, turning the meat frequently.

Bake the roast in a 350-degree oven for an hour and a half to two hours, or until tender. Then remove the meat, and cool. The meat should really be cooked the day before, so that it can be well cooled in the refrigerator. To serve it, slice it paper thin, with something resembling a razor. Accompany the meat with a strong mustard. The accompanying cocktail should be a very cold and a very dry martini.

Devotees of Chinese food know that Cantonese Egg Rolls are practically a "must" as an hors d'oeuvre at Chinese restaurants, or Chinese dinners at home. About the best I have ever tasted were served at the Shangri-La Restaurant on North State Street in Chicago. So I went to Jimmy Moy, who at that time was host at Shangri-La, and asked him how I could get the recipe. He took me down in the restaurant's immaculate kitchen, introduced me to Jimmy Chang, the head chef, and asked him to show me how to make the egg rolls. On that same visit I also learned how to prepare and cook four other wonderful Chinese dishes—May May Pike,

Tahitian Shrimp Feast, Cantonese Beef with Noodles, and Bali Bali Chicken, the recipes for which are in my *With a Jug of Wine*.

Here is the recipe for the Cantonese Egg Rolls.

CANTONESE EGG ROLLS

½ lb. fresh shrimps
1 cup finely chopped pork
    (or veal or beef)
1 cup finely chopped celery
½ cup Chinese water chestnuts
½ cup chopped little green
    onions
2 tsp. salt
¼ tsp. Ac'cent
⅛ tsp. dark Oriental seasoning
⅛ tsp. black pepper
1 tsp. melted butter
1 tbsp. peanut butter
Noodle dough
Beaten egg
Peanut oil

Cook the fresh shrimps, unshelled, in gently boiling water for about 7 to 8 minutes if the shrimp are large, or 5 minutes if they are medium-sized. Let the shrimps remain in the water until almost cool. Then shell, remove the veins, and chop into very small pieces. This should give about 1 cup of chopped shrimps.

In a large bowl combine the chopped shrimp, the chopped meat (I think pork is best), the celery, the water chestnuts (they should be measured after peeling), chopped not too fine, the little green onions (bulbs and tops), minced, salt, Ac'cent, dark Oriental seasoning, black pepper, melted butter, and peanut butter. Work everything well with your hands until thoroughly blended. If the mixture appears too dry, add a little more melted butter. The mixture should appear moist, but not too wet or too dry. Cover and store in the refrigerator.

The noodle dough may be purchased in Chinese noodle factories or Chinese bakeries. It comes in 7-inch squares and is more economical and satisfactory than homemade noodle dough. There are about 18 squares to the pound. Keep them in their original wrapper, covered with a very damp towel, and store in the refrigerator until ready to serve. They should be used within three days of purchase.

Cut off about 1½ inches from 2 corners of each square, and 1 inch from the other two corners. Measure ½ cup of filling solidly packed, and form a 6-inch roll. Place the filling on the wide end of the dough nearest you. Brush the edges of the dough with well beaten egg, and roll up, turning the edges while rolling. Keep the rolls on wax paper until all have been completed.

As soon as the rolls are completed, heat the peanut oil to 360-375 degrees. Drop the rolls in the hot fat carefully, and fry until *very lightly colored* and set. Lift out and drain on paper toweling. If they are to be kept more than an hour before serving, cover and store in the refrigerator. About 30 minutes before serving remove from refrigerator, and let stand at room temperature. When ready to be served, drop again into the hot peanut oil (360 to 375 degrees) and fry until golden brown and crisp. Remove from fat, drain, and cut each roll crosswise into 3 or 4 pieces, and serve at once.

This recipe will make 8 large egg rolls. The dark Oriental seasoning can be purchased in almost any Chinese grocery store. The water chestnuts, of course, can be purchased in cans in most grocery stores or chain stores.

Not long after the above recipe was published in my weekly syndicated newspaper column, "For Men Only!" I began to receive letters asking for a recipe for the dough used in the Cantonese Egg Rolls. Most of the letters were from men and women who lived in towns that did not have a Chinese section, and therefore did not boast any Chinese bakeries or grocery stores. As one man put it, "I realize it [the noodle dough] can be bought in noodle factories and bakeries, but out here in the sticks we are on a pork and potato diet, and a Chinese bakery would starve to death."

Inasmuch as I have always lived in cities which have a Chinese section, I have never had to make the noodle dough myself. But Henry Low's excellent cookbook, *Cook at Home in Chinese,* has a recipe for the dough, which should be authentic. So I offer it for those who are devotees of Cantonese Egg Rolls, and have no Chinese acquaintances.

CANTONESE EGG ROLL DOUGH

2 *beaten eggs*　　　　　　3 *cups water*
4 *cups sifted flour*　　　　*Peanut oil*

Beat the eggs and stir in the flour. Beat well, then add the water, and stir until smooth.

Use a 9-inch frying pan or skillet. Grease the pan thoroughly, and heat until very hot. Put about 4 teaspoons of batter into the hot pan, shaking and tilting the pan to spread the batter into a tissue-thin layer. Pour any excess back into the bowl. When the cake is slightly brown (watch it, because it will burn easily), turn over and heat the other side until thoroughly dried.

To make the egg rolls, proceed with the directions in the preceding recipe.

It was at a dinner party given by Otto Eitel at his Bismarck Hotel in Chicago that I was introduced to one of the most delicious German dishes I have ever tasted—*Zwiebelküchen,* or Onion Cake. It was served before dinner as an accompaniment to *apéritifs*. I pestered Theodore Meyer, the executive chef of the Bismarck, for the recipe, and he finally broke down and gave it to me.

ZWIEBELKÜCHEN
(Onion Cake)

1 *cup butter*	2 *whole eggs*
4 *tbsp. milk*	1 *egg yolk*
Pinch salt	¾ *cup sour cream*
Pinch sugar	Salt
2 *cups flour*	Pepper
6 *strips bacon*	1 *tsp. chopped chives*
4 *large onions, diced*	Pinch caraway seeds

Mix together gently the butter, milk, salt, sugar, and flour, and put the resultant dough in the refrigerator until it is able to be handled. Then roll the dough out and put into two 8-inch pie tins. Bake in a 350-degree oven for 10 minutes, or until half done.

Next, fry the bacon, diced, in a skillet, and when done, remove the bacon and fry the diced onions in the fat. When they are tender, but not brown, drain off the fat and add the 2 whole eggs and the extra egg yolk, well beaten together, the cooked bacon, the sour cream, salt and pepper to taste, and the chopped chives. Pour this mixture into the already half-baked pie crusts, sprinkle a generous pinch of caraway seeds over the tops, and bake in a 350- to 375-degree oven for 12 to 15 minutes. Serve warm, cut into small wedges. This recipe will serve 8 to 10.

Not long ago I received a very nice letter about my first cookbook, *With a Jug of Wine,* from Mrs. I. Keith Neece, of Decatur,

Illinois. Along with the letter she sent me two recipes of her own for me to try. One was for Beef Strogonoff, and the other was for an easy-to-make onion pie. She said it was an excellent substitute for potatoes with a meal, but I found it made a pretty terrific hot hors d'oeuvre. It is an interesting variation of the Bismarck Hotel's *Zwiebelküchen*.

ONION PIE, NEECE

Rich pie shell   *½ cup cream*
Cream   *½ tsp. cracked pepper*
2 large onions   *1 tsp. salt*
3 tbsp. butter   *Dash grated nutmeg*
1 beaten egg   *Grated Parmesan cheese*

Make a rich pie shell from your favorite recipe, and when it is in a pie tin, pat the bottom of the shell with cream (this seals the bottom) and chill.

Cut in half and slice the onions, and sauté them in the butter until transparent. While the onions are cooking, bake the pie shell in a 400-degree oven for 2 minutes. Remove from the oven, and when the onions are cooked, place them in the pie shell, and spoon over them the well-beaten egg and the cream mixed together. Season with salt and pepper and nutmeg. Then sprinkle the top generously with the grated Parmesan cheese, and bake in a 350-degree oven for 30 minutes until golden brown, or until the custard is set.

Karl Peter Koch is an enthusiastic gourmet in Chicago. When my first cookbook came out, I autographed a copy for him, and shortly thereafter I received a letter of thanks. He wrote: "Thanks for the inscription and autograph in your book. Of course, I read cookbooks from cover to cover. Have just finished your chapter on Hors d'Oeuvres, and I am so damned hungry I won't need an appetizer this evening. But let me give you one—it doesn't sound like much, but it leaves the caviar go begging every time."

BRISLING SARDINES À LA KOCH

White bread toast   *Brisling sardines*
Garlic butter   *Little green onions*
                Canned pimiento strips

Toast slices of white bread, after removing the crusts, spread with garlic butter (you can use Lawry's garlic spread very nicely, which is easier than making garlic butter), and halve each slice of bread. On each half slice place 2 brisling sardines, with little green onions sliced lengthwise. Across the sardines and onions place 2 strips of canned pimiento.

As I mentioned in the beginning of this chapter, the ancient Greeks were very fond of vegetables as appetizers. Nicander, the Greek poet who lived in the second century before Christ, tells of diners eating as an appetizer turnips done in vinegar and mustard. However, I think we can get along very well without turnips as an appetizer, but there are some vegetables that make delightful appetite whets. Crisp, cold celery is one, but celery stuffed with a piquant filling such as the following has a lot of zest.

PIQUANT STUFFED CELERY

4 oz. Roquefort or Blue cheese	½ tsp. dill seed
4 tbsp. mayonnaise	½ tsp. dry mustard
1 3-oz. pkg. cream cheese	½ tsp. Worcestershire sauce
1 tsp. anchovy paste	Small pinch cayenne pepper
1 tsp. Madeira wine	Paprika
Celery stalks	

In a mixing bowl combine all the ingredients except the paprika and celery stalks, and thoroughly blend into a smooth paste. Refrigerate at least overnight.

Cut the chilled celery stalks to desired length, and fill the stalks with the mixture. Dust with paprika, and keep refrigerated until ready to serve. This recipe will stuff 15 to 20 celery stalks, depending on their size.

The above mixture also makes a delicious spread for crackers or rounds of thinly sliced rye bread.

Cucumbers quartered lengthwise often appear on vegetable appetizer trays. But sliced stuffed cucumbers are vastly superior as an appetite whet.

STUFFED CUCUMBERS

1 3-*oz. pkg. cream cheese*	1 *tsp. dry sherry wine*
1 *tbsp. chopped chives* (*or*	2 *tbsp. mayonnaise*
little green onions)	1 *tsp. paprika*
½ *tsp. chopped parsley*	1 *small cucumber*

Using an apple corer, remove the seed part from a small, crisp, unpeeled cucumber. Then stuff the cavity with the following mixture:

Mash the cream cheese with the chives, the chopped parsley, the dry sherry, and the mayonnaise. Then stir the paprika into the mixture.

Place the stuffed cucumber in the refrigerator for an hour, or until thoroughly chilled.

To serve, cut the stuffed cucumber in ½-inch slices, and place the slices on small buttered rounds of icebox rye bread, cut silver-dollar thin.

A few years ago I attended a most delightful cocktail party. The guests were interesting and sprightly; the *apéritifs* were skillfully blended and very cold; and the hors d'oeuvres most intriguing. On the buffet table were four Lazy Susans, each holding a different vegetable appetizer—asparagus spears wrapped in cheese and ham; Brussels sprouts fried in a breadcrumb and peanut batter; flowerettes of cauliflower with a dip of sour cream and anchovies, and lima beans skewered on toothpicks with a dip of sweet-sour sauce. These may sound fancy, but they are amazingly easy to prepare. And they are real appetite whets.

ASPARAGUS IN A BLANKET

1 *pkg. frozen asparagus spears   Boiled ham*
Grated Parmesan cheese

Cook the frozen asparagus as directed on the package, and then drain. Cut each spear into 2 pieces crosswise. Cut 5 thin slices from a boiled ham (or use the packaged boiled ham) into 6 or 7 pieces each. Place a piece of asparagus on each piece of ham, and sprinkle with grated Parmesan cheese. Roll the ham around the asparagus, fasten with a toothpick, and broil about 5 minutes.

GEORGIA BRUSSELS SPROUTS

1 *pkg. frozen Brussels sprouts*
1 *slightly beaten egg*
1 *tsp. milk*
1 *tsp. dry sherry*

1 *tsp. grated onion*
½ *tsp. salt*
¼ *cup fine breadcrumbs*
¼ *cup finely chopped peanuts*

Butter

Cook the frozen Brussels sprouts as directed on the package, and then drain. Mix the slightly beaten egg with the milk, sherry, grated onion, and salt. Combine the breadcrumbs and the finely chopped salted peanuts.

Dip the cooked Brussels sprouts in the egg mixture, then roll in the crumb and peanut mixture. Fry in butter, turning to brown on all sides. To serve, spear each Brussels sprout on a toothpick.

CAULIFLOWER PIQUANT

1 *pkg. frozen cauliflower*
½ *cup sour cream*
1 *tsp. red wine vinegar*
1 *tsp. dry red wine*
1 *tbsp. chopped parsley*

2 *tbsp. finely chopped anchovy filets*
½ *tsp. grated onion*
½ *tsp. salt*
¼ *tsp. pepper*

Cook the frozen cauliflower as directed on the package. Drain, and then cut the flowerettes into finger-size pieces.

Combine and blend well the remaining ingredients. Heat, and serve as a dip for the cauliflower.

Instead of cooked cauliflower, fresh raw cauliflower may be used. Simply break the cauliflower into finger-size flowerettes, and dip in the sauce.

LIMA BEANS EN BROCHETTE

1 *pkg. frozen Fordhook lima beans*
5 *slices bacon*
3 *tbsp. bacon fat*
1 *tbsp. flour*

¾ *tbsp. dry mustard*
¾ *tbsp. salt*
½ *cup dry white wine*
3 *tbsp. vinegar*
1 *tsp. sugar*

⅛ *tsp. paprika*

Cook the frozen Fordhook (large) lima beans according to the directions on the package, and drain. Cut the bacon slices crosswise into 1-inch pieces, and fry. Then, on a toothpick, skewer 2 lima beans, 1 piece of bacon, and 2 lima beans.

Make a sweet-sour sauce by combining the remaining ingredients, except the paprika. Bring to a boil, then add the paprika, stir, and serve as a dip for the Lima Beans En Brochette.

One of my favorite eating and drinking companions in Chicago was Franklyn Kohler, who, incidentally, writes a syndicated cooking column, "The Skillet Club for Men." His favorite pastime was giving unusual dinners in his Michigan Avenue apartment. Sometimes his brother Jack acted as co-chef, sometimes Frank did it all himself, and always the hostess was the very charming and gracious mother of the two boys. One dinner I'll always remember was a Mexican one. Chapultepec cocktails were served in the living room, accompanied by various Mexican appetizers. The dinner menu was *Arroz con Pollo,* Corn and *Napolitos* (canned cactus bits), hot tortillas, a guacamole salad, and slices of honeydew melon served with fresh limes. With the demitasses came *Coco en Almibar* and cream cheese, with toasted tortillas. The beverage with the dinner was Mexican Carta Blanca beer, and the liqueurs were Almondrado and Kahlua.

The guacamole salad was served on tomato slices bedded on shredded lettuce. But guacamole also makes a very delicious dunk to accompany predinner libations.

GUACAMOLE DUNK

2 *ripe avocados*	*Garlic salt*
1 *tbsp. fresh lime juice*	*Freshly ground black pepper*
6 *tbsp. mayonnaise*	*Cayenne pepper, pinch*
2 *tbsp. freshly grated onion and juice*	1 *tsp. chili powder*
	Dash Tabasco sauce

Peel and pit the avocados, and cut up into small dice. Then sprinkle the diced avocados with the lime juice, and put through a ricer.

Combine the riced avocado, mayonnaise, grated onion and juice, garlic salt, and freshly ground pepper to taste, cayenne pepper, chili powder and Tabasco sauce. Blend everything thoroughly, and chill.

Serve in a bowl surrounded by pumpernickel crackers, wheat thins, triscuits, or rye crisp.

Have you ever had friends drop in on you unexpectedly? If you haven't, you're a *rara avis,* if I may borrow a phrase from Juvenal's *Satires* (dig that erudition, man!). Anyhow, friends do drop in, and you want to offer a drink of some sort, and something to nibble on, but you discover there's not even a can of peanuts on the pantry shelves.

Well, the Spice Islands Company have come up with an easy-to-make hors d'oeuvre that is a honey. You make up what seems to be about a six months' supply, but don't worry. It can be stored in the refrigerator in airtight containers, and you'll be amazed at how quickly they can disappear. In no time at all, you'll need a new supply of "Nuts and Bolts."

NUTS AND BOLTS

1 *pkg. Cheerios*
1 *pkg. Rice Chex*
1 *pkg. Wheat Chex*
2 *cups small pretzel sticks*
2 *cans salted peanuts*
¼ *cup pecans*
¾ *lb. butter*
1 *tsp. Spice Islands marjoram*
1 *tsp. Spice Islands summer savory*

1 *tbsp. Spice Islands Beau Monde seasoning salt*
1 *tbsp. Spice Islands smoke-flavored salt*
½ *tsp. Spice Islands garlic powder*
½ *tsp. Spice Islands onion powder*
⅛ *tsp. Spice Islands cayenne pepper*

In a large baking pan carefully mix the three cereals, the pretzel sticks (if the sticks are too long, break them in half), and the nuts. Hand-pulverize the marjoram and summer savory, and blend them with the other seasonings. Then blend the seasonings and herbs with the cereals, pretzel sticks, and nuts. Cut the butter in small chunks over the entire surface. Then place in a 250-degree oven for 45 minutes. Stir gently during the toasting period, being careful to keep the cereals whole.

The first serving of Nuts and Bolts may be served warm. Store what remains in airtight containers in the refrigerator. They can be served cold, or slightly warmed in the oven. Either way they are wonderful with cocktails, highballs, or what have you. This recipe makes about 6 quarts.

The foregoing hors d'oeuvres, or appetizers, are largely accompaniments for cocktails and other predinner libations. But there will come times when you will want to give a rather swanky dinner party, and serve an appetizer as a first course at the dinner table. Of course, there are an almost countless number of first-course appetizers, but the preparation of a large number of them requires the skill of a professional chef, to say nothing of a great amount of time and expensive ingredients. So I've gathered together a few first-course appetizers which are really superlative, and yet do not require horribly expensive items, nor a skill beyond that of the average cook.

This first one is sort of a cross between cocktail appetizers and a first course appetizer. It is a canapé, but a "fork" canapé rather than a finger canapé. I personally think it should be served at the table, for you need three hands to manage a cocktail, a canapé, and a fork. But use your own judgment as to when you want to serve it.

CANAPÉ FRANCISCO

6 3-inch rounds white bread
Butter
1¼-inch slices canned tomato aspic
1 medium avocado, peeled and thinly sliced
1 cup of flaked cooked or canned crab meat

¾ cup mayonnaise
3 tbsp. lemon juice
Salt to taste
⅛ tsp. Ac'cent
Paprika
Watercress or parsley for garnishing

Sauté the bread rounds gently in butter until golden brown, turning to brown both sides. Then set aside to cool.

To assemble the canapés, just before serving place a sautéed bread round on each of 6 salad plates. Place an aspic slice on each bread round. Cover the aspic slices with avocado slices, and top with a mound of the crab meat.

Mix the mayonnaise, lemon juice, salt, and Ac'cent, and spoon the mixture over the crab meat. Dust with paprika and garnish each canapé with a small bouquet of watercress or parsley.

About three years ago the American Spice Trade Association played host to food writers in a "Golden Era Dinner" given in the elegant Grand Ballroom of the Hotel Astor in New York.

The seven-course dinner was patterned after luxurious affairs of the late nineteenth and early twentieth centuries. It was designed to dramatize the Spice Trade's belief that, due to improved food storage and transportation, and the greater availability of seasonings, today's average housewife can serve her family delicious dishes which were rare and expensive fifty years ago.

The Association kept faithfully to the period it portrayed throughout the evening. A champagne reception opened the affair in the hotel's stately Coral Room. When the guests entered the Grand Ballroom for dinner, the huge hall was lighted entirely by candles. Potted palms fringed the room, and each table was elaborately decorated with floral pieces, silver candlesticks, and delicate china and crystal. At each place there was a menu, beautifully printed in gold and black, welcoming the diners into the Golden Era.

The first course was Lobster Crème à la Lillian Russell. This famous toast of New York had a normal appetite which the most ingenious corsetières had trouble combating. The lovely Lillian loved Lobster Crème, and restaurateurs teased her with it wherever she went. To aid in her reducing, it is said that "Diamond Jim" Brady bought her a gold-plated bicycle with mother-of-pearl handles and diamonds and rubies on the spokes! But apparently the exercise only increased her appetite for Lobster Crème.

LOBSTER CRÈME

½ lb. lobster meat, shredded   ½ tsp. salt
½ can condensed cream of   ¼ tsp. cayenne pepper
   mushroom soup   Breadcrumbs
2 tbsp. dry sherry   1 tbsp. butter
1 tbsp. chopped pimiento   12 2-inch toast rounds

Combine the lobster meat, mushroom soup, sherry, pimiento, salt, and cayenne pepper in the top of a double boiler. Also combine the breadcrumbs and the melted butter. Heat the lobster mixture until very hot. Then spread on the toast rounds, cover with the breadcrumb mixture, and place under the broiler until browned. This makes 12 canapés.

At the dinner, La Ina pale dry sherry was served with this course, but a dry white wine could be served instead, continuing on with a fish course that might follow.

There is hardly anything that teases the appetite more than cold boiled lobster. The half of a small cold, boiled lobster, with an accompaniment of just lemon juice or mayonnaise, makes a delectable and colorful first course. Another is lobster meat, cut into bite-size pieces, marinated in French dressing, and served in lettuce cups with a sprinkling of paprika over the lobster meat. To my mind, the best accompaniment is mayonnaise mixed with a little prepared Dijon mustard, and an added touch is to sprinkle over the lobster meat a few drained capers.

Many people like a more piquant sauce with the lobster meat, so here is my nomination for a lobster cocktail.

LOBSTER COCKTAIL

2 *cups diced cooked lobster*   ⅓ *cup dry sherry*
    meat   1 *tbsp. Worcestershire sauce*
1 *heart of celery*   ½ *tsp. prepared Dijon mustard*
1 *small head of lettuce*   1 *tbsp. chopped chives*
¼ *cup mayonnaise*   *Salt to taste*
½ *cup tomato catsup*   *Lettuce, or lettuce cups*

Combine the cooked lobster meat, cut in ½-inch cubes, the diced celery heart (2, if they are small), and the chopped heart of a small head of lettuce.

Mix together the remaining ingredients (except the lettuce leaves or cups). When they are well blended, combine the sauce with the lobster mixture, and serve in lettuce cups, or compotes lined with lettuce. Of course, the lobster mixture and the sauce should be well chilled before being combined. This recipe should serve 4 generously.

The Pan American Coffee Bureau sends out to food writers each month an interesting *Coffee News Letter,* filled with very interesting data on coffee, and always a couple of recipes, one of which calls for coffee as an ingredient. Not long ago they had a recipe for a salad that caught my eye. So I made it, but served it not as a salad, but as a first-course appetizer. And it was sensational, not only from the point of view of taste appeal, but eye appeal as well. It was called an avocado and seafood salad, but as an appetizer I have called it Seafood Stuffed Avocados.

SEAFOOD STUFFED AVOCADOS

1 6½-oz. can lobster meat
2 6-oz. pkgs. frozen crab meat
2 cups cooked shrimps (fresh,
    frozen, or canned)
2 tbsp. olive oil
1 tbsp. white wine vinegar
½ tsp. garlic salt

1 pinch black pepper
1 pinch dry mustard
1 pinch dried tarragon leaves
3 ripe avocados
½ cup mayonnaise
½ cup sour cream
1 tbsp. chopped chives

1 tbsp. Worcestershire sauce

Break the lobster meat and the crab meat (after having defrosted and drained the crab meat) into medium pieces, being sure to remove any bits of shell. If fresh lobster meat is used, or if there are any large pieces, reserve them. Also reserve at least 6 whole shrimps, and cut the remainder of the shrimps into pieces.

Combine the olive oil, white wine vinegar, garlic salt, black pepper, dry mustard, and the dried tarragon leaves, and blend well. Then blend that with the combined lobster, crab, and shrimp pieces, so that they are well coated, and place in the refrigerator to chill.

When ready to serve, cut the avocados in half and remove the pits. Then fill the cavities with the seafood mixture. Distribute the mixed mayonnaise and sour cream dressing, to which the chopped chives have been added, over the 6 filled avocado halves, and top each with the reserved lobster meat and whole shrimps. Serve the stuffed avocados on lettuce leaves or cups.

Fresh crab meat, when it is available, makes a delicious first course. I like it best when it is served in a cocktail compote without any garnishing. But I suppose the cocktail compote has to be fancied up for a dinner party, so line it with crisp lettuce leaves.

FRESH CRAB MEAT COCKTAIL

¾ cup mayonnaise
2 tbsp. Lawry's garlic spread
½ fresh lime, juice of
4 tsp. hot mustard

2 tsp. A-I sauce
½ tsp. dried tarragon leaves
8 dashes Angostura bitters
1 tsp. brandy

Fresh crab meat

Blend all of the ingredients except the crab meat thoroughly, and chill. Also chill the crab meat.

To serve, gently mix the sauce with the crab meat, and place in compotes which have been lined with crisp lettuce leaves. The above ingredients for the sauce make approximately ¾ cup, which should do for 4 generous cocktails. Or maybe 6, depending on how much sauce you like. The amount of crab meat necessary again depends on how much you want to serve. But don't make the servings too large.

Incidentally, when I originated this recipe, I meant it just for fresh crab meat. But it can be used with fresh lobster or shrimp. As a matter of fact, we fell so much in love with the sauce that we find ourselves also using it on broiled sole and halibut.

One of the most celebrated appetizers, or hors d'oeuvres, which can be served with predinner libations (champagne preferred) or as a first course is *Quiche Lorraine.*

Samuel Chamberlain, in his wonderful volume, *Bouquet de France,* defines *Quiche Lorraine* as "at heart an honest and simple tart, not difficult to make and delicious when hot." He further describes it as "a hot, flaky crust filled with cream and bacon, and often fortified with eggs, onions or ham."

For some strange reason, the word *Quiche* is not to be found in French dictionaries, at least in the three that I have. Lorraine is, of course, an ancient province of France, bordered by Germany. And *Quiche Lorraine* is probably the most famous specialty of that region.

There are a number of recipes for *Quiche Lorraine,* but the one I like best is that of a very cherished friend, Elva Van Meter, of San Francisco. Elva, and her late husband, Dr. Abram Lee Van Meter, were two of the most ardent gastronomes I have ever known, and I have never eaten more perfect dinners, in every detail, than those they frequently served in their beautiful home. Elva, by the way, is a graduate of the famous Cordon Bleu Cooking School in Paris, and the doctor, having made two different wine tours of France, had a profound knowledge of wines.

Here is Elva Van Meter's recipe for *Quiche Lorraine*.

QUICHE LORRAINE

Unbaked pie crust shell	*4 tbsp. minced onion*
White of 1 egg	*3-4 eggs*
½ lb. grated Gruyère cheese	*1-2 cups rich milk, or cream*
1 tbsp. flour	*Salt*
6 slices bacon	*Dash cayenne pepper*

Make your favorite rich pie crust shell (9 inches), and brush the entire surface with white of egg after the shell is in the pie tin. This prevents any sogginess in the crust.

Dredge the grated Gruyère (or imported Switzerland) cheese with the flour, mixing well. Fry the bacon slices in a skillet until nicely crisp. Drain them on paper toweling, and cut in small pieces.

In the bacon fat sauté the minced onion until limp, then distribute the onion and the bacon pieces over the bottom of the unbaked pie shell. Cover the onion and bacon pieces with the mixture of grated cheese and flour.

Beat 3 eggs with 1 cup of rich milk (or 4 eggs with 2 cups of rich milk for a deeper tart), salt to taste, and add the small pinch of cayenne pepper. Pour this custard over the cheese.

Bake in a 400-degree oven for 15 minutes, then reduce the temperature to 325 degrees, and bake for 30 minutes longer, or until a knife comes clean from the custard. This recipe will serve 6 generously, or 8 scantily.

For authentic and delicious Swiss cuisine, I don't know of any restaurant in America that can compare with the Swiss Pavilion Restaurant on East Fiftieth Street in New York City. The proprietor, handsome Paul Burger, managed the Swiss Pavilion restaurant at the New York World's Fair, which was outstanding among the many restaurants for its distinctive food.

Paul, by the way, is a delightful host, and a unique raconteur. I mean unique in the true sense of the word, because Paul tells various dialect stories with a Swiss accent, and you'll roll off your chair laughing. If you can ever corner Paul, ask him to tell you the "Bon Voyage" story. That alone is worth twice the price of the dinner.

One of the specialties of the Swiss Pavilion Restaurant is *Delices d'Emmenthal* (feather-weight hot cheese croquettes that melt in your mouth). He gave me the recipe, and, believe me, it will rate raves at your next dinner party.

DELICES D'EMMENTHAL
(Cheese Croquettes)

2 *oz. butter*	3 *beaten egg yolks*
5 *tbsp. flour*	1 *whole egg*
10 *oz. milk*	¼ *cup milk*
2 *oz. dry white wine*	1 *tbsp. olive oil*
Salt and pepper	*Flour*
½ *lb. Switzerland cheese,*	*Fine breadcrumbs*
grated	*Butter*

Melt 2 ounces of butter in a saucepan over a low flame, add 5 table-spoons of flour, and stir until golden-colored. Then thin with 10 ounces of milk and the dry white wine, and stir until smooth. Cook slowly for about 10 minutes, stirring constantly. Season with salt and pepper to taste, and remove from the fire. Add the Switzerland cheese, grated, and stir until dissolved. Then add 3 beaten egg yolks, and stir well.

Spread the mixture into a well-buttered shallow baking dish about 6 by 9 inches. Let cool, then cover with wax paper and chill for at least 2 hours, or until needed. When ready to prepare for serving, cut the cheese mixture into about 18 pieces, each piece about 1 inch wide and 3 inches long, and mold into croquettes.

Beat 1 whole egg with ¼ cup of milk and 1 tablespoon of olive oil. Roll each croquette in flour, dip into the egg mixture, drain well on wax paper, and then cover completely with fine breadcrumbs. Fry in plenty of butter over a medium flame on all sides until golden brown. These can be served as is, or with a tomato sauce poured over them.

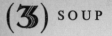 S O U P

Would you like to have a unique recipe for making soup? A recipe that is not to be found in any other cookbook ever written or published? Very well, here it is, and it's simply called "Soup."

SOUP

1 *good bonfire*
Several round, smooth stones
1 *animal-skin bag*

Several bones of animals or birds, with particles of meat adhering to them

Water

Build a good bonfire, and after it is really going, place the stones in the fire, and let them get very hot.

Fill the bag (made from animal skins) with several split bones of animals and/or birds which have particles of meat adhering to them. Add a quantity of water. Remove the hot stones from the fire and drop them into the bag filled with water and bones. When the stones have cooled, drink the liquid from the bag.

Sounds incredible, doesn't it? Yet that was the way soup was first made by prehistoric man—the beginning of the art of soup making —not long after the discovery of fire.

Later, when man learned to devise pots and kettles whose contents could be heated over a fire, the science of soup making improved. Soup kitchens, which are usually the first things to appear in time of a catastrophe, are said to have originated in the Middle Ages. And so, down through the centuries, soup has been a mainstay of man's diet.

Soup should be but a prelude to a meal—the prologue to the play, so to speak—unless it be the main course, or the whole meal.

Soup is said to prepare the stomach for the voluptuous activity to follow, and at the same time to stimulate the palate to a keener anticipatory pitch. I might go along with that premise if the soup is a clear consommé, cunningly concocted from taste-teasing ingredients. But heavy soups, at least as far as I am concerned, take the hungry edge from appetite, even though the serving be but a cup. However, in all fairness, I should point out that I am well beyond the first flush of youth, when it is almost impossible to fill up a yearning tummy. Nor am I a pick-and-shovel man, a woodsman, a logger, or a tramper of the fields. And I still have a yearning (so far satisfied) to look down while standing erect and see that my shoes are well polished!

In Grandmother's day (that is, if Grandmother was cooking before the twentieth century) every kitchen had a coal range with a stock pot simmering on it. But in these modern times the can opener has superseded the stock pot, and I can't honestly say that we've lost thereby. To my mind one of the most delightful dinner openers during the summer is jellied consommé served in a cup with a wedge of lemon squeezed over it. The only labor necessary to produce this delectable is to put a can of condensed consommé in the refrigerator, let it remain a day or so, then open it with a quick and easy can opener, and serve. The same holds true for Consommé Madrilène. Both of these clear soups, as well as others, have most of the virtues of Grandmother's soup stocks, and with 99 and 95/100 less work. For instance, take Consommé Florida.

I first tasted Consommé Florida at the Drake Hotel in Chicago. The occasion was the annual meeting of the Chicago Wine and Food Society. As a rule I don't care too much for clear hot soups, but I was so intrigued with this one that I later asked Lee Schoenbrunn, the general manager of the hotel, for the recipe. A few days later John L. Kaufmann, executive chef of the Drake, sent me the recipe.

The basis of Consommé Florida is a beef consommé. The recipe for this called for the slow boiling for 2½ hours of 2 quarts of beef stock, to which have been added chopped onion, garlic, celery, stewed tomatoes, a leek, parsley root, parsley greens, 8 ounces of lean beef shanks ground up very coarse, whole peppercorns, mixed spices, and 1 egg white and the shell. That is the way Grandmother (or Great-grandmother) would have made beef consommé, and the way a chef in the kitchen of a great hotel (with several stock pots always simmering at the back of huge ranges) would make it.

But when I serve Consommé Florida, as I often do for important guests, I do not make beef consommé myself. Instead of spending around three hours to prepare it, I make it in about fifteen minutes, and it is just exactly as delicious as though I made my own beef consommé instead of using Campbell's Condensed Beef Bouillon.

CONSOMMÉ FLORIDA

4 *cans condensed beef bouillon*   1½ *tsp. anisette*
2 *10-oz. cans green turtle meat*   1 *oz. arrowroot*
                                3 *oz. dry sherry wine*

Remove the turtle meat from the cans, discard the thickened broth, and dice the meat in small cubes. Combine the diced turtle meat, the beef bouillon, and the anisette in a saucepan. Bring to a boil, then lower the flame and simmer for 10 minutes.

Mix the arrowroot (a dry, powdery thickening agent like cornstarch, only much better, for it is more easily digested) with the dry sherry, stirring well, and add to the consommé mixture. Blend well, then bring the whole to a boil, and continue boiling for 3 minutes. Serve very hot, and preferably with cheese sticks. This recipe will serve 8 to 10 people if bouillon cups are used.

Turtles have always been regarded as delicious, albeit expensive, food. Because of its glutinous quality, the turtle is highly esteemed by the Chinese. This animal (it is neither fish nor fowl) has another virtue—it is supposed to be highly aphrodisiacal! (Gentlemen, please walk, do not run, to the nearest turtle emporium!)

The green turtle (which isn't green at all, but is so-called because of the color of its fat) is probably the most highly prized of all the turtles. However, people living in the vicinity of Chesapeake Bay will undoubtedly violently disagree with such a statement, because to them the diamondback terrapin is the queen of all turtles.

Anyhow, Green Turtle Soup is an epicurean delight. It is at its best when fresh turtle meat is used. But I have successfully used canned green turtle put out by the More and Company Soups, Incorporated, under the trade name of "Bon Vivant."

GREEN TURTLE SOUP

1 *lb. green turtle meat*	3 *cloves*
½ *medium-sized onion*	3 *bay leaves*
½ *green pepper*	*Dried marjoram*
1 *carrot*	*Dried thyme*
1 *stalk celery*	*Dried basil*
3 *tbsp. olive oil*	*Salt and pepper*
1 *pint beef bouillon*	*Dash Angostura bitters*
1 *pint cold water*	2 *sprigs parsley*
8 *peppercorns*	⅔ *cup dry Madeira wine*

Slices of fresh lime

In a skillet in the olive oil, sauté the chopped onion, chopped green pepper, chopped carrot, chopped celery, the green turtle meat cut in small dice, and a pinch of salt, for about 10 minutes.

In a pot put the beef bouillon and the cold water. Add the peppercorns, cloves, bay leaves, parsley, a generous pinch each of dried marjoram, dried thyme, and dried basil, salt and pepper to taste, and a dash of Angostura bitters. Then add the sautéed turtle meat and the sautéed vegetables. Cover, and let simmer for 1 hour, or until the turtle meat is tender. Strain, skim off the fat, and add the dry Madeira wine. Reheat, and serve hot, adding a thin slice of lime to each cup. This will serve 8 to 10, using bouillon cups.

In that era of fabulous dining during the late nineteenth and early twentieth centuries, chefs, not only in hotels but in private homes, took a great deal of time to devise special dishes for great occasions. In 1909 the Iowa Society gave a most elaborate dinner at the Hotel Astor in New York. The highlight of the ten-course dinner was a most unusual consommé created by the chef of the hotel. He called it Spiced Consommé with Quenelles. (In case you were not listening to the $64,000 Question the night Captain Richard McCutcheon hit the jackpot, *quenelles* are forcemeat balls made of pounded meat or fish, and used as a garnish for soups.)

I had this wonderful consommé at the Golden Era Dinner given by the American Spice Trade Association at the Hotel Astor, which I have mentioned earlier. The Association furnished each guest with all the recipes, and I hereby pass this one on to you. It takes time to make, but it is well worth the trouble, and it will be a conversation piece at and after any dinner party which includes it.

SPICED CONSOMMÉ WITH QUENELLES

2½ *quarts water*	1 *tsp. curry powder*
2 *lbs. beef bone and shank meat*	2 *small tomatoes, cut up*
2 *medium carrots, sliced*	2 *tsp. dried parsley flakes*
2 *stalks celery, sliced*	1 *bay leaf*
½ *clove garlic*	¼ *tsp. powdered thyme*
3 *whole cloves*	1 *tsp. salt*
⅛ *tsp. black pepper*	1 *tbsp. quick-cooking tapioca*
1 *leek, sliced*	*Quenelles*

2 *leeks, cut in very thin strips*

Place the meat and bones in a large kettle and add the water. Bring slowly to a boil. Skim, then add the next 12 ingredients. Simmer slowly, covered, for 4 to 5 hours. Strain, add more salt to taste, then add the tapioca, the *quenelles,* and the 2 leeks. Simmer 10 minutes longer. This recipe serves 8.

QUENELLES

⅓ *lb. very finely ground veal*	¾ *tsp. curry powder*
2 *egg whites, unbeaten*	½ *tsp. salt*
4 *tbsp. heavy cream*	*Pinch black pepper*

Mix the veal with the egg whites, one at a time. Beat well. Then add the remaining ingredients, and blend thoroughly. Shape into small balls the size of small walnuts. Add the *quenelles* to the consommé as directed above.

One of America's most celebrated soups is, or was, Bookbinder Red Snapper Soup, a famous creation of the original Bookbinder Restaurant in Philadelphia. Over a period of years I was asked time and time again to publish the recipe for this soup in my newspaper column. Each time a request came in I would comb through my library of cookbooks for the recipe, search through my food files, and make inquiries among my gourmet friends and correspondents. But I was always out of luck.

Early in my search I approached the management of the Drake Hotel in Chicago. Their Cape Cod Restaurant served Bookbinder Red Snapper Soup, and I had had it in all its deliciousness, but the recipe was guarded possibly better than Fort Knox guards our gold supply.

However, I am a persistent cuss, particularly when it comes to digging out food facts. I pestered Lee Schoenbrunn, the manager, and I needled Eddie Brashears, the president of the hotel. Finally, they broke down and gave me the recipe. In the letter accompanying it, Lee Schoenbrunn wrote:

This recipe was obtained by Mr. Edwin L. Brashears, from the original Bookbinder Restaurant in Philadelphia with the understanding that if we ever released the recipe, due credit would be given to their restaurant.

Well, I published the recipe in my column, giving due credit both to the Bookbinder Restaurant and the Cape Cod Room of the Drake Hotel. I was happy to be rid of the whole thing, but alas, I had not counted on alert readers.

Three days after the recipe appeared, I had a letter from a dear and valued friend in Washington, D.C., Arthur Sears Henning, who is one of the best known and best beloved newspaper correspondents in the capital, and at that time, head of the Washington Bureau of the Chicago *Tribune*. Arthur wrote:

Your readers are greatly indebted to you for the recipe for the Cape Cod Room's Bookbinder Red Snapper Soup. But are you sure you have told all the story?

What puzzles me is how Mr. Brashears could have obtained the recipe from Bookbinder, inasmuch as Bookbinder's famous snapper soup is not made of fish, but of snapping turtle. The gourmets of Philadelphia are divided on the question whether Bookbinder or the Union League Club makes the better snapping turtle soup.

Does this whet your reportorial interest?

It's things like that that sometimes make me wonder if I wouldn't have been better off as a clerk in the Government Printing Office.

Well, I transmitted Mr. Henning's letter to the management of the Drake Hotel. Four days later I received an answer from the president, Mr. Brashears. He wrote:

It is entirely possible that Mr. Henning is correct regarding the famous snapping turtle soup, but the recipe which we have used for the snapper soup is one which we obtained from Bookbinder's many years ago.

The occasion is still fresh in my memory because of the fact that this snapper soup has become a great favorite in our Cape Cod Room.

Ben Marshall, the former president of our company, and I were dining in Bookbinder's Philadelphia restaurant many years ago—I do not remember the exact date. We opened our luncheon with one of the most delicious snapper soups we had ever tasted, and Mr. Marshall, being somewhat of a gourmet himself, and tremendously interested in food and unusual recipes, requested the recipe for this soup.

Quite naturally, under the circumstances, Bookbinder declined, stating that such recipes were part of his stock in trade, and that a great deal of loving care had gone into their preparation. Mr. Marshall recognized that fact, and stated that, if obtained, the soup would be featured in our Cape Cod Room as Bookbinder's Red Snapper Soup, and that forever after, full credit would be given to Bookbinder's famous recipe.

But Arthur Sears Henning, indefatigable newspaperman that he is, finally cleared up the whole matter, and wrote me. He said: "In Philadelphia the other day Mrs. Henning and I lunched at Bookbinder's. We called for Red Snapper Soup. The head waitress, who said she had been there 6 years, had never heard of it, said their only snapper soup was made of snapping turtle. Mr. Peterson, the manager, said they originated Red Snapper Soup many years ago, but abandoned it because of the difficulty in getting fresh Red Snapper in Philadelphia. Your faithful reporter, with best regards."

Well, now that due credit has been given to all concerned, let's get on to the recipe.

BOOKBINDER RED SNAPPER SOUP
As served in the Cape Cod Room of the Drake Hotel

2 *pints fish stock*
¼ *cup diced onions*
½ *cup diced celery*
1 *diced green pepper*

1 *pint tomato and brown sauce*
1 *cup diced Red Snapper*
2 *tbsp. butter*
1 *cup dry sherry wine*

Fish Stock

Fish trimmings (*head, fins, and bones*)
3 *pints water*
1 *cup dry white wine*
1 *medium onion*
Few cloves

6 *peppercorns*
½ *bay leaf*
1½ *tsp. salt*
2 *sprigs parsley*
1 *carrot*
Pinch dried thyme

Tomato and Brown Sauce

3 *tbsp. flour*
¼ *lb. lard*

3 *pints beef or chicken stock*
1 #2 *can purée of tomato*

First, make the tomato and brown sauce. In a saucepan brown the flour in the lard. When the flour is golden brown, add the beef bouillon (or chicken broth) and the purée of tomato. Simmer this slowly for 2½ hours. This recipe makes about 1 quart of sauce, and the unused portion can be saved for about a week by placing it in a covered jar in the refrigerator.

Next comes the fish stock. In a kettle put the trimmings of the fish, and extra fish trimmings which you can get from your fish market. The extra trimmings will make the stock even richer. Cover the fish trimmings with water (about 3 pints), and add the dry white wine, the onion stuck with a few cloves, the peppercorns, bay leaf, salt, parsley, the carrot cut into thin strips, and the thyme. Simmer all this 25 to 30 minutes, then strain.

Now for the soup itself. Smother the diced onion, diced celery, and diced green pepper in the butter and the 2 pints of fish stock until all is brought to a boil. Then add 1 pint of the tomato and brown sauce, and bring to a boil again. Then add the diced red snapper, and let cook until the fish is tender (about 12 minutes). Just before serving, add the sherry wine, reheat, and serve piping hot.

I don't know of any shellfish that doesn't make wonderful soups, bisques, chowders, or gumbos. Incidentally, if you are interested in semantics, *bisque* is the culinary name of a purée, or thick soup, but the word is largely restricted to shellfish soups. Properly made, the shellfish is marinated in a white wine courtbouillon, then cooked, the shell removed and pounded in a mortar, and then strained into the soup. This gives color to the lobster, shrimp, and crayfish bisque.

Chowder comes from the French *chaudière,* which is a large cauldron in which the peasants cook their soups and stews, particularly those made with seafood.

Gumbo is the name given to a rich Creole soup, which must contain okra, and also filé powder.

Of all the soups we have ever served in our home, the one which never fails to draw extravagant praise is Crab Bisque Helen. It is the creation of Helen Gruber, of Carmel, California, wife of Brigadier General William Gruber, USA, Retired. The following recipe is reprinted from my *Fisherman's Wharf Cookbook*.

CRAB BISQUE HELEN

12 oz. (1½ cups) crab meat   ½ tsp. sugar
2 oz. butter   1 tsp. chili powder
½ small green pepper   2 tbsp. flour
1 medium onion   1 pint thin cream
                  4 tbsp. dry sherry

Melt the butter in a saucepan, and in it sauté the green pepper, seeded and finely minced, and the onion, also minced, until they are transparent, but not browned. While they are cooking, mix the sugar, chili powder, and flour together in a bowl, blending the ingredients well and being sure that any little lumps of chili powder are smoothed out.

When the green pepper and onions are transparent, add the flour-sugar-chili-powder mixture slowly to the saucepan, stirring constantly so that everything is well blended. Then add the cream, continuing to stir all the time. Let this simmer slowly until it has the consistency of a cream sauce—about 10 minutes or so.

Put the crab meat in the top of a double boiler and add the sherry to it. Let this heat through, then add the crab meat and sherry to the sauce, mixing it in gently so that the crab meat will not be broken up too much. Serve very hot.

For those who cannot obtain fresh crab meat, canned crab meat can be used. But the best substitute for fresh crab meat is fresh-frozen crab meat. My favorite is Wakefield's Ocean Frosted King Crab Meat. The Alaskan king crabs are caught, cleaned, cooked, and frozen at sea aboard trawlers. This frozen crab meat is ideal for any cooked crab-meat dishes, or for cocktails and appetizers. Of course, it should be completely defrosted. I have found the best way to do this is to spread the frozen crab meat as it comes from the package out on towels, so that every bit of water will be absorbed.

One of my favorite restaurants in America, and I think one of the finest, is the Imperial House in Chicago. The co-owner, Max Guggiari, is an old and dear friend of Mrs. Wood's and mine. Many times the three of us have sat together for hours over superlative food and vintage wines, and talked of the subject dearest to our hearts, the preparation of fine food. Max is a perfectionist, and everything that is served at Imperial House is flawless. All of the ingredients that go into the superb dishes are the best obtainable. If any are unobtainable locally, Max has them flown in—strawberries from Florida, salmon from Nova Scotia, game birds and sole from England, and king crabs from Alaska.

One of the dishes Imperial House is noted for is Crab Gumbo Imperial. It is so popular that in one month a couple of years ago I received four requests to have the recipe published in my syndicated food column. The following recipe was given to me by Max.

CRAB GUMBO IMPERIAL

1 cup diced celery

1 cup diced onions

1 cup diced leeks

1 cup diced green pepper

2 oz. butter

1 cup fish stock or clam juice

2 cups stewed tomatoes

2 cups beef bouillon or broth

3 bay leaves

3 whole cloves

pinch dried rosemary

½ cup okra

¼ tsp. Ac'cent

Salt and pepper

½ lb. crab meat

1 cup cream

1½ oz. Madeira wine (or dry sherry)

Sauté the diced celery, onions, leeks, and green pepper in the butter until the vegetables are half-cooked. Then add the fish stock (or clam juice), the tomatoes, and either beef bouillon or chicken broth. In a small sack, such as an empty tea bag, place the bay leaves, cloves, and dried rosemary. Tie the sack up, and add to the other ingredients. Simmer for 45 minutes.

Five minutes before removing from the heat add the okra. If canned okra is used, it should first be warmed. If fresh okra is used, cook it in water until it is tender, or can be pierced with a fork—about 15 minutes. Also add the Ac'cent and salt and pepper to taste. About 3 minutes before serving add the crab meat, which has first been heated, the cream, and the Madeira wine.

I think this is an opportune time to say something about Madeira wine. Madeira is a fortified wine, made on the island of Madeira. There are three types of Madeira, *Sercial,* which is dry, *Bual,* rich, and *Malvasia,* or *Malmsey,* which is sweet. This latter is a rich dessert wine.

In nearly all cases of cooking with Madeira wine, the *Sercial* should be used. But Sercial Madeira is fairly expensive, and difficult to get in some areas. When I have been out of Sercial Madeira, I have used 1 part of sweet (or cream) sherry to 2 parts of a good dry, or cocktail sherry, and had excellent results.

The Sherman Hotel in Chicago has long been noted for its fine and unusual restaurants. For many years its College Inn Restaurant was famous from coast to coast. I believe it was the first restaurant in America to have a skating rink. Most of the famous name bands in America played at the College Inn at one time or another.

The old College Inn has been replaced by the Porterhouse Room, and a few years ago another restaurant was added, named the Well of the Sea. The décor and lighting of the large room gives one the impression that he is really under the sea, and it is a most exotic and delightful place for luncheon or dinner.

Of course, almost any seafood dish imaginable can be had in the Well of the Sea. One of my favorite dishes is Cuban Shrimp Soup, Carola. I strongly suspect that this luscious dish is named after the charming and beautiful Cuban wife of Colonel Leon Mandel, owner of the Chicago Department Store, Mandel Brothers.

CUBAN SHRIMP SOUP, CAROLA

8 *raw shrimps*	¼ *cup tomato purée*
¾ *lb. African lobster tails*	2 *qts. chicken broth*
⅛ *lb. butter*	*Salt and pepper*
¾ *cup diced onion*	1 *tsp. Ac'cent*
¾ *cup diced celery*	2 *tbsp. brandy*
1 *cup Minute rice*	6 *tbsp. dry sherry*
1 *tsp. curry powder*	6 *tbsp. cream*

Peel and clean the shrimp, and remove the lobster meat from the tail, and cut up coarsely.

Using a large soup pot or kettle, melt the butter, and in it sauté the onions and celery until golden brown. Add the lobster meat and the shrimp, and continue cooking until they are tender (prolonged cooking toughens shellfish). Add the uncooked rice and sauté for a few minutes. Then add the tomato purée and the curry powder, and mix everything well. Then add the chicken stock (or broth) and let the whole thing simmer for 1 hour, stirring occasionally to keep the rice and vegetables from sticking to the pan. Season to taste with salt and pepper, and add the Ac'cent. Then remove from the fire, and take out about ½ of the lobster meat from the pot. Strain the remainder through a coarse strainer, forcing as much of the remaining ingredients through as possible, and discard the solids. Dice the lobster meat that has been removed and return it to the soup. Just before serving, add the brandy, sherry, and cream, reheat, and serve. This recipe will serve 4 to 6 persons.

Colonel Leon Mandel is one of Chicago's most enthusiastic gourmets, and has one of the finest private wine cellars in America. Although he has a very fine chef in his fabulous Oak Street home, Leon loves to whip up unusual dishes, and he could well be a distinguished chef in his own right. From time to time he has given me recipes that are out of this world. Two outstanding ones are for Roast Beef Hash (which will be detailed later) and what he calls Chilean Soup. This latter he made originally with the little conchita, a type of scallop found off the coast of Chile. But inasmuch as this item is not obtainable in America, he advises using the small bay scallop, or shrimp, as a substitute. The result is something between a milk fish soup and a broth, and, I can assure you, is a taste-teasing delectable.

CHILEAN SOUP À LA MANDEL

1 *cup consommé*
½ *cup scallops* (*or shrimps*)
½ *cup milk*
1 *egg yolk*
Small pinch dried thyme

Small pinch dried marjoram
Small pinch freshly ground
    pepper
1 *tbsp. sweet* (*unsalted*) *butter*
Paprika or cayenne pepper

In a saucepan put the consommé and scallops (or shrimps), first having cleaned them. Allow to boil for about 5 minutes. Then turn down the flame and add the milk with the egg yolk beaten into it, stirring to be sure that it does not separate. Also add the dried thyme, marjoram, and the black pepper. Let all this simmer until the mixture is well heated. Just before serving add the sweet butter, and stir until the butter is melted. On serving, sprinkle over the top either paprika or cayenne pepper lightly, depending on how highly seasoned you like your food.

The island of Hawaii, largest of the Hawaiian Archipelago, is the realm of the fire goddess, Pele, who rules the sleeping craters of Mauna Loa and Mauna Kea. In Hilo, the largest city on the island, orchids border the green lawns of modest homes as well as mansions. In the surrounding country great fields of orchids lie like undulating pools of velvet in the sunshine. Along the Kona Coast, which is rich in history and legends, one finds the last bits of the primitive beauty that once lay over all the islands. Here you escape from the tumult of the modern world into the enchanting serenity of Old Hawaii, where the natives live somewhat as did their ancestors before the white man came.

In the town of Kailua, on the coast, is the peaceful, quaint Kona Inn, celebrated for its wonderful food, which is prepared by chef Max I. Mori. Chef Mori, knowing my interest in unusual foods, gave me some of his choicest recipes, one of which is Kona Inn Fish Chowder. Its unusual and delightful flavor is imparted by coconut milk. It is quite a job to prepare, but your efforts will be well rewarded.

KONA INN FISH CHOWDER

3 *lbs. firm-fleshed fish, with*
    bones and head
1 *gallon water*
2 *bay leaves*
3 *cloves garlic*
½ *lb. diced salt pork*
½ *lb. potatoes, diced*
½ *lb. turnips, diced*

2 *onions, chopped*
1 *pint heavy cream*
1 *cup coconut milk**
½ *lb. butter*
5 *tbsp. flour*
1 *tsp. salt*
1 *tsp. Ac'cent*
2 *oz. dry sherry wine*

1 *fresh coconut*

Put the water in a deep pot or kettle, and add the fish, with the bones and head included, the bay leaves and the garlic. Bring to a boil, and continue to boil until the meat of the fish falls off the

---

* To make the coconut milk, first grate the meat of a coconut and spread it on a shallow pan. Moisten it with the milk from the inside of the coconut, and set the pan in a warm oven for a few moments to loosen the oils of the coconut meat. The coconut meat must by no means become hot—only slightly warmed. Then it is put into a strong, though loosely woven cloth, and wrung hard over a bowl until all the milk is obtained. What remains in the cloth is discarded.

bones. Then strain out the liquid, reserving it, and remove the meat of the fish, flaking it, and reserve. Bones, head, bay leaves, and garlic are discarded.

In a saucepan or skillet cook the salt pork, potatoes, turnip, and onions until the vegetables are tender. Strain out the liquid, reserve, and reserve the cooked vegetables.

Combine the fish liquid and the pork drippings, and simmer them until they are reduced to about 2 quarts. Then add the cream and the coconut milk. When the liquids are thoroughly heated, add the cooked ingredients, including the flaked fish, that have been reserved, blend everything well, and strain again, reserving the liquid and the cooked ingredients.

Melt the butter, then add the flour, salt, and Ac'cent. Cook until well blended, then gradually add the reserved liquid, stirring constantly, and cook until smooth. Then add all the cooked ingredients, including the flaked fish, blend well, and just before serving, add the dry sherry.

A couple of hours after Mrs. Wood and I arrived in San Francisco, in 1951 (this was the first time for me), I was introduced to the famed Fisherman's Wharf. I haven't gotten over it yet, and I hope I never will. The place, and the seafood served there, so intrigued me that I set about collecting recipes for most of the delectable dishes served on the wharf. These I finally included, along with other unusual seafood recipes from across the country, in *The Fisherman's Wharf Cookbook,* which was published in 1954.

This showcase of San Francisco's potent fishing industry is reminiscent of a Mediterranean scene. In the placid lagoons are scores of blue, white, and green fishing craft, ranging in size from tiny crab boats to Diesel-powered tuna clippers.

Seafood repasts are offered at quaint sidewalk grottos, as well as at large and modern restaurants. There are at least a dozen places where huge, pink West Coast crabs are stacked edgewise on large tables, cooked and ready to take home. There are vendors of the little bay shrimps, so small that it would take eight or ten to make up the size of a jumbo shrimp, or prawn; of squids, and of many other kinds of seafood, cooked or raw.

Our daughter Betty selected a restaurant, and the three of us went in and ordered. The magic word *Cioppino* met my eyes, and without further exploring the menu I ordered it, along with a bottle of California wine, a Grey Riesling.

The waiter came up and tied a white bib around my neck, and quickly came back with a large, steaming bowl, whose fragrant fumes sent a delightful shiver through my taste buds until they were doing nip ups. This was *Cioppino* (pronounced cho-*peen*-o) at its best.

Cioppino is something like *bouillabaisse,* yet to my mind it is more lusty and flavorsome than any bouillabaisse one can get in America. *Cioppino* usually consists of various shellfish and pieces of fish, put in a pot, then covered with a rich garlic sauce, and cooked for 15 to 20 minutes. That first *Cioppino* I ate had the shellfish left in their shells (which makes it more toothsome, to my mind). But it can be made with the shellfish removed from their shells.

I have not been able to find the word *Cioppino* in any Italian dictionary (but then, I am no authority on the Italian language). It has been said that *Cioppino* is a corruption of the Italian *Cuoco,* which means "cook." However, in May of 1956 I received a letter from Mrs. Winfield G. Wagener of Palo Alto, California, in which she gave a very logical explanation of the word. She wrote:

As to the origin of the word [*Cioppino*]—I may be able to shed some light, since my father was Quarantine Officer in San Francisco for several years before World War I, with headquarters on Meigg's Wharf, as Fisherman's Wharf was then named.

Cioppino was a familiar dish, always brought into being with a familiar ritual: someone making the rounds of the moored boats, calling out for contributions to a common, festive stew. One fisherman would toss into the proffered bucket a nice, fat fish, another would drop in a crab. I was once allowed to pour, with small girl pride and care, four double handfuls of shrimp into the pail. From the little shops and restaurants came herbs, onions and vegetables. Usually a wicker-covered demijohn appeared, but sometimes the Quarantine Officer was allowed to furnish the price of a few bottles of wine. After all, the man had no ingredients to contribute.

The cry that instigated this wonderful stuff was "Chip in! Chip in!" But coming from an Italian throat, this delightfully used American slang had to end in a vowel. And the "in" was "een." So—"chip-eeno." We all pronounced it that way, for fun, but we all knew what it meant. If there were an Italian origin for the word, it escaped not only my young self, but my elders as well, among the Americans.

By the way, there were no bibs with mottos. If chip-eeno was being eaten in one of the restaurants, big napkins were tied around the neck, but on the wharf or the deck of a boat, where it was usually served forth from the communal bucket, we leaned over and let 'er drip. Some swabbing was done with cotton waste and we rinsed in freshly-drawn bay water.

You know, *Cioppino* eaten sedately (well ALMOST sedately) in a restaurant on Fisherman's Wharf has always seemed to me to lack something of the flavor of those long ago buckets of chip-eeno. Perhaps it is the rosemary of remembrance.

The following recipe, which I devised, is sort of a composite of different recipes from Fisherman's Wharf restaurants.

CIOPPINO

¼ cup olive oil
8 oz. butter
2 medium onions, chopped
1 leek, diced
2 green peppers, diced
4 cloves garlic, minced
2 #2 cans solid pack tomatoes
1 6-oz. can tomato paste
2 cups canned tomato sauce
1 bay leaf
2 pinches dried oregano
2 pinches dried thyme

2 pinches dried basil
6 whole peppercorns
1 pinch cayenne pepper
Salt and pepper
1¾ cups dry white wine
¼ cup Marsala wine
2 medium lobsters
4 hard-shell crabs
1 lb. raw shrimps
12 oysters
24 clams
2 lbs. firm-fleshed fish

In a large skillet heat the olive oil (use only the best, which to my mind is Old Monk) and butter, then add the onions, chopped, the leek, diced, the green peppers, seeded and diced, and the garlic, minced. Sauté these until lightly browned, then add the tomatoes, tomato paste, canned tomato sauce, bay leaf, dried oregano, dried thyme and basil, the peppercorns, slightly bruised, cayenne pepper, and salt and pepper to taste. Cover, and cook the sauce very, very slowly over the lowest possible flame, stirring frequently, for 2 hours. Then add the dry white wine and the Marsala wine, and cook for 10 minutes more.

In the meantime cook the lobsters, crabs, and shrimps (these last should be shelled and deveined) in boiling salted water until tender, 10 to 15 minutes. Allow the oysters and clams, covered with fresh water, to stand for 1 hour, then scrub the shells thoroughly. Have 2 lbs of flaky fish, such as sea bass, rock cod, red snapper, or other firm-fleshed fish, cleaned, boned, and cut in 2-inch pieces.

Place the seafood in layers in a deep pot or kettle (split the lobsters in half and crack the claws), pour the sauce over all, cover the pot, and simmer on top of the stove for 15 to 20 minutes. Serve in deep soup plates, and accompany with hot garlic bread, and chilled dry white wine. This recipe may serve 8, depending upon appetites.

Frankly, some of the foregoing recipes take time and work to prepare. However, for the busy housewife (I get your thought right at this point—what housewife isn't busy!), career girls, and working bachelors, I am going to give a recipe for a seafood chowder, courtesy of the American Can Company.

In a two-page color advertisement in some of the leading national magazines, the American Can Company featured a Pacific Coast Chowder supper. Most of the major ingredients for the four courses came out of cans, believe it or not. The advertisement said, in part, "No matter where you live . . . even if it's hundreds of miles from any coast . . . you can share their [Pacific Coasters] fresh-from-the-ocean catches and their 'catchy' way of cooking. For all the major foods in this typical West Coast-style supper are available at your grocery in Canco cans . . . the cans made by the American Can Company."

For the above paragraph and the following recipe, I may be criticized by pedantic gourmets, who have an aversion to anything that comes out of cans. But I, for one, think that the canning industry, by bringing high perfection to its art in the majority of instances, has rendered a very great service to housewives all over the land, and has made the preparation of fine food immeasurably easier, and oftentimes much less expensive.

Anyhow, boys and girls, here is the recipe for the Seafood Chowder. I hope the American Can Company won't object to a bit of tampering which I, being I, couldn't resist when I made it. To wit: I added ½ cup of dry sherry. To those who are against the use of alcohol I earnestly say: don't blame the American Can Company for this vandalism!

SEAFOOD CHOWDER

1 *can condensed cream of*
  tomato soup
1 *can condensed cream of*
  mushroom soup
1 *cup milk*
1 *can (1 lb. 4 oz.) white*
  potatoes

1 *can (8 oz.) peas*
1 *can (7-8 oz.) tuna or salmon*
1 *can (6½ oz.) crab meat*
2 *tbsp. grated onion*
1 *cup light cream*
½ *cup dry sherry wine*

Blend the tomato soup, cream of mushroom soup, milk, and dry sherry wine. Add the potatoes, drained and cut in quarters, peas, tuna (or salmon), crab meat, and onion. Heat thoroughly. Just before serving, add the cream, heat well, but do not boil. This recipe, as a main course, will serve 4.

Fall and winter call for hot, thick soups, and their number is legion. Among my favorites for a one-dish meal are such soups as *Minestrone,* Black Bean Soup, *Borsch,* Lentil Soup, Mulligatawny, Turkey Soup, Creole Gumbo, and clam chowders. Recipes for all of these are contained in my first cookbook, *With a Jug of Wine,* so I won't repeat them here, because I have too many new recipes to record. But I have added to my list of favorites the following two recipes, both of which are savory and taste-teasing.

Unfortunately, Cream of Fresh Mushroom Soup cannot be duplicated in cans, especially the following recipe, for it has a pungent, spicy flavor and aroma, which makes a new dish from an old favorite.

CREAM OF FRESH MUSHROOM SOUP

4 *tbsp. butter*
½ *lb. sliced fresh mushrooms*
1 *small onion*
3 *tbsp. flour*

Salt and pepper
1 *cup beef bouillon*
1¾ *cups thin cream*
2 *oz. dry sherry wine*
8 *dashes Angostura bitters*

Melt the butter in a heavy pan, and when it is hot add the sliced fresh mushrooms and the small onion, sliced. Cook over a low flame until the mushrooms and onion are tender, about 10 minutes. Then stir in the flour, and add salt and pepper to taste. When the flour has been absorbed, gradually stir in the beef bouillon, and then add the cream. When all is blended thoroughly, let it cook over a very low flame for about 10 minutes, or until the soup thickens slightly. Remove from the fire, stir in the sherry (which has been warmed) and the Angostura bitters. Serve in well-warmed soup plates to 4.

Cheese soups are not too common, except where grated Parmesan cheese is sprinkled over the top of the soup. So, being very fond of cheese, I really loved this cheese and vegetable chowder.

CHEESE AND VEGETABLE CHOWDER

4 tbsp. butter
1 clove garlic
3 tbsp. minced onion
½ cup chopped carrots
½ cup diced celery

4 tbsp. flour
½ cup dry sherry wine
1¾ cups milk
2 cups grated, sharp aged
    Cheddar cheese

Melt the butter in a large saucepan, and when it is hot, add the sliced clove of garlic. When the garlic browns, remove it, and add to the butter the minced onion, chopped carrots, and diced celery. Cook until the vegetables are just tender. Remove from the heat, and blend in the flour. Then add the sherry and milk, stirring constantly until all is the consistency of a thin white sauce. Then add the grated cheese, and stir until the cheese is melted and blended. This serves 4.

As a rule I am not too fond of cooked cabbage. My mother and father loved a New England boiled dinner, but when I was served, I used to tell Dad to "skip the cabbage." However, I really go for the following combination of ham and cabbage, and I think you will too some frosty night.

HAM AND CABBAGE SOUP

2 tbsp. butter
¼ cup chopped onion
¼ cup chopped celery
¼ cup chopped green pepper
3 cups boiling water
3 tbsp. flour
2 cups shredded cabbage

2 cups cubed cooked ham
1 bay leaf
¼ tsp. salt
⅛ tsp. pepper
¾ cup sour cream
2 oz. Madeira wine
2 tbsp. chopped parsley

In a heavy pan lightly fry the onion, celery, and green pepper in the butter until the vegetables are clear. Remove from the heat and blend in the flour. Then slowly add the boiling water, stirring constantly to blend well. Return to the heat and add the cabbage, ham, bay leaf, and salt and pepper to taste. Cook 8 to 10 minutes, or until the cabbage is tender. Remove the bay leaf and add the sour cream, mixing it in well. Let heat, and just before serving stir in gently the Madeira wine. In serving, sprinkle chopped parsley over each portion. This serves 4.

Now let's jump right out of cold winter weather to the heat of summertime. Outside it is hotter than the hinges of hell, and inside it is still hotter (unless you have air conditioning). The appetite is just as wilted as one's collar or blouse. This is a time when a cold soup will snap your appetite to attention quicker than the sudden appearance of a general snapped you to attention in the Army (if you were never a soldier, ask Dad—he knows!).

Cold soups, as we know them today, scarcely existed in Grandmother's time. Oscar, of the Waldorf, doesn't list a single cold soup in his famous cookbook. One of the great bibles of French cookery, *L'Art Culinaire Moderne,* first published in 1935, mentions only three cold consommés: Consommé Madrilène ("should be thick with meat and fowl so that when it is cold, it jells"), Iced Tarragon Consommé, and Iced Consommé Strozzi (which is thickened with tapioca).

Today, thanks to modern refrigeration, many soups can be enjoyed in hot weather. I have mentioned jellied consommé and jellied Consommé Madrilène. In addition, there are infinite combinations of canned soups that make enticing appetite whets when chilled. *Look Magazine* a number of years ago published a list of eight recipes for chilled soups that would make you drool just reading them. There were such combinations as cream of chicken soup, cream of pea soup, cream, and grated Parmesan cheese; spinach soup, mushroom soup, cream, and curry powder; cream of asparagus soup, cream, onion salt, garlic salt, paprika, and marjoram; tomato soup, pea soup, cream, basil, and sherry; and spinach soup, cream, mayonnaise, chili powder, and coriander seeds.

As I have mentioned before, I am very fond of black bean soup (my grandmother's recipe for this marvelous soup is in my *With a Jug of Wine*). Recently, I had a chilled black bean soup, and I thought it was terrific.

CHILLED BLACK BEAN SOUP

1 *can Campbell's condensed*
    black bean soup
1 *can Campbell's condensed*
    consommé

1 *can water*
1½ *tbsp. dry sherry*
Lemon slices

Stir the black bean soup well, then add the consommé. Stir in the water (using the measurement of an empty can of either one of the foregoing soups) and the sherry. Chill for 4 hours. Serve in icy cold bowls, garnishing each serving with a lemon slice. This will serve 4.

In the preceding chapter I told about Professor Otto G. Graf's appetizer for the start of a Mandarin dinner, which was Chinese Cold Roast Pork. His second course was called simply Chinese Soup.

CHINESE SOUP

2 *tbsp. chopped mushrooms*
Butter
4 *cups condensed beef bouillon*
    or chicken broth
1 *tbsp. chopped celery*

½ *cup chopped spinach*
½ *cup raw, lean pork*
1 *tsp. Ac'cent*
1 *egg*
2 *tbsp. cornstarch*

Salt and pepper

Brown the chopped mushrooms in a bit of butter (about 1 teaspoon) in a saucepan over a low flame until they are soft, about 6 minutes.

In another saucepan heat the beef bouillon, then add the sautéed mushrooms, the chopped celery and spinach, the raw, lean pork cut into very thin strips, and the Ac'cent. Bring to a boil, then stir in the beaten egg. Then add the cornstarch, which has been made into a thin paste by the addition of a little water. Stir, adding a pinch each of salt and pepper, and then serve, very hot.

Back in the Golden Era of dining one of the most popular restaurants in New York was Rector's. One of the foremost patrons of Charles Rector's establishment was that fabulous character, "Diamond Jim" Brady.

James Buchanan Brady was a highly successful salesman of railroad supplies around the turn of the century. It has been said that he had three passions—diamonds, food, and blondes! I have never found out which was the dominating passion, but he went for luxurious food in a big way. One evening, when he was in Paris, he dined at the old Café Marguery, and fell in love with their famous Filet of Sole. Upon his return to New York he went immediately to Charles Rector and demanded that Filet of Sole Marguery be served to him. But for once Rector had to deny his imperious patron, explaining that the recipe for Sauce Marguery was a closely guarded secret.

But "Diamond Jim" was not to be denied. He finally persuaded Rector to take his son George out of Cornell and send him to Paris to obtain, by hook or crook, the recipe.

George Rector, who later became famous in his own right, went to Paris. He spent more than a year working in various top Parisian restaurants as a busboy, waiter, kitchen helper, and apprentice cook. Finally he obtained employment at the Café Marguery as a chef. And, after nine months of intensive effort, he learned the secret of Monsieur Marguery's sauce.

On his return to New York, "Diamond Jim" was waiting at the wharf as George's ship docked. Seeing George by the rail, Brady shouted to him, "Have you got the sauce?" George nodded an emphatic "yes," and that very night he made Filet of Sole Marguery for the bediamonded salesman, who pronounced it perfect. Charles Rector was so delighted that he made his son a partner on the spot!

In "Diamond Jim" Brady's time filet of sole was an expensive delicacy, particularly for those who lived away from seacoasts. Today, however, due to improved transportation and frozen food packing, it is a budget item in almost any part of the country. Sauce Marguery is also relatively inexpensive. Its exquisite flavor is due to an artful blending of herbs, all of which are on the shelves of practically all groceries. So, why don't you try this wonderful dish?

FILET OF SOLE MARGUERY

10 *small filets of sole*
¼ *cup carrots, sliced*
2 *leeks, sliced*
1 *tbsp. parsley flakes*
10 *peppercorns, bruised*
1 *bay leaf*
⅛ *tsp. dried thyme*

6 *cups water*
½ *tsp. salt*
⅛ *tsp. pepper*
8 *mussels* (*or oysters*)
8 *small shrimps, boiled*
4 *oz. dry white wine*
¼ *lb. butter*

4 *egg yolks*

Place 2 of the filets of sole in a large pot. Add the carrots, leeks, parsley, peppercorns, bay leaf, dried thyme, and water. Bring to a boil, then simmer until the liquid is reduced by half, then remove from the fire and strain, reserving the broth and discarding the solids. This is your fish stock.

Place the remaining 8 filets of sole in a baking dish and cover with 1 cup of the reserved fish stock. Place in a 375-degree oven and simmer for 10 to 15 minutes, or until fish is tender. Drain off the stock, and simmer it again in a saucepan until it is reduced to about 4 tablespoons. Gently fold each filet in half and sprinkle with salt and pepper. Top each filet with 1 shrimp and 1 mussel (or oyster).

Place the 4 tablespoons of reduced fish stock in the top of a double boiler. Add 3 ounces of the dry white wine, then the butter, and cook over very gently boiling water in the bottom of the double boiler until butter is melted. Beat the egg yolks until lemon-colored, then add to them the remaining 1 ounce of wine. Add this egg-yolk-wine mixture to the butter-stock-wine mixture, stirring constantly, and cook until it is the consistency of a medium cream sauce. Strain this sauce over the filets, and place under a medium broiler flame until lightly browned. Serves 4 to 6.

The sole that you will find in most fish markets and on the

menus of most restaurants is really flounder, and, incidentally, very good. As far as I have been able to find out, Dover sole is the true English sole. About the only place you will encounter it is in the top-flight restaurants in America, and it is expensive. I doubt if any fish market in America carries Dover sole, because it has to be flown in from England.

One of my favorite filet of sole dishes is Filet of Sole Bonne Femme. My old friend, Max Guggiari, who has made such a tremendous success of Imperial House, Chicago's top restaurant, prepares Filet of Sole Bonne Femme in a way that causes diners to go into ecstasies, myself included. Of course, he uses the imported Dover sole, but you can use flounder, and get almost the same luscious dish.

FILET OF SOLE BONNE FEMME

2 1-*lb. soles, fileted*
3 *oz. butter*
2 *oz. shallots* (*or little green onions*)
1 *cup dry white wine*
½ *bay leaf*
½ *cup fish stock*
3 *oz. sliced fresh mushrooms*
Salt and pepper
½ *cup cream*

Place the soles, which have been fileted, in a shallow pan, and add the butter, the shallots (shallots are bulbs, somewhat like garlic, but much more delicate. If you can't get them, use little green onions), finely chopped, the dry white wine, bay leaf, fish stock or broth, the sliced fresh mushrooms (a scant ¼ pound of fresh mushrooms), and salt and pepper to taste. Cover the pan and poach the filets for 10 minutes. Remove the filets from the pan very carefully, and place on a hot, fireproof platter. Reduce the sauce for 5 minutes by adding the cream. Then pour the sauce over the filets, and put under the broiler for about 1 minute. Serve very hot. This should serve 4.

The Well of the Sea Restaurant in the Hotel Sherman in Chicago serves a very delicious sole fish, called Filet of English Dover Sole à la Tour d'Argent. In the restaurant Tour d'Argent in Paris this is a luxurious and costly dish, as most of the dishes are in that restaurant.

I'd like to digress for a moment and tell you about a French publication, the *Guide Michelin*. It is primarily a guidebook of hotels and restaurants in France. For the restaurants they have unique designations: crossed knives and forks, and stars. The highest rank a restaurant can obtain is five crossed knives and forks, and three stars. In Paris, as of 1953, there were only two of such category—the Café de Paris and the Restaurant Lapérouse. Five other restaurants in Paris had the next lower rank, five crossed knives and forks and two stars. They were the Lucas-Carton, Maxim's, Plaza Athénée, the Ritz, and the Tour d'Argent. The third-ranking restaurants, five crossed knives and forks and one star, are the Crillon, George V, and Fouquet's. The lowest-ranking restaurants have only one crossed knife and fork, and no stars. Such restaurants are designated "plain, but fairly comfortable." If one star is added, it means "a good meal"; if two stars are added it signifies "excellent cuisine." The only restaurant in that classification was La Boule d'Or, in the 12th Arrondissment. This place specializes in Quiche Lorraine and Filets of Sole Vermouth.

If you are going to Paris, or France, be sure to provide yourself with a *Guide Michelin*. It will tell you everything you will want or need to know about hotels and restaurants; information which has been gleaned not only by inspectors of the Michelin Touring Service, but from dependable comment from travelers from all over the world.

But to get back to Filet of Sole à la Tour d'Argent. It is a very elegant and impressive dish, and consequently takes a bit of doing, particularly the making of the puff pastry, which is a long, involved process. I have an authentic and tested recipe for puff pastry in my *With a Jug of Wine,* but I have found a much easier recipe in that finest of basic cookbooks, *The New Fannie Farmer Boston Cooking-School Cookbook*. It is almost as flaky as the real puff pastry. This I have used in this recipe.

FILET OF ENGLISH DOVER SOLE À LA TOUR D'ARGENT

2 *filets of sole*
½ *cup dry white wine*
2 *chopped shallots*
Salt and pepper
4 *pats butter*
4 *heads fresh mushrooms*

Flour (for roux)
Butter (for roux)
1 *cup cream*
2 *tbsp. chopped chives*
1 *oz. dry white wine*
3 *eggs (whites only)*

Grated Parmesan cheese

Simplified Puff Pastry

2 *cups sifted pastry flour*   ⅓ *cup lard*
½ *tsp. salt*   ⅓ *cup ice water*
½ *tsp. baking powder*   ⅓ *cup butter*

Poach 2 small filets of sole with ½ cup dry white wine, the finely chopped shallots (or an equal amount of finely chopped little green onions), salt and pepper to taste, the butter, and the mushroom heads, until the fish is tender (about 10 minutes). Then remove the filets and the mushroom heads from the stock, and keep warm.

To make the sauce add the *roux* (equal parts of butter and flour creamed together) to the stock, whipping it in until it is smooth. Add the cream, blend well, then strain the sauce. To the strained sauce add the finely chopped chives and 1 ounce of dry white wine.

Using the puff pastry as a base, cut the 2 filets in half and pile them on the crust, alternating the fish with the mushroom heads, until a dome is formed. Pour the wine sauce over all.

To decorate, whip the whites of 3 eggs until they have a stiff consistency. Put the whites into a pastry bag and squeeze out, covering the fish dome by starting at the bottom, and circling around to the top. Sprinkle grated Parmesan cheese over the dome, and bake in a very hot oven until golden brown. This recipe is for an individual serving.

To make the simplified puff paste, sift the flour with the salt and baking powder, work in the lard, and add the water, sprinkling it over the flour, stirring in with a fork until enough has been added so that you can pat the dough lightly together to form a ball.

Roll the dough out. Dot with ⅓ of the total amount of butter (⅓ cup), roll up like a jelly roll, pat, and roll out again. Repeat this operation twice more, using the two remaining thirds of butter. Chill, shape, and bake.

I want to be perfectly honest and say that *this recipe is not for the novice to attempt*. It is a showy, expensive, and difficult dish, and only an expert should attempt it. But it is a famous example of *haute cuisine*.

In case you are all worn out, or discouraged, after reading the foregoing recipe, I shall encourage you with an extremely simple, yet notable, filet of sole, or filet of flounder, recipe. It's so easy to prepare that you can assemble part of the recipe and store it in the refrigerator overnight. Then, when dinnertime rolls around, the dish can be cooked in half an hour, with little fuss or bother.

FILET OF SOLE, MUSHROOM SAUCE

4 *filets of sole*	1 *tbsp. chopped parsley*
¼ *lb. fresh mushrooms*	*Pinch dried thyme*
½ *clove garlic*	*Pinch dried marjoram*
2 *tbsp. chopped little green*	*Flour*
onions	*Salt and pepper*
1 *tbsp. chopped chives*	½ *cup dry white wine*
	Butter

Chop the mushrooms, and add to them the minced ½ clove of garlic, the little green onions, chives, parsley, dried thyme, and marjoram. Mix well together, and put in a covered bowl in the refrigerator until ready to use.

A half an hour or so before dinner roll the filets of sole (or flounder) in seasoned flour. Then lay them flat on the table with the tapered ends toward you, and roll the filets gently but firmly, and fasten with a toothpick. Put the rolled filets in a flat baking dish. Cover them with the mushroom mixture you have already prepared, and pour over all a generous ½ cup of dry white wine. Dot the whole with butter, and bake in a 325-350-degree oven for about 30 minutes, or until the fish is tender and done.

The prewar era, from repeal to Pearl Harbor, seems to many of us, these troubled days, like the true "Golden Age." It was a time of "midnight sailings" from New York, and the gayest were usually aboard the ships of the French Line. A great many Americans going abroad favored the line because passage on board one of its ships gave them an extra four or five days "in France."

One of the chief attractions was the exquisite cooking—truly French—prepared by French master chefs. M. Emmanuel le Runigo was the *chef de cuisine* aboard the S.S. *Paris*. Today he presides over the kitchens of the French Line's newest luxury vessel, the *Liberté*. One of his outstanding culinary masterpieces is Filet of Sole Vigneronne à l'Angostura. Despite its formidable name, almost any housewife or amateur chef can prepare it in the home kitchen. And it is really captivating.

FILET OF SOLE VIGNERONNE À L'ANGOSTURA

1 *filet of sole*	1 *tsp. brandy*
Butter	1 *tsp. vermouth*
½ *cup white seedless grapes*	2 *dashes Angostura bitters*

Flour

Flour the filet of sole, and sauté it in butter (about 1 tablespoon). When the fish is tender, remove the filet to a hot dish and put about another tablespoon of butter in the pan. Then add the grapes, and cook lightly for 2 or 3 minutes. Add the brandy, vermouth, and bitters. Let heat through, and pour the sauce over the filet. This recipe serves 1. For more, multiply it for number.

One of the delectables in San Francisco is Rex Sole. It is a firm-fleshed fish, rather small, as fishes go, with a sweet and delicate flavor. Unfortunately for gourmets at large, it cannot be obtained outside of California. I have had it in a creamy, golden yellow sauce, whose piquancy and subtle flavor make it a perfect companion to the delicate flavor of the sole. But you can obtain practically as perfect results by using filets of sole, or even filets of halibut, haddock, or other filets of firm-fleshed fish.

FILET OF SOLE ANGELO

6 *tbsp. butter*	1 *tsp. prepared mustard*
6 *tbsp. flour*	½ *tsp. Worcestershire sauce*
2 *cups milk*	1 *tsp. Ac'cent*
½ *cup cream*	*Dash celery salt*
½ *cup dry white wine*	*Dash onion salt*
2 *tbsp. dry sherry*	*Dash garlic salt*
1 *lemon, juice of*	*Salt and pepper*
1 *tbsp. anchovy paste*	2 *tbsp. chopped parsley*

1½ *lbs. filets of sole*

Melt the butter and stir in the flour. When thoroughly blended, add the milk, cream, and dry white wine. Cook, stirring constantly, until the mixture is smooth and thickened. Then add all the other ingredients except the filets of sole, and blend well.

Arrange the filets of sole in 4 greased shallow individual baking dishes. Pour the sauce over the fish, and bake in a 375-degree oven for 25 minutes, or until the fish flakes when tested with a fork. This serves 4. Shoestring potatoes and a mixed green salad are ideal accompaniments.

When it is at its best, salmon is said to be the king of all fish. Pliny the Elder, the great Roman naturalist and writer, wrote more than eighteen hundred years ago that the salmon of the Acquitaine (southwest France) surpassed all fishes of the sea.

There are two groups of salmon; the Atlantic salmon, known as the Kennebec, and the Pacific, which is divided into five groups. These are, in the order of their importance, the chinook, the red, or sockeye (which is largely canned), the pink (also canned), the silver, and the chum (largely canned).

The love life of the salmon is fantastic, and I guess volumes have been written on it. From the little I have read on the subject, I have come to the conclusion that the guy in the old song who would climb the highest mountain, or swim the deepest river was a piker when compared to salmon. It is said that the Pacific salmon is the only fish that dies immediately after spawning.

The flesh of the salmon is rich and delicious in flavor, and may be cooked in almost any manner. It is equally savory when served cold. And, as an added feature, salmon always has terrific eye appeal.

I have experimented until I have come up with what I consider the most delicious broiled fresh salmon I have ever tasted. And it is very easy to prepare and cook.

BROILED FRESH SALMON

2 *medium-sized fresh salmon*	Salt
steaks, 1 inch thick	*Freshly ground pepper*
Lime juice	4 *pinches dried tarragon leaves*
Butter	4 *oz. dry vermouth*

Place the salmon steaks in a shallow, fireproof baking pan and squeeze lime juice over them. Then dot them liberally with butter, sprinkle with salt and freshly ground pepper, and a pinch (for each steak) of dried tarragon leaves. Pour about 4 ounces of dry (French) vermouth in the pan around the steaks, but not over them.

Place the pan under the broiler, about 4 inches from the flame. Cook for about 10 to 12 minutes, basting carefully once or twice during the latter part of the cooking, so that the herbs will not be "washed off" the surface of the steaks. Then turn the steaks, season as before, and broil for about 5 to 6 minutes, again basting with the vermouth after the seasonings have been "set" by the heat. If necessary, add a little more vermouth to the pan.

The steaks will be moist, tender, and have the most intriguing flavor you have ever tasted. With this, serve parsley potatoes, a good coleslaw, and a chilled dry white wine. Serves 2.

The Charles Krug Winery at St. Helena, California, bottles some of California's best wines. Their Traminer is really superb. The two Mondavi boys, who operate the winery, have gone far in promoting public interest and education in wine. To this end they publish, under the guidance of Francis Gould, an always interesting brochure called *Bottles and Bins*. In the April issue of 1954 they had a recipe for Baked Salmon with Wine, from Miss Lillian Ryan, of Los Angeles. It is so good that I think it deserves inclusion in any cookbook dealing, even in part, with seafood.

BAKED SALMON WITH WINE

3 *lbs. salmon*	1 *small bay leaf*
Salt and pepper	4-5 *sprigs parsley*
4 *tbsp. butter*	1 *stalk celery*
1 *carrot*	2 *cups dry white wine*
1 *onion*	1 *tsp. flour*
Pinch dried thyme	*Small cooked mushrooms*

Clean a 3-pound salmon (or salmon trout) and season with salt and pepper to taste. A long salmon steak (cut at least 2 inches thick) may be used instead of a whole fish.

Melt 2 tablespoons of butter in a pan long enough to hold the fish, and in it sauté the carrot and onion, both finely chopped, until the vegetables begin to turn golden. Then place the fish on the vegetables. Add the dried thyme, bay leaf, parsley, celery, and dry white wine. Cover the fish with a piece of buttered wax paper (or aluminum foil) and bring the wine to a boil. Then cover the pan and cook in a 425-degree oven for 45 to 50 minutes, or until the fish is done. Baste from time to time.

Place the fish on a warm serving dish and remove the skin. Strain the pan liquid into a saucepan, discarding the solids, and cook over a brisk flame until reduced by half. Then stir in the flour blended with 2 tablespoons of butter, and cook until the sauce is thickened. Add salt and freshly ground pepper to taste. Garnish with the mushrooms, and pour the sauce over the fish. Serves 4.

In the glasses, a chilled dry white wine—naturally, Krug's Traminer!

I think canned tuna fish is the savior of many an impromptu dinner. A clever wife, arriving home late from an extended bridge or canasta (or Bolivia) game, can whip up a tuna fish dish out of a can that will win plaudits from husband and/or children.

During the Lenten season, particularly, it is no easy matter to dream up a variety of appetizing meatless dishes throughout the six-week period, but a family's interest can be kept up with a new recipe now and then.

Attractive enough for company, yet unbelievably quick to make is a delectable Supreme of Tuna served in a springlike green rice ring. The ripe olives, used in the creamed tuna and as a garnish for the ring, enhance the delicate coloring so that the whole is a feast to the eyes as well as the palate.

SUPREME OF TUNA

⅓ cup butter	¼ tsp. dried rosemary
⅓ cup flour	2½ cups milk
1 tsp. salt	½ cup dry sherry wine
Pinch pepper	½ cup sliced ripe olives
1 tsp. paprika	2 cups cooked white onions

1 7-oz. can tuna

Green Rice Ring

1 pkg. precooked rice	2 tbsp. minced onions
1 cup minced parsley	¼ cup melted butter

Melt the butter in a saucepan, and blend in the flour, salt, pepper, paprika, and dried rosemary. Then add the milk and the sherry, and cook over a low flame, stirring constantly until smooth and thickened. Then add the sliced ripe olives, onions, and flaked tuna. Heat well, and serve in a green rice ring. This serves 6.

To make the green rice ring prepare 1 package (1½ cups) of precooked rice as directed on the package. Or cook your favorite rice in your own manner. Add the minced parsley, the minced onion, and the melted butter. Then form into a ring on a serving platter.

Tuna fish is a natural for luncheons, but too often it is served without imagination. Here's an inviting variation that can be prepared quickly, for either luncheon or dinner.

TUNA AVOCADO SCALLOP

2 avocados

Salt

1 cup cream mushroom soup

2 oz. dry white wine

1½ cups canned tuna fish

Cheese-flavored potato chips

Lemon wedges

Cut the avocados in half lengthwise, remove the pits, and sprinkle with salt.

Combine the condensed cream of mushroom soup, the dry white wine, and the flaked tuna fish in the top of a double boiler, and heat thoroughly.

Place the avocado halves in a baking dish containing ¼ inch of warm water. Fill the avocado halves generously with the tuna mixture, and cover the tops with crushed cheese-flavored potato chips. Bake 10 to 15 minutes in a 325-degree oven. Garnish with lemon wedges and serve immediately. Be careful not to overcook. Serves 4 as a light luncheon dish, but only 2 as a dinner dish.

Here is an unusual recipe for noodles and tuna fish which depends upon the blend of tropical spices in Angostura bitters for a rare taste tang.

EPICURE'S DELIGHT

2 cups (about 4 oz.) noodles

2 tbsp. butter

1½ tbsp. flour

¾ tsp. salt

1 cup milk

¾ cup drained canned asparagus tips

¾ cup flaked tuna fish

2 tbsp. minced green pepper

Small pinch paprika

1 3-oz. can button mushrooms, drained

⅔ cup grated Cheddar cheese

1 tsp. Angostura bitters

Parsley

Cook the noodles in salted boiling water. When tender (about 12-14 minutes) drain through a collander. Then pour cold water over the noodles and drain again.

Melt the butter in a saucepan. Add the flour and blend well. Add

½ teaspoon of salt and add the milk gradually. Cook until it just begins to bubble. Add the noodles, asparagus tips, tuna fish, green pepper, paprika, ¼ teaspoon of salt, and the mushrooms. Add the Angostura bitters last, and mix everything gently but well. Put in a buttered casserole dish and sprinkle the grated cheese over the top (incidentally, I prefer grated Parmesan cheese). Bake in a 350-degree oven for 40 minutes. Serve hot, garnished with parsley. This recipe serves 6.

If you desire to use fresh mushrooms and asparagus tips, clean the asparagus and cook until tender, and use only the very tender top part. In using fresh mushrooms, wash and sauté them about 5 minutes in the 2 tablespoons of butter before making the white sauce.

Here's a simple, yet hearty and delicious dish in which tuna fish is combined with cooked chicken and rice.

TUNA-CHICKEN CASSEROLE

1 7-oz. can solid-pack tuna, drained	1 large onion, chopped
	¼ cup chopped green pepper
1 cup chopped cooked chicken	½ cup chopped celery
1 cup cooked rice	1 tsp. salt
1 #2 can tomatoes	⅛ tsp. pepper
2 oz. dry sherry wine	Buttered crumbs

Break the tuna into large pieces with a fork. Combine the tuna, chicken, rice, tomatoes, and dry sherry. Cook over a low flame for 10 minutes. Then add the onion, green pepper, celery, salt and pepper, and mix well. Turn into a greased 1½-quart casserole and top with buttered crumbs. Bake in a 350-degree over 1 hour. This recipe serves 4 to 6.

Pompano en Papillotte (pompano cooked in paper cases) is probably one of the swankiest and most delectable dishes in the realm of fish cookery. In the first place pompano, with its rich, delicately flavored flesh, is considered to be one of the choicest of salt-water fishes. And the cooking of it in a sealed paper bag, laved with an ambrosial sauce made with shellfish and wine, only enhances its deliciousness.

Antoine's Restaurant, in the old French Quarter of New Orleans, is one of the finest restaurants in the world. Its age (over a hundred years), its picturesqueness, and its high culinary tradition carried on by three generations of the Alciatore family, make it unique. And it was in this restaurant that *Pompano en Papillotte* was originated.

According to Roy Alciatore, the present owner, this is how it happened. A famous balloonist who had done fancy stunts on errant air waves at the French Army maneuvers was to be entertained at Antoine's. Jules Alciatore—Roy's father, then proprietor of the restaurant, was told to prepare a dish which would resemble the gas envelope of a balloon. So he set to work with a pair of scissors and cut some large hearts from parchment paper. Then he poached filets of pompano in white wine. He also made a seductive sauce of crab meat and shrimp, fish stock, white wines, garlic, and onions. Then he placed the filets on the parchment hearts, spooned some of the sauce over each, sealed the hearts into a bag, and baked the result in the oven. When the bags were browned and puffed up, they were brought to the table, the bags split open, and the gustatory triumph eaten amidst terrific acclaim.

The following recipe is the original one as devised by Jules Alciatore. It was given to me by my dear friend Roy Alciatore, Jules' son, with special permission for its use in this book. Its preparation is tricky work, but Roy gives the assurance that anyone can turn out this specialty.

POMPANO EN PAPILLOTTE
Antoine's

3 *medium-sized pompano*	½ *clove garlic, minced*
3 *cups water*	8 *chopped onions* (1½ *cups*)
1 *chopped shallot* (*or* 2 *tbsp.*	*Pinch dried thyme*
chopped onion)	1 *bay leaf*
6 *tbsp. butter*	2 *cups fish stock*
2¼ *cups dry white wine*	2 *tbsp. flour*
1 *cup crab meat*	2 *egg yolks*
1 *cup diced cooked shrimps*	*Salt and pepper*

Clean the pompano, and cut them into 6 filets, removing head and backbone (your fish dealer can filet the pompano for you, but be sure you get the head and bones, as this is the basis for the fish stock). Combine the head and bones and water, and simmer until there are 2 cups of stock remaining. Sauté the shallot (or the 2 tablespoons of chopped onion) and the filets of pompano in 2 tablespoons of butter for a couple of minutes, then add 2 cups of dry white wine, cover, and simmer the whole gently until the filets are tender, about 5 to 8 minutes.

In another saucepan sauté the crab meat and shrimps and ¼ clove of garlic, minced, in 1 tablespoon of butter for a minute or so, then add the other ¼ clove of garlic and the 1½ cups of chopped onion, and cook for 10 minutes. Add the thyme, bay leaf, and 1¾ cups of fish stock, and simmer for another 10 minutes. Blend together 2 tablespoons each of butter and flour, and gradually add the remaining ¼ cup of fish stock. Add this to the crab meat-shrimp mixture along with the wine stock drained from the filets. Cook, stirring constantly, until thickened. Beat the egg yolks, and add the hot sauce and the remaining ¼ cup of dry white wine. Mix thoroughly, and place in the refrigerator until firm.

Cut 6 parchment paper hearts 8 inches long and 12 inches wide. Oil well, and lay a poached filet on 1 side of the heart, and cover the filet with spoonfuls of sauce. Fold the heart over, and hand-seal the edges. Lay the sealed hearts on an oiled baking sheet, and bake in a 450-degree oven for 15 minutes, or until the paper hearts are browned. Serve immediately in the paper hearts. This recipe serves 6.

Filets of fresh salmon, sea bass, striped bass, sole, or flounder may be used instead of pompano.

The Cape Cod Room of the Drake Hotel in Chicago serves *Pompano en Papillotte,* and it is excellent. Their recipe is much simpler than the original recipe of Antoine's. It differs also in the shellfish used, and in the wine. Perhaps you can try your hand at this one, and then, sometime when you are in a more adventuresome mood, you can try Antoine's recipe.

POMPANO EN PAPILLOTTE À LA CAPE COD ROOM

6 *selected filets of pompano*   2 *oz. butter*
2 *oz. diced, cooked lobster*   2 *chopped shallots*
1 *cup light dry red wine*   4 *oz. water*
3 *large mushrooms*   *Arrowroot*

Combine in a large pot the wine, lobster meat, the mushrooms, cut julienne, the butter, the shallots and the water. In this mixture poach the filets of pompano for 20 minutes. When the pompano is tender, remove carefully from the poaching liquor and keep warm. Then thicken the poaching liquor with arrowroot to the consistency of heavy cream.

Form your *papillottes* as under the directions in Antoine's recipe. The Drake recipe says that a wax sandwich bag of the right size will also do nicely, although I have never tried it.

Lay the filets on the hearts (or in the sandwich bags), spoon the sauce over the filets, seal, and bake in a 425-degree oven until the bags begin to puff up. Serve from the paper container, or place on a hot platter with the sauce, and serve while piping hot.

In some localities a good fish market is hard to find sometimes, and in others there are none. But thanks to the frozen food industry, fish filets can be obtained wherever there is a grocery or meat market with a frozen food department. These filets may be from any number of fishes, and while I do not believe that frozen fish can retain the delicacy of fresh fish, nonetheless the frozen filets can be excellent. And certainly they are no bother to clean and prepare. The following recipe makes a very tasty dish.

FILETS OF FISH AUX FINES HERBES

4 *fish filets*	4 *oz. dry white wine*
Salt	1 *tsp. lemon juice*
Paprika	2 *tsp. minced parsley*
Flour	2 *tsp. minced chives*
2 *tbsp. butter*	¼ *tsp. dried tarragon*
	⅛ *tsp. dried thyme*

Follow the directions on the package of fish filets for preparing to cook. I think the best way is to defrost them first, and pat dry with paper toweling on a cloth.

Sprinkle the filets with salt and paprika and just a bit of flour, then brown them ever so slightly in about 2 tablespoons of butter (or olive oil) in a skillet on top of the stove. When you turn the filets, use a large spatula or a pancake turner. Next add the dry white wine, lemon juice, parsley, chives, tarragon, and thyme. Now cover the skillet and let the fish poach 5 minutes longer, and then serve at once. If the filets are small, they will probably only serve 2.

Haddock is a native of the North Atlantic waters, not only in America but in Europe. It is closely related to the cod, and is a very firm, white-meated fish of very pleasant flavor. When smoked, it is called finnan haddie, and this is a much favored fish in England and Scotland. They broil it and spread it with pats of sweet butter, or boil it in milk and serve it with a butter sauce. Creamed Finnan Haddie is a wonderful dish, and can be made by following a good recipe for Lobster Newburg, substituting flaked finnan haddie for the lobster.

People in the state of Maine are particularly adept at cooking haddock, and two dishes are oustanding in my memory—Haddock filets with an oyster stuffing and sauce, and what the State-of-Mainers call Haddock à la Rarebit.

OYSTER STUFFED HADDOCK FILETS

2 *haddock filets*   ½ *tsp. salt*
½ *cup chopped oysters*   ⅛ *tsp. pepper*
½ *cup dried breadcrumbs*   2 *tbsp. melted butter*
2 *tbsp. chopped celery*   *Lemon juice*
              4 *slices salt pork*

Oyster Sauce

3 *tbsp. butter*   ¾ *cup hot milk*
3 *tbsp. flour*   ¼ *cup dry white wine*
¼ *tsp. salt*   12 *oysters, chopped*
⅛ *tsp. pepper*   *Lemon juice*
¼ *tsp.* fines herbes, *dried*   1 *tbsp. minced parsley*
              Lemon wedges

Combine the oysters, breadcrumbs, celery, and salt and pepper with the melted butter.

Wipe the haddock filets with a damp cloth, and place 1 filet in a greased shallow baking dish, skin side down. Sprinkle with additional salt and pepper and lemon juice, then spread the stuffing over it. Over the stuffing place the other filet. Sprinkle it with salt and pepper, and cover with additional breadcrumbs. Place the salt pork slices on the top and bake in a 375-degree oven for about 25 minutes. Remove to a hot platter, and pour the hot oyster sauce over the filets.

To make the oyster sauce melt the butter, add the flour mixed with the salt, pepper, and dried *fines herbes,* then cook and stir until all is well blended. Then add the hot milk and the dry white wine, stirring constantly until the sauce is smooth and thickened. Then add the chopped oysters and any oyster liquor. Heat through, but do not boil. Season with lemon juice, sprinkle with the minced parsley, and pour over the filets. Garnish the whole with lemon wedges. Parsley potatoes go well with this dish.

And here is the other recipe, deliciously using cheese.

HADDOCK À LA RAREBIT

3½-lb haddock   1 *heaping tsp. dry mustard*
1 *cup grated sharp Cheddar*   2 *heaping tsp. flour*
    cheese   ½ *tsp. salt*
1¼ *cup sweet milk*   *Dash pepper*
¼ *cup dry sherry*   *Paprika*

Have the haddock skinned and boned (your fish dealer will do this for you). Wash the fish, and arrange it in a flat, buttered baking dish.

In the top of a double boiler melt the grated, sharp aged Cheddar cheese. Add ¾ cup of sweet milk and the dry sherry, and heat slowly.

Into ½ cup of cold milk stir the dry mustard, the flour, and the salt and pepper, and blend smoothly. Pour this into the hot cheese-milk-sherry mixture and stir constantly until it thickens. Then pour the sauce over the fish, sprinkle with paprika, and bake in a 375-degree oven for about 30 minutes. This recipe serves 4.

If you find haddock unobtainable, flounder, or small fresh cod, or any similar fish may be substituted.

In San Mateo, California, where I live, I am very fortunate in having a wonderful fish market. It is part of the Shop Rite Store, and is owned and run by the Taub family—Dan, Della, daughter Elaine, Mrs. Taub's mother, Mrs. Dora Dichter, and sometimes son Jerry, when he is home from college. They are all such pleasant and obliging people, and everything they have to sell (poultry as well as seafood) is of the finest quality, and wonderfully fresh.

Mrs. Taub is an excellent cook. One day we were discussing cooking fish, and she asked me if I had ever fixed fish in the Hawaiian manner. I told her I hadn't, so she gave me a recipe of her own, and suggested that I try it. I did, and found it really taste-teasing. Here is the recipe, and I have named it after Della.

FISH HAWAIIAN À LA DELLA

1 *green pepper*	1 *small can pineapple chunks*
2 *carrots*	1 *tsp. sugar*
1 *Bermuda onion*	¼ *tsp. cornstarch*
½ *tsp. soy sauce*	⅛ *tsp. paprika*
	Fish filets

Cut the green pepper, carrots, and onion into bite-size pieces. Put them in a saucepan with the soy sauce, and steam them until they are tender but not mushy. Then add the pineapple chunks and their juice, sugar, cornstarch, and paprika. Bring to a boil, then remove from the fire.

Broil any firm, white fish filets in the usual manner. When done, sprinkle the filets with lemon juice, and pour the sauce over them. Serve at once. This recipe will serve 2.

SHELLFISH

The late Ernest Byfield, of Chicago, gourmet extraordinary and restaurateur supreme, was not a gentleman chef. To use his own words, he was "not even an every-other-inch-a-gentleman chef." But he could, and did, invent some superb dishes.

At luncheon one day he told me about one of his creations, Crab Meat Louise. It seems that some years ago Grace Moore asked him to produce a dinner menu for a special party that she was going to give in the Pump Room of the Ambassador East Hotel, which was owned by the Byfields. So Ernie "dreamed up" the principal dish.

"Miss Moore's cosmopolitan palate," he said, "approved the dish very highly, and we added it to our Pump Room menu. It is terrific in flavor, and," he added with a grin, "terrific in calories."

Crab Meat Louise à la Byfield is indeed a terrific shellfish preparation. So, sometime when you want to splurge, toss your calorie counter in the fireplace, and try a truly ambrosial dish.

There are three parts to the dish—Crab Meat Maryland, French pancakes, and a Sauce Mousseline. The following recipe is reprinted from my *Fisherman's Wharf Cookbook*.

CRAB MEAT LOUISE À LA BYFIELD

Crab Meat Maryland

3 *tbsp. butter*	1 *lb. fresh crab meat*
2 *tbsp. flour*	*Salt to taste*
1 *cup cream*	*Freshly ground pepper to taste*
1 *tbsp. chopped chives*	¼ *cup dry sherry wine*

Lemon juice

French Pancakes

3 *eggs*	*Few grains salt*
2 *tbsp. twice-sifted flour*	1 *tbsp. cold water*

½ *tsp. butter* (*per cake*)

Sauce Mousseline

4 *egg yolks*	2 *drops cold water*
½ *lemon* (*juice of*)	4 *oz. butter*

Brandy or cognac

First, make the Crab Meat Maryland. Melt the butter in the top of a double boiler, the lower section half filled with boiling water. Blend the flour with the cream until smooth, and add to the melted butter. Stir constantly until the mixture begins to thicken (about 5 minutes), then add the chopped chives and cook 5 minutes more, stirring constantly. Now add the picked-over fresh crab meat (or fresh-frozen crab meat that has been defrosted and dried), stir well but gently to avoid breaking up the crab meat, and heat through for 5 minutes. Season to taste with salt and freshly ground pepper, then add the sherry wine and a few drops of lemon juice. Turn the heat well down and keep the crab-meat mixture hot over the hot water in the bottom of the double boiler.

Next, make your French pancakes. In a mixing bowl place the eggs, the twice-sifted flour, the cold water, and a few grains of salt. Beat the mixture vigorously until it has the consistency of thin cream. In a small frying pan (5 inches in diameter) place ½ teaspoon of butter, and when it begins to bubble pour in about 1 generous tablespoon of batter, or just enough to cover the bottom of the pan. Shake the pan so as to distribute the batter evenly, and cook over a medium flame for 1 minute, then turn the pancake and cook another minute. Stack the cakes on top of each other until all are baked, and keep warm.

The third step is the Sauce Mousseline, which is essentially equal quantities of Hollandaise sauce and stiffly whipped cream stirred very carefully and constantly until the sauce is thoroughly heated, and seasoned to taste with salt and white pepper. Or it can be made by putting the yolks of 4 eggs in a small earthenware bowl, adding the juice of half a small lemon, a couple of drops of cold water, and 4 ounces of butter cut into small pieces. Stand the bowl in a saucepan full of boiling water and stir quickly with a wooden spoon; in a minute or two the sauce will be like soft cream, as it should be.

To complete the Crab Meat Louise, distribute the Crab Meat Maryland on the pancakes and roll them up. Then cover the rolled pancakes with the Sauce Mousseline. In serving, ladle burning cognac or brandy over each serving.

In the chapter on soups I gave the recipe for Crab Bisque Helen. However, with a few additions, this makes a wonderful luncheon or supper dish, and, believe me, you and your guests will go into ecstasies over it.

CRAB MEAT SUPREME

½ cube butter (2 oz.)	1½ cups milk
1 finely chopped onion	¾ cup mayonnaise
½ green pepper, chopped	Dash Tabasco sauce
½ tsp. salt	12 oz. fresh, frozen, or canned
Generous pinch pepper	crab meat
1 tsp. chili powder	3 tbsp. dry sherry wine
2 tbsp. flour	Breadcrumbs
Paprika	

Sauté the finely chopped onion and green pepper in the butter until they are soft, then sprinkle with the salt, pepper, and a rounded teaspoon of chili powder mixed with 2 tablespoons of flour. Blend thoroughly, then remove from the heat and stir in the milk a little at a time. Then return to the heat and let cook slowly, stirring constantly, for about 10 minutes, or until the sauce is thickened to the consistency of thin cream. Then blend in the mayonnaise and the Tabasco sauce well, and remove from the heat.

In the top of a double boiler over gently boiling water in the lower half, heat the crab meat and the dry sherry for several minutes. Fresh crab meat is best, of course. If you can't get it, or it is out of season, use the fresh-frozen crab meat, defrosted and well drained. If you use canned crab meat, get the very best quality, and use it drained.

When the crab meat and sherry are thoroughly heated through, add to the cream sauce and mix gently, but well. Divide the mixture into ramekins or individual casseroles, sprinkle with fine breadcrumbs, dot with butter, and dust with paprika. Place in a 350-degree oven for about 10 minutes, or until top is lightly browned.

Serve with a salad of tossed greens, a chilled white wine, and a Florida Lime Pie for dessert. There is a luncheon!

Ernie Byfield was famous for his Crab Meat in a Skillet, and I suspect that the Baked Imperial Crab Meat that is served in the Well of the Sea Restaurant of the Hotel Sherman in Chicago is a concoction that he devised. Anyway, it is a very piquant and delicious dish.

BAKED IMPERIAL CRAB MEAT

1 lb. fresh or frozen crab meat	1 tsp. salt
¼ cup butter	6 drops Tabasco sauce
4 shallots (or ¼ onion)	½ lemon, juice of
2 tsp. A-1 sauce	2 tsp. dry white wine
1 tsp. Worcestershire sauce	1 egg
1 cup white breadcrumbs	1 tsp. dry mustard

Break the crab meat into large pieces. Chop shallots or onion finely and sauté in about 1 tablespoon of butter until transparent. Combine the remaining ingredients, reserving about ½ the breadcrumbs, and mix well. Add the crab meat. Melt the remaining butter in skillet and add the crab-meat mixture. Cook until the breadcrumbs are slightly browned.

Fill 4 scallop shells or shallow baking dishes with mixture, and top with buttered breadcrumbs, using reserved breadcrumbs and added butter. Bake in a 350-degree oven for about 30 minutes. This serves 4 portions.

I don't suppose there is any better known lobster dish than Lobster à la Newburg. It was supposed to have been invented during the Civil War by a man named Wenburg. I believe that it reached the height of its popularity during the Gay Nineties and the early twentieth century, when the chafing dish was one of the most important articles in the dining rooms of the elite. And now that the popularity of the chafing dish has once more zoomed, Lobster à la Newburg is more popular than ever.

There are a great many recipes for Lobster à la Newburg, and they are to be found in a great many cookbooks. But I have developed a slight variation, by adding six ingredients, and dropping two, from my original recipe in my *With a Jug of Wine*. I brazenly call the following recipe Lobster Newburg à la Wood, and I think all of your taste buds will have a rousing convention when you taste it.

LOBSTER NEWBURG À LA WOOD

4 *oz. butter*	3 *cups cooked lobster meat*
1 *tbsp. chopped parsley*	2 *oz. brandy*
3 *tbsp. flour*	¼ *tsp. Worcestershire sauce*
1 *tbsp. grated onion*	*Salt*
Dash Angostura bitters	*Freshly ground pepper*
¼ *tsp. dry mustard*	2 *oz. dry Madeira wine*
Dash paprika	½ *lemon, juice of*
Pinch cayenne pepper	1 *tbsp. butter*
1 *cup cream*	1 *tbsp. flour*

In the top of a double boiler over gently boiling water in the lower half melt 2 ounces of butter, add the chopped parsley, and 3 tablespoons of flour. Stir the flour in slowly so that no lumps develop. Then add the grated onion, Angostura bitters, mustard, paprika, and cayenne pepper, and stir well. Then slowly add the cream, and again blend well.

In a saucepan melt 2 ounces of butter, and when it is hot add the lobster meat, cut in fairly large dice. Then pour over the lobster meat the brandy, which has been warmed. Set the whole alight, and let the flame die out.

Add the lobster meat and the juices from the saucepan to the cream sauce in the top of the double boiler. Also add the Worcestershire sauce and salt and freshly ground pepper to taste, and stir well. Then add the dry Madeira wine and the lemon juice.

Make a *roux* of 1 tablespoon of butter and 1 tablespoon of flour, and when blended stir the *roux* into the lobster and sauce mixture. Again blend everything well, and allow to heat for about 5 minutes. Serve over buttered toast, buttered English muffin halves, or Melba toast.

To make this in a chafing dish, make the sauce in the blazer pan placed in the outer pan, in which there is water. The lobster meat can be prepared in a saucepan (use that beautiful Revere Ware with the copper bottom) and brought to the table. Then pour the brandy over it, set it alight, and when the flame has died out, pour the contents of the saucepan into the sauce heating in the blazer pan. Continue on from there with the following recipe steps.

An old friend and confrere on the Chicago *Tribune* is the peripatetic Phil Maxwell. He is less known as a gourmet than as a public speaker, a radio personality, or as the director of the Chicago *Tribune's* Annual Chicagoland Music Festival. As if that was not enough, he, and his charming and gracious wife Helen, have composed a number of songs. Nevertheless, in his travels on land, sea, and air, he always has a weather eye cocked for a dainty morsel, a succulent dish, or a fabulous meal.

One year when he was in Florida he sent me a recipe that he thought I would like. In transmitting it, he said: "We've been here on a lazy island on upper Matecumbe Key for two days, at the Casa Islamorada. What food! Mrs. Bessie Bland (everybody calls her Miss Bessie) is said to be the best cook on the Keys, and I am enclosing her recipe for her own creation, Lobster Key Pie. What a dish!"

Well, Phil was right—it is delicious. And I doff my hat to Miss Bessie.

KEY LOBSTER PIE

2 *small cooked lobster tails*	2 *tbsp. finely chopped onions*
1 *can cream of mushroom soup*	2 *oz. dry sherry*
1 *tsp. dry mustard*	*Grated Parmesan cheese*
	Paprika

Cook 2 small lobster tails in salted boiling water for about 10 to 12 minutes. Then remove the meat from the shells and dice it.

Heat the contents of a can of condensed cream of mushroom

soup and add it to the diced lobster meat, along with the mustard, finely chopped onions, and dry sherry. Heat this all well, after stirring thoroughly, and then put the mixture into 2 ramekins or individual casseroles. Cover the tops with grated Parmesan cheese, sprinkle with paprika, and place under the broiler until the tops are browned.

As *Homard à l'Americaine* is the classic French lobster dish, Lobster Cantonese, or to give it its Chinese name, *Chow Loong-Har,* is the classic Chinese lobster dish. It is actually fried lobster with a pork sauce. It can be prepared with canned or frozen lobster meat, but, to be authentic, it should be made with live fresh lobsters which are cut up and fried, shell and all. Jimmy Moy, when he was host at Chicago's excellent Chinese restaurant, Shangri-La, and Jimmy Chang, the chef, showed me how to prepare Lobster Cantonese a few years ago, and the following recipe is genuine, with one exception. I have substituted dry sherry wine for the Chinese rice wine. However, if you can get the Chinese rice wine, use it by all means.

LOBSTER CANTONESE

2 *1-lb. live lobsters*

2 *tbsp. peanut oil*

½ *tsp. salt*

1 *tbsp. Black Bean Garlic Sauce*

Dash pepper

2 *little green onions*

½ *lb. ground lean raw pork*

2 *tbsp. dry sherry wine*

1 *tsp. sugar*

1 *tsp. soy sauce*

1½ *cups chicken broth*

1 *beaten egg*

1 *tsp. Ac'cent*

1 *tbsp. cornstarch*

Black Bean Garlic Sauce

¼ *cup Chinese black beans*

2 *large cloves garlic*

1 *tsp. fresh ginger root*

¼ *tsp. black pepper*

1 *tbsp. soy sauce*

1 *tbsp. peanut oil*

½ *tsp. salt*

Sever the cord of the lobsters by inserting a sharp knife between the body and the tail. Wash the lobsters thoroughly under cold running water. Cut off the heads and split the lobsters in half lengthwise. Remove the dark vein and small sac back of the head and discard. However, do not remove the coral. Then cut the lobster halves crosswise through the shell into 1-inch pieces. If Eastern lobsters are used, remove the claws and crack them.

Heat the peanut oil in a heavy skillet, adding to it the salt, the Black Bean Garlic Sauce, the pepper, and the little green onions (bulbs and tops) chopped fine. Sauté over a medium flame for ½ minute, stirring constantly (the Chinese call such cooking "stir fry"). Then add the lean raw ground pork, and cook for about 5 minutes, stirring constantly with a fork to separate the meat particles and keep from scorching. Then add the lobster pieces and stir fry for about 5 minutes. Next add the sherry wine (or 1 teaspoon of Chinese rice wine if you can get it), the sugar, soy sauce, and 1 cup of chicken broth. Mix, then cover and cook for 2 minutes. Uncover and add the beaten egg, and stir fry for ½ minute. Finally add the Ac'cent and cornstarch mixed together in ½ cup of chicken broth. Continue to cook, stirring constantly, until the gravy thickens. Serve on hot, flaky rice, or fried rice.

To make the Black Bean Garlic Sauce wash the Chinese black beans thoroughly in running water, then drain. Then combine the beans with the garlic cloves, finely chopped, and the fresh ginger root, finely shredded (if you can't obtain fresh ginger root, use ½ tsp. of powdered ginger). The beans can be chopped, or left whole.

Place the beans, garlic, and ginger in a bowl, add the pepper, soy sauce, peanut oil, and salt. Mix well, and keep this tightly covered in the refrigerator until ready to use. It may be kept for several days.

Coming to the third course in Professor Otto Graf's Mandarin dinner (the first course was detailed in the chapter on appetizers, and the second course in the chapter on soup), we come to the main courses, the first of which is Steamed Lobster with Pork.

In transmitting the menu to me, Professor Karl Litzenberg added some of his own notes on Chinese cookery, which I think are interesting.

"The main thing in Chinese cookery," he wrote, "is to get the food very hot, without overcooking the vegetables. These are always put in last, on high heat, and stirred constantly. A special Chinese deep-sided pan is useful for this, but not entirely necessary. Another thing about the vegetables is that most of them, like celery, are cut Chinese style, ergo: fairly thin and on the bias. Onions are not sliced against the grain, but with it. Tomatoes are usually quartered or cut in eights, depending on their size, and with, not across the pulp."

And now to the first entree of Professor Graf's Mandarin dinner.

STEAMED LOBSTER WITH PORK

2 *large lobster tails*   ½ *tsp. salt*
2 *little green onions*   ½ *tsp. sugar*
2 *cloves garlic*   2 *tbsp. hot peanut oil*
1 *lb. lean raw pork, ground*   1 *tsp. chopped fresh ginger*
2 *eggs*   1 *tsp. Ac'cent*
                 Dash Tabasco sauce

Remove the meat from the lobster tails and cut into small cubes. Put the cubed lobster meat in an oiled metal or ovenproof glass baking dish.

Mix thoroughly the little green onions, finely chopped, the cloves of garlic, finely chopped, the raw lean pork, finely ground, the eggs, the salt and sugar, the hot peanut oil, the fresh ginger, finely chopped (or ½ tsp. of powdered ginger), the Ac'cent, and the Tabasco sauce. Spread this well-blended mixture over the diced lobster meat. Place the container or baking dish on inverted cups in a large cooker containing 4 inches of water. Cover tightly and steam for 30 minutes. Uncover, slice, and serve very hot.

The second entree of the Mandarin dinner is Tomato and Green Peppers with Pork, which will be detailed in the chapter on meats. The third entree is curried shrimps, which follows.

CURRIED SHRIMPS

1 *lb. raw shrimps*   1 *tsp. sugar*
4 *large green peppers*   ½ *tsp. salt*
1 *large onion*   1 *cup consommé*
4 *tsp. curry powder*   2 *tsp. cornstarch*
Dash Tabasco sauce   *Cold water*

Remove the shells and the veins from the shrimps, wash in cold water, and drain. Clean and seed the green peppers, and cut into small squares, and peel and slice the onion.

Put the shrimps, green peppers, and onion in a well-greased skillet. Mix, and stir fry for 2 minutes. Then add the curry powder, Tabasco sauce, sugar, salt, and consommé. Cook for 2 minutes, then add the cornstarch which has been made into a thin paste by the addition of a little cold water. Stir this well into the mixture until it is thickened, and then serve very hot.

Jambalaya is a highly seasoned Creole dish of rice, ham, shrimps, tomatoes, and green peppers. No printed or spoken word can describe its deliciousness—you've just got to eat it in Louisiana. It traditionally calls for ham, for the very name is a mixture of French and African, *jambon à la ya. Jambon* is French for ham, and *ya* is sort of African for rice.

At the International Rice Festival in 1951 a Shrimp Jambalaya recipe won first prize in the rice and fish division of the Creole Rice Cookery contest. It makes a mighty toothsome dish, but I was slightly amazed that the recipe doesn't call for ham as one of the ingredients. To the purist, it isn't a true Jambalaya, but we can sometimes say, "To hell with the purists!" See if you don't agree with me.

SHRIMP JAMBALAYA

2 *tbsp. bacon drippings*	¼ *tsp. dried thyme*
1 *tbsp. flour*	1 *tbsp. Worcestershire sauce*
½ *cup chopped onions*	3 *cups cooked rice*
1 *minced clove garlic*	2 *cups cooked shrimps, cut in*
1 *cup canned tomatoes*	*pieces*
½ *cup dry white wine*	10 *whole cooked shrimps*
1 *green pepper, chopped*	1 *cup tomato juice*
½ *tsp. salt*	½ *cup grated cheese*
¼ *tsp. red pepper*	2 *tbsp. parsley*

Melt the bacon drippings in a skillet, stir in the flour, and blend thoroughly. Add the onions, and cook until they are limp. Then add the finely minced garlic, tomatoes, dry white wine (this is an addition of mine, because the original recipe called for water), finely chopped green pepper, salt, red pepper, dried thyme, and Worcestershire sauce. Cook until the green pepper is tender, stirring occasionally. Then add the cooked rice, the 2 cups of cut-up shrimps, and the tomato juice. Pour the whole into a greased baking dish. Sprinkle the grated cheese (an aged, sharp Cheddar cheese) and the parlsey over the top. Place the whole shrimps about the top. Place in a 350-degree oven and bake for 15 minutes. This recipe makes 6 servings.

Speaking of Jambalaya reminds me of a "For Men Only!" column I had a lot of fun doing, and which evidently brought a lot of fun to my readers, and sympathetic reactions particularly from fathers.

A few weeks before a Father's Day I received a communication addressed to food editors from the National Father's Day Committee which offered some suggestions for a Father's Day feature. One of them was, and I quote:

"Perhaps you might wish to feature the head of the household as the official chef and host on Father's Day, using the small fry as Associate Chefs. Milady could be told of the thrill that comes to many dads when they are allowed to take control of the kitchen (sic). Emphasis should be put on the importance of allowing the young 'uns to participate in the activities." Unquote.

Now, this suggestion was all very well, and very meritorious, except Father would probably be in a state bordering on collapse and/or coma by dinnertime if he had spent the afternoon in the kitchen preparing dinner with one or more small fry complicating things, as small fry are apt to do, no matter how charming and helpful. However, let's suppose Father had elected to make that noble dish Jambalaya, from the recipe in my *With a Jug of Wine*.

Get out a large earthenware casserole, a saucepan, a wooden board for chopping, 2 bowls, and a colander. Remove toy fire truck, building blocks, water pistol, and jigsaw puzzle from kitchen table.

Get ham and shrimps out of refrigerator. Dice 1½ cups of ham and place in a bowl. Remove Junior's hand from the shrimps. Shell and peel shrimps. Dice another ½ cup of ham to replace that the children have sampled.

Peel 2 onions, chop them, and place them in another bowl. Measure out 1 cup of rice, put it in the colander, and place under running water. Get dustpan and brush up pieces of bowl and onion that Betty has accidentally knocked off the table. Get out another bowl, and peel and chop 2 more onions. Chop ½ green pepper and mince ½ clove of garlic. Remove onion and garlic peelings which Junior has placed in the saucepan, and place saucepan over a low flame.

Answer telephone. Return to kitchen. Go to casserole and remove shrimp shells which one of the small fry have placed therein. Put 2 tablespoons of olive oil in the casserole, and heat. Add diced ham to the casserole. Remove 3 marbles from the shelled and peeled shrimp. Add shrimps to casserole, and sauté lightly.

Go to refrigerator. Remove Junior's chemical set and Betty's teddy bear from the refrigerator and get out butter. Add 1½ tablespoons to the shrimp and ham. Also add chopped onions, garlic, bay leaf, and salt and pepper.

Answer doorbell. Return to the kitchen and wonder if you added salt or sodium chromate from Junior's chemical set to the casserole. Open can of tomato paste.

Answer telephone again. Return to the kitchen. Wipe from Margaret's fingers the tomato paste with which she has been drawing pictures on the wall. Add drained rice to the casserole, and sauté until brown. Fish pieces of jigsaw puzzle out of the consommé, which Betty had added, and add consommé to casserole. Get out and open another can of tomato paste and add to the casserole.

Answer telephone. Return to the kitchen to find Junior putting potassium permanganate into the casserole. Head for Junior, who flees, knocking casserole off the stove.

Clean up mess. Wash kitchen floor, kitchens walls, and dishes. Call up nearest restaurant and order dinner for five. Take a double slug of bourbon. Retire to bedroom, lock the door, and collapse on bed!

Shrimps combined with artichoke hearts in a casserole will make a delightful luncheon dish that the ladies of your bridge, canasta, or Bolivia foursome will rave over. It also serves as the *pièce de résistance* for a Lenten dinner, which should elicit compliments from hubby.

SHRIMP AND ARTICHOKE HEARTS EN CASSEROLE

1 #2 can whole artichoke hearts	¼ tsp. pepper
¾ lb. shelled, cooked shrimps	Dash cayenne pepper
½ lb. fresh mushrooms	1 cup cream
4 tbsp. butter	1 tbsp. Worcestershire sauce
2½ tbsp. flour	¼ cup dry sherry
½ tsp. salt	¼ cup grated Parmesan cheese
	Paprika

Drain the can of artichoke hearts and arrange them in a buttered shallow baking dish. Spread over them the shrimps (crab meat may also be used instead, fresh, frozen, or canned). Sauté the coarsely sliced mushrooms in 2 tablespoons of butter for about 6 to 7 minutes, then add them, and the butter in the pan, to the contents of the baking dish.

In the meantime have made a medium cream sauce by melting 2 tablespoons of butter in a saucepan and stirring in the flour. When smooth, add the salt, pepper, cayenne pepper, and the cream. Cook, stirring constantly, until the sauce is smooth, then add the Worcestershire sauce and sherry. Blend these in well, then pour the sauce over the artichoke hearts, shrimps, and mushrooms. Sprinkle the top with grated Parmesan cheese, and dust the top with paprika. Bake 20 minutes in a 375-degree oven. Serve from the casserole to 4.

In the chapter on Hors d'Oeuvres I told about the Lawry Spaghetti Sauce Mix. While I believe it was originally intended for making a quick and easy, yet palatable and delicious sauce for spaghetti and other pastas, it has many other uses. For example, it makes a delightful and zesty Shrimp Creole.

SHRIMP CREOLE

1 *pkg. Lawry's Spaghetti* *Sauce Mix*	¼ *cup olive oil*
	½ *lb. raw, cleaned shrimps*
1 #2 *can tomatoes*	¼ *tsp. Lawry's seasoned salt*
¼ *cup dry red wine*	

Place the contents of the package of spaghetti sauce mix in a saucepan. Add the canned tomatoes, and stir until well blended. Bring to a boil, then lower the flame, cover the saucepan, and simmer the contents over a low flame for 15 minutes. Add the oil, shrimps, and seasoned salt. Cover again and simmer over a low flame for 15 minutes. Add the dry wine, heat, and serve with or over boiled rice.

A half pound of cooked, cleaned shrimps may be used. However, in preparing this variation, simmer the sauce for 30 minutes, then add the olive oil and shrimp, and stir thoroughly. Add salt if needed. Just before serving add the dry red wine, reheat, and serve.

Oysters have been a favorite article of food for about twenty centuries, as far as I have been able to find out. Before the Christian Era the Greek Poet and writer, Alexis of Thuril, wrote in his comedy, *The Apothecary:* "First, then, I spied oysters, wrapped in seaweed. . . . I grabbed them; for they are the perfect prelude to a daintily ordered dinner."

Tiberius, the second Roman Emperor, is said to have lived on oysters practically all of his life. To the Romans, oysters were the "dainty manna of the sea." They were considered to be the crowning touch to a banquet. Slaves were sent as far as the Atlantic seacoast to gather oysters. Many Roman homes had great tanks of water in which the oysters were kept fresh for the tables. In a more recent time Emperor Napoleon III is said to have established two "Imperial Oyster Parks" in the shallow Bay of Arcachon. These were underwater farms to produce oysters. And of course oysters were highly prized by the American Indians.

For those who are oyster enthusiasts, perhaps a little run-down on the different kinds might be interesting. For those who don't like oysters, skip the next thirteen paragraphs.

BLUEPOINTS are possibly the most widely known variety of oysters. They are fairly small, delicious, and come from the Great South Bay on the south side of Long Island.

GREENPORTS have a salty flavor all their own, and come from Long Island Sound.

TANGIERS come from the Eastern Shore of Maryland, and are one of the sweetest and most succulent of oysters. It is said that Pocahontas fed Tangiers to Captain John Smith—with famous results, if you know your early American history!

CHINCOTEAGUES, regarded by many epicures as the supreme aristocrat among oysters, come from Cape Cod.

COTUITS come from Massachusetts, and are a delicious middle-size oyster.

LYNNHAVENS, the very large oyster that was the favorite of "Diamond Jim" Brady, come from the south side of Chesapeake Bay. Perhaps I should say "did come," for a correspondent of mine, George Debnam, of Baltimore (who seems to be a walking encyclopedia on oysters), wrote me that Lynnhavens haven't been caught during the last twenty years in Chesapeake Bay. Too many ferry-boats and other ocean vessels apparently are to blame.

CAPE CODS are delicious, with a special flavor that seems to endear them to New Yorkers.

DELAWARE BAY oysters are excellent, and are said to have been a favorite of William Penn.

CHERRYSTONES (and I don't mean clams!) come from Cherrystone Creek, just north of Cape Charles, Virginia. Mr. Debnan considers them the best-flavored large oyster.

OLYMPIA oysters, no larger than your thumbnail (they are so small that they run 1,600 to the gallon), have an exquisite flavor. But you rarely get them away from the Pacific Coast.

OYSTER BAYS, coming from the north shore of Long Island, have a sweet-flavored and darker meat.

ROYAL WHITSTABLES and COLCHESTERS are the two favorite oysters in England.

Mr. Debnan wrote me that the largest and best oysters he had ever tasted came from Morro Bay on the coast of California. He said he had them when a guest at William Randolph Hearst's castle at San Simeon, in California. These were probably Japanese oysters, first planted in California waters in 1902, and called the WILLA-POINT. They are sometimes as big as a man's hand!

Incidentally, the best and most interesting run-down on oysters I have ever found is in Iles Brody's book, *On the Tip of Tongue,* published by Greenberg. There are eleven pages of history, anecdote, and recipes.

Oysters are versatile little creatures, because they can be eaten and enjoyed any time at any meal; creamed oysters over waffles is an elegant breakfast dish, and *La Mediatrice* (fried oysters in a loaf of French bread) is a most gratifying very late evening or very early morning snack.

I guess it's about time to get down to some really enticing oyster dishes. Let's start with Oysters Florentine, which calls for fresh oysters on the half shell.

OYSTERS FLORENTINE

36 *oysters on half shell**	⅛ *tsp. pepper*
1 *cup cooked, chopped spinach*	1 *medium lemon, juice of*
Butter	¾ *cup mayonnaise*
Salt and pepper	2 *oz. dry white wine*
¼ *cup minced onion*	½ *cup milk*
1 *tsp. Ac'cent*	*Paprika*
½ *tsp. salt*	3-4 *tbsp. butter*
1 *cup dry breadcrumbs*	

* In place of the half-shell service, the ingredients for this dish may be layered in a shallow, buttered baking dish, and baked as directed later for 30 minutes.

Drain the chopped, cooked spinach well, and season to taste with salt, pepper, and about 1 teaspoon of melted butter. Then add the minced onion, and mix well. This is your spinach mixture.

Wash the oysters to remove any sand, after having removed them from their shells. On each oyster half shell place 1½ teaspoons of the spinach mixture, and then place the oysters on top of the spinach mixture in the shells. Sprinkle the oysters with a mixture of the Ac'cent, ½ teaspoon of salt, and ⅛ teaspoon of pepper. Also sprinkle the oysters lightly with lemon juice.

Mix together the dry white wine and the mayonnaise, and then add the milk. The mixture should be reasonably thick, and not runny. Better add the milk a little at a time to the mayonnaise, so that you can judge when you have added enough. Spoon this mixture over the oysters. Then on top of the mayonnaise sauce sprinkle 1 cup of buttered breadcrumbs, which are prepared by mixing 1 cup of dry breadcrumbs with 3 to 4 tablespoons of melted butter. Then sprinkle paprika over the breadcrumb topping.

Place the oysters in their shells in pans filled with rock salt, or on a large cookie sheet covered with rock salt. This will hold them steady while cooking.

Bake the oysters in a 350-degree oven for 20 to 25 minutes, or until the crumbs are brown. This makes 6 servings.

Oysters Casino also call for oysters on the half shell, but they are broiled. I think they have a slightly more exciting flavor than Oysters Florentine.

OYSTERS CASINO

24 *oysters on half shell**	*Salt and pepper*
2 *slices lean bacon, diced*	1 *chopped pimento*
2 *tbsp. butter*	1 *tsp. dry sherry*
1 *small onion, minced*	*Dash Worcestershire sauce*
½ *green pepper, minced*	*Few drops lemon juice*

See that the oysters and their shells are free from sand and clean.

Place the diced bacon in a skillet, and fry slowly over a low flame until crisp—about 3 minutes.

* In place of the half-shell service, distribute the oysters equally on 4 toasted half slices of English muffins, which have been spread with mayonnaise, place in a buttered shallow baking dish, and cover with the sauce. Place under the broiler, 3 inches from the flame, and broil for 3 minutes. Serve on individual hot plates.

In a saucepan melt the butter over a medium flame, and add the minced onion and green pepper, and salt and pepper to taste. Sauté for about 5 minutes, or until the vegetables are tender. Then pour the contents of the saucepan into the skillet with the diced bacon, and add the chopped pimento, dry sherry, dash of Worcestershire sauce, and a few drops of lemon juice. Mix everything well.

Cover the oysters in their half shells with the above mixture, distributing it evenly over the oysters. Bed the oysters in their half shells in rock salt on a cookie sheet or in pans, and place under the broiler, 3 inches from the flame, and broil for 3 minutes. This serves 4.

To savor the delicacy of oysters to the utmost, they should be freshly opened and eaten on the half shell, with only a little lemon juice squeezed over them, or even just a sprinkling of black, freshly ground pepper. To my mind, one of the worst gastronomic crimes is to dunk fresh oysters in a highly spiced cocktail sauce.

Next, in order of succulence, to oysters on the half shell would come oyster stew. Not the skimmed milk and tough bivalve concoction that one encounters all too often, but a rich, steaming bowl of oyster stew that intrigues your eyes as its fragrance makes your mouth water. One of the best oyster stews I have ever eaten was in the Oyster Bar of the Grand Central Terminal in New York City. But, immodestly, I think it runs second to the one that I devised. The recipe is at its best if you use freshly opened oysters, but it is still tops if you use bulk oysters.

OYSTER STEW, M.W.

3 *pints oysters*	1 *bay leaf*
4 *tbsp. butter*	1 *tsp. salt*
1 *clove garlic*	⅛ *tsp. white pepper*
2 *medium onions, minced*	*Dash cayenne pepper*
2½ *cups milk*	½ *cup dry white wine*
2½ *cups cream*	*Chopped parsley*
½ *cup chopped celery tops*	*Paprika*

In a saucepan lightly brown the crushed clove of garlic and the minced onions in 3 tablespoons of butter. Then discard the garlic.

Put the milk and the cream in the top of a double boiler to heat over gently boiling water in the lower part. Then add the cooked onions and the butter they were cooked in, the chopped celery tops, bay leaf, and 1 pint of oysters which have been coarsely chopped (the remaining 2 pints should not be chopped, but left whole). Mix all, and let this heat for about 20 minutes, but do not allow to boil. Then strain the mixture through a fine sieve, discarding the solids, and return the strained liquid to the top of the double boiler.

In a saucepan put the remaining 2 pints of whole oysters (and their liquor, if they are bulk oysters) to heat, together with the salt, white pepper, and cayenne pepper. Just as the edges of the oysters begin to curl, add them and their liquor to the strained milk and cream. Also add the remaining 1 tablespoon of butter and stir in the dry white wine. Cook for a minute or two longer, or until the mixture is thoroughly heated. Serve in heated bowls, with a sprinkling of chopped parsley over the top, and a dusting of paprika. This may serve 6, but you'd be safer in figuring on 4.

In closing this chapter on fish and shellfish, I'd like to mention my *Fisherman's Wharf Cookbook,* if I'm not being too immodest. If you are interested in seafood recipes, I think you will enjoy it, and profit by it. Prudence Penny, writing in the New York *Daily Mirror,* said, "One of the most valuable recipe collections that could be acquired by the average person with no more than mild enthusiasm for seafood is, in my opinion, 'The Fisherman's Wharf Cookbook' . . . Gourmet-author is Morrison Wood."

This book is entirely devoted to fish and shellfish, and contains over 160 unusual and easy-to-follow recipes that have been gathered from all over the country, or devised by me. Included in it are recipes for the finest dishes that are served in the various restaurants on San Francisco's famed Fisherman's Wharf.

(5) MEATS

Hanging on the wall of my study is a painting depicting a gay and colorful scene. The setting is a banquet hall of an English castle. In the foreground, and crowded in the background around a huge, heavily laden table, are gaily caparisoned men wearing doublet and hose, and ruffs around their necks. The central figures are two servants, kneeling, supporting between them a great platter of meat, and a commanding figure, standing before an ornate chair. This haughty, bearded man, with ermine-trimmed vestments, has his jeweled sword extended in front of him, its point resting on the meat. Legend has it that this English King is saying:

"I dub thee—Sir Loin of Beef!"

The re-enactment of this knighting of a loin of beef is carried out even in our day on special occasions. I recall very vividly a similar tableau that a group of men put on several years ago at a Knighting of the Beef Dinner at the South Shore Country Club in Chicago. A stage had been built at the end of the dining room, and on it, in front of velvet drapes, a heavily laden table had been set up. Seated at the table were gaily caparisoned men in doublet and hose, and at the center of the table sat a bearded man with ermine-trimmed vestments. Great tankards of ale were quaffed frequently by the group (it wasn't really ale at all, for the ceremony took place during prohibition—it was heavily spiked bootleg beer!).

Suddenly two servants appeared, bearing between them a huge loin of beef on a platter. They placed it in front of the King. He rose, and stood a little unsteadily, trying to draw his jeweled sword (that spiked bootleg beer was mighty potent). Finally the King got the sword out of the scabbard, and he brought it down on the beef with such a resounding smack that grease flew in all directions. Slightly disconcerted for the moment, he forgot his line. Then it came to him.

"I dub thee Sir Loin of Beef!" he shouted.

At the same time he brought the sword again down on the beef with a mighty blow, and again grease spouted out. All of the people in the dining room applauded. That is, all except those seated at tables in front of the stage, one of whom was my wife.

After the party was over, Mrs. Wood and I departed for home. Most of the way the silence in the car was pregnant. Finally I asked casually, "How did you like the tableau, dear?"

"Oh, it was just dandy," she answered brightly—a little too brightly, I thought. "The table roistering that went on in Merrie Old England was certainly faithfully reproduced. But why, in Heaven's name, did you have to strike that roast of beef twice with your sword?"

I regretted having brought the subject up, and had nothing to say. But my Better Half exercised the time-honored prerogative of having the last word.

"And furthermore," she added succinctly, "I don't want to hear one peep out of you when the bill comes in for a new formal."

Well, what I started out to say was that I know of no other meat that so richly deserves an accolade as beef. In America steaks and roast beef are the most popular meat throughout the country. In England roast beef and steak and kidney pie are national dishes, and in France *Pot au Feu* is an institution.

To my mind the most elegant, and one of the most delicious beef dishes is broiled tenderloin of beef, or filet of beef, as it is also called, with a mushroom sauce. This is a dish that is literally "fit for a king," and is an ideal entree for a party of ten or twelve. Of course the filet, or tenderloin, is the most tender cut of beef that can be had, and if it comes from prime or choice beef its flavor and texture are unsurpassed. The whole tenderloin will weigh between five and six pounds, and it is broiled whole. When you buy it, have your butcher remove all of the fat and trim it, and then lard it well. Also have him grind the trimmings, which you will use in the sauce.

The best procedure, I think, is to make the sauce first. It can be started a little while before you put the tenderloin under the broiler, or it can be made a little in advance. But it must always be kept hot, because it must be instantly available the moment the tenderloin is removed from the broiler.

BROILED BEEF TENDERLOIN, MUSHROOM SAUCE

1 *beef tenderloin, 5-6 lbs.*   *Pinch dried marjoram*
3 *oz. butter*   *Pinch dried thyme*
1 *large clove garlic*   *Pinch hickory smoked salt*
½ *lb. fresh mushrooms, sliced*   *4 drops Tabasco sauce*
2 *medium onions, sliced*   *2 dashes Worcestershire sauce*
Ground trimmings from meat   *5 oz. dry red wine*
2 *tbsp. chili sauce*   *2 oz. condensed beef bouillon*
1 *tbsp. Escoffier Sauce Diable*   *Salt and pepper*
                    ½ *tsp. flour*

For the sauce, melt the butter in a fairly large skillet. Peel a large clove of garlic and cut it lengthwise into slivers. Put these slivers into the hot butter, and add the sliced fresh mushrooms and the onions, sliced. Sauté for about 5 minutes, or until the onions are limp. Then add the ground trimmings from the tenderloin (or about ¼ pound of ground hamburger), and break up the meat with a fork, stirring constantly. At the end of about 4 or 5 minutes add the chili sauce, Sauce Diable, the dried marjoram and thyme, a generous pinch of the hickory smoked salt, the Tabasco sauce, Worcestershire sauce, dry red wine, beef bouillon, a sprinkling of salt and pepper, and the flour. Stir this mixture well, and let it just barely simmer until ready to pour over the tenderloin when it is put in a roaster.

To cook the tenderloin, preheat the oven for 15 minutes, with the broiling pan in, at 550 degrees. Also have your beef tenderloin at room temperature. Put the larded tenderloin on the broiling pan, not more than 2 inches from the flame or heat units, and cook under the broiler at its highest heat for 8 minutes. Then turn the tenderloin and cook for about 7 minutes on the other side. Then take it from under the broiler and place it in a roaster, pour the sauce over it, and put it in a 350-degree oven for about 10 minutes. Remove the tenderloin to a hot platter, pour the sauce over it, and serve.

Remember, one of the greatest culinary crimes is to overcook a tenderloin of beef. When it is sliced the center should be definitely pink, shading to a crisply done outside.

While the art of broiling meat on skewers is one of the oldest methods of cooking, it was rarely practiced in the home. Then the craze for barbecuing captured the imagination of amateur chefs, and soon the steel skewer became an indispensable item.

But preparing food *en brochette* need not be confined to the outdoor barbecue pit or oven. It can be done very simply and easily in the kitchen oven or broiler with mouth-watering results. And you can cook a surprising number of meats, fish, and shellfish combinations on skewers.

One of the most toothsome dishes I have ever tasted is *Tenderloin en Brochette* served on a bed of wild rice with sort of a Bordelaise sauce. It is the famed specialty of one of San Francisco's top restaurants, Ernie's, on upper Montgomery Street.

In a town loaded with fine restaurants, Ernie's is outstanding, not only for its food and service, but for its décor. It is an intimate restaurant, and one instinctively feels, sitting at a candlelit table and surrounded by red brocaded silk walls, that here is a bit of Old San Francisco. The bar at the front of the restaurant is long, massive, and gleaming, and is said to have come to San Francisco around the Horn. And the moment you enter the place you are made to feel completely welcome by either Victor Gotti, or Mario DeFenzi, the owners and hosts.

Here is Mario's recipe for the restaurant's most popular dish.

TENDERLOIN EN BROCHETTE, ERNIE'S

2 *lbs. tenderloin of beef*	16 *button mushrooms*
Green peppers	*Salt and pepper*
Bacon	*Olive oil*

Risotto of Wild Rice

1 *cup wild rice*	2 *oz. butter*
3 *little green onions*	4 *small bay leaves*
½ *green pepper*	*Pinch dried thyme*
2 *cloves garlic*	1½ *cups beef bouillon*
Pinched dried rosemary	*Salt and pepper*

Sauce

1 *celery branch*	4 *oz. strong beef stock*
½ *small carrot*	4 *oz. dry red wine*
½ *small onion*	1 *lemon, juice of*
2 *cloves garlic*	*Pinch nutmeg*
4 *oz. butter*	2 *egg yolks*
1 *tsp. pickling spices*	*Salt and pepper*
Pinch dried rosemary	*Chopped parsley*
4 *oz. tomato purée*	*Grated Parmesan cheese*

Get 2 pounds of well-pared tenderloin of beef free from all fat and sinews. Cut into 16 pieces about 1 inch thick. Prepare also 16 squares of green pepper, cut to the same size as the meat pieces. The green peppers should first be boiled for 2 minutes, drained, and allowed to cool before cutting. Also prepare 16 bacon squares (of the same size as the green pepper squares), and have ready 16 button mushrooms.

On four 10-inch-long wire skewers spear first a piece of meat, then a piece of pepper, then a piece of bacon, then a mushroom. Repeat until you have used 4 pieces of everything on each skewer. Salt and pepper to taste, dip the filled skewers in olive oil, and then put on a rack under the broiler, and broil at 550 degrees for 2 minutes, medium rare, or 1½ minutes rare.

For the *Risotto* of wild rice you will need 1 cup of well-washed wild rice. Finely mince the little green onions (bulbs and tops), the the green pepper, and the cloves of garlic. In a saucepan sauté these in the butter, to which a pinch of dried rosemary has been added, until the vegetables are tender and start to brown (approximately 2 minutes), tossing several times. Then add the wild rice, crumbled bay leaves, and dried thyme, and cover the whole with the condensed beef bouillon. Salt and pepper to taste, and allow to cook slowly until the rice absorbs all the liquid and becomes fluffy and tender.

For the sauce cut the celery branch and the half small carrot into 2-inch lengths, chop the onion, and mince the garlic. Put these vegetables, the pickling spices, and the dried rosemary in a saucepan with 2 ounces of butter, and sauté until the vegetables are well browned. Then add the tomato purée, beef stock, dry red wine, lemon juice, and the nutmeg. Bring to a boil, and then let the liquids reduce to half their volume, then pass the whole through a fine strainer, discarding the solids. Add the strained sauce to the well-beaten egg yolks, and beat all together until well integrated. Add salt and pepper to taste. Keep hot, but do not allow to boil. Just prior to serving beat in 2 ounces of butter, and finish with the chopped parsley.

To serve, divide the wild rice among four plates, and sprinkle with grated Parmesan cheese Place one skewer of the meat on each bed of rice, hold the skewer down with a fork, and withdraw the skewer from the meat. Then cover each with the sauce.

French cooks are notoriously frugal, and with them it is a cardinal sin to waste anything that is still edible. Consequently, their ragouts and stews are usually out of this world. Scraps of this, scraps of that, scraps of something else, a little wine, an herb or two, a little leftover meat stock go into the pot or casserole, and what comes out of it later is so good you can hardly believe it.

However, there are some leftovers that are too delicious in themselves to be made into stews or ragouts. I'm thinking in particular of a prime roast of beef, or a wonderfully flavored pot roast. But the French have an answer to that—Miraton of Beef. The "miraton" simply means sliced, cooked meat warmed over with onions and a rich sauce. The next time you have a roast of beef, save about a pound of it, and try this recipe.

MIRATON OF BEEF

Thin slices cooked roast beef	*6 oz. canned beef bouillon*
2 medium-sized onions	*4 oz. dry red wine*
1 tbsp. butter	*1 tsp. tomato purée*
1 tsp. red wine vinegar	*1 tsp. chopped parsley*
½ tbsp. flour	*Salt and pepper*
Pinch powdered thyme	*½ cup sliced fresh mushrooms*
	Butter

Chop the onions rather fine, and sauté them in the butter in a heavy skillet until they are evenly browned. Then sprinkle over the onions the red wine vinegar, and the flour which has the powdered thyme mixed with it. Stir well until the mixture is thoroughly blended, then add the beef bouillon and the dry red wine. Continue to stir until the mixture is smooth, then blend in the tomato purée, chopped parsley, salt and pepper to taste, and the sliced fresh mushrooms which have previously been sautéed in about 1 tablespoon of butter for a few minutes.

Let the above mixture cook for 2 or 3 minutes, then lay in the sauce the medium-thin slices of cooked roast beef and spoon the sauce over them. Cover the skillet and simmer for about 5 minutes, or until the slices of beef are thoroughly heated. Serve on a very hot deep platter, and surround the slices of beef and the sauce with a border of mashed or riced potatoes, or hot, flaky rice, or cooked noodles.

I am very fond of thick cold slices of rare roast beef, but my wife doesn't care for rare roast beef when it is cold. So one night I dreamed up something that I thought she might like, while I had my rare roast beef cold. But it turned out so delicious that the next time we had cold rare roast beef, I went for it too.

DEVILED ROAST BEEF

2 *slices cold roast beef,*
   (*⅜ inch thick*)
Hickory smoked mustard
Fine breadcrumbs
6 *oz. roast beef gravy*
1 *oz. Escoffier Sauce Diable*
4 *dashes Tabasco sauce*

Generous pinch dry mustard
1 *tsp. Worcestershire sauce*
1 *tsp. Hot-N-Tot Barbecue*
   Sauce
1 *tbsp. chili sauce*
½ *cup consommé*
Garlic salt
Freshly ground pepper

Cut the cold roast beef in slices about ⅜ inch thick. Spread the slices on both sides with the hickory smoked mustard, and then cover both sides of each slice with fine breadcrumbs. Place the prepared slices on a cookie sheet, or in a shallow fireproof dish, and broil under a medium flame until the slices are brown and sizzling (about 5 minutes on each side). In the meantime, have the sauce prepared.

If you have ¾ cup of roast beef gravy left, use it. If not, use the same amount of Franco-American canned beef gravy, or, lacking that, stir 1 teaspoon of meat extract into 6 ounces of boiling water, and then blend in 1 tablespoon of flour.

Place the gravy in a saucepan, and add the Sauce Diable, Worcestershire sauce, Tabasco sauce, dry mustard, the teaspoon of the bottled Hot-N-Tot sauce, chili sauce, consommé, a generous sprinkling of the garlic salt, and 5 or 6 turns on a pepper mill of freshly ground black pepper. Mix all this well, and cook for about 5 minutes.

To serve, pour the sauce over the sizzling roast beef slices. This recipe serves 2.

If you still have any roast beef left over, there's always roast beef hash which, to my mind, always closes out a grand roast beef in a blaze of glory. I've never tasted any roast beef hash that can compare with that my wife makes, but here is an entirely different and enticing version of roast beef hash as devised by my good gourmet friend, Colonel Leon Mandel.

ROAST BEEF HASH À LA MANDEL

1 *large baking potato*   *Cooked roast beef, chopped*
Heavy cream   *Brown sauce or beef gravy*
Butter   *Grated Parmesan cheese*

After baking a fairly large-sized potato, remove most of the inside and put it in an Osterizer with enough heavy cream and butter to make it whip into a fluffy mass. Take this out of the blender and add about twice the amount of leftover cooked roast beef, chopped, that you have of the potato mixture. Also add to the potato-roast-beef mixture as much of any good brown sauce (your own, or a high-grade commercial sauce or brown gravy) as the mixture will absorb. Then restuff the potato skin with the mixture, put a slight sprinkling of grated Parmesan cheese over the top, and return the stuffed potato to the oven, or under the broiler, to brown.

To most men, and many women, a steak rates top ranking in the field of meats. Some people prefer sirloins, some porterhouse, some T-bones, and some the elegant filet mignon. But, regardless of the cut, they are all super, provided, of course, that the beef is properly aged and of top quality, and, equally important, that the steak is cooked properly.

Without going into technicalities, the two best grades of beef are prime and choice. On both grades the fat is white, or creamy white and firm. Both are well marbled (the deposit of fat in the fine network of connective tissues which binds the muscle fibers together; i.e., the fine streaks of fat in the meat itself). This "marbling" adds greatly to the tenderness of a cut, and enriches its flavor.

As far as I can see, the only difference today between the grades "prime" and "choice" is that an animal graded prime has spent about a month longer in the feed lot than the animal graded choice, and consequently has more fat. The steaks and roasts I buy are graded choice, and I can't imagine anything better in flavor, tenderness, and succulence.

Parenthetically, in the There-Is-Always-Something-New department, a different kind of beef has made its appearance on the market in selected localities. It is called "bourbon beef."

"Bourbon beef is a new Kentucky product to please the most discriminating tastes," it says in the brochure that I received. "First prime and choice feeder calves are selected by competent cattle feeders. Then comes the slow fattening process on balanced rations enriched with liberal quantities of distillers' dried grains. High in proteins, minerals and vitamins from dried yeast, these feeds are by-products of Kentucky's famed distilling industry. Months later, loin, rib, and round are developed to the fullest—streaks of marbleizing white have interspersed the tender meat, and over all a smooth, creamy covering protects and retains the flavoring juices of this taste-tempting delicacy."

If the serving of bourbon beef becomes widespread, I shall expect to overhear in restaurants something like the following:

"How about another piece of steak, Joe?"

"No thanks, no more for me. I'm driving, you know."

Perhaps you might be interested in a quick run-down on the various cuts of steaks. *Porterhouse* is the aristocrat of steaks. It has a large tenderloin and quite a bit of fat. *T-Bone* is from the same loin, but has less tenderloin. *Tenderloin* is often called *Filet Mignon,* the most tender cut of beef. *Club Steaks* are essentially the same as porterhouse, except that they are smaller, with less fat and tail. *Sirloin* is next in palatability to the preceding cuts. However, it contains portions of bone.

Fine steaks should be broiled. I always allow a steak to stand at room temperature for about an hour before broiling, after first having rubbed the finest olive oil into both sides of the steak. Then I put it under the broiler, the top of the steak about 2 to 2½ inches from the flame. Depending upon thickness, I let it broil about 6 minutes (for a steak 1½ inches thick). Then I salt and pepper it, and turn it over and broil the other side for about 4 to 5 minutes (this leaves the steak well browned outside, and a little pink on the inside—rare, but not raw). That side is salted and peppered, generously dotted with butter, and served on a hot platter.

The following recipe will give you what I and my wife consider the most luscious steak we have ever tasted.

PIQUANT BROILED STEAK

1 *porterhouse steak, 1½ inches*	*Garlic powder*
thick	*Worcestershire sauce*
Olive oil	*Soft butter*
Minced fresh ginger root	*Dry mustard*
Hickory smoked salt	*Freshly ground pepper*
	Paprika

Rub olive oil into both sides of the steak, and allow to stand at room temperature for at least an hour. Just before broiling, sprinkle one side of the steak with finely minced fresh ginger root.

Place the steak under the broiler, with the side sprinkled with the ginger root up. Broil for about 6 minutes. Then sprinkle with hickory smoked salt, freshly ground pepper, and a pinch of garlic powder. Then turn the steak, sprinkle the uncooked side with minced fresh ginger root, and broil for about 4 to 4½ minutes (if you want to test the doneness of a steak, cut a small gash with a sharp knife along the edge of the bone, bend the meat back, and note its color. Do this after about 4 minutes if broiling the second side. If there is any rawness visible, let it cook for about ½ to 1 minute more). When the second side is finished, repeat the seasoning of the first side. Then remove the steak to a hot platter.

Cover the top with 1 to 2 tablespoons of soft butter, sprinkle over the top a generous pinch (about ½ teaspoon) of dry mustard, a generous sprinkling of Worcestershire sauce (about 1 teaspoon), and a sprinkling of paprika. Then turn the steak over, and follow the same procedure on the other side, and serve.

This is really not saucing the steak; rather, it is a seasoning. When you slice the steak (I usually remove the T-shaped bone from the steak with a sharp knife the moment it is on the platter) the juices of the steak mingle with the butter-mustard-Worcestershire-sauce-paprika seasoning (which I spoon over each serving), and you get the wonderful flavor of the meat, which is enhanced by the marvelous piquancy of the seasoned juices.

In San Francisco, Trader Vic operates one of the best-known restaurants in America (I should say in San Francisco and Oakland, because the original Trader Vic's was in Oakland, and his San Francisco restaurant was opened in 1953).

Victor Bergeron is a character; his restaurants are exotic; his rum drinks are famous all over the world; and his food is tops. Originally, I believe, he served only Polynesian and Cantonese food, but more recently, in San Francisco, he has added other better-known comestibles, such as poached chicken with truffles, rack of lamb, steaks, fresh frogs' legs, flambéed kidneys with sour cream, and seafood.

Recently, I had a most unusual and exciting entree at Trader's San Francisco restaurant. Bobby Gee, the captain (an old friend from my first days at the Fairmont Hotel's Tonga Room), gave me the recipe.

BUTTERFLY STEAK, HONG KONG STYLE

1 10-oz. filet mignon	1 tsp. Worcestershire sauce
1 oz. butter	Dash A-1 sauce
Salt and pepper	Dash Tabasco sauce
Mai Kai (or Ac'cent)	3 tbsp. beef bouillon
1 tsp. Dijon mustard	1 oz. brandy

Cut the filet mignon by splitting it nearly in half, and opening it out in the shape of a butterfly wing. Grill the steak in the butter for about 3 minutes to each side. Then remove the steak to a hot platter, season with salt and pepper, and a sprinkling of Mai Kai seasoning powder (or Ac'cent).

To the juices in the skillet add the Dijon mustard (imported from France), Worcestershire sauce, A-1 sauce, and Tabasco sauce. Blend these ingredients, and then add the beef bouillon, and blend the whole to a smooth sauce. Put the steak back in the skillet, along with any juices which may have seeped out. Set the warmed brandy alight, and pour it over the steak, spooning the liquid over the steak until the flame dies out. Serve very hot. This recipe is for a single serving. Incidentally, this recipe may be prepared in a chafing dish most effectively.

One of the most famous Hungarian dishes is Beefsteak à la Eszterhazy (in Hungarian, *Eszterhazy Rostelvos*), named after one of the oldest and richest families of the Hungarian nobility. I am sure that Prince Nicholas Eszterhazy never personally prepared the dish to which his name has been given, but I believe that he would have approved of this version, which I have devised.

BEEFSTEAK À LA ESZTERHAZY

6 small steaks, 1 inch thick
3 slices bacon, diced
4 tbsp. butter
Salt and pepper
3-4 tbsp. hot lard
2 carrots, chopped
2 medium onions, chopped
2 small parsnips, chopped

2 stalks celery, chopped
½ cup sliced fresh mushrooms
1½ tbsp. flour
¾ cup sour cream
½ cup beef consommé
2 tbsp. drained capers
1 tsp. paprika
¼ cup dry Madeira wine

First, prepare the sauce. In the hot lard (or bacon drippings) in a skillet lightly sauté the chopped carrots, onions, parsnips, celery, and the sliced mushrooms. When the vegetables are soft (about 7 minutes), sprinkle in the flour, and then blend in well the sour cream, consommé, drained capers, and paprika. Let all this heat thoroughly over a low flame.

Fry the diced bacon slices in a skillet until they are half done. Then drain the fat from the skillet and add the butter. In this sear the 6 individual small steaks over a high flame. Season the steaks with salt and pepper to taste, and then place them with the contents of the skillet in a large casserole. Add the sauce to the casserole, cover it tightly, and bake in a 325-350 degree oven for 25 minutes.

Remove the cover from the casserole and add the dry Madeira wine. Recover the casserole and bake 5 minutes more. Serve from the casserole to 6 people. Buttered noodles are, of course, the ideal accompaniment.

There was a time when you never encountered a pot roast of beef on the tables of New York's "Four Hundred," or comparable groups in cities across America. It comes from an inexpensive cut of beef, which in the old days was considered suitable only for those in the lowest income groups.

Actually, a pot roast, properly prepared, is a mighty fine dish. It is full of flavor, and its fairly long cooking renders it tender. One of the most famous pot roasts is the German *Sauerbraten,* which is really spiced beef. For all pot roasts the top or bottom round is excellent, also pieces from the rump, chuck, or neck. About 4 pounds, all in one piece, will serve anywhere from 4 to 6 people, depending upon their appetites, and what other foods are served with the meal.

The following recipe for pot roast is of my own devising, and I can guarantee its enticing flavor.

POT ROAST OF BEEF WITH BRANDY

4 *lbs. beef, in one piece*
Brandy
2 *small cloves garlic*
Salt
Freshly ground pepper
Flour
2 *tbsp. bacon drippings*
2 *tbsp. olive oil*
4 *tbsp. brandy*
1 *bay leaf*
Pinch dried thyme
Pinch dried marjoram

1 *tsp. salt*
1 *tsp. pepper*
2 *medium-sized onions, sliced*
4 *medium-sized carrots,*
    quartered
½ *cup chopped celery*
2 *fresh tomatoes, sliced*
1 *cup dry red wine*
½ *lb. sliced fresh mushrooms*
2 *oz. butter*
½ *cup sour cream*
2 *tbsp. flour*
2 *tbsp. butter*

Wipe a 4-pound piece of beef, preferably cut from the top of the round, with a cloth dampened with brandy. Then quarter the cloves of garlic, make small incisions in the top of the meat, and insert the garlic slivers in them. Then sprinkle the meat on all sides with seasoned flour, patting it into the meat.

In a heavy iron kettle melt the bacon drippings and add the olive oil. When hot, put in the meat and sear it well on all sides until nicely browned. Then pour over the meat in the kettle 4 tablespoons of brandy, and set it alight. (CAUTION: turn out the flame under the kettle, and be sure the kettle is not under anything, because the flame will mount about a foot above the kettle). Let the brandy blaze until the flame dies down, and then extinguish it with the top of the kettle.

Put the kettle back over the flame, and add the bay leaf, crumbled, the pinches of dried thyme and marjoram, salt and pepper, the onions, sliced, the carrots, quartered lengthwise, the chopped celery, the tomatoes, sliced, and the dry red wine. Place a tight-fitting lid on the kettle, and let the contents simmer slowly for 3½ to 4 hours.

When the cooking time has elapsed, remove the meat to a hot platter and, with a slotted spoon, remove the vegetables, spooning them on top of the meat. Place the platter in a warm oven and proceed to make the gravy.

Sauté the sliced fresh mushrooms in the butter in a skillet. When they are tender (about 6 minutes), put them into the gravy in the kettle. Also add the sour cream. Make a *roux* of the 2 tablespoons each of butter and flour, and add this *roux* to the gravy, stirring and blending well until smooth. Allow the gravy to cook briskly until thickened and smooth, than pour it into a gravy boat or tureen.

Serve buttered noodles with the pot roast, and slice the beef, including in each portion some of the vegetables. Pour the gravy over the meat, and the noodles too, if you like it that way.

A tossed green salad goes excellently with the entree, particularly if it has a blue cheese or Roquefort dressing. The same wine that went into the pot roast should be served with the dinner. A dessert suggestion? Cherry pie and coffee.

A favorite dish among the middle-class British families is a hot-pot of steak and tripe, and it really is delicious.

Hot-Pot, Hotch-Potch, and Hodge-Podge are different names for the same stew of meat and vegetables, and undoubtedly sprung from the French word *hochepot*. In French, *hocher* means "to jog or shake," hence, to stir. Q.E.D., a *hochepot* is a pot that is stirred.

In the North of England the hot-pot is usually made of mutton, and takes the place of an Irish stew. But I like it best when it is made from pieces of beef from the chuck or round, and that savory variety meat, tripe.

CASSEROLE OF STEAK AND TRIPE

¾ lb. lean beef	½ tsp. cracked pepper
2 tbsp. bacon drippings	1 bay leaf
2 cups chopped onions	Pinch dried thyme
1½ cups chopped celery	Pinch dried marjoram
2 cups carrots, sliced	¼ tsp. grated lemon rind
½ cup sliced leeks	1½ lbs. honeycomb tripe
2 tsp. salt	1 cup dry red wine

In a heavy skillet heat the bacon drippings, and when hot add the beef (chuck or round) cut in cubes about ¾ inch in size. Brown the beef cubes on all sides over a fairly hot flame.

In a large bowl mix together the onions, celery, carrots, thinly sliced, and the leeks. Place this vegetable mixture in an earthenware casserole. On top of it place the browned cubes of beef and the fresh honeycomb tripe, which has been washed in cold water and then cut into strips about ½ inch wide and 2 inches long.

Sprinkle over the contents of the casserole the salt, cracked pepper, the pinches of dried thyme and marjoram, and the grated lemon rind. Then pour over all the dry red wine, cover the casserole tightly, and simmer slowly on top of the stove for 1½ to 2 hours, or until the tripe is tender. Serve very hot from the casserole. This recipe serves 4 to 6.

I have a correspondent who lives in New York, and is a great gourmet. He follows my syndicated newspaper column, "For Men Only!" regularly in the Chicago *Tribune,* and every once in a while he will write me and ask for some special German or French recipe.

A year or so ago he wrote and asked if I had, or could unearth, a recipe for *Rinder Rouladen* made with beer. But neither in my food files, recipe files, nor among my hundreds of cookbooks could I find a recipe for *Rinder Rouladen* made with beer. So I sent out an S.O.S. in my column.

The response was heartwarming. Scores of recipes were sent to me from all parts of the country; not only from German cooks, but from Danish, Swedish, and Swiss cooks, and an excellent recipe came from a celebrated amateur chef in Duluth, Minnesota, who is a dentist, and, I believe, Scotch!

The preparation of *Rinder Rouladen* varies, but essentially it consists of pieces of flank or round steak covered with a stuffing, rolled, tied with a string, browned in butter, and then simmered until the rolls are tender. They are served with a gravy.

Inasmuch as my correspondent asked for a recipe using beer, I selected one which came from Charles Zuellig, of Groverstown, Indiana. He had been a chef for the Fred Harvey System for twenty-five years. Mr. Zuellig, in his letter, said that his recipe was the one from which the dish is prepared in Switzerland. It is really wonderful.

RINDER ROULADEN

2½ lbs. beef	Butter
Salt and pepper	2 tbsp. chopped cooked ham
Powdered thyme	1 onion, finely sliced
1 medium onion	1 bay leaf
2 tbsp. celery leaves	1 sprig thyme
4 slices bacon	3 sprigs parsley
1 tbsp. chopped parsley	2 tbsp. flour
Flour	1 bottle dark beer

1 cup brown sauce

Cut the beef into 6 oblong pieces, and flatten them with a cleaver until they are about ½ inch thick. Trim the slices neatly, rub each slice with mixed salt, pepper, and powdered thyme, and then arrange them on a board.

Put the trimmings through a meat grinder together with the onion, celery leaves, and the bacon. Mix well, season to taste with salt and pepper and 1 tablespoon of chopped parsley. Divide this mixture among the 6 beef slices, then roll each slice tightly, and secure with kitchen thread. Dredge the rolls lightly with flour, and fry slowly in butter in a skillet until golden brown on all sides.

Remove the rolls from the skillet and arrange them side by side in a shallow baking dish, on the bottom of which has been placed the chopped, cooked ham, the finely sliced onion, and a bag containing the bay leaf, sprig of thyme, and the sprigs of parsley (if you haven't the fresh thyme, use ¼ teaspoon of dried thyme. The bag can be an emptied tea bag). Drain off all but 2 tablespoons of fat from the skillet, then blend in 2 tablespoons of flour, and brown lightly over a gentle flame. Then stir in the dark beer, bring to a boil, then reduce the flame and simmer gently for a few minutes. Then add 1 cup of brown sauce (or canned beef gravy), season to taste with salt and pepper, and pour the sauce over the rolls and vegetables. Cover tightly, and set in a 350-degree oven and cook slowly, turning the rolls once, until they are tender.

Add more heated beer if necessary in order that the rolls may be covered with the sauce. At the end of the cooking time remove the bag of herbs, and serve. This should serve 6.

During roundup time on the great cattle ranches of Arizona, Montana, and Texas, the chuckwagon, and its absolute monarch, the cook, are the most important things in life to the cowboy, except, perhaps, his horse.

In case you don't savvy the word, podner, a chuckwagon is a portable range kitchen. Amazingly enough it will carry, besides a stove and kitchen utensils, enough provisions to feed maybe fifty or more hungry cowboys for five or six weeks! However, their food wants are simple—biscuits, beans, and beef. About the only food that is fresh is the beef. In the morning cookie and a cowpoke cut a yearling steer out of the herd, slaughter and butcher it, and hang it up for perhaps a day.

The meat menu? Steaks and roasts and stews. All edible meat, from the animal's tail to his tongue, is utilized. Probably the most famous roundup dish is (lower your eyes discreetly, and hide your blushes, ladies) Son-of-a-Bitch Stew. That is its actual name. This stew is composed of brains, liver, marrow gut, sweetbreads, heart, kidneys, and scraps of meat left over from the slaughtering of the day before, with onions and seasonings added. In case you are curious about its preparation, *Roundup Recipes,* published by World Publishing Company, contains five recipes for this stew that cowboys drool over.

In the College Inn Porterhouse Room of the Sherman Hotel in Chicago they make and serve a Chuckwagon Stew that is really appetizing. In an atmosphere of the cow country (ranch vistas are painted on the walls, waiters wear unborn-calf jackets, and a real Indian, complete with war bonnet, serves the coffee), you'll love this glorified stew. But you can make it at home with profit to the taste buds, and the delight of all concerned.

CHUCKWAGON BEEF STEW

1 *lb. beef tenderloin*	6 *medium-sized mushrooms*
24 *small pearl onions*	2 *green peppers*
4 *oz. butter*	*Salt and pepper*
4 *tbsp. flour*	1 *cup sour cream*
2 *cups consommé*	1 *cup dry red wine*
	2 *cups raw rice*

Cut the beef tenderloin julienne style, about 2 inches long. Sauté the meat and the onions in the butter until well browned. Remove the onions from the skillet or pot, and dust the meat with flour until all the butter in the pan has been absorbed. Then add the consommé, stirring constantly until a thin sauce is formed (it should be light brown in color). Then add the onions, the mushrooms, sliced, the green peppers cut julienne, and season with salt and pepper to taste. Cover, and simmer slowly for about 20 minutes. Uncover, and add the sour cream and the dry red wine. Heat, and serve over boiled, fluffy rice. This recipe will yield 4 servings.

With all due respect to the talented chef at the Sherman, I have made a slight variation in his recipe. The original recipe called for 2 cups of sour cream and 12 ounces of beef. But I like a little more meat, and I substituted 1 cup of dry red wine for the second cup of sour cream. Personally, I think the red wine gives an added piquancy to the dish.

Hungarian cuisine is said to rank next to French cuisine in importance. While there may be disputants to such a statement, certainly Hungarian dishes are interesting and exciting. They are apt to be highly spiced, but not nearly so "hot" as the curried dishes of the Far East, or the food of Latin America. True Hungarian paprika, for instance, is rather mild and sweet, rather than "hot," and many Hungarian dishes are thickened with sour cream or tomato pulp, which tempers any sharpness of the paprika. You will find this true in the following popular dish.

HUNGARIAN PAPRIKA BEEF STEW

2 *lbs. lean round steak*	¼ *tsp. freshly ground pepper*
2 *tbsp. lard*	1 *clove garlic*
4 *medium-sized red onions*	¾ *cup dry red wine*
1 *tbsp. Hungarian paprika*	2 *tbsp. tomato paste*
½ *tsp. salt*	1½ *cups sour cream*
¼ *tsp. caraway seeds*	½ *cup mayonnaise*

Cut the lean round steak into strips about 1½ inches long and ¼ inch wide. Be sure and cut the meat across the grain to avoid tough and stringy meat.

In a casserole or Dutch oven melt the lard (or bacon drippings) and add the red onions, chopped fine (ordinary onions can be used, but the red make for strength), and the Hungarian paprika. Fry gently until the onions are limp, and then add the strips of beef. Sauté until the beef is golden in color.

Add the salt, caraway seeds, freshly ground black pepper, clove of garlic, minced, dry red wine, and tomato paste. Cover and simmer gently for about 1 hour, or until the meat is tender. Then uncover the casserole and stir in the sour cream and mayonnaise, which have been blended together. Let all heat thoroughly, but do not allow to bubble. Serve from the casserole to 6 people.

Rib ends, or short ribs of beef, come from either rib roasts or the upper part of the plate. They naturaly include a considerable amount of bone, but nevertheless they are most succulent. They are always braised or stewed, and one of the favorite dishes in the Wood household is Short Ribs of Beef Burgundy.

Recently, however, I discovered a new way of cooking short ribs —broiling them, believe it or not. But before detailing the method, I'd like to go back exactly six years.

Early in April of 1950 I was invited to lunch to meet a man named Lloyd Rigler, from Los Angeles. Over coffee, Mr. Rigler pulled a small bottle out of his pocket and handed it to me.

"You'll probably be interested in this," he said. "It's a seasoned meat tenderizer. This may sound incredible, but this product will make tough cuts of meat tender and mouth-watering."

As Rigler went on to explain his product, I listened with somewhat skeptical amusement. But I accepted the sample, and agreed to try it. On the way home that day, I bought the toughest piece of beef that can be bought, and in my kitchen I cut it in half. On one half I sprinkled the meat tenderizer evenly over both sides, and let the meat stand for 45 minutes. The other half I left untreated.

I had decided to pan-broil the meat, which is the worst possible way of cooking a piece of bottom round. I preheated a heavy iron skillet, and put both pieces of meat in it. When both sides of the two pieces of meat were seared, I turned down the flame and let the meat cook to the degree of doneness that I prefer—brown on the outside and pink in the center.

The first thing I noticed was that the treated piece of meat had not shrunk or shriveled, but the other piece had. And when I served a piece of each of the two halves, the treated piece was as tender as a fine steak and had a delicious flavor, while the untreated piece was so tough that it could scarcely be chewed, and was completely devoid of flavor.

I was so impressed with the results obtained from Adolph's Seasoned Meat Tenderizer that I devoted the whole of my column, "For Men Only!" to it in the Chicago *Tribune* of April 14, 1950. In the last paragraph of the column I said that Mr. Rigler had very generously offered a sample of the meat tenderizer to anyone sending in a request, and accompanying the request with a self-addressed stamped envelope.

On Saturday morning my mail contained over 3,000 requests for samples; by the end of the following week, the number of requests had reached an astounding total of 10,116, and before the month was over, the total of requests had exceeded 14,000! And they came from every state in the Union!

In February of 1953 the *Reader's Digest* ran an article on Adolph's Seasoned Meat Tenderizer. Then later the International Editions (printed in twelve languages) carried the story, and inasmuch as my experience with the product was part of the story, and my name and the name of the Chicago *Tribune* were given, I began receiving mail from *all over the world,* asking where Lloyd Rigler and his partner, Larry Deutsch, could be contacted for the product. I never kept track of the number of requests, but it ran into the thousands. I even had to enlist the aid of the foreign department of the Bank of America in San Francisco to devise replies in the various languages.

Today Adolph's Meat Tenderizer is available in almost every part of the civilized world. And the partners are finding new things the product will do. Lentils, split peas, lima and navy beans, soaked overnight in water to which a tablespoon of Adolph's has been added, cook in half the time. Soups and broths made from tenderized meat or fowl are tastier. And for some time Ruth Rigler, Lloyd's sister, has been experimenting in her own home, and as she devises tasty new dishes, she sends the recipes for me to try. In this chapter I am including three of them—Broiled Short Ribs of Beef Oona Loa, Roast Leg of Lamb au Sherry, and Roast Shoulder of Pork à la Normande. They are all wonderful, and, of equal importance, they are thrifty dishes.

BROILED SHORTRIBS OF BEEF OONA LOA

3 lbs. lean beef shortribs
1½ tsps. Adolph's Seasoned
    Meat Tenderizer
1 cup pineapple juice
¼ cup soy sauce

1 tbsp. brown sugar
¼ cup honey
¼ cup water
1½ tsp. ground ginger
6 slices pineapple

Sprinkle the ribs evenly with the meat tenderizer and pierce generously from all sides with a kitchen fork or skewer. Place in a single layer on a plate, cover loosely, and store in the refrigerator overnight.

The next morning mix the pineapple juice, soy sauce, brown sugar, honey, water, and ground ginger together, and pour this sauce over the shortribs, and return the ribs to the refrigerator for 4 or 5 hours. When ready to cook, drain the meat, place on a broiler rack (or barbecue rack) about 3 inches from the flame or heat unit. Broil until the meat is well browned. Then turn, spoon well with the sauce, and broil until richly brown.

Five minutes before taking up the meat, brush the pineapple slices with the marinade sauce, and arrange on rack with meat. Let them heat through and brown slightly at the edges. These make a very pretty garnish for those shining brown ribs. Serves 6.

I consider Restaurant La Rue, out on Sunset Boulevard in Hollywood, another of the outstanding restaurants in America. In a town which leans heavily on tinsel and glamor, La Rue's is quietly and tastefully luxurious, but without ostentation.

Bruno is the host, and he welcomes you with a smiling courtesy that is definitely Old World. You don't have to be a personage, or a cinema star (although you will find plenty of both eating there almost every night), to warrant his meticulous attention to your food and service. But if you obviously know and enjoy fine food, he will beam.

Orlando Figini, the chef and co-owner, is one of the most renowned master chefs in America. He was selected by the Italian Government as chef of its Italian Pavilion at the New York World's Fair, which was hailed as the finest restaurant on the grounds during the run of the Exposition. His expert knowledge of Italian cuisine is reflected in the wonderful dishes that are served at La Rue's, although the restaurant is more continental than Italian.

Some time ago I chronicled in my "For Men Only!" newspaper column a recipe for Shrimps La Rue (which is also in my *Fisherman's Wharf Cookbook*). Several weeks later I received a request for another justly famous dish served at La Rue's. My correspondent wrote:

"I wonder if you could get and publish one of the most delectable dishes that I have ever eaten, which I once had at La Rue's. I don't know the name of it, but it was a casserole of meatballs in a rich, sour cream gravy. If you can give it to your readers, I am sure they will bless you for it."

The recipe referred to is *Biftoks La Rue,* and chef Orlando Figini sent me the recipe for 4 people. It takes a little time and effort to prepare, but, believe me, it is worth it.

BIFTOKS LA RUE

1 *lb. lean round beef, ground very fine*	2 *oz. dry white wine*
	1 *pint sour cream*
2 *tbsp. chopped onions*	1 *cup cream sauce*
6 *oz. butter*	*Few drops lemon juice*
Salt and pepper	*Flour*
1 *pint heavy cream*	¼ *lb. sliced fresh mushrooms*
1 *medium onion, sliced*	*Pinch dried tarragon leaves*

Smother 2 tablespoons of chopped onions in ½ ounce (1 tablespoon) of butter in a covered saucepan until the onions are tender. Then combine them with the beef, ground very fine, and salt and pepper to taste (if possible, force the seasoned beef and onions through a coarse sieve). Place the mixture on ice and allow to get very cold. Then add the heavy cream slowly to the beef mixture, mixing with a wooden spoon to obtain a smooth white paste. Further add 1 ounce (2 tablespoons) of butter that has been lightly browned in a saucepan (*beurre noisette*), stirring the whole mixture fast and constantly until well blended. Then place the mixture in the refrigerator for 2 hours.

In the meantime, make the sauce. Smother 1 sliced medium-sized onion in 2 ounces of butter (4 tablespoons) for a few moments, then remove the cover and add the dry white wine (a Chablis type is best), and cook until the onions are tender. Then add 1 pint of commercial sour cream, and a cup of cream sauce, and cook until the whole is reduced to a sauce consistency. Add a few drops of lemon juice, and salt and pepper to taste, then set aside.

Make 12 patties, or balls, out of the chilled beef mixture, and keep flouring them lightly during the shaping. Sauté the meatballs in 2 ounces (4 tablespoons) of butter until they are a rich, golden brown. Then place them in a casserole and keep warm.

Pour the sauce, which you have set aside, into the same pan that the meatballs were cooked in, bring to a boil, and boil for a few minutes, stirring constantly. Then strain the sauce, and add to it the sliced fresh mushrooms which have been previously sautéed in ½ ounce (1 tablespoon) of butter for about 7 minutes, and the pinch of dried tarragon leaves. Blend the whole, and pour the sauce over the meatballs, and serve. This recipe serves 4 persons.

This wonderful dish should be accompanied with a rice pilaf, or mashed potatoes, and fresh peas in butter. The wine can be a chilled Chablis, or a Rosé.

The Germans have a justly famous meatball dish which is, I believe, indigenous to East Prussia. But these meatballs are unlike any other meatballs that have been devised for the delight of the palate. Perhaps they might be likened to hamburgers, but they are boiled, not fried, and then they are simmered in a caper and sardellan sauce.

KÖNIGSBERGER KLOPS

¾ lb. chuck beef, ground
¾ lb. veal, ground
¼ lb. pork, ground
2 small hard rolls
½ cup light cream
1 medium onion, chopped
6 tbsp. butter
4 anchovy filets
2 beaten eggs
1 tsp. salt

¼ tsp. freshly ground pepper
Lemon juice
2 tsp. Worcestershire sauce
2 tbsp. chopped parsley
¼ tsp. dried marjoram
5 cups beef bouillon
1 cup dry white wine
4 tbsp. flour
1 tsp. dry mustard
2 small boneless sardines

⅓ cup drained capers

Have the beef, veal, and pork ground twice. Also break up the hard rolls and soak them in the cream for about 10 minutes, then press the excess liquid from them. Also sauté the chopped onion in 1 tablespoon of butter until lightly browned.

Put the ground meats, the moistened hard rolls, the sautéed onions, and the anchovy filets through the food grinder, using the finest blade. Then add to this the lightly beaten eggs, salt, freshly ground pepper, 1 tablespoon of lemon juice, the Worcestershire sauce, 1 tablespoon of chopped parsley, and the dried marjoram. Mix everything thoroughly, and shape the mixture into 12 balls.

Heat the condensed beef bouillon and the dry white wine in a deep skillet or an iron kettle. When the liquid is boiling, carefully drop the meatballs in, turn down the flame, and simmer slowly for 15 to 20 minutes, covered. Then remove the meatballs from the stock, and keep them hot while the gravy is being made.

Mix the dry mustard with the flour, and cream that mixture together with 4 tablespoons of butter. When the *roux* is smooth, add enough of the hot stock the meatballs were boiled in to make a thin paste, free from lumps. Turn up the flame under the stock, then stir the *roux* into the stock. Cook and stir until smooth and boiling.

Mash the sardines with 1 tablespoon of butter, and then stir into the gravy, blending well. Then add the drained capers (if you're fond of capers, use ½ cup), 1 tablespoon of chopped parsley, and the juice of half a lemon. When all is blended, add the meatballs to the gravy, reheat, and serve.

This will serve 4 to 6, depending upon the capacity of the diners. Boiled parsley potatoes, riced potatoes, or noodles go best with *Königsberger Klops*. Personally, I like cold mugs of beer best with this meal, but a good Rhine wine, chilled, is excellent. Coleslaw is a grand side-dish. For dessert, if you have room, there is nothing better than a good cheesecake.

The Scandinavian countries are noted for their meatballs. The Swedish meatballs are called *Köttbullars,* the Danish *Frikadellers,* and the Norwegian *Kjöttbollers*. I once did a column on Scandinavian meatballs, but it stirred up such a hornet's nest among my Swedish, Norwegian, and Danish readers that I'm not going to make that mistake here. Instead, I'm going to give you a wonderful recipe for meatballs that was dreamed up by my wife, who is of English extraction. She is a wonderful cook, and this is one of her damn good recipes.

BEATRICE'S MEATBALLS

1 *lb. ground round steak*   *Salt and pepper*
½ *lb. sausage meat*   *Pinch dried thyme*
1 *onion, chopped*   2 *tbsp. chopped parsley*
1 *green pepper, chopped*   *Dash Worcestershire sauce*
1 *clove garlic*   1 *egg, beaten*
½ *cup chopped celery*   *Tomato juice*
½ *cup fine breadcrumbs*   *Flour*
2 *tbsp. bacon drippings*

Mix together the ground round steak and the sausage meat, breaking the latter up with a fork. Then add the chopped onion and green pepper, the clove of garlic, minced, the chopped celery, the fine breadcrumbs (or cracker crumbs), salt and pepper to taste, generous pinch of dried thyme, the chopped parsley, the Worcestershire sauce, 1 beaten egg, and enough tomato juice to moisten the mixture. Work all these ingredients well together, mold into 18 balls, and roll each ball thoroughly in flour.

In a large skillet heat the bacon drippings, and when hot add the meatballs. Brown on all sides, and then add enough tomato juice to nearly cover the meatballs. Let the whole thing simmer very slowly for about 45 minutes, and then serve. This should serve about 6 people.

Remember the old days, along toward the end of the week, when a meat loaf was Mother's solution to the problem of stretching the remaining food dollars to the utmost, and yet you ate well? It was made from ground meat leftovers padded out with ground beef, or from the cheaper cuts of beef, pork, and veal ground together. The aroma that came from the kitchen while the meat loaf was cooking was tantalizing, and you were drooling when you sat down to the table. If any of the meat loaf was left, it was served cold for Saturday or Sunday night supper, or it made a wonderful snack, with a glass of cold milk, before bedtime.

One night at the Maison Wood we developed a yen for meat loaf. So the next day we got some ground chuck beef, lean shoulder of veal, beef liver, and sausage meat, and the two Woods collaborated on a meat loaf. Mrs. W. dug into her memory of her mother's meat loaf, and I added a few touches of my own. The result was an epicurean masterpiece, if I may be so bold.

THE WOODS' MEAT LOAF

1 *lb. lean chuck beef*	⅛ *tsp. allspice*
1 *lb. lean shoulder of veal*	⅛ *tsp. dried thyme*
1 *lb. beef liver*	½ *tsp. paprika*
1 *lb. sausage meat*	4 *tsp. Worcestershire sauce*
2 *onions*	*Freshly ground pepper*
½ *green pepper*	*Salt*
½ *lb. fresh mushrooms*	*Butter*
1 *cup celery leaves*	¼ *cup water*
1 *tbsp. parsley*	½ *cup chili sauce*
1 *cup stale breadcrumbs*	1 15½-*oz. can solid pack*
½ *cup dry Madeira wine*	*tomatoes*
3 *eggs, lightly beaten*	¼ *cup red wine garlic vinegar*
¼ *cup beef bouillon*	1 *small can pimientos*
½ *cup dry red wine*	½ *tsp. chili powder*
2 *cloves garlic*	1 *tsp. hickory mustard*

Put the beef, veal, liver, and sausage meat through the meat grinder twice. Place the ground meat in a large bowl, and combine with it 1 onion, the green pepper, the sliced fresh mushrooms, the celery leaves, and the parsley, all of which have been finely chopped. Then add the stale breadcrumbs which have been soaked in the dry Madeira wine, the lightly beaten eggs, the beef bouillon, and ¼ cup of dry red wine, 1 clove of garlic, finely chopped, the allspice, dried thyme, paprika, 2 teaspoons of Worcestershire sauce, and salt and freshly ground pepper to taste. Stir the whole together to get a thorough blend (one's own hands is the best method). If the mixture seems too dry, add a little more wine and bouillon to it. After the mixing, cover the bowl with cheesecloth, and allow to stand for 30 minutes to an hour in a cool place.

When ready to cook, shape the mixture into an oblong loaf, and place in a roasting pan. Preheat the oven to 375 degrees, and, after having brushed the top of the loaf with melted butter, put it in the oven and cook for 30 minutes. Then reduce the heat to 350 degrees, and allow to cook for 1 hour. Remove the loaf to a hot platter and cover.

Skim off all the fat from the roasting pan, and then add ¼ cup of dry red wine and the water to the pan. Stir and scrape the pan so that the juices remaining and any meat particles clinging to the pan are mixed. Then pour all this into the sauce, which has been made while the loaf is cooking.

For the sauce mix together the chili sauce, the solid pack tomatoes, the red wine garlic vinegar, 1 finely chopped onion, 2 teaspoons of Worcestershire sauce, the canned pimientos, chopped, 1 clove of garlic, minced, the chili powder, the hickory mustard, and ½ teaspoon of salt. Let this all simmer for about 1 hour. Then add the drippings from the roasting pan.

To serve, slice the loaf in ¾-inch slices, and pour some of the sauce over each slice. Parsley new potatoes or buttered noodles sprinkled with grated Parmesan cheese go beautifully with the meat loaf. Serve the same dry red wine as was used in the preparation of the meat loaf.

I never thought I would live to see the day when I would regard Mother Goose as a prophet. But harking back to the nursery rhyme, "Hey diddle diddle, the cat and the fiddle, the cow jumped over the moon," and then reading the price tags, from left to right, in any meat market today, it's easy to see that the old gal wasn't kidding!

Let's face it—if you want to be thrifty you have to forego choice cuts of beef. But, praise be, there's always ground beef, or hamburger.

Once a dish of scant repute, the hamburger today graces gourmet tables, and many swank restaurants feature it on their menus, sometimes pricing it, with trimmings, at $2.50 a copy. Or they call it Salisbury Steak, which is merely fancied-up hamburger, or ground beef, usually served with a sauce or gravy. Properly prepared, this latter dish is delectable, and a very felicitous variation from regular hamburgers.

SALISBURY STEAK

2 lbs. lean ground chuck
1 medium onion
1 tbsp. bacon drippings
½ green pepper, minced
1 stalk celery, minced
1 clove garlic, minced
2 tbsp. chopped chives
2 tbsp. chopped parsley
½ tsp. dry mustard
Pinch dried marjoram
Pinch dried thyme

Generous sprinkle paprika
Salt and pepper
Flour
Olive oil
3 tbsp. butter
¼ lb. sliced fresh mushrooms
⅓ cup chili sauce
1 tsp. lemon juice
1 tsp. Worcestershire sauce
Dash Tabasco sauce
2 oz. dry white wine

In a large mixing bowl combine the twice-ground beef, the finely minced onion which has been sautéed in the bacon drippings until limp, the finely minced green pepper, celery and garlic, the finely chopped chives and parsley, the dry mustard, the dried marjoram and thyme, the paprika, and about ½ teaspoon each of salt and pepper. When all is thoroughly blended, shape the mixture into 6 individual patties about ¾-inch thick. Brush them with olive oil, sprinkle them lightly with seasoned flour, and place them under the broiler, about 3 inches below the flame. Broil for 2 to 3 minutes on each side, depending on how you like them done.

For the sauce, melt the butter in a saucepan, and when it is hot, add the thinly sliced fresh mushrooms. Let them sauté for about 5 minutes, then sprinkle over them ½ tablespoon of flour. Stir and blend gently, then add the chili sauce, Worcestershire sauce, Tabasco sauce, lemon juice, 1 tablespoon of chopped parsley, the dry white wine, and salt and pepper to taste. Blend everything well, and bring almost to the boiling point. Arrange the patties on a hot platter, pour the sauce over them, and serve immediately.

Not long ago I was really put to a challenge. A letter came to me, in care of the Chicago *Tribune,* and it was simply signed "Teenager."

"One of the most popular 'eatings' these days," he or she wrote, "is beef barbecues. I have tried a number of recipes for it—one was so thin it soaked up the buns, one tasted flat, one didn't taste, period, and one made so much the family ate it for a week. I don't mean the patties with a barbecue sauce on top, but the ground beef just browned and chopped up and cooked in the sauce.

"Why don't you sneak a real good one using about a pound of meat (not with wine) in your 'For Men Only!' column one of these Fridays soon."

I must confess that I did a lot of worrying over that letter, because many teenagers have as critical tastes as a lot of fastidious gourmets. Young people who like to eat know exactly what they want, and if what they get doesn't measure up to their standards, they won't pussyfoot about it.

Well, with considerable qualms I took the bull by the horns—or perhaps I should say by the chuck—and offered a recipe. And I said in the column, "Believe me, Mr. or Miss Teenager, I would appreciate your reaction in honest terms. And you don't have to spare the horses!"

Here's the recipe that I devised.

TEENAGER BARBECUE BEEF ON BUNS

1½ lbs. ground chuck
2 tbsp. bacon drippings
1 clove garlic (optional)
1½ cup chopped onions
1 cup chopped green pepper
1½ cups chili sauce
1 tbsp. Worcestershire sauce
1 tbsp. cider vinegar

1 tsp. fresh lime juice
3 tbsp. A-1 sauce
1½ tsp. salt
1 tsp. dry mustard
1 tsp. brown sugar
1 tsp. chili powder
Dash Tabasco sauce (optional)
Split buns

Sweet onion rings

Put the bacon drippings (or butter or margerine) in a heavy skillet and let it get hot. Add the crushed clove of garlic, and when it browns remove it. However, if you don't care for garlic, skip it. Then add to the fat the chopped onions and chopped green pepper. Sauté these for about 5 minutes, stirring occasionally.

To the onions and green peppers in the skillet add the ground beef. Sauté the meat until it browns, breaking up the meat with a fork as it cooks.

When the beef is browned, stir in the chili sauce, Worcestershire sauce, cider vinegar, lime juice, A-1 sauce, salt, dry mustard, brown sugar and chili powder. If you like the sauce hot, add a small dash of Tabasco sauce. Simmer everything, mixing well, for about 20 minutes, so that the flavors will be well blended.

Spoon the mixture over split buns (toasted, if you like them that way) and garnish the top with sweet onion rings. This recipe should serve 8, depending upon appetites, of course.

A few weeks after the above recipe appeared in my column, I received a very short note about my effort. It read:

Dear Mr. Wood:

Thanks for the recipe for the beefburgers. I made it several times already, and my crowd thought it was lush.

That Teenager

In all sincerity, I am prouder of that letter than any other I have ever received. I only wish the writer could know how happy and proud it made me.

In the lives of most families there comes a time (all too frequently, alas) when the food budget suddenly falls apart at the seams. And no leftovers.

Unfortunately, hunger and appetite never went to school, and consequently they are unaware of the simple problems of mathematics. That's why housewives become prematurely gray, and otherwise model husbands place two dollars across the board on a longshot in the fifth at Pimlico, Tanforan, or Washington Park.

However, there is a haven for harassed housewives and hungry husbands in jars of baked beans, cans of kidney beans, or packages of frozen lima beans, combined with ground beef. It is really surprising how many ways they can be made into taste-teasing dishes that not only fill the tummy, but thoroughly satisfy.

In the following recipe, which is elegant to savor, either baked beans, kidney beans, or lima beans can be used, and you'll get a dish with a different flavor from each.

BEEF-BEANS SKILLET

1 *lb. ground chuck beef*
2 *cups lima, baked, or kidney beans, cooked*
½ *cup chopped onions*
½ *cup diced celery*
2 *tbsp. bacon drippings*
1½ *cups canned tomatoes, drained*

¼ *cup catsup*
1½ *tsp. Worcestershire sauce*
Dash Tabasco sauce
1 *tsp. salt*
⅛ *tsp. pepper*
¼ *tsp. dried oregano*
¼ *cup dry red wine*
1 *tbsp. A-1 sauce*

Heat the bacon drippings in a skillet, and then add the chopped onions and the diced celery, and cook until the onions are clear. Then add the ground beef, and cook until it is well browned, breaking up the meat with a fork while cooking, about 10 minutes. Then add the kind of beans you prefer (if you use baked beans, get the kind without tomato sauce), the drained canned tomatoes, the catsup, Worcestershire sauce, Tabasco sauce, salt, pepper, dried oregano, A-1 sauce, and the dry red wine. Cover and simmer 15 to 20 minutes, until the flavors are well blended. This makes about 4 generous servings.

Another lima bean casserole dish that is a favorite of ours is part Mexican and part Spanish.

LATIN LIMA BEAN CASSEROLE

1 *pkg. frozen lima beans*	2 *oz. grated Parmesan cheese*
1½ *cups chopped onion*	1 *tsp. salt*
¾ *cup chopped green pepper*	1 *tbsp. chili powder*
1 *clove garlic, minced*	1 *6-oz. can tomato paste*
¼ *cup olive oil*	½ *cup dry sherry*
1 *lb. ground round steak*	¼ *cup fine breadcrumbs*
1 *cup chopped ripe olives*	1 *tbsp. grated Parmesan cheese*

Cook the frozen lima beans according to the directions on the package, undercooking rather than following the time exactly. Then drain, reserving any liquid that remains.

Sauté the chopped onion, chopped green pepper, and the minced garlic in the olive oil in a skillet until the vegetables are tender. Then add the ground beef, and continue cooking until the meat is lightly browned. Next add the cooked lima beans, whatever liquid remained, the chopped ripe olives, 2 ounces grated Parmesan cheese, salt, chili powder, tomato paste, and the dry sherry. Mix gently but well, and place the whole in a greased casserole. Sprinkle the top with the fine breadcrumbs which have been mixed with 1 tablespoon of grated Parmesan cheese. Bake in a 350-degree oven for 30 minutes. This will serve 4.

One of Italy's most tantalizing dishes is *Canneloni.* It consists of *rigatoni* (a large, tubular *pasta* cut in 3-inch lengths) stuffed with a savory filling, covered with an Italian sauce, and baked in the oven. But for some strange reason recipes for *Canneloni* are very difficult to find in cookbooks, even Italian ones.

Oddly enough, the great Italian composer, Gioacchino Rossini (who was also a famed gourmet and cook), laid the foundation for *Canneloni*. It is said that he stuffed equal lengths of cooked macaroni with a purée of *pâté de foie gras,* using a syringe! These he placed in a dish, covered them with a thick white sauce, sprinkled them with grated Parmesan cheese, and baked them in the oven. Incidentally, the word *Canneloni* is said to have originated in the Chinese kitchen, and was taken to Italy by Marco Polo.

While *rigatoni* can be bought in Italian grocery stores, it may be difficult to obtain in many communities. So my good friend and culinary confrere, Emily Chase Leistner, devised a substitute for *rigatoni*—pancakes! While Italians may miss their national comestible, I think the stuffed pancakes make quite as delectable a dish as the one with the *rigatoni*. The stuffing and sauce, which I devised, are, however, truly Italian.

CANNELONI

Pancakes

1 *cup sifted all-purpose flour*	3 *well-beaten eggs*
1½ *tsp. salt*	1½ *cups milk*

Butter

Filling

2 *tbsp. olive oil*	1 *cup drained cooked spinach*
1 *clove garlic, minced*	⅛ *tsp. dried oregano*
1 *medium onion, chopped*	*Salt and pepper*
1 *lb. ground beef*	6 *chicken livers*

1 *tbsp. butter*

Sauce

1 *large onion, chopped*	1 *small can tomato paste*
1 *clove garlic, minced*	1 *cup dry red wine*
2 *tbsp. olive oil*	1 *cup condensed beef bouillon*
3 *cups Italian canned tomatoes*	1 *cup grated Parmesan cheese*

Salt and pepper

First, make the pancakes. Mix the sifted all-purpose flour and salt in a bowl. Combine the well-beaten eggs and the milk and add this gradually to the flour and salt, stirring until smooth. Cook the pancakes one at a time in a well-greased 6½-inch skillet, turning once. Use ¼ cup of batter for each pancake, and tilt the skillet as you pour in the batter so that the batter covers the bottom of the skillet evenly. Stack the cooked pancakes on a plate and let cool.

To make the filling, heat the olive oil in a skillet, and add the minced garlic and the finely chopped onion. Sauté for about 5 minutes, or until the onions are limp. Then add the ground beef, and continue to cook until the beef is browned, breaking it up as it cooks with a fork. Drain off the fat, and mix in the well-drained and finely chopped cooked spinach, the dried oregano, and salt and pepper to taste. Sauté the chicken livers in the butter for about 5 minutes, then chop them, and add them to the beef-spinach mixture.

For the sauce sauté the chopped onion and minced clove of garlic in the olive oil until the onions are golden brown. Then mix in the canned Italian tomatoes (the best are pear-shaped) and the tomato paste, and simmer for about 5 minutes. Then add the dry red wine (Chianti type is best), condensed beef bouillon, grated Parmesan cheese, and salt and pepper to taste. Bring to a boil, then lower the flame and let simmer for about 30 minutes, stirring occasionally.

To assemble the dish divide the filling among the 12 pancakes (about ¼ cup to each). Roll up loosely, and place the rolls side by side in 1 large or 2 smaller greased baking dishes. Pour the simmering sauce over the pancakes and bake in a 375-degree oven for about 20 minutes, or until the sauce bubbles. Sprinkle the top with grated Parmesan cheese just before serving. This recipe serves 6.

If you can get *rigatoni,* and would like to have the *Canneloni* fixed the Italian way, boil 1 pound of *rigatoni* in 2 quarts of salted water for 5 minutes, then drain. Stuff the *rigatoni* with part of the filling and place in a lightly greased casserole. Spread the remaining filling over the stuffed *rigatoni,* then pour over the sauce, and bake in a 450-degree oven for 15 minutes, then brown under the broiler. In this method, the grated Parmesan cheese is served separately, rather than incorporated in the sauce.

Bourke Corcoran is a bachelor gourmet I have known for a great many years. The last few years Mrs. Wood and I lived in Chicago, Bourke had an apartment in our building. He loved to give dinners, and at least once a week he would have my wife and me down to his apartment for a wonderful meal, to say nothing of very expertly mixed cocktails before dinner, a fine wine with dinner, and liqueurs afterward.

One night he announced that he had a very special entree for us as we sat sipping our cocktails, but refused to name it. When we were seated at the dinner table, he brought on a platter of gorgeous baked potatoes, and a covered silver dish. When he opened it up, I could see it was chipped beef in cream, which I heartily disliked.

Bourke is such a grand guy I simply couldn't hurt his feelings, so I accepted my plate without comment, and, summoning a great deal of courage, I lifted a forkful of chipped beef and cream to my mouth. And was I surprised! It was absolutely delicious. It was more than that—it was absolutely epicurean. And here's how he did it.

CHIPPED BEEF AND CREAM À LA CORCORAN

8 oz. chipped beef   ¼ tsp. pepper
3 tbsp. butter   1 cup milk
3 tbsp. minced onion   1 cup cream
3 tbsp. minced green pepper   1 tbsp. chopped parsley
3 tbsp. flour   2 tbsp. dry sherry
                ¼ tsp. paprika

Melt the butter in a saucepan, and when it is hot, add the minced onion and the green pepper. Sauté until the vegetables are a light brown, then sprinkle in the flour and the pepper (if you can get spiced pepper, use it, if not use freshly ground pepper). Then slowly add the mixed milk and cream, stirring constantly until well blended.

When the sauce is blended and smooth, add the chipped beef, which you have separated. Mix the chipped beef well with the sauce, and then simmer the whole until the mixture is thickened. Then remove from the flame and add the chopped parsley, the paprika, and the dry sherry. Mix gently, and serve, with a baked potato split open and topped with butter, salt and pepper to taste, and a dab of sour cream.

I don't know of any city in the United States that has as many superlative Chinese and Cantonese restaurants as San Francisco. Of course, that is only natural, since San Francisco has the largest Chinese quarter in the United States.

On Grant Street (the main thoroughfare of San Francisco's Chinatown) is Johnny Kan's Restaurant. You have to walk up to the second floor to reach it, but I would walk up four or five flights to savor Johnny's food, for there is no finer or more authentic Chinese food served in all of Chinatown. It is also a rendezvous for stage and motion picture celebrities.

Johnny personally supervised our dinner the first time Mrs. Wood and I ate there. And what a meal it was—Bird's Nest Soup, Pekin Duck with Thousand Layer Buns, Kan's Gourmet Vegetables, Pineapple Pork Sweet and Sour, Asparagus Beef Cantonese, and a special Fried Rice.

Both my wife and I were so intrigued by the Asparagus Beef that I asked Johnny for the recipe. A few weeks later Johnny sent it to me, explaining that the delay was caused by Mrs. Kan's efforts to adapt the restaurant's recipe to home use, since cooking in a skillet and a Chinese "Wok" are entirely different techniques. So here it is, adapted for the American home kitchen.

KAN'S FRESH ASPARAGUS BEEF WITH BLACK BEAN SAUCE

(Lee Sun Gnow Yuke)

2 cups fresh asparagus
2 cups boiling water
4 tbsp. vegetable oil
1 tsp. salt
1 lb. flank steak

1 tbsp. Chinese salted spiced
*   black beans*
1 clove garlic
1 tbsp. soy sauce
Asparagus liquid

1 tbsp. cornstarch

Place the fresh asparagus (cut diagonally in ¼-inch slices) in a saucepan containing the boiling water. Cover pan with a lid and cook for 3 minutes. Remove the asparagus from the liquid, retaining the liquid for the gravy.

Place the vegetable (or salad) oil, salt, and the flank steak (cut diagonally in ⅛-inch slices) in a preheated large skillet. Brown the meat slightly for about 2 or 3 minutes, and then remove it from the skillet.

Mash the Chinese salted spiced black beans with the finely chopped and crushed garlic, and add to this the soy sauce. Place in the skillet and add 1 cup of the asparagus liquid (the water the asparagus was boiled in). Cook for about 5 minutes, then add the asparagus and meat.

Make a thin, smooth paste of the cornstarch and ¼ cup of the asparagus liquid. Combine this with the other ingredients in the skillet, stirring constantly until the gravy thickens. Serve immediately with hot steamed rice. This recipe will serve 3 to 4 people as a course in a Chinese or Cantonese dinner.

Lamb was a favorite on the menus of New York society's incredible dinners during the 1880's, 1890's, and the early 1900's. It was a period in which American creation and appreciation of exquisite food seems to have reached its peak, not only in the gilded rooms of Delmonico's, but in the glittering palaces of society's leaders and gastronomes. Socialites vied with each other to achieve the epitome of elegance at elaborate dinners of many courses. It was common practice first to serve oysters or melons, then two soups, an hors d'oeuvre, a fish course, a relevé (a French term for a course of a substantial nature, consisting of large joints of game or meat), an entree (on two menus before me as I write, one lists turkey and the other Supreme of Chicken), a roast (the foregoing menus list woodcock on one, and canvasback duck on the other), two or three vegetables, a salad, and at least two desserts!

At one of the dinners, on opening her napkin, each fair lady guest found a gold bracelet with her monogram in chased gold in the center.

In 1890 Ward McAllister, the social arbiter of the era, wrote a fascinating book called *Society As I Have Found It*. I have a copy of the book, and, although it is a faithful and factual presentation of the times, it reads today like a fairy tale. The book is devoted to descriptions of parties, balls, cotillions, dinners, food, and wines.

Ward McAllister was very fond of lamb and mutton, and not only did he serve it frequently, but when he gave picnics at his Newport farm, he hired an entire flock of Southdown sheep to give his place a pastoral and animated look.

At the Golden Era Dinner given by the American Spice Trade Association in New York, which I have mentioned before, Roast Baron of Lamb Rosemary was served (a baron of lamb is the name applied to the two loins which have not been cut apart). However, as a baron of lamb is several touches too large to get into the home oven, this recipe has been adapted to a leg of lamb, and I have taken the liberty of adding a touch or two of my own, which certainly will not detract from the finished dish.

ROAST LEG OF LAMB ROSEMARY

1 6-*lb. leg of lamb*	2 *leeks, sliced*
1 *tbsp. butter*	2 *cups water*
1 *carrot, sliced*	2 *cups dry white wine*
1 *stalk celery, chopped*	¾ *tsp. powdered rosemary*
	Salt and pepper

In a saucepan sauté the sliced carrot, chopped celery, and the sliced leeks in the butter for 5 minutes, stirring frequently. Then add ½ cup each of the water and dry white wine.

Place the leg of lamb in a roasting pan, and sprinkle with salt and pepper and ¼ teaspoon of the powdered rosemary. Then pour in the vegetables and their liquid around the lamb. Roast in a 325-degree oven for 2½ to 3 hours. Add more water and wine in equal proportions to the pan as necessary. When the lamb is done, remove it and keep it warm. Skim off any grease in the pan, and add 1 cup each of water and the dry white wine, and ½ teaspoon of the powdered rosemary. Season to taste with salt and pepper. If a thickened gravy is desired, add a flour and butter *roux*. Blend well, bring to a boil, and then strain. Slice the lamb on a platter, pour the gravy over the meat, and serve.

I think many people abuse a leg of lamb by overcooking it. The next time you get a leg of spring lamb, try it cooked just a tiny bit on the pink side, and you'll find it has a delightful new taste and flavor. For other legs of lamb, regardless of the grade, I have found that Adolph's Seasoned Meat Tenderizer not only makes the lamb more tender, but also improves the flavor. The following is Ruth Rigler's recipe, and it is wonderful.

SHERRY-GLAZED LEG OF LAMB

1 5- *to* 6-*lb. leg of lamb*	1 *tsp. dried mint leaves*
Clove garlic	¼ *tsp. dried thyme*
Adolph's Seasoned Meat	⅓ *jar mint or currant jelly*
Tenderizer	2-3 *oz. dry sherry wine*

Make gashes in the leg of lamb with a sharp knife, and in the gashes insert slivers of garlic. Force the slivers deep into the lamb in various spots. Then sprinkle the leg of lamb witht Adolph's Seasoned Meat Tenderizer (allowing ½ teaspoon per pound of the weight of the leg of lamb) over all surfaces of the meat. Pierce deeply with a long-tined fork at intervals of 1 inch. Crush the mint leaves and mix with the dried thyme, and rub this mixture well into the surfaces of the meat. Cover loosely, and allow to stand overnight in the refrigerator.

To cook, place the leg of lamb on a rack in a roasting pan, and cook 25 to 30 minutes per pound. During the last half hour of cooking, cover the top of the meat with either mint or currant jelly mixed with the sherry wine. This gives a very attractive glaze, and a wonderful flavor to the drippings for the gravy.

Leftover lamb from a roast is, to my mind, an advantage rather than a problem. I have a few favorite methods of using cooked lamb, some of which I would like to detail. The first is slices of cooked lamb in Madeira.

LAMB SLICES IN MADEIRA

Slices cold roast lamb	*Salt*
1 *tbsp. butter*	*Pinch cayenne pepper*
¼ *tsp. crushed dried rosemary*	1 *tbsp. currant jelly*
	½ *cup Madeira wine*

Melt the butter in a large skillet, and stir into it the crushed dried rosemary. When the butter is sizzling hot, add enough slices of cold roast lamb to cover the bottom of the skillet. Keep turning the slices until they are thoroughly heated, then season them with salt to taste and the cayenne pepper. Then add the currant jelly and the Madeira wine. Simmer for 5 or 6 minutes, then take up the lamb slices and serve immediately.

If you prefer a thicker gravy, add a *roux* of about ½ teaspoon of butter creamed with the same amount of flour. Stir this into the gravy after the lamb slices have been removed, let the gravy cook for a minute or two, and then pour over the lamb.

Ladies, how often has the following situation arisen in your home?

HUSBAND (Kissing the Little Woman goodbye as he departs for the office): What's for dinner tonight, dear?

L. W. (Mentally reviewing a badly bent food budget): Well, I think we ought to eat up the rest of the roast lamb. There's ample for dinner tonight.

HUSBAND: But, honey, we've been eating on that lamb for three nights!

L. W.: I know, but we simply can't throw it away. Don't worry, I'll fix it up nicely.

HUSBAND: Okay, sweetheart. 'Bye.

Time passes, as time will. Then about four o'clock in the afternoon the telephone rings, and the Little Woman answers. It's friend husband.

HUSBAND: Say, honey, I'm terribly sorry, but Ransom just called me and wants me to go to dinner with him. I'm after a big order from him, and I just couldn't say no. But I'll be home early. 'Bye now.

It's true that many people have a prejudice against leftovers, but there is no reason for it if leftovers are treated with imagination. If the above Little Woman had answered Hubby's question about what they were going to have for dinner that night by saying, "We're going to have a surprise dish tonight, one that Helen got the recipe for in Paris, and don't be late!" chances are that the man of the house would never have invented Ransom's dinner, or would have turned it down. And he'd probably never (well, almost never) believe that he'd been served lamb hash.

GOURMET LAMB HASH

2 cups cooked lamb	¾ cup consommé
1 large onion, chopped	½ cup dry white wine
1 medium green pepper, minced	Dash Worcestershire sauce
1 tbsp. butter	1 tsp. salt
1 tbsp. chopped parsley	¼ tsp. pepper
Pinch dried rosemary	Mashed potatoes
3 small tomatoes	Cream
	Grated Parmesan cheese

Sauté the finely chopped onion and the minced green pepper in the butter in a skillet for about 5 minutes, or until the vegetables are tender. Then add the chopped parsley, pulverized dried rosemary, the tomatoes, chopped, the consommé, the cooked lamb, chopped fairly fine, the dry white wine, Worcestershire sauce, and the salt and pepper. Cover the skillet and simmer for about an hour, stirring from time to time. Then correct the seasoning, if necessary, and place the contents of the skillet in a fireproof casserole, or baking dish. Cover the top with mashed potatoes which have been whipped with a little cream, and sprinkle grated Parmesan cheese over all. Place under a hot broiler and brown, then serve. This will serve 3 to 4.

There is one leftover lamb dish that, to me, makes it worth while to cook a leg of lamb just for the leftovers, if you get what I mean. That is lamb curry. In my *With a Jug of Wine* there is my recipe for a lamb curry that I have been told many times is the finest lamb curry ever devised. I am inclined to agree, but then, I am prejudiced.

In the interim, I had another lamb curry that is wonderful. It was served to Mrs. Wood and me at the home of Franklyn Kohler, as the main entree of a Dutch East Indian dinner. Accompanying the curry were popadams (these are imported, and come in cans, and are deep-fried), and 12 condiments, or "boys." The vegetables were baked bananas and french-fried eggplant, and the salad was a tossed green one. Melons with a slice of lime was the dessert, and Heinecken's beer, very cold in stone mugs, was the beverage.

KOHLER'S BENGAL CURRY

⅔ *cup finely chopped onion*	2 *tsp. salt*
4 *tbsp. butter*	¼ *tsp. pepper*
2½ *cups lean cooked lamb,*	½ *tsp. granulated sugar*
cubed	2 *cups milk*
6-8 *tsp. curry powder*	3 *tbsp. preserved ginger*
¼ *tsp. ground cloves*	1 *cup coconut milk*
¼ *tsp. dried mint*	½ *cup rich cream*
½ *cup fresh lime juice*	

I am quoting Frank's letter on the instructions:

To prepare—and don't forget, the large earthen casserole and the wooden spoons are absolute musts, as is the freshly grated coconut. I bring the casserole up to temperature on top of the stove on an asbestos pad, then in it sauté the onion in 1 tablespoon of butter until golden, but not brown. Then push the onion to one side, add the remaining butter, and sauté the lamb, cut in about ¾-inch cubes, until it is lightly browned. I like to stir the curry powder and other dry ingredients with a little of the milk to form a paste which will spread more smoothly through the mixture—first the curry powder, then the cloves, dried mint, sugar, salt and pepper, and add this to the casserole along with the milk and finely chopped preserved ginger. Mix well, then cover and cook very slowly for an hour, stirring occasionally. Then add the grated coconut and coconut milk,* stir some more, and continue to cook until the meat is very tender and the sauce is giving out an aroma that causes everyone within range to drool. Fifteen minutes before serving stir in the cream and fresh lime juice. As you know, we bring the casserole to the table, and serve the curry with rice, and pass the condiments, or "side boys."

* To make the coconut milk if there isn't any in the coconut, or enough, add ½ cup of grated coconut to 1½ cups of hot milk. Let it stand and cool for 2 hours, then drain, and add to the casserole as indicated.

For the condiments, have small dishes with a small spoon in each (demitasse spoons) filled with the following: (1) Major Grey's Chutney (Sun Brand) (2) toasted flaked salt codfish (3) minced crisp bacon (4) minced white and yolks of hard-cooked eggs mixed together (5) finely chopped little green onions (6) finely chopped green pepper (7) grated fresh pineapple (8) grated fresh coconut (9) chopped dried herring (10) grated orange peel (11) chopped cashew nuts, toasted brown (12) plump, boiled seedless raisins.

In serving this Bengal Curry, place a mound of rice on your plate, spoon a generous amount of curry over the rice, and then sprinkle the whole with a little of each condiment. Mix this all up, and go to it!

Many fastidious gourmets would wrinkle their noses in disdain at the thought of eating such a lowly dish as lamb stew. And one would imagine that a great master chef would scorn a dish that seems to be so uninspired. Yet I have known one or two epicures who, in the privacy of their own homes, prepared (and ate) lamb, or Irish, stew with relish; and one of the great chefs of America has admitted that, on his day off, he dearly loves to sit down to a dish of savory lamb stew.

True Irish stew has mutton as its foundation, with, of course, potatoes and onions, and other vegetables on occasion, as ornaments. But mutton, in America, is far less tasty than the mutton one finds in the British Isles, so in this country lamb is used. And if you are of the opinion that a lamb stew can't be taste-tantalizing, just try this recipe.

LAMB STEW

2 *lbs. lamb shoulder, cubed*
1 *tsp. salt*
¼ *cup flour*
3 *tbsp. bacon drippings*
1 *medium onion, sliced*
1 *clove garlic, minced*
1 *cup light red wine*
4 *cups boiling water*
½ *tsp. Ac'cent*

1 *tsp. salt*
¼ *tsp. pepper*
½ *tsp. dried rosemary*
2 *cups potatoes, cubed*
1 *cup snap beans*
1 *cup diced carrots*
6-8 *small white onions*
5 *tbsp. flour*
5 *tbsp. water*

Get the shoulder of lamb cut in about 1-inch squares. Wipe with a damp cloth. Sprinkle with about 1 teaspoon of salt, and roll in flour.

In a heavy pot heat the bacon drippings, and then add the floured lamb cubes. Brown them well over a medium flame on all sides, then add the sliced onion and the minced garlic. When the onions are browned lightly, pour off all the fat from the pot and add to the pot the light dry red wine, the boiling water, the Ac'cent, the salt and pepper, and the dried rosemary. Cover the pot tightly, and simmer slowly until the meat is almost tender, about 1½ to 2 hours.

Next add to the pot the cubed potatoes, the green beans, cut as desired, the diced carrots, and the small white onions. Continue cooking until the vegetables and meat are tender, about 20 to 30 minutes.

Blend together the flour and water to form a smooth paste, and add this paste to the stew, stirring it in carefully so that no lumps will form. Then reheat the whole thing until it comes to a boil, and boil gently for half a minute. Then serve to 6.

To many people the only satisfactory way to cook chops is to broil or fry them. This is particularly true of lamb chops (broiled) and pork chops (fried). Mutton chops do not have the vogue in America that they have in England, for Americans believe mutton is strong in flavor and is apt to be tough. Yet the so-called English mutton chop, from yearling mutton and with the kidney in the center, is a delicious dish.

However, there is a wide variety of ways of cooking chops other than the usually accepted ways, and many are delicious and temptingly different. I shall detail some in writing of pork and veal later in this chapter, and right now I'll suggest lamb chops baked in a casserole in red wine. It's a mighty good dish, and doesn't require baby spring lamb either.

LAMB CHOPS EN CASSEROLE WITH RED WINE

4 *loin lamb chops, 1½ inches
    thick*
1 *clove garlic*
Seasoned flour
8 *tiny white onions*

2 *medium carrots*
1½ *ozs. butter*
1½ *cups dry red wine*
Pinch dried marjoram
4 *large mushroom caps*

Butter

Rub the lamb chops with a split clove of garlic on both sides, and dust them with seasoned flour. Parboil the whole tiny white (pearl) onions in boiling salted water for 15 minutes, and cut the carrots julienne (in small matchlike strips).

Heat the butter (3 tablespoons) in a skillet. Add the parboiled onions, the julienne carrots, and the lamb chops. When the chops are lightly browned on both sides, transfer them and the browned vegetables to a casserole. Pour in the dry red wine (a claret type preferably) and sprinkle in a generous pinch of dried marjoram over all. Cover the casserole tightly and place in a 325-degree oven and cook for 1 to 1½ hours, or until the chops are tender.

Transfer the chops and vegetables to a hot platter, top each with a large mushroom cap which has been sautéed in butter for about 8 minutes, and pour the gravy over all. This will serve 4, unless you have a hearty enough appetite to get away with 2 chops, which may possibly be the case if they are not large. Hashed brown potatoes are an excellent accompaniment, as well as stewed tomatoes. Serve the same type of wine that was used in cooking the chops.

Another enticing and different lamb-chop entree is Lamp Chops Strogonoff.

LAMB CHOPS STROGONOFF

8 *small frenched lamb chops*	2 *small onions, sliced*
Brandy	1 *tbsp. bacon drippings*
Flour	1 *tomato, cut up*
Fine breadcrumbs	1 *thin slice dill pickle*
½ *tsp. mace*	1 *tsp. grated lemon rind*
2 *oz. butter*	1 *cup sour cream*
	2½ *oz. Madeira wine*

Have the fat all trimmed away from the rib lamp chops, and break off the long bone. Wipe each chop with a cloth soaked in brandy, and then pound into each chop (with the blunt side of a heavy kitchen knife) a little flour mixed with fine breadcrumbs and mace. Sear the chops in a heavy skillet or Dutch oven in the hot butter until the chops are brown. Then add to the skillet the onions, which have been thinly sliced and lighty fried in the bacon drippings, the cut-up tomato, the thin slice of dill pickle which has been diced, and the grated lemon rind. Pour over all this the commercial sour cream which has been mixed with the dry Madeira wine. Cover the skillet closely and simmer for 1 hour, or until the chops are tender. Flaky boiled rice goes wonderfully with this entree. The recipe is designed for 4 people, because the chops are small, and each person should be served 2.

Incidentally, in my never-ending search for new ways to use mayonnaise, I devised a very different and savory lamb chop dish. When I presented it to the testers in the Table Products laboratories, makers of Nu Made mayonnaise, eyebrows were raised, because it sounded rather weird. But once it was tried, they were enthusiastic. So don't let the title of the recipe fool you.

GRILLED LAMB CHOPS WITH MAYONNAISE

6 *thick loin lamb chops*	1 *beaten egg*
Salt	*Pinch dried basil*
Fine breadcrumbs	1 *tbsp. dry white wine*
	Ice-cold mayonnaise

Trim away all the excess fat from the loin lamb chops, and reduce the tails to the strictly edible portions. Rub the chops with salt, and then cover them with fine breadcrumbs on both sides. Then dip them in beaten egg to which a pinch of dried basil and the dry white wine has been added. Again cover them on both sides with the fine breadcrumbs, and press the breadcrumbs down on the chops. Let the crumbed chops stand at room temperature for 15 minutes or so.

Place the breaded chops under the broiler and cook for about 10 minutes on one side, then turn and cook for about 10 minutes on the other side. When they are done serve them very quickly, covering each chop with a coating of ice-cold mayonnaise. You'll get an unexpected taste thrill.

One day a gourmet friend of mine, who is one of the chief editorial writers on the Chicago *Tribune,* called me on the phone and said, "Morry, you have a lot of succulent and high-grade recipes in your 'For Men Only!' columns, but how about a recipe for something that can be bought in a butcher shop where you'll have some change left out of a five-dollar bill—say, a pork roast?"

For some strange reason there are few unusual recipes for a pork roast in the majority of cookbooks. Going through several scores of them, I found only fifteen recipes that went beyond just roasting a loin of pork and making a gravy. The Danes marinate a pork roast in claret, and, after cooking, pour a cream laced with Madeira wine over it. The Viennese sprinkle the roast with carraway seeds and minced garlic. The Poles rub the loin with mustard and sugar, and top it with an applesauce combined with cloves and cinnamon. The Italians insert rosemary and garlic into the loin before roasting. And down in South America the Brazilians stuff the loin with onions, green peppers, tomatoes, rice, and seedless raisins, all spiked with chili powder.

Well, I got busy dreaming up things that could be done to a pork roast, and I finally worked out a recipe that makes one of the most tantalizing dishes imaginable. And here it is.

HERBED PORK ROAST

1 4- to 5-lb. pork loin roast	Flour
Olive oil	1 cup chicken broth
Salt	½ cup sour cream
Freshly ground pepper	¾ cup dry white wine
Dried thyme	1 clove garlic
Dried oregano	⅛ tsp. ground nutmeg
Fennel (or anise) seed	2 tbsp. flour
Medium onion, thinly sliced	2 tbsp. butter

Rub the pork loin roast lightly with the very best olive oil (I have tried a great many kinds, but years ago I settled on the Old Monk brand as the best I could find anywhere. It is made in Nice, France, and I have found that many of the leading restaurants in America use only the Old Monk Imported Olive Oil).

After annointing the meat with the olive oil, sprinkle it with salt, freshly ground pepper, dried thyme, dried oregano, the fennel (or anise) seeds, and flour. Lightly pat the roast, so that the herbs will adhere to it. Then fasten the onion slices, cut almost paper-thin, over all the meat with toothpicks. Wrap the prepared roast in Saran Wrap, and let it stand in the refrigerator for about 12 hours, so that the flavor of the herbs will be absorbed.

Just before putting the roast in the oven, make the basting liquor. Cook together in a saucepan for about 5 minutes the chicken broth (or canned chicken bouillon), the dry white wine, the minced clove of garlic, and grated nutmeg. Keep this warm.

To cook, remove the meat from the refrigerator, remove the wrapping, and place the meat in a roasting pan, rib side down. Place in a preheated 375-degree oven for 30 minutes. Then pour in the basting liquor, turn the oven down to 325 degrees, and let the roast cook for about 35 minutes to the pound (or, if a meat thermometer is used, roast until the thermometer registers 185 degrees for the inside of the roast), basting frequently.

To prepare the gravy, remove the roast to a hot platter and keep warm (leave the onion slices pinned on the roast; they will be almost black, but they have the most delicious flavor imaginable). Skim the excess fat from the basting liquor in the roaster, and add enough chicken broth and dry white wine (in equal parts) to make 2 cups of liquid. Have a *roux* prepared of 2 tablespoons each of flour and butter. Mix this *roux* with the liquid in the roaster (or add a little of the hot liquid to the *roux* and stir until it is a thin paste), and add the commercial sour cream. Cook, stirring constantly, until the gravy is thickened and smooth. Serve the gravy separately.

A couple of years after I had devised the Herbed Pork Roast I learned of another and different method of cooking a pork roast from a White Russian friend of mine. This too has a most unusual flavor.

MUSHROOM STUFFED LOIN OF PORK

1 4- to 5-lb. loin of pork	Fennel (or anise) seeds
Lemon juice	Salt
1 cup fresh mushrooms	1 cup consommé
Seasoned salt	1 cup dry sherry
1 tbsp. butter	½ cup commercial sour cream

Get the center cut of a loin pork and rub it with lemon juice, then allow it to stand at room temperature for 20 to 30 minutes. During that time, slice the fresh mushrooms (about ¼ pound) in fairly thick strips (about ¼ inch) and sprinkle them lightly with seasoned salt (Spice Islands Beau Monde seasoning is perfect). Let the mushroom strips stand for a few minutes, then make small slits in the top of the pork roast on the fatty surface about 1¼ inches apart. You should be able to make about three regular rows. Into each slit place a strip of mushroom, getting the strips well down into the meat.

Put the butter in a roasting pan to melt, sprinkle the pork roast well with salt and the fennel (or anise) seeds, and brown the roast in the butter in a 450-degree oven. Then turn the oven down to 325 degrees, and let the roast continue to cook until it is done, about 2½ hours, or when the meat thermometer registers 185 degrees. Baste the roast often with the combined consommé and sherry.

When the roast is done, remove it to a hot platter. Skim the fat off the gravy and stir in the commercial sour cream, blending the whole well. Any one of the sweet potato recipes in the chapter on potatoes goes with this roast like mustard goes with hot dogs.

The third of Ruth Rigler's recipes is for a roast shoulder of pork. It has a delectable, rich flavor imparted to it by the apple butter and apple cider.

ROAST SHOULDER OF PORK À LA NORMANDE

1 4- to 5-lb. shoulder of pork	⅓ cup apple cider (or juice)
Adolph's Seasoned Tenderizer	⅛ tsp. cloves (or cinnamon)
⅓ cup apple butter, or jelly	⅛ tsp. dried thyme

Sprinkle all sides of the shoulder of pork with Adolph's Seasoned Meat Tenderizer (½ teaspoon per pound). Use no additional salt. Plunge a long-tined fork into all sides at 1-inch intervals. Don't be afraid of losing the juices, as Adolph's retains the juices within the meat. Allow to remain at room temperature for 1 hour, or cover loosely and return to the refrigerator overnight.

Place the treated shoulder of pork on a rack in a shallow roasting pan, and roast in a 300- to 325-degree oven for 30 minutes to the pound. Combine the remaining ingredients and spread evenly over the pork during the last hour of cooking. Baste frequently with the drippings in the roaster.

In this melting pot which is America, Christmas food is prepared in many different ways by many different people. The standard holiday fare among Americans is either turkey, goose, or a handsomely decorated ham. But in the early nineties a favorite Christmas viand was roast suckling pig, and I don't believe even the golden splendor of a roast turkey can match the festive air that a roast suckling pig, with an apple stuck in its mouth, cranberry eyes, and a wreath of holly around its neck, gives to a Christmas table.

I think the most amusing story concerning a roast suckling pig has to do with two Americans who were visiting Paris for the first time.

Cecil Shapiro and Sam Wykofsky were the proprietors of a small cloak and suit factory on the lower East Side of New York. Competition being what it is, they didn't make very much money. However, reading about the fabulous amounts of money that were being made in uranium, they decided to take their vacation in the West, and do a little prospecting. And, as luck would have it, they made a strike. Not long afterward, they sold their claim for a quarter of a million dollars.

With riches of which they had never dreamed, they decided to make a European trip. Nothing was stinted—they bought fancy wardrobes, expensive luggage, they had a suite on the *Queen Mary,* and they stopped only at the most luxurious hotels.

When they got to Paris, they really began to live it up. The first night of their arrival they went to the Café de Paris. The maitre d' came up to them, and Sam tendered him a twenty-dollar bill, saying, "If you'll be so kindly, please, we would like your very best table." Naturally, they were seated at a select table, and the solicitous maitre d' said to Sam, *"Qu'est-ce que vous desire, messieurs?"*

Sam looked blank. "Nu, he's asking questions, Cecil!"

Cecil waved his hand. "Naturally, he's asking us if we would like some champagne, Sam." He turned to the maitre d'. "Coitindel we'd like some champagne. But the best."

The maitre d' beamed. *"Ah, oui, Messieurs. Vitement!"*

After the champagne was served, the waiter handed them a menu. Cecil and Sam studied it for some minutes, then Sam leaned closer. "Cecil, I'm not making head or tail to this menu. It must be in French, and I can't understand a word of it."

"Nu, what did you expect, Sam, Yiddish already?" Cecil replied. "Coitindel it's in French."

"But what are we going to do, Cecil? We can't read French."

"Who's saying WE can't read French? Don't forget, Sam, I had a good education. I'll take care of the ordering. Just sit back and relax."

Cecil studied the menu for several minutes more, then beckoned the waiter. "If you'll be so kindly please, bring us this," and he pointed to an item on the menu. The waiter seemed quite impressed as he wrote down the order, then bowed low, and departed for the kitchen.

Sometime later, after they had drunk a second bottle of champagne, the waiter appeared, bearing a huge silver tray with a cover. He deposited it on the table, and, with a flourish, removed the cover. And there, resting on a bed of watercress, was a golden-brown roast suckling pig. Sprigs of holly were about its ears, and in its mouth was a luscious, huge apple.

Sam gasped. "Cecil, what have you done? It's a roast pig! It's pork! We can't eat that!"

Cecil shrugged his shoulders. "So I should know how they serve a baked apple in Paris!"

But back to our roast suckling pig.

ROAST SUCKLING PIG

1 *suckling pig*	1 *tbsp. chopped chives*
Salt	1 *clove garlic*
Pepper	1 *large onion*
Powdered marjoram	¼ *tsp. dried thyme*
Powdered thyme	¼ *tsp. dried marjoram*
1½ *lbs. chestnuts*	¼ *tsp. dried tarragon*
½ *cup cooking oil*	¼ *tsp. sage*
1 *cup consommé*	2 *oz. butter*
2½ *cups soft breadcrumbs*	*Butter*
Madeira wine	*Flour*
1 *tbsp. chopped parsley*	1 *cup dry sherry*

Most authorities agree that the ideal size for the piglet should be about 12 pounds, or 4 to 5 weeks old. Have your butcher draw and clean it thoroughly. Wash the pig well, inside and out, with a coarse towel, then rub the inside well with a mixture of salt, pepper, powdered marjoram, and thyme. Master Pig is now ready for stuffing.

Heat the chestnuts (after scoring the flat sides with a sharp knife) in the cooking oil for 3 or 4 minutes, shaking the pan constantly. Then take out the chestnuts, drain on paper toweling, and when the chestnuts are cool enough to handle, remove the shells and skin, and simmer the chestnuts in the consommé until tender. Then cool them and slice.

Moisten the soft breadcrumbs in the Madeira wine, and then squeeze them dry. To the crumbs add the chopped parsley and chives, the clove of garlic, grated or minced, the onion, chopped, the dried thyme, marjoram, tarragon, and sage, and salt and freshly ground pepper to taste. Sauté this mixture in the butter in a skillet over a gentle flame for 5 minutes, stirring constantly.

Cool the mixture, then add the sliced chestnuts, mixing everything gently but well. If too dry, add a little Madeira wine, but the stuffing should not be soggy. Stuff the pig with this, and sew up the opening. Truss the piglet with the hind legs back and the forelegs forward, in a large roasting pan. Wrap the ears with oiled cheesecloth, and put a wooden block in the mouth to keep it open.

Rub the pig all over with butter and flour mixed in equal parts, pour in the pan the sherry and the consommé the chestnuts were cooked in, and place in a 350-degree oven, allowing 25 to 30 minutes per pound for the cooking time. Baste frequently with the pan juices.

When the pig is done, transfer it to a large platter, remove the mouth prop and insert an apple, cranberries for the eyes, and a wreath of holly around the neck. Thicken the gravy with a flour and butter *roux,* and serve it in a separate gravy boat.

One of my favorite pork dishes is pork tenderloin patties, which was devised by my wife. We have it at home at least once a month, and both of us look forward to it. It is not too expensive, since there is no waste and it is easy to prepare. It is one of the top dishes on the pork parade, as far as I am concerned.

PORK TENDERLOIN PATTIES WITH WINE

1 *pork tenderloin, frenched into 6 patties*	½ *cup consommé*
	½ *cup dry white wine*
Seasoned flour	*Salt*
1 *tbsp. bacon drippings*	*Freshly ground pepper*
1 *tsp. flour*	*Celery salt*
½ *cup water*	*Garlic salt*

Dash Worcestershire sauce

Have your butcher divide a pork tenderloin into 6 parts, and french them. Shake them in seasoned flour. Put the bacon drippings into a skillet, and when hot brown the tenderloin patties on both sides over a medium flame (if they show a tendency to stick, add a teaspoon or more of bacon drippings).

When the patties are nicely browned, sprinkle in and around the patties 1 heaping teaspoon of flour, and stir into the fat to make a *roux*. Then add the water, consommé, and dry white wine, salt and freshly ground pepper to taste, a sprinkle of celery salt and garlic salt, and a couple of dashes of Worcestershire sauce. Cover, and simmer over a low flame slowly for 45 minutes, stirring occasionally, and moving the patties in the gravy so they won't stick. This recipe will serve 3.

With the patties serve new boiled potatoes with parsley butter, green string beans, a green salad with Thousand Island dressing, and the same dry white wine (chilled) that was used in the preparation of the patties. And, of course, an apple pie.

I think the two most tantalizing aromas coming from the kitchen are those of bacon frying and pork chops cooking. There are a number of ways of cooking pork chops beside pan-broiling them, and each way adds its own little distinctive flavor. This recipe I call Pork Chops Beatrice, in honor of my talented Better Half, who devised it.

PORK CHOPS BEATRICE

4 *lean pork chops*   ½ *cup chicken broth*
1 *tsp. bacon drippings*   ½ *cup dry white wine*
1 *generous tsp. flour*   1 *large onion, sliced*

Get the pork chops cut about 1 inch thick. In a heavy skillet put the bacon drippings (just enough so that the chops will not stick to the pan), and when it is hot put in the pork chops, and sear them slowly on both sides. When they are nicely browned, drain most of the renderings, leaving only enough to form the basis for a *roux*. Remove the chops for a moment, and into the renderings sprinkle the flour.

Mix the flour and renderings thoroughly until smooth, and then put the chops back in the skillet. Add the chicken broth (canned will do very nicely) and the dry white wine. Peel and slice thinly the onion, spreading the slices over the chops. Cover the skillet and let the chops simmer for about 45 minutes. This recipe will serve 4 or 2, depending upon capacities. The ideal accompaniments are either baked sweet potatoes or fried sweet potatoes, lima beans with plenty of butter, and a salad of grapefruit segments alternated with Belgian endive halves on a bed of romaine, with a tart French dressing.

The Italians have a delicious way of cooking pork chops. After the chops are seared on both sides (pan-broiled), sprinkle a few anise seeds over them, and let them continue cooking until done. The anise flavor in conjunction with pork is both unusual and taste teasing.

I don't know why so many dishes utilizing pineapple are labeled "Hawaiian." One might think that if pineapple is used in the preparation of a dish, it must have originated in Hawaii, which, of course, is silly. True, the greatest pineapple plantations in the world are in Hawaii, but on the other hand there is scarcely a grocery store in the country that doesn't have canned pineapple on its shelves.

Well, be that as it may, here is a succulent dish of pork chops called:

HAWAIIAN BRAISED PORK CHOPS

3 *lean center-cut pork chops*   ⅓ *cup pineapple juice*
1 *tbsp. cornstarch*   ¾ *tsp. salt*
⅔ *cup chilled dry white wine*   *Pinch powdered cloves*
                  2 *slices pineapple*

Get large pork chops, cut at least 1 inch thick. Heat a heavy skillet until it is hot, then rub the skillet with the fat on the edge of the pork chops. Then brown the chops well on both sides in the skillet, being careful not to brown too fast, for pork should be well cooked. When the chops are nicely browned, remove them from the skillet, drain off excess fat, and keep the chops warm.

Mix the cornstarch with the dry white wine and the pineapple juice. Add the salt, the powdered cloves, mix well, and pour the liquid into the skillet. Then add the pineapple (canned or fresh) cut in ½-inch wedges. Cook until the mixture is thick, and then return the browned pork chops to the skillet. Simmer, uncovered, for about 15 minutes. This serves 3 people, or better 2, which gives each 1½ chops for a serving.

I am very fond of peanut butter. An old friend of mine in the advertising and radio business in Chicago, Katherine Avery, knowing my predilection for it, suggested that I cook pork chops in peanut butter, making a gravy out of the peanut butter and water. The idea intrigued me, so I set to work one evening. And I came up with what I thought was a marvelous pork chop dish. But I added something else instead of water.

PORK CHOPS AND PEANUT BUTTER

2 *thick center-cut pork chops*   1 *onion, chopped*
Seasoned flour   ⅓ *cup peanut butter*
Bacon drippings   1 *cup dry sherry*

Roll the pork chops in seasoned flour, and brown them on both sides in a heavy skillet lightly greased with the bacon drippings. Then put them in a casserole and sprinkle the chopped onion over them. Thoroughly mix the peanut butter and the dry sherry until the consistency is about that of thin cream. Pour the sherry-peanut-butter mixture over the chops and onion, cover the casserole, and bake in a 325-degree oven for about 45 minutes. But watch the baking, for if baked too long the sherry will quickly evaporate, leaving only the moist peanut butter. It should be a rather thick sauce.

The following is practically a whole meal in one dish, for pork chops are combined with rice and vegetables in a casserole that is so palatable that it's apt to bring forth the request for a second helping.

PORK CHOP VEGETABLE CASSEROLE WITH RICE

6-8 *lean pork chops*	*½ cup water*
½ cup chopped onion	*½ cup dry sherry*
½ cup chopped green pepper	*3 cups cooked rice*
1 10-oz. can cream of mush-	*2 cups cooked peas*
room soup	*1 tsp. salt*
	⅛ tsp. pepper

Place the pork chops in a lightly greased heavy skillet and brown them on both sides, then remove and keep warm. Enough fat should cook out of the chops so that it is not necessary to add any more. Place the chopped onion and green pepper in the skillet and cook until tender. If necessary, add a little bacon drippings, so that the onions and green pepper will not stick to the pan.

When the onions and green peppers are tender, add the mushroom soup, water, dry sherry, cooked rice, cooked peas, and the salt and pepper. Mix all together well, then pour half of the mixture into a greased baking dish. Arrange half of the pork chops over the rice and peas. Top the pork chops with the balance of the rice and peas, and then add the other half of the pork chops. Bake in a 350-degree oven for about 30 minutes. This recipe will make

6 to 8 servings depending upon the number of pork chops used. Please bear in mind I said "servings," not "people."

From Luxembourg comes a dish that flavorably combines pork chops, sauerkraut, bacon, and applesauce. It is really unusual, and unusually delicious. This recipe was sent to me by my old friend, Ted Sills, who blows the trumpets for various comestibles.

LUXEMBOURG KRAUT

8 *slices bacon, diced*
1 *tbsp. brown sugar*
Dash freshly ground pepper
¼ *tsp. paprika*
1 *tsp. prepared mustard*
3 *tbsps. vinegar*

1 *oz. dry white wine*
1 #2½ *can sauerkraut*
1 *cup applesauce*
1 *tbsp. butter*
4 *shoulder pork chops*

Fry the diced bacon in a heavy skillet, and pour off all of the drippings except for ¼ cup, which reserve. Combine the bacon, the ¼ cup of drippings, the brown sugar, pepper, paprika, mustard, vinegar, dry white wine, the sauerkraut, and the applesauce (canned applesauce can be used nicely). Mix everything together well, and turn into a lightly greased casserole.

Melt the butter in the skillet over a low heat, and brown the pork chops well on both sides. Place the browned chops on top of the sauerkraut mixture, and bake in a 350-degree oven for 1 hour, or until the chops are tender. This recipe makes 4 servings.

As if hosts and hostesses don't have enough problems in these days of soaring prices, a new problem has reared its disquieting head—"To barbecue or not to barbecue."

Formerly confined to the South and Southwest, this cooking fad has spread across the whole United States, and nearly everybody who has a tiny plot of ground behind the home has an outdoor barbecue. Even those who live in apartment houses are, in increasing numbers, buying portable barbecues and setting them up in their kitchens.

I think the most complete comment on barbecuing was contained in a recent syndicated column called "Stanton Delaplane's San Francisco Postcard," which appeared in the San Francisco *Chronicle* on September 30, 1955. Mr. Delaplane's columns appear daily in the *Chronicle,* and other papers, and for my money they are rarely anything but priceless.

The Burning Question, Sir

As an outdoor living man (with an outdoor liver that gives me fits at times), I am happy to report that we are nearly back living in the kitchen.

This report comes from my neighbor, Scofflaw, who hasn't cooked in the kitchen since he got the portable barbecue.

No sooner did the Scofflaws start cooking on the terrace than we must do the same. It seems only squares cook in the kitchen these days. All us up-to-date people eat steaks cooked in the Great Outdoors.

Scofflaw took a nosy interest in my house even while it was under construction.

"Whereya gonna put the barbecue?" said Scofflaw.

"What barbecue?"

"Whereya cook," said Scofflaw patiently. "You aren't gonna cook in the kitchen?"

So the Scofflaws shouldn't sneer at us, we started with a hibachi.

A hibachi is a Japanese job. It is a kind of bucket. You put charcoal in this thing and touch it off. If you put a steak over it, it usually cooks the hand right off of you without even taking the chill off the steak.

Socially, though, we couldn't have gotten along without it.

Scofflaw regarded this like a Leica fan talking to a boy with a box Brownie.

Mr. Scofflaw's barbecue is made of brick. It has a spit that turns the meat and a rack you can raise and lower.

On rainy and cold days, Mr. Scofflaw has a portable barbecue—I kid you not—a portable barbecue he can move INSIDE the house.

Mr. Scofflaw has asbestos gloves to handle the hot stuff. He has a chef's cap and an apron with funny sayings, "Say When!", "Crying Towel." And so on.

The way this meat is prepared is like this: You start the fire. There is a new fuel you pour over the charcoal, makes it light right up.

Scofflaw is now a busy man. He has a patent sprayer which sprays water on the blaze and cuts them down to coals again. He has forks with three-foot handles and long-armed spatulas. He has a house painter's brush.

He dips this brush in a mixture of catsup and vinegar and old varnish. And he paints the steaks like crazy. He burns himself pretty regularly.

"Gotta keep the fire down—OUCH! Or the steaks get too much—WOW!—crust. BLAST! And keep the sauce going. AYE!"

Grease pops all over the terrace. Smoke gets in everybody's eyes and a little film of soot swims on the martinis.

At the proper moment, Scofflaw flings the meat on the platter, slices it and everybody sits down and SHHHHHHHHHIVVVVVVERRRRRRS in the cold evening air.

All except Scofflaw. That dumb rabbit is half cooked himself.

Well, as I said, there is a move back to the kitchen. Or, rather, modern technology is swallowing up the Outdoor Life. Like the jungle swallows up man's ruins.

It started when Scofflaw hooked his spit up to electricity.

I liked this idea. Because I used to be spit dog for Scofflaw. When I came to dinner, I turned the spit. Crank. Crank. Crank. While Scofflaw, the artist, belted the martinis and mixed the sauce.

I was still thinking we would have to put in a brick barbecue. Or be sneered out of the neighborhood. A hibachi is O.K. but temporary. Like a camp cot in the bedroom.

However, Mr. Scofflaw has bought a new gadget. It is shiny and wired for electricity.

"Know what it is?" he said proudly. "Call this a Lite-R-Rite. Put it under your charcoal and switch on. Lights the charcoal by ELECTRICITY!"

Well, now we have the electric spit and the electric lighter. And I think I will hang on to the hibachi.

All we have to do is put a roof over the terrace. And, hey-ho, kids. We're back in the kitchen.

In the opinion of many of my friends out here in California, I am still living in the horse and buggy era because I do not have (a) an outdoor barbecue, nor (b) own an indoor barbecue or rotisserie The closest I have come to barbecue cooking is in my wonderful Rheem Wedgewood gas range, which has an Ember-Glow broiler. Around the broiler burner are special radiants. During the broiling operation these radiants glow red and give off rays that penetrate the meat, speed the broiling process, and help to give meats that delicious charcoal taste. So, I turn out mighty succulent barbecued chicken, *shish kebabs,* corn, and spareribs right in my kitchen, either under the broiler or in the oven.

Take spareribs, for instance. Not long ago I made barbecued spareribs, which I called Piquant Spareribs. The guests may not have enjoyed them, but it's the first time I ever saw sparks fly from knives and forks!

PIQUANT SPARERIBS

4 *lbs. lean spareribs*
1 *cup Nu Made mayonnaise*
2 *oz. dry sherry*
2 *oz. soy sauce*
1 *tsp. chili powder*
1 *tsp. powdered ginger*
2 *cloves garlic, minced*
2 *tbsp. Worcestershire sauce*
1 *tsp. hickory smoked salt*
2 *tsp. horseradish*

1 *tsp. dry mustard*
2 *tbsp. tomato paste*
½ *tsp. black pepper*
3 *tbsp. brown sugar*
6 *oz. pineapple juice*
1 *tsp. onion juice*
4 *tsp. white wine tarragon*
   vinegar
½ *tsp. oregano*
½ *tsp. celery salt*

Mix all the ingredients (except spareribs) until sauce is well blended. It will make a scant 3 cups.

Put the spareribs, cut into about 4-inch pieces, into a roaster, and place in a preheated 500-degree oven. Let them cook for about 30 minutes. Pour off the accumulated fat.

Cover the spareribs with about ⅓ of the sauce, and put in the oven, after reducing the heat to 300 degrees. After 30 minutes add the second third of the sauce, and cook for another 30 minutes. Then add the balance of the sauce, and cook for another 30 minutes, or until the spareribs are tender.

Remove the spareribs to a hot platter, skim off any fat that has accumulated, and then pour the sauce over the spareribs, and serve. This will serve 4 people generously.

If ribs are barbecued, do not cut them in pieces. Brush them liberally and frequently with the sauce while cooking. The sauce may be kept warm while the ribs are cooking, and any remaining sauce may be poured over the spareribs.

Not long ago I received a letter from a Detroit reader of my newspaper column, "For Men Only!" signed Ross H. Johnson. He wrote, in part:

I am a chef by trade, but I cook because I like it. This includes a bit of puttering around the kitchen at home simply for the fun of it, and has resulted in several recipes which I think are fairly good, not too expensive, and while they involve a little time, there isn't too much labor involved.

One of my favorites is a Bar-B-Que Sauce, a little different from the average inasmuch as it is a sweet-sour sauce, not of the too spicy-hot type. It goes well with chicken, ribs, or sliced leftover roasts, and may be made, stored in the refrigerator almost indefinitely, and used at any convenient time.

Along with the sauce recipe came his method of cooking spareribs, so I am including both under one recipe. And, believe me, both are mighty good.

ROSS JOHNSON'S BARBECUED SPARERIBS

5 *lbs. lean spareribs*	1 *tsp. black pepper*
½ *lb. diced bacon*	3 *tsp. salt*
1 *cup ¼ inch diced celery*	3 *tbsps. prepared mustard*
2 *cups ½ inch diced onion*	1 #2 *can tomatoes*
3 *cloves garlic, chopped*	2 #2 *cans tomato juice*
3 *tsp. allspice*	3 *lemons (juice)*
3 *tsp. chili powder*	⅓ *cup wine vinegar*

1½ *cups brown sugar*

Sauté together in a heavy skillet the bacon, the celery cut in ¼-inch dice, the onions, cut in ½-inch dice, and the chopped garlic. When the bacon is done, add all the other ingredients except the spareribs, simmering slowly until reduced by half, stirring frequently. This takes 30 to 45 minutes.

Have the butcher break the ribs into 4-inch squares. Place the squares of ribs in a shallow container, salt lightly, and place under a medium broiler for 20 minutes, turning once. Drain off the excess fat and place the ribs in an uncovered roaster, pour the sauce over the ribs, and bake in a 350-degree oven, turning the ribs so the sauce browns but does not burn. The baking time will be from 45 minutes to an hour, but test for doneness by slipping the ribs from the tissues surrounding them. When the ribs slide out easily without breaking the meat up, they are just right to eat.

The foregoing recipe is for the indoor barbecue chef, but the outdoors one can barbecue his ribs over his pit, using the sauce for basting. This recipe serves 4.

If you've lived on, or visited, a Pennsylvania Dutch farm, you've probably learned the delights of scrapple. This dish, to the uninitiated, is a mixture of pork, liquid, and cornmeal, and, after it has been cooked and cooled, it is sliced and lightly fried, and then served with fried eggs.

Butchering day down on a Pennsylvania Dutch farm occupies everyone from dawn to dusk. Among other things, women cook the meat for liverwurst, and the water is saved to make the scrapple. In some parts scrapple is called *pann haas,* which literally means "pan rabbit." I have been told that the scrapple season was once as limited as the oyster season, running from the first week in September to the middle of March.

One of the most enthusiastic scrapple fanciers I know of is Lieutenant Colonel Von Kolnitz. In writing to me about scrapple, he said:

My wife, Mildred, is from Philadelphia, and she makes the most edible scrapple I have ever tasted. . . . Probably there is more hog meat ruined and served to the innocent public in the name of scrapple than even a congressional investigating committee could uncover. It's easy to make, but tricky to cook, and that is where the dyspepserias reduce what may have been passable scrapple to a gooey mess. But, please, don't ever tell anyone to serve scrapple drowned in syrup like hot cakes. That is treason!

Well, here is Mildred Von Kolnitz's recipe for scrapple.

SCRAPPLE VON KOLNITZ

2 *lbs. lean ground pork*	1 *tsp. red chili pequins*
2 *quarts bouillon*	1 *tsp. poultry seasoning*
½ *tsp. freshly ground pepper*	1 *tbsp. Worcestershire sauce*
½ *tsp. sage*	1½ *tsp. salt*
½ *tsp. dried thyme*	1½ *cups yellow corn meal*

Simmer the ground pork in the bouillon for about 1½ hours, or until tender. After the meat is tender, draw off 1 quart of the stock, place in a saucepan, and add the pepper, sage, thyme, red chili pequins, crushed (these are bottled by Spice Islands Company, and are on sale at the better stores), the poultry seasoning, the Worcestershire sauce, and the salt. Bring the whole to a boil.

When the mixture is boiling rapidly, beat in over a low flame the yellow corn meal and cook until the mixture thickens (the best way to beat the corn meal in is with an electric beater to keep the mixture from lumping). Then add the meat mixture, and cook for another 5 minutes. Stir the mixture into two 9 x 5 x 3-inch loaf pans, and refrigerate overnight so the mixture will solidify.

When ready to cook the scrapple, slice it with a sharp ham slicer in ⅛-inch thick slices, being careful not to break the slices. Rub a heavy frying pan with a thin coating of fat, but make certain that there is no excess fat in the pan. Place the first batch in a cold pan, and cook over a medium-low flame. When it has browned on one side, use a pancake turner, inverted, and carefully cut the strip of scrapple from the pan, turn, and brown on the other side. The second batch will be easier to turn.

This is really a breakfast delicacy, and should be served with fried eggs. But the cooked scrapple, as finger pieces or hot hors d'oeuvres, goes excellently with beer.

And now my Chinese department recommends these two delectable pork dishes. The first is from the hand and heart of Johnny Kan, of San Francisco.

KAN'S SWEET AND SOUR PUNGENT PORK

2 *cups lean pork*	5 *slices canned pineapple*
1 *beaten egg*	1 *tbsp. onion*
½ *tsp. Ac'cent*	1 *medium green pepper*
½ *tsp. salt*	2 *tbsp. cornstarch*
1 *cup flour*	2 *tbsp. soy sauce*
Peanut oil	¼ *cup brown sugar*
⅓ *cup chicken broth*	⅔ *cup pineapple juice*

1 *tbsp. catsup*

Cut the lean pork into ½-inch pieces, coat them well with the beaten egg, and place them in a bag containing the Ac'cent, salt, and flour (this is seasoned flour, but without pepper). Shake until all the pieces of pork have been well coated. Then remove the pieces of pork from the bag and shake off the excess flour.

Heat enough peanut (or vegetable) oil in a large skillet to cover the pork pieces. When the oil is hot, brown the pork pieces over a moderate flame until done, about 7 to 10 minutes. Remove the pork pieces and drain on absorbent paper toweling. Drain all the oil from the skillet except 1 tablespoon. Then add the chicken broth (or consommé), the slices of pineapple cut into 1-inch pieces, the onion cut into ¼-inch pieces, and the green pepper cut into ¼-inch pieces. Cook this for 5 minutes, then add the pork pieces, blend all together thoroughly, and cook over a low flame for 10 minutes.

Mix together the cornstarch, the soy sauce, the brown sugar, the pineapple juice, and the catsup. Add this to the pork mixture, stirring constantly while cooking until the juice thickens and the mixture is hot. Serve immediately with fried rice. Serves 4 to 6.

The second pork dish is from Professor Otto Graf, the previously mentioned expert on Chinese cooking. It is the third entree in his Mandarin dinner.

TOMATOES AND GREEN PEPPERS WITH PORK

2 *lbs. lean pork*	2 *tsp. sugar*
4 *large tomatoes*	1 *tsp. Ac'cent*
2 *large green peppers*	1 *tbsp. soy sauce*
1 *clove garlic, chopped*	½ *tsp. fresh basil*
1 *cup consommé*	2 *tsp. cornstarch*

Cut the tomatoes (slightly underripe) and the green peppers, seeded, into cubes. Brown the pork, cut into cubes, in a well-greased skillet, then add the garlic, finely chopped, and cook 1 minute. Then add the consommé, the sugar, the Ac'cent, the soy sauce, and the basil (use ¼ tsp. of dried basil if you haven't the fresh). Cover and cook for 30 minutes, until the pork is almost tender. Then add the green peppers, and cook 3 minutes. Next add the tomatoes, and cook 2 minutes. Stir in the cornstarch (made into a thin paste with a little water), and continue stirring carefully until the sauce is thickened. Serve very hot. This recipe makes 4 to 6 servings.

On Easter Sundays, if you follow the traditional American (or French or old Russian) custom, you will serve a baked ham. Or you may well serve it on any other festive occasion, for it is exciting to look at when brought to the table, and its succulent goodness is highly gratifying to the taste buds.

If your ham is not tenderized, or precooked, you will soak it overnight in water, then boil it, and finally bake it, perhaps serving it with some special sauce.

"Pigs is Pigs," wrote Ellis Parker Butler, and as ham comes from pigs, it might follow that ham is ham, no matter how you slice it. But that is not true. There are many varieties of ham, both in this country and abroad. Two famous American hams are Virginia hams and Kentucky hams. The Virginia variety comes from pigs known as razorbacks, which are fed on peanuts, acorns, and peaches, and which, when slaughtered, are cured over fires of apple and hickory wood, then aged for at least a year.

The Kentucky hams are from the finest Hampshire hogs. They are dry salted for thirty days and then smoked over a fire of hickory wood and corncobs for another thirty days. Then they are aged for from one to two years.

The best-known European hams are York hams from England; Irish hams, from northern Ireland, which are peat-smoked; Westphalian hams from Germany; Prague hams from Bohemia; and Prosciutto hams from Italy.

Well, how shall we cook our ordinary American whole ham, which is pretty hard to beat? Are you feeling opulent? Then bake it in a good domestic champagne.

HAM BAKED IN CHAMPAGNE

1 *whole ham*	1 *cup brown sugar*
Whole cloves	½ *cup prepared mustard*
Champagne	3 *tbsp. brandy*

If the ham is tenderized, boiling it first is not necessary. Remove any rind or excess fat, and score the remaining layer of fat with a sharp knife, dot liberally with whole cloves, and place in a large roaster. Pour 1 quart of good domestic champagne over the ham, then place it in a 300-degree oven, and cook for about 15 minutes to the pound, basting occasionally with the champagne.

While the ham is cooking, make your glaze. Make a paste of 1 cup of brown sugar and ½ cup of prepared mustard (if you can get it, use the imported Dijon mustard, which is made with white wine). Moisten the paste with about 3 tablespoons of brandy, or enough to make the paste about the consistency of marmalade.

When the ham is done, remove it from the oven and cover the top with the paste, over the cloves. Replace the ham in the oven, adding a little more champagne if necessary, raise the oven heat to 425 degrees, and let it cook for about 20 to 25 minutes more, basting with the liquid in the roaster, until the ham is well glazed and brown.

Another tantalizing way of cooking a whole ham is with Madeira wine. I first heard of it as Jubilee Ham.

JUBILEE HAM

1 *whole tenderized ham*	½ *tsp. dried marjoram*
3 *carrots*	½ *tsp. dried thyme*
4 *medium onions*	1 *quart dry white wine*
5 *stalks celery*	*Water*
5 *sprigs parsley*	*Whole cloves*
1 *clove garlic*	8 *oz. Madeira wine*
	Dark molasses

First you prepare a broth for the tenderized ham to cook in. Slice the carrots and onions, and put them in a deep kettle with the celery stalks, the parsley, the split clove of garlic, the dried marjoram and thyme, and the dry white wine. Place the ham in this liquid, and add enough water so the liquid will cover the ham in the kettle, and boil gently for 1 hour.

Then turn the heat very low, and let the ham simmer, without boiling, for 2 hours. Then remove the ham from the liquor, and peel off the skin and some of the fat. Score the fat, and stick cloves all over the top. Place the ham in a roaster, pour the Madeira wine over it, and then spread it with dark molasses. Glaze in a 425-degree oven for about 10 minutes, basting often, then serve.

Not long ago we had a problem in the Wood household. With guests expected for a Sunday night dinner, I bought a large half ham, which was baked. However, two of the guests were unable to make the dinner, and, although those present ate lustily, it seemed that only a slight dent was made in the ham.

Mrs. Wood and I had two dinners of cold ham; we had ham sandwiches one night after a hearty luncheon in town; we had eggs scrambled in chopped ham for Sunday brunch, and still there was ham left. So late one afternoon I started improvising, and what came to the table that night was out of this world. I'll call it Ham Pilaf.

HAM PILAF

3 *tbsp. olive oil*	¼ *cup dry sherry*
1 *medium onion*	½ *tsp. Worcestershire sauce*
½ *cup chopped celery*	*Salt*
¼ *cup chopped green pepper*	*Pepper*
2 *cups diced cooked ham*	1 *4 oz.-can chopped mushrooms*
¾ *cup raw rice*	1 *tbsp. chopped parsley*
1¼ *cups chicken broth*	½ *cup pitted ripe olives*

Heat the olive oil in a skillet, and in it sauté the onion, chopped, the celery, and the green pepper, chopped, for 5 minutes. Then add the ham, mix in well, and continue to sauté for 5 minutes more. Then add the uncooked rice and cook for about 2 minutes, stirring well.

To the contents of the skillet add the chicken broth, the dry sherry wine, the Worcestershire sauce, and salt and pepper to taste. Turn up the flame and, after stirring well, bring the contents of the skillet to a boil. Then remove from the heat and pour the contents of the skillet into a greased casserole, cover, and bake in a 375-degree oven for 30 minutes.

Take the casserole out of the oven, uncover, and gently stir in the can of chopped mushrooms, drained, the chopped parsley, and the pitted ripe olives, coarsely chopped. Cover, return to the oven, and cook about 10 minutes more. Serve from the casserole to 4 people.

This ham pilaf, or *Risotto,* or whatever you want to call it was so wonderful that Mrs. Wood and I ate two-thirds of it, instead of half of it. So two nights later we added the remainder of the ham (about 1 cup, diced), and ½ cup of *Bulghour* cooked with onion and chicken broth, heated the whole in a low oven, and we enjoyed it as much, if not more, than we had the original dish.

Succulent ham topped with tender rice and rings of apples is truly a main dish with sparkling good flavor. The cheese makes a golden halo for the flavor beneath, and basting with the molasses goodness, in which the ham has baked, brings a gourmet touch to the rice and apples.

APPLE TOPPED HAM SLICE

2 *cups cooked rice*   ½ *cup sherry*
1 *ham slice (about* 12 *ounces*)   1 *cup grated cheese*
¼ *cup molasses*   *About* 7 *apple slices partially
                                cooked*

First cook your rice according to your favorite method. In a baking
dish soak the ham in the molasses for 15 minutes. Add the sherry
and bake in a 350-degree oven for 40 minutes or until the ham is
tender. Frequently baste the ham with the molasses and sherry.
Mix the rice with half of the cheese. Cover the ham slice with the
rice. Top the rice with the apple slices. Sprinkle with the remaining
cheese. Turn the oven to 450 degrees and cook about 10 minutes
or until the cheese is browned. Before serving, baste with some of
the molasses and sherry. This recipe makes 5 servings.

One of the most famous and delicious dishes in the realm of
gastronomy is *Wiener Schnitzel*. But don't confuse it with the
breaded veal cutlets that are served in some tearooms and even in
many high-class restaurants. Such an atrocity is usually a thick
slab of veal coated with breadcrumbs, fried too much and too long,
and served with a catsup-like liquid called tomato sauce.

The true *Wiener Schnitzel,* prepared in the traditional style of
old, prewar Vienna at such restaurants as Sacher's or the Hotel
Bristol, is a delicate morsel that will set your taste buds tingling
with delight. If the meat comes from young, milkfed calves (as it
should), it will come out, when cooked, as white and tender as the
meat from a chicken breast. And *Wiener Schnitzel* is very simple
to prepare.

WIENER SCHNITZEL

2 *lbs. young veal*   2 *eggs*
Lemon juice   2 *tbsp. dry white wine*
½ *lb. butter*   1 *cup fine breadcrumbs*
Salt   ¼ *cup flour*
Freshly ground pepper   12 *anchovy filets*
                Pinch paprika

Have the veal cut from the leg in slices ¼ inch thick. Trim, and cut the cutlets into individual serving pieces. Place the pieces between several thicknesses of waxed paper, and pound gently with a flat-faced wooden mallet, or the flat side of a cleaver, until the pieces are ⅛ inch thick. Then marinate the pieces for 1 hour in enough lemon juice to cover the meat. Then remove them from the lemon juice, dry, and sprinkle both sides with salt and freshly ground pepper.

Beat 2 whole eggs lightly in a bowl with the dry white wine. Draw each of the veal pieces through the beaten egg, first on one side then on the other. Dredge the pieces with fine breadcrumbs mixed with the flour, and gently pat the coating in. Allow to stand for 15 to 20 minutes.

Melt the butter in a large skillet and let it foam well. Reduce the flame and sauté the cutlets for 1½ minutes on each side. The cutlets are done when the coating turns to a golden brown. Drain the sautéed cutlets on paper toweling, then place on a very hot platter.

To the butter in the skillet (add more if necessary) add the 12 mashed anchovy filets and a generous pinch of paprika. When blended, pour over the cutlets, first having sprinkled them lightly with lemon juice. Serve immediately. Buttered noodles are almost a must with *Wiener Schnitzel.*

The foregoing is the plain *Wiener Schnitzel,* but in many continental restaurants the cutlets are garnished in the following manner: On top of each cutlet place a thin slice of lemon; in the center of the lemon place a pitted olive wrapped with an anchovy filet; sprinkle a few capers around the meat; chop the yolks and white of hard-cooked eggs separately, and place them alternately around the edges of the dish.

Another variation is *Wiener Schnitzel Holstein,* in which a fried egg is placed on top of each cutlet in place of the lemon and other garnishes.

One day my wife spent the afternoon at the beauty shop getting a permanent (so I'm giving away family secrets—she doesn't have naturally curly hair!). We hadn't discussed dinner plans beforehand as we usually do, so it was up to me to choose the entree at the butcher shop. What I selected was something that my wife is not too enthusiastic about—a veal steak.

Now, the payoff of this story could be that the veal steak was fixed so deliciously that my wife went into ecstasies over it. But that is exactly what happened when she savored Veal Madeleine. The moral—if you think you do not like veal, try Veal Madeleine. It's a thick veal steak, pan-browned, smothered with golden brown onions, simmered in wine, and set on a bed of noodles which have been paprika'd, buttered, sprinkled with almonds, and served with a sour cream, herb, and sherry sauce.

VEAL MADELEINE

1 *veal steak, 1½ inches thick*	1 *cup commercial sour cream*
¼ *cup flour*	2 *tbsp. dry sherry*
1 *tbsp. paprika*	¼ *tsp. dried oregano*
1 *tsp. salt*	*Cooked noodles*
3 *tbsp. bacon drippings*	*Butter*
3 *medium onions*	*Slivered almonds*
1 *cup dry white wine*	*Sliced stuffed olives*

Combine the flour, paprika, and salt. Dredge the veal steak thoroughly with this mixture.

In the bacon drippings (or olive oil) in a heavy skillet sauté the onions, sliced thin, over a low flame until they are soft and golden brown, then remove them from the skillet. Brown the floured veal steak well on both sides in the same skillet that the onions were sautéed in. When browned, place the sautéed onions on top of the veal steak in the skillet. Add any remaining seasoned flour mixture to the skillet along with the dry white wine. Cover the skillet and simmer until the veal is tender—about 1 hour. Remove veal and onions to a hot platter.

To make the gravy, after the veal and onions have been removed from the skillet they were cooked in, add the sour cream, the dry sherry, and the dried oregano to the skillet juices. Stir and blend thoroughly and heat to serving temperature. Surround the veal and onions with cooked noodles which have been buttered and sprinkled with paprika and the slivered almonds. Garnish the top of the veal steak and onions with sliced stuffed olives. Serve the gravy separately.

Belgian endive is to me one of the greatest salad delicacies. It is grown from specially selected chicory roots. The white heads are made up of thick, fleshy leaves, anywhere from 4 to 6 inches long, and the width of the heads runs from 1 to 2 inches. In salads, the leaves can be separated, washed and dried, and arranged on a bed of lettuce or watercress. Or the heads can be split in half, and bedded the same way. The best dressing is a tart French one, or a Roquefort cheese one.

One of the great Belgian dishes combines veal and endive to make what I think is a gastronomic masterpiece. It is called *Veau aux Chicorées,* and it is quite simple to prepare, and not too expensive, as entrees go.

VEAL WITH ENDIVE

4 lbs. veal
1 tsp. salt
¼ tsp. freshly ground pepper
Pinch powdered thyme

Flour
2 oz. butter
2 lbs. Belgian endive
Consommé
Dry white wine

The breast of veal is excellent for this dish. Cut the meat into pieces about 2 by 3 inches. Make a mixture of the salt, pepper, and powdered thyme, and rub the pieces of veal with it. Then flour them. Melt the butter in a skillet and sauté the meat until the pieces are a light golden brown. Then transfer the pieces of veal to a baking dish, and lay 10 to 12 washed and drained endives around the meat.

Butter a piece of wax paper and lay it over the top of the baking dish, buttered side down. Bake in a 300-degree oven for about 2 hours. Baste the contents of the dish frequently with a mixture of half consommé and half dry white wine, using a little at a time. You may need about 1½ cups of basting liquor altogether.

After basting, always replace the waxed paper, as this prevents too great browning. When the veal is tender, there should not be too much gravy; however, if too much has accumulated, remove the meat and endive to a hot platter (the meat in the center and the endive around it), put the baking dish on top of the stove over an asbestos pad, and, with a hot flame, allow the gravy to reduce a bit. The gravy should be light golden-colored, and not too thick.

During my travels across the country I have been amazed at the lack of enthusiasm over veal. In some states it is practically unobtainable, and in others one rarely finds it on menus. In a cookbook which deals with home cooking across the country, I was unable to find a single recipe for veal.

Yet veal, properly cooked, yields some exquisite dishes. I've already detailed Vienna's greatest dish, *Wiener Schnitzel;* Luxembourg Veal Stew is almost a national dish; Veal Scallopini Marsala cannot be topped among Italian dishes; and the famous old Russian dish, Veal Chops with Madeira and Mushrooms, is a gourmet's delight (recipes for all of these are given in my *With a Jug of Wine*).

And *G'schnetzlet's* (it's pronounced exactly the way it's spelled) is a veritable symphony of flavors. Theodore Meyer, the executive chef of the Bismarck Hotel in Chicago, makes the best *G'schnetzlet's* (all right, call it minced veal à la Suisse) I have ever tasted. And with very little trouble you can duplicate it right in your own home.

G'SCHNETZLET'S
(Minced Veal à la Suisse)

1 *lb. tender part of veal leg*	1½ *cups half and half (cream*
3 *oz. butter*	*and milk)*
1 *medium onion*	*Salt*
2 *mushrooms*	*Freshly ground pepper*
1 *tbsp. flour*	1 *cup dry white wine*
1 *tbsp. chopped parsley*	

Cut the veal in slivers, or thin slices. Sauté the veal pieces in a pan with 1½ ounces of butter until light brown.

In another pan sauté the onion, chopped, and the large mushrooms, sliced, in 1½ ounces of butter until they are a light brown. Then put the sautéed veal in with the onions and mushrooms, adding the flour and the thin cream (half and half). Mix well, and allow everything to cook for 5 to 6 minutes, seasoning with salt and freshly ground pepper to taste. Then add the dry white wine and the chopped parsley. Let this simmer for a few moments, and then serve.

The perfect accompaniment to *G'schnetzlet's* is sautéed french-cut green beans and Roesti potatoes. These are boiled potatoes cut julienne style (matchlike sticks), sautéed in butter until brown on one side, and then flipped over to brown on the other side.

Slices of meat, covered with a seasoned mixture and then rolled up and braised in a pot, and served with a rich gravy, is a favorite dish in a number of European countries. The Italians call them *Bracciole,* the Poles name them *Zraziki po Krakowski* if they are made with beef, and *Zraziki Cielece* if they are made with veal; and the French name for them is *Paupiettes de Veau.* But I call them delicious in any language.

The Polonaise Restaurant in New York serves Polish *Zarzi,* which are very thin strips of beef covered with a mixture of cooked mushrooms and onions, to which matzoth meal has been added, and then rolled, tied, and simmered in bouillon. Cream and flour are added to the gravy. A correspondent of mine in New York writes that he has had a similar dish, but with a Madeira sauce rather than a cream sauce. This improves it mightily, to my way of thinking.

The Dominique Restaurant, in the Montparnasse section of Paris, serves a dish they call Zrazys Nelson. These are not beef rolls at all, but a very unique and delicious dish nevertheless. Rounds of boiled potatoes are sautéed in butter and then placed on a serving platter. Sliced cucumbers and mushrooms are sautéed in butter, then thickened with flour and water, and a little tomato purée is added. Small filets of beef are sautéed in butter, then placed over the fried potatoes, the cucumber and mushroom sauce is poured over all, and the whole topped with french-fried onions.

But here is a treasured Polish recipe for *Zraziki* that I think is tops.

ZRAZIKI
(Stuffed Veal Rolls)

1½ lbs. veal cutlets	1 tbsp. chopped parsley
4 tbsp. butter	2 tbsp. butter
5 chicken livers	½ cup dry Madeira wine
½ cup chopped onions	½ cup condensed consommé
½ cup chopped mushrooms	1 cup sour cream
¼ tsp. dried marjoram	1 tbsp. grated Parmesan cheese

Salt and pepper

Get the veal cutlets cut in slices about ¼ inch thick, and pound them with a mallet until the slices are very thin. Then cut the veal into oblong pieces about 3 by 4 inches.

Sauté the chicken livers, onions, and mushrooms in 2 table-spoons of butter for about 8 minutes. Then, while they are in the skillet, finely chop the chicken livers. Sprinkle over all the dried marjoram and chopped parsley, and mix everything well.

Lightly salt and pepper each slice of veal, and on each slice spread the above mixture evenly until all is used. Then roll up the veal slices and secure either with toothpicks or thread. Put the rolls into a heavy skillet with 2 tablespoons of butter, and cook until the rolls are evenly browned all over. Then add the Madeira wine and the consommé to the contents of the skillet, cover, and simmer gently until the rolls are tender, about 45 minutes. If needed, add a little more consommé and Madeira wine, in equal parts, while cooking.

When the veal rolls are tender, remove them to a hot platter, and to the juices in the skillet add the sour cream, and sprinkle in a generous tablespoon of the grated Parmesan cheese. If the gravy seems too thin, add a little flour and water paste. Bring the gravy to a boil, stirring constantly. Then pour it over the veal rolls and serve.

If desired, the veal rolls may be placed first on slices of toasted French bread, and the gravy poured over all.

Veal chops, properly prepared and cooked, will win devotees and influence appetites. My two favorite veal chop dishes are veal chops (with the kidneys attached) cooked with Madeira and mushrooms, and Veal Chops Parmesan with White Wine. These two recipes are in my *With a Jug of Wine,* so I won't repeat them in this book. But here is a third favorite of mine, Veal Chops Baked in White Wine.

VEAL CHOPS BAKED IN WHITE WINE

4 *veal chops,* 1½ *inches thick*	*Tiny pinch poultry seasoning*
Dry white wine	*Flour*
1 *clove garlic*	2 *tbsp. olive oil*
Salt and pepper	1 *small can mushrooms*

Trim off most of the fat from the thick veal chops. Place them in a deep bowl and cover with dry white wine, also adding a sliced clove of garlic (or small minced onion). Weight down the meat with a small plate to keep the chops covered with the wine, and refrigerate several hours, or overnight.

When ready to cook, remove the chops from the marinade, drain, sprinkle with salt and pepper and a tiny pinch of poultry seasoning, dredge with flour, and brown the chops well in the olive oil in a heavy skillet. Then remove the chops to a casserole, pour off the olive oil from the skillet, and put in the skillet a small can of mushrooms and their liquid, and the wine in which the chops were marinated. Mix well, heat, and pour the sauce over the chops. Cover the casserole, and bake in a 350-degree oven for 45 minutes. Then uncover, increase the heat to 400 degrees, and bake for 10 or 15 minutes longer, or until most of the liquid is evaporated.

Noodles go perfectly with veal dishes, but so does rice. For the above dish, toss hot, flaky cooked rice with sliced toasted almonds and sautéed fresh mushrooms which have been coarsely chopped.

And finally, a most intriguing taste combination, veal chops with an onion cream sauce. This is company fare.

VEAL CHOPS IN ONION SAUCE

4 *veal rib chops*	⅓ *cup dry sherry*
Flour	2 *tbsp. tomato paste*
3 *tbsp. bacon drippings*	½ *tsp. Ac'cent*
1 *can* (10 *oz.*) *condensed onion*	
soup	

Flour the thick veal rib chops, then brown slowly in the bacon drippings in a heavy skillet. When the chops are browned on both sides, pour off almost all of the drippings.

Combine the condensed onion soup, dry sherry, tomato paste, and Ac'cent. Pour this into the skillet with the chops, cover, and simmer gently for 1 hour or more, or until the chops are tender. During the cooking, turn and baste the chops occasionally. Serve with buttered noodles or mashed potatoes to 4.

Tallyrand, the great French statesman, once said that all successful men know how to hold their tongues. I'd like to paraphrase that by saying that all successful chefs know how to cook their tongues.

Many people dislike tongue, probably because they have never eaten it prepared properly. Many more eschew tongue because it is a variety meat.

My wife is one of the latter. Although she is fond of liver, kidneys, and sweetbreads, she has always shied away from tongue. So, at a dinner when the entree turned out to be tongue, I had a bad moment wondering what she would do (she had a few bad moments herself, she admitted afterward).

The occasion was a delightful dinner party given by Helen Evans Brown in her home in Pasadena, California. Not only is Mrs. Brown a noted authority on food and the author of four wonderful cookbooks (*Chafing Dish Cookbook, Patio Cookbook, Holiday Cookbook, and West Coast Cookbook,*—all tops), but she is distinguished for her culinary creations. And that evening it was Tongue Tarragon.

And how did my wife acquit herself? Nobly! After the first taste, she gave me a sly grin, which as much as said, "Okay, Morry, it's wonderful, and I take back all I ever said about tongue." And she proceeded not only to eat every bit of her serving, but eagerly accepted a second helping!

Helen sent me the recipe (a variation is in her *West Coast Cookbook* under the designation, Braised Tongue Tulare). And here it is.

TONGUE TARRAGON

1 *fresh beef tongue*	*Flour*
Water	¼ *cup butter*
Salt	1 *carrot, chopped*
8 *sprigs parsley*	2 *stalks celery, chopped*
1 *large bay leaf*	1 *onion, chopped*
5 *sprigs green celery tops*	½ *lb. fresh mushrooms*
1 *sprig thyme*	1 *cup dry white wine*
1 *sprig marjoram*	1 *cup tongue stock*
1 *sprig basil*	1 *tbsp. dried tarragon*

Submerge the beef tongue with enough salted water to cover (1 teaspoon of salt for each quart of water) and place a *bouquet garni* in the pot (if you have fresh herbs tie together the parsley, bay leaf, green celery tops, thyme, marjoram, and basil. If you haven't fresh ones, put the dried ones in a little cheesecloth bag). Bring the water to a boil, then lower the flame and let the tongue simmer gently for 2 to 3½ hours, or until tender (Helen says the knowing fork is the only reliable test).

When tender, take the tongue out of the liquid, and remove the skin and throat bones and trim off the surplus fat. Rub the tongue well with flour, and brown in a heavy skillet in ¼ cup of butter. Then remove the browned tongue to a casserole.

In the butter the tongue was browned in (add a little more, if necessary) put the chopped carrot, the chopped celery, the chopped onion, and the sliced fresh mushrooms. Cook all this until wilted, then add to the casserole. Also add the dry white wine (a California Pinot Blanc is perfect), and 1 cup of tongue stock. Add the dried tarragon, correct the seasoning, and cook in a 350 degree oven until the top is browned, and the sauce slightly thickened.

Tongue, either smoked or fresh, may be prepared in a number of ways. Of course, the simplest is to boil it in water until tender, with herbs and spices added to the water, and then serve it with some sort of sauce (my favorite is a creamed horseradish sauce). Tongue also may be baked, grilled, or braised. A very delectable, yet inexpensive, tongue dish is called Spiced Tongue with Burgundy.

SPICED TONGUE WITH BURGUNDY

1 2 to 3-lb veal tongue	2 bay leaves
Boiling water	1 medium onion, minced
Salt	2 carrots, sliced
2 cups dry red wine	½ cup celery, chopped
2 cups tongue broth	1 cup raisins
½ tsp. allspice	Flour
12 whole cloves	Lemon slices

Watercress

Scrub the veal tongue well, place in a kettle, and cover with boiling water to which a small amount of salt has been added. Cook about 2 hours. Then remove the tongue, peel off the skin, and remove the root ends.

In a deep iron pot heat the dry red wine and the tongue broth. Add the allspice, the cloves, bay leaves, the minced onion, the sliced carrots, the chopped celery, and the raisins. Place the tongue in this, and cook for an hour longer.

Remove the tongue and cut it in thin slices and arrange them on a hot platter. Thicken the sauce with a little flour and water paste, heat, and then pour over the slices of tongue. Garnish the platter with watercress and lemon slices.

Here's a delicious tongue and cheese preparation that utilizes cooked tongue.

TONGUE AND CHEESE EN CASSEROLE

1 *lb. sliced cooked tongue*	1 *tsp. salt*
2 *cups consommé*	⅛ *tsp. pepper*
¼ *cup wine vinegar*	1 *cup browned breadcrumbs*
1 *tsp. pickling spices*	½ *cup grated Parmesan cheese*
	½ *cup dry white wine*

Simmer the sliced cooked tongue in the consommé, wine vinegar, pickling spices, and salt and pepper for 10 to 15 minutes. Then place a layer of the tongue slices in a greased casserole.

Have mixed together the browned breadcrumbs and the grated Parmesan cheese. Sprinkle the layer of tongue slices with the breadcrumb-cheese mixture, add another layer of tongue slices, then breadcrumb-cheese mixture, and repeat until all the tongue is used, with the breadcrumb-cheese mixture on top. Pour over this the dry white wine, and bake in a 350-degree oven until the top is browned.

Here is a delicious recipe for Smoked Beef Tongue with a spicy raisin sauce that utilizes beer.

SMOKED BEEF TONGUE WITH BEER
AND RAISIN SAUCE

1 3½-*lb. smoked beef tongue*	½ *cup seedless raisins*
Water	2 *tbsp. butter*
1½ *cups beer*	¼ *tsp. salt*
Vinegar	¼ *tsp. cinnamon*
1 *bay leaf*	⅛ *tsp. cloves*
4 *peppercorns*	½ *cup currant jelly*
½ *cup sugar*	1 *tsp. cornstarch*

Cover, in a pot, the smoked beef tongue, with cold water. Add to the pot 1 cup of beer, ⅔ cup of vinegar, the bay leaf, and the peppercorns. Cover the pot and simmer about 3 hours, or until the tongue is tender. Then remove it from the liquid, skin, slice, and serve with the following sauce.

In a saucepan combine ½ cup of beer and the sugar. Cook them together for about 5 minutes, stirring until the sugar is dissolved. Then add the seedless raisins, the butter, 1 tablespoon of vinegar, the salt, cinnamon, cloves, and currant jelly. Mix all this well, and bring to a boil. Dissolve the cornstarch in a little of the hot sauce, and add to the saucepan. Stir the whole over a low heat until the sauce thickens slightly. This should yield 6 servings.

It is too bad that so many Americans pass up kidneys. Throughout Europe kidneys are a great delicacy. Almost every country has a special way of preparing and cooking them. *Rognans de Veau à la Liégeoise* is one of the gastronomic achievements of the Walloons of southern Belgium. *Rognans sauté au vin blanc* is a favorite French luncheon dish. *Riñones de Carnere à la Señorita* is one of Madrid's most popular dishes.

Both the people of Holland and England are very fond of kidney toast, in which kidneys are cooked with sherry and onions, and then spread on toast. One of the best known of all German soups is *Nierensuppe,* or kidney soup. The Russians cook beef kidneys with dill pickles, potato slices, and sour cream, and their *Potchki v Madeiry* (kidneys cooked in Madeira) is one of the European continent's greatest epicurean dishes.

My veal kidney dish differs from the Russian one in that I do not use sour cream, and I do use onion. I think you will find it unusually delicious.

KIDNEYS AND MUSHROOMS IN MADEIRA AND BRANDY

6 *veal kidneys*	2 *oz. brandy*
Salt and pepper	1 *tsp. (rounded) flour*
6 *tbsp. butter*	½ *cup Madeira*
6 *tbsp. chopped onion*	½ *cup dry white wine*
1 *tsp. dried chervil*	⅓ *cup beef bouillon*
2 *tsp. chopped parsley*	½ *lb. fresh mushrooms*

Chopped chives

Remove the outer skin and fat from the kidneys, and cut them in not too thin slices (about ¾ inch in thickness). Season the slices with salt and freshly ground pepper.

In a heavy skillet melt 4 tablespoons of butter, and when hot, add the chopped onion, and cook until the onion begins to become limp. Then add the kidneys and sauté quickly until the kidneys begin to brown slightly. Sprinkle them with the chervil and chopped parsley. Toss for 2 minutes over a hot flame, shaking and rocking the pan frequently so they won't stick. Then warm the brandy in a ladle, ignite, and pour the burning brandy over the contents of the skillet.

Sprinkle over the whole a rounded teaspoon of flour. Sauté for a few seconds, then moisten the whole with the Madeira and white wine and beef bouillon. Bring to a quick boil, then turn down the flame to the lowest possible point, cover the skillet, and simmer very gently for about 5 minutes. Then uncover and add the sliced mushrooms, which have been sautéed in 2 tablespoons of butter for about 7 minutes. Simmer the whole for about 5 minutes longer, then transfer the contents of the skillet to a hot platter, and sprinkle with finely chopped chives. Spread the kidneys over triangles of bread fried in butter. Serves 6.

Incidentally, in the initial preparation of kidneys for cooking, the thin, white covering tissue, or skin, and the fat should first be removed. This is usually done by the butcher. Then the white core, or center, and the tubes should be removed (after the kidneys have been cut in half lengthwise). A sharp-pointed knife will do the trick, but the easiest way is to use a curved pair of scissors, such as manicure scissors. I happen to have a heavy pair of surgical scissors with curved blades, which enables me to operate on the kidneys in almost nothing flat. After the cores and tubes have been removed, soak the kidneys in cold, salted water for an hour or so. Lamb and veal kidneys are usually split lengthwise before preparing and cooking; beef kidneys are usually sliced or cut into segments.

The following is a very simple and easy kidney dish, and follows the old Russian custom of using sour cream. Either veal or lamb kidneys may be used.

KIDNEYS SAUTÉED WITH MADEIRA AND SOUR CREAM

2 *kidneys* (*lamb or veal*)	1 *tbsp. sour cream*
Flour	½ *cup Madeira wine*
2 *tbsp. butter*	*Salt and pepper*

Prepare the kidneys for cooking, and then slice them very thin. Powder the kidney slices lightly with flour, and sauté them in the butter for only 4 minutes, stirring the slices around in the pan once or twice. Then remove the kidneys from the skillet, and put in the skillet the sour cream and the Madeira wine. Allow to boil up, season lightly with salt and freshly ground pepper, stir well, and then pour the sauce over the kidneys. This recipe serves 2.

When you have run out of ideas for dinner, some night try a casserole of kidneys and mushrooms, flambéed with brandy and simmered in white wine. It is unbelievably delectable.

CASSEROLE OF KIDNEYS AND MUSHROOMS

12 *lamb kidneys*	¾ *cup dry white wine*
¼ *cup butter*	*Pinch dried tarragon leaves*
12 *little green onions*	½ *tbsp. butter*
¾ *lb. fresh mushrooms*	½ *tbsp. flour*
2 *oz. brandy*	*Salt and pepper*

Prepare the kidneys for cooking, then slice them thin.

Melt ¼ cup of butter in a casserole (earthenware, if you have one) and add the little green onions (tops and bulbs), chopped very fine, the sliced kidneys, and the fresh mushrooms, sliced. Sauté over a gentle flame until the kidneys are lightly browned and tender, about 5 minutes. Then remove the casserole from the fire, and pour over the warmed brandy, which has been ignited. When the flames have died out, put the casserole back over the flame, add the dry white wine, and a small pinch of dried tarragon leaves. Cover the casserole and simmer very gently for 1½ hours, adding more dry white wine if necessary. Cream together ½ tablespoon each of butter and flour to make a *roux,* and add to the gravy, blend in well, and continue to cook until the gravy is thickened, seasoning to taste with salt and freshly ground pepper. This serves 6 from the casserole. Riced or mashed potatoes, or saffron rice, are the best accompaniments, and of course a chilled dry white wine, the same you used in the preparation of the kidneys.

In Norse mythology, Valhalla was the great hall where Odin received and feasted the souls of heroes who had fallen in battle.

But across the bay from San Francisco, in the waterfront town of Sausalito, there exists another Valhalla. Once the rendezvous of Jack London, politicians, moviemakers, and rum runners, the present-day Valhalla Inn is where Sally Stanford, expertly assisted by her chef, Jerry Lee Smith, receives and feasts the very much alive bodies of fastidious gourmets.

Sally Stanford, the very active owner of Valhalla Inn, is a fabulous personage in and around San Francisco. On first seeing her, one would take her to be a youngish, middle-aged dowager. She is always impeccably gowned, and a fine figure of a woman, with black hair piled high on her head and flashing eyes. When she comes into her restaurant, you instinctively feel that here is a presence. Her graciousness is charming, but there is a quality of reserve about it. And if you can get her to sit down at your table, you will find that she is an accomplished conversationalist.

But it is not the foregoing qualities alone that make Sally fabulous. For many years (strictly according to hearsay, I can assure you) she owned a House That Was Not a Home (if I may borrow the title of a fairly recent book by New York's famous Polly Adler) on Pine Street in San Francisco.

Today, Sally Stanford is strictly a business woman. The décor of the bar and cocktail lounge of her Valhalla Inn is astonishing. It is mid-Victorian and plush, with red-upholstered straight-backed chairs and settees, old-fashioned table lamps, and gaily decorated china potties holding books of matches. Oh yes, there is a huge parrot that wanders about the cocktail lounge who can cry just like a baby, or sing in a high falsetto.

Valhalla Inn is one of those rare restaurants where you can demand an epicurean dish, even if it isn't on the menu, and get it, superbly prepared. On my first visit I selected Chicken *Cacciatora* as the entree, which was on the menu, and which I found worthy of a top Italian chef. But a couple of times later when Mrs. Wood and I dined there I asked for an item that wasn't on the menu—sweetbreads. And damned if I didn't get one of the most ambrosial sweetbread dishes I have ever tasted. I invaded the kitchen after dinner, and asked Jerry for the recipe, and here it is.

SWEETBREADS VALHALLA

3 *pairs sweetbreads*
Water
1 *lemon*
1 *onion, sliced*
1 *bay leaf*
1 *tsp. pickling spices*
Salt
2 *tbsp. butter*
2 *tbsp. fine olive oil*
Flour
¼ *tsp. dried rosemary*
¼ *tsp. dried basil*
¼ *tsp. Ac'cent*
¼ *tsp. dried tarragon*
¼ *tsp. crushed peppercorns*
¼ *tsp. salt*
¼ *tsp. chopped garlic*
¼ *tsp. seasoned salt*
1 *cup sliced mushrooms*
1 *cup little green onions,*
    chopped
½ *cup dry sherry*
¼ *cup beef bouillon*
1 *cup brown sauce*

Soak the sweetbreads for 2 hours in cold salted water. Then remove them, and cook them in sufficient water to cover, to which has been added the lemon, split, the sliced onion, the bay leaf, the pickling spices, and about 1 teaspoon of salt. Bring the water to a boil, and then turn down the flame and let simmer for 15 minutes. This is the parboiling, or "blanching," after which you place the sweetbreads in cold water, then peel off the tubes and membranes, being careful not to tear the tissues.

Next, heat the butter and olive oil in a large skillet. Flour the sweetbreads, and sauté them with the dried rosemary, dried basil, Ac'cent, dried tarragon, crushed peppercorns, salt, chopped garlic, and the seasoned salt. Let the sweetbreads cook until golden brown.

Then add the sliced fresh mushrooms, and the chopped little green onions (bulbs and tops). Continue cooking until the mushrooms and little green onions are tender. Then add the dry sherry and the condensed beef bouillon. Cook until the liquid is reduced by half.

Now add 1 cup of brown sauce (or Franco-American beef gravy) to the skillet, and continue cooking until the sweetbreads are glazed. This should be about 6 minutes, cooked slowly. Serve hot, and after eating, doff your hat to Jerry Smith! Serves 6.

For many years frankfurters, or "weenies," were largely eaten out of doors at picnics, ball games, beach parties (remember the weenie roast on the beach?), country fairs, amusement parks, and race tracks. Occasionally they would be eaten at home, accompanied by sauerkraut or potato salad, and washed down with beer.

But there was seldom anything fancy about them, and they were almost never found in the better homes. But things are different now. Frankfurters have an important part in barbecue menus, Saturday night suppers, and after card game snacks.

Barbecued frankfurters make a delightful entree for dinner, when they are baked in the oven in a tangy sauce, like this:

BARBECUED FRANKFURTERS

8 *frankfurters*	1 *tbsp. prepared mustard*
2 *tbsp. butter*	1 *tbsp. Worcestershire sauce*
1 *large onion*	¾ *tsp. salt*
⅓ *cup catsup*	¼ *tsp. freshly ground pepper*
2 *tbsp. vinegar*	¼ *tsp. horseradish*
1 *tbsp. brown sugar*	*Dash cayenne pepper*
	¾ *cup beer*

First make the sauce. Melt the butter in a saucepan, and when hot, add the onion, chopped, and cook it until tender, but not browned. Then add the catsup, vinegar, brown sugar, prepared mustard, Worcestershire sauce, salt, freshly ground pepper, horseradish, cayenne pepper, and the beer. Simmer this mixture for about 20 minutes.

Place the frankfurters in a lightly greased casserole. Then pour over them the sauce, and bake the whole in a 400-degree oven for about 20 minutes, basting the frankfurters occasionally with the sauce. This recipe serves 4.

Macaroni and cheese goes excellently with this dish, and of course cold beer is the beverage.

(6) GAME

I don't believe there is any phase of cookery which elicits more tumult and shouting than the cooking of game, particularly ducks.

I have seen men who were normally mild-mannered, temperate of speech, and thoroughly pleasant in manner become red-in-the-face, snarling, shouting maniacs during a discussion of the proper way and the proper length of time to cook a duck. I know a man in Chicago who wouldn't touch a steak or a piece of roast beef if it had more than the faintest tinge of pink in it, but who would go into ecstasies over a duck that had come out of the oven no more than just warmed through, with the blood running out.

I am the kind of a guy who likes to live in amity with my fellow men. I refuse to say that blood-rare duck is horrible, or that over-cooked duck is a gastronomic crime. Who am I to set standards of taste? Very early in my career I had a very definite lesson on the folly of saying this or that was good or bad.

I was living in New York State and Eddie Cantor brought one of his shows to Rochester for a two-day run. The morning following the first performance all the critics panned the show unmercifully. I attended the second performance, and the audience loved the show. At the final curtain the audience kept applauding, so that Eddie Cantor took seven or eight curtain calls. Finally, he held up his hand for quiet, and made a very short speech.

"I can never tell you," he said, "how grateful I am for your appreciation and so evident enjoyment of our efforts to entertain you. I must confess that I was pretty blue this morning after reading the newspaper reviews. But tonight I am really very happy. And I have only this to say. I have every right in the world to say that I don't like apple pie. But I have absolutely no right to say that apple pie is no good. Thank you, ladies and gentlemen."

First of all, let me state that I am, by no stretch of the imagination, an authority on the preparation and cooking of ducks or game. I thoroughly enjoy wild ducks; I am exceptionally fond of pheasants, quail, partridge; and I dearly love venison, when it is properly prepared and cooked. I have eaten bear steak and enjoyed it; I am very partial to filet of moose or elk. But in most cases I am quite content to turn to others who are admittedly experts in the field of game cookery.

As to the initial preparation of ducks, I am in full accord with Charles Browne, who wrote in his very excellent *Gun Club Cookbook*, published by Charles Scribner's Sons:

> . . . we read in cookbooks written by well intentioned and otherwise moral women, statements like these: "to remove the game taste from a wild duck, soak it in salt water overnight, parboil it ½ hour and roast 40 minutes to the hour" or "stuff it full of onions to take away (or disguise?) the game flavor." Now, it is perfectly obvious that these outrageous procedures would not only remove the "game taste" from the ducks, but all other tastes as well . . . as for removing the "game taste," which is the epicure's delight, it would be just as sensible to say, when writing of a Welsh rabbit, "to remove the strong cheese taste from the Welsh rabbit, add 1 or 2 ounces of tincture of asafoetida, or ½ bar of laundry soap!"

From extensive reading on the subject, I have gathered that the sane way to prepare a duck for cooking is merely to wipe the duck out with a damp cloth, or a cloth soaked in brandy, salt and pepper it inside, and put it in the oven, unless you are going to stuff it. That makes sense to me.

There are those who like, or pretend to like, a duck practically raw. I have heard duck connoisseurs say that a duck shouldn't be in the oven for more than eight minutes. Okay, if they really like it that way, let them eat it that way. On the other hand, an outstanding authority on ducks prescribes cooking a duck 3½ hours!

I think most sane duck lovers will agree that a duck should be rare but not raw—the meat red, but not purple, and no blood following the slicing.

So you pays your money and you takes your choice. I am going to give you two recipes for roast wild duck which should be authoritative, and which encompass the two extremes I have mentioned. The first is from a recipe published in a brochure gotten out by Ducks Unlimited, of San Francisco.

ROAST MALLARD DUCK

1 *mallard duck* (1½ *lbs.*)   ½ *pared cored apple*
1½ *tsp. salt*   1 *small peeled onion*
⅛ *tsp. pepper*   2 *thin slices salt pork*

Wash the duck and wipe dry. Sprinkle the body cavity with ½ teaspoon of the salt. Sprinkle the remainder of the salt, and the pepper, on the outside of the body. Place apple and onion in the body cavity. Truss bird and place on a rack in an uncovered pan or roaster. Lay the slices of salt pork over the breast. Place bird in a very hot oven of 500 degrees, and roast for 15 to 20 minutes, if liked rare. If preferred well done, roast for 30 minutes. Serves 2. Gravy may be made from the drippings in the pan if desired. Duck may be stuffed with wild rice stuffing, if desired.

In the magazine *Outdoors in Illinois,* published by the State of Illinois Department of Conservation, the following recipe was given by L. H. Barkhausen, Illinois chief of Ducks Unlimited:

DUCK À LA BARKHAUSEN

Brace of ducks   *Quartered apples*
Prunes   *Water*

Stuff the ducks with prunes and quartered apples.

Place ducks in an open roasting pan, breasts down, without any lard or butter, and place in a hot preheated oven (450 degrees). Leave there until ducks are very brown, ¾ to 1 hour.

When ducks are brown, add 2 cups of water, cover roaster, and return to oven—reduce temperature to 350 degrees.

Add water if needed and cover roaster until the ducks are done, which should be after 3 to 3½ hours of roasting. When ducks are done, the meat will easily break away from the breastbone.

Remove surplus fat from the pan, thicken gravy, turn ducks breast up and baste in gravy, and return to oven without cover until ready to serve.

See what I mean?

Baring my breast to the slings and arrows of possibly outraged duck authorities throughout this fair land, I make bold to give my recipe for a roast wild duck. It ain't raw, it ain't burned to a crisp, and it ain't bad! As a matter of fact, my wife and I have found it damn good, and so have duck-loving guests who have savored it.

WOOD'S ROAST WILD DUCK

1 *wild duck* (1½ *lbs.*)	*Salt and pepper*
1 *small apple*	*Brandy*
1 *small onion*	1 *cup orange juice*
1 *small stalk celery*	1 *cup dry red wine*
1 *slice bacon*	1½ *tbsp. orange curaçao*
2 *slices orange*	3 *tbsp. sour cream*
Butter	

Rub the well-cleaned duck inside and out with a brandy-soaked cloth. Then sprinkle with salt and pepper inside and out.

Cut a small peeled and cored apple in quarters, and insert it, together with a small onion and a small stalk of celery, in the duck's cavity. Truss the duck, and rub the breast with soft butter. Lay the duck in a roasting pan, and place two half slices of bacon across the breast, and top the bacon slices with 2 thin orange slices.

Put the duck into a preheated 450-degree oven for about 8 minutes. Then pour in ½ cup each of orange juice and dry red wine in the roaster, and reduce the oven heat to 375 degrees. Baste the duck from time to time. After about 30 minutes of roasting, the liquid in the roaster will be almost dried up, and at that point add another ½ cup each of orange juice and dry red wine. Continue to roast the duck for about an hour from the time the oven heat was reduced.

Remove the duck to a hot platter and keep warm while making the gravy. Place the roaster on top of the stove, over a medium flame, and scrape the bottom to dislodge any particles of duck that might adhere. To the liquid in the pan add 1½ tablespoons of orange curaçao and 3 tablespoons of sour cream. Blend well until the gravy is smooth, then pour into a gravy boat. Serves 2.

Perhaps the most celebrated duck dish is *Duck à la Presse*. The method of preparing and cooking it calls first for roasting the duck, or ducks, for just a few minutes, then carving the breast meat from the duck (and removing the legs) and then putting the carcass in a duck press, and extracting all the juice and blood. Then a sauce is prepared, and the duck breasts are simmered in that sauce.

In all my eating experience I have never tasted *Duck à la Presse* that measured up to the recipe of my very old and dear friend Ric Riccardo, who passed away a year or so ago in Chicago. He called his masterpiece Duck à la Frederic Riccardo, and the recipe for it is given in my *With a Jug of Wine*. However, L. H. Barkhausen of Chicago, gave me his recipe, which is most felicitous.

DUCK À LA PRESSE

2 *ducks*
2 *stalks celery*
1 *tsp. butter*
1 *tsp. beef extract*

1 *tbsp. currant jelly*
1 *tbsp. Worcestershire sauce*
3 *tbsp. Madeira wine*
1 *duck liver*

Insert a stalk of celery with leaves into the cavity of each cleaned duck. Place the ducks in an open pan and roast in a 500-degree oven for 8 to 10 minutes. They only need to be heated through.

Remove the ducks from the oven and carve the breasts from the birds. Remove the legs (the meat may be carved from them). Remove the skin from the breast pieces.

Remove the celery from the duck carcasses and chop the carcasses in several pieces, and put the carcasses into a duck press (if you haven't a duck press, which most people won't have, use a stout potato ricer). Crush the carcasses until every drop of juice and blood is extracted. Put the breasts aside until the sauce is prepared.

In a heavy skillet over a slow fire put the butter, the extracted duck juices, the beef extract (or 1 bouillon cube), the currant jelly (or any tart jelly), the Worcestershire sauce, the Madeira wine, and 1 duck liver pressed through a sieve. Let all this heat together without boiling. When thoroughly heated, place the duck pieces in the sauce, and sauté gently as long as desired. For rare, sauté for approximately 1½ minutes on each side; for medium, sauté for approximately 2 to 3 minutes on each side; for well done, approximately 4 to 5 minutes on each side. This will serve 4 or 2, depending on one's fondness for ducks.

Ducks Unlimited is an organization with which most duck hunters are familiar. It is a non-profit group made up of sportsmen and fanciers of waterfowl, and is dedicated to eliminating, as far as possible, the natural enemies of wild duck, such as drouth, predatory animals, fire, and devastated breeding grounds.

The San Francisco branch of Ducks Unlimited gets out an attractive brochure containing recipes for cooking wild duck by famous chefs. There are about sixteen recipes, including one on how to prepare game stock, which is very important to game cooking.

As you might guess from the title, the following recipe is an old Southern one. It is for a stuffed wild duck, and I can guarantee its deliciousness. It is also one recommended by Ducks Unlimited.

MAMMY'S ROAST WILD DUCK

1 *wild duck*
1 *cooked sweetbread*
½ *cup lean salt pork*
2 *tbsp.* (*altogether*) *of*
    chopped parsley
    chopped chives

chopped mushrooms
chopped shallots
Salt and pepper
Small pinch dried thyme
Small pinch of mace
4 *oz. fine port wine*

Prepare the stuffing of the cooked sweetbread, diced small, the lean pork, chopped fine, a total of 2 tablespoons of the chopped parsley, the chopped chives, the chopped mushrooms, and the chopped shallots (½ tablespoon each), salt and freshly ground pepper to taste, a small pinch of dried thyme, and a few grains of powdered mace.

Fill the cavity of the cleaned, singed wild duck with the stuffing, then sew and truss. Roast in the usual way in a 400-degree oven, basting profusely with the port wine, removing the fat as it comes down the dripping pan. If necessary, add more port wine for basting.

Serve the duck dressed on a hot platter, with the gravy on the side.

The next recipe must have come from a Texas member of Ducks Unlimited, for their brochure calls it Wild Duck, Texas Style. This is also a stuffed duck recipe, and, as everything else in Texas, it is really great. (But wait until you come to the recipe from a Texan for Wild Duck and Spaghetti later on in this chapter, which is the most fabulous recipe I have ever encountered!)

WILD DUCK TEXAS STYLE

2 2- to 2½-lb. wild ducks	½ cup scalded milk
1 cup diced celery	6 slices bacon
1 cup minced onion	1 cup catsup
1 cup seedless raisins	½ cup chili sauce
1 cup chopped pecan meats	¼ cup Worcestershire sauce
4 cups soft breadcrumbs	Watercress or parsley
1½ tsp. salt	Orange slices
2 eggs, beaten	Currant jelly

Combine the diced celery, minced onion, seedless raisins, and pecan meats with the breadcrumbs and salt, then add the beaten eggs, and mix well. Add the scalded milk and blend the whole well.

Stuff the ducks, after having been cleaned and singed, with the breadcrumb mixture. Sew up the slit in the body as well as the one in the crop. Place 3 strips of bacon across the breast of each duck, place the ducks on a rack in an uncovered roaster or baking pan and roast, allowing 60 minutes per pound (drawn weight of the largest of the birds). For the first 15 minutes of roasting, the oven temperature should be 500 degrees. Then reduce the oven heat to 350 degrees, and continue roasting for the remainder of the time.

One half hour before removing the ducks from the oven, mix the catsup, chili sauce, and the Worcestershire sauce, and pour over the ducks. (If desired, the chili sauce mixture can be omitted, and an equal amount of dry red wine substituted, which I prefer.

When the roasting is completed, arrange the ducks on a hot platter, garnishing with watercress or parsley, and thin slices of orange topped with the currant jelly. If the chili sauce mixture is used, after the ducks are removed from the roaster, skim the fat from the sauce at the bottom of the roasting pan, and thicken if necessary. This will give a very spicy gravy. If the red wine is used, follow the same procedure for making the gravy as directed with the chili sauce mixture. This recipe serves 4 to 6.

A *salmi,* in culinary French, is a highly finished hash made with game or wildfowl, cut up and prepared in either a rich gravy or sauce. So a *salmi* of wild duck is an ideal way to use up leftover duck, or even underdone duck that you didn't care for. This recipe is adapted from one in a mid-Victorian cookbook published in 1885.

SALMI OF WILD DUCK

2 *cups cooked duck meat*	1 *celery top*
1 *tbsp. butter*	1½ *cups chicken broth*
1 *small onion, minced*	4 *oz. port wine*
1 *tbsp. flour*	12 *pitted green olives*
small pinch cayenne pepper	*Salt*
small pinch dried thyme	*Freshly ground pepper*
1 *small bay leaf*	*Lemon juice*

Orange juice

In a saucepan, melt the butter, and when it is hot add the minced onion, and lightly sauté until the onion is golden brown. Then add the flour, blend well, and continue to cook until the flour is lightly browned. Then add the cayenne pepper, dried thyme, the bay leaf, crumbled, the celery top, chopped. Mix well, then add the chicken broth and the port wine. Stir, and simmer gently for about 30 minutes.

Strain the sauce into another saucepan, discarding the solids, and add to it the cut-up duck meat and 12 pitted and coarsely chopped green olives. Season to taste with salt and freshly ground pepper, and simmer the whole until quite hot. Just before serving add a few drops of lemon juice and about an ounce of orange juice (the original recipe called for the juice of a sour orange). Serve with wild rice.

For those who enjoy ducks, a nimrod in the household is indeed an asset. But while wild ducks are an epicurean delight, the domestic duck, usually called "Long Island duck," is still mighty tasty eating.

Among the classic duck recipes, Duck Bigarade is always a favorite. If you are the fortunate possessor of a brace of wild ducks, you roast them in the usual way, according to your preference as to doneness, place them on a hot platter, surround with orange sections, lemon slices, and watercress, and serve them with a Bigarade sauce. Or, you can braise your wild ducks, if they are older birds, and add a Bigarade sauce of sorts. But even if you buy your ducks at the market, you can enjoy Braised Duck Bigarade.

BRAISED DUCK BIGARADE

1 5½- to 6-lb. duck
1½ tsp. Ac'cent
1 tsp. salt
Flour
3 tbsp. bacon drippings

1 cup consommé
1 cup orange juice
3 tbsp. grated orange rind
2 tbsp. dry vermouth
⅓ cup brown sugar

Flour and butter roux

Cut your duck into serving pieces, and sprinkle with the Ac'cent and salt. Then coat the pieces thoroughly with flour.

In a large, heavy skillet heat the bacon drippings, and when hot, brown the duck pieces on all sides over a moderate flame. Then pour off all the fat, add the consommé, cover tightly, and simmer slowly for 1 hour. Then uncover, and add the orange juice, the grated orange rind, the vermouth, and the brown sugar. Continue simmering until the duck is tender, about 1 hour, basting occasionally.

Remove the duck pieces to a hot platter, and thicken the gravy, if necessary, with a flour and butter roux, or a little arrowroot. (This latter is a highly nutritive and easily digested form of starch, and is a wonderful thickening agent.) Pour the gravy over the duck, and serve with wild rice or braised rice. This recipe makes about 6 servings.

Some years ago I sent out a cry for help regarding duck recipes through my syndicated column, "For Men Only!" The response was splendid, and I received a number of recipes. Two were unusual. The first of them came from Oleg Tupine, premier danseur with the Ballet Russe de Monte Carlo, which was appearing at the Civic Opera House in Chicago at that time.

Mr. Tupine has two hobbies outside of dancing—collecting stamps and cooking. His recipe was for a Bulgarian Duck Stew.

BULGARIAN DUCK STEW À LA HELENE

1 duck
2 tbsp. olive oil
1 lb. carrots, sliced
Salted water

1 #2 can tomatoes
2 onions
Salt and pepper
½ lb. dried prunes

Remove all the meat from an uncooked duck, and sauté it in the olive oil (or bacon drippings) until the meat is lightly browned on all sides. In the meantime, cook the scraped and sliced carrots in a small amount of salted water for about 10 minutes. Then add to the carrots the sautéed duck meat, the tomatoes, and the onions, which have been sliced and sautéed to a golden brown in the pan in which the duck meat was sautéed. Salt and pepper to taste, and cook, covered, for from 15 to 20 minutes. Then add the dried prunes, which have been washed but not soaked. Cover again and cook slowly until the prunes are soft and the duck meat tender. The prunes absorb a lot of liquid, so be sure there is enough in the pot. Additional liquid can be a light, dry red wine.

With this duck stew, Tupine and his wife, who is also in the ballet, serve thinly sliced cucumbers seasoned with salt and pepper and plenty of chopped dill, and mixed with sour cream.

The second duck recipe worthy of note came from Mrs. J. A. Balderson, of Chicago. It is a Bohemian recipe for stewed wild duck.

BOHEMIAN STEWED WILD DUCK

2 *wild ducks*	1 *stalk celery, cut up*
Water	1 *carrot, cut up*
½ *tsp. dried thyme*	1 *slice bacon*
2 *bay leaves*	1 *thin slice lemon*
Small piece ginger root	2 *tbsp. red wine vinegar*
6 *cloves*	2 *tbsp. Burgundy wine*
6 *allspice berries*	2 *tbsp. butter*
Large sprig parsley	1 *tbsp. flour*

Put the cleaned and singed wild duck in a large stewing pan and add enough water to just cover the ducks. Add a small bunch of fresh thyme (or the dried thyme), the bay leaves, the ginger root, the cloves, allspice berries, the parsley, the cut-up celery and carrot, the bacon, and the slice of lemon. Let the whole simmer gently. When the ducks are about half done, add the red wine vinegar and the Burgundy wine. When the ducks are tender, remove them from the pan and quarter them, and place them on a hot platter. Thicken the gravy with the butter, heated and blended with the flour. Stir and cook until the gravy is golden brown, strain, and pour over the ducks. The gravy should be like a thin sauce, and of course dumplings go with the duck, as any good Bohemian would know.

A duck hunt is one of the major attractions for sportsmen in southwest Louisiana (and everywhere else, I guess). However, down thar, one will find small lodges, scattered along the edges of the marshland, that will furnish guides to take small parties deep into the marsh, where the limit is certain to be bagged. On the return to the lodges, the happy hunters generally sit down to a real duck dinner. One of the cooks has a rice stuffing for ducks that the customers rave about. It is a departure from the usual wild rice stuffing.

LOUISIANA RICE STUFFING FOR DUCKS

1½ cups raw rice	½ cup dry sherry
2 tbsp. bacon drippings	2 tbsp. poultry seasoning
3 tbsp. minced onion	Salt
6 large fresh mushrooms	Freshly ground pepper
2½ cups consommé	1 whole egg

In a large saucepan, fry the minced onion in the bacon drippings until they are tender, then add the mushrooms, chopped, and the raw rice. Simmer until the rice is golden brown, then add the condensed consommé, the dry sherry, the poultry seasoning, and salt and freshly ground pepper to taste. Stir well, then cover the saucepan tightly, and steam for about 20 minutes, or until the rice has absorbed all the liquid, and is tender and flaky. Remove from the fire, add 1 beaten egg, and mix well, and correct seasoning if necessary. Cool, and then stuff the ducks.

And now, ladies and gentlemen, it is my great pleasure to introduce to you the most super colossal, stupendous, and fabulous recipe that it has ever been my privilege to present! (At this point there should be a fanfare of trumpets, but unfortunately this book is not wired for sound.)

In Beaumont, Texas, I have a gourmet friend who not only is a fervid disciple of duck hunting, but a terrific chef as well. Like everything else in Texas, Phil Justice is big, jovial, and full of enthusiasm. His hospitality is boundless. A mutual friend told a story on him one afternoon while we were enjoying libations in the Cork Club of the Shamrock Hotel in Houston.

It seems that Phil and a friend lunched together, and after luncheon they visited the Cadillac showrooms, inasmuch as Phil's friend wanted to buy a new Cadillac. The salesman showed various models, but the prospective buyer shook his head at all of them, each time asking if there wasn't a more expensive car. Even the El Dorado didn't suit him. Finally, the salesman took the two men back into the warehouse, where a covered car stood. The salesman removed the cover, and there was the jewel of jewels among motorcars. It had air conditioning, a built-in portable bar and refrigerator, a television set, a record player, and a telephone. All the mountings inside were solid gold. Phil's friend asked the price of the car, and the salesman replied that it cost twenty-five thousand dollars. The man said, "I'll take it," and started to write out a check, but Phil stopped him.

"Just put your checkbook away," he ordered. "You paid the luncheon check; this is on me."

Of course, the story wasn't true, but Phil is the sort of man who would do something like that.

Well, back to this recipe that out-recipes all recipes. In its accompanying letter Phil wrote:

This recipe is for a strictly one-dish meal, invented specifically to satisfy the lusty but nonetheless appreciative appetites of the author's duck-calling, duck-hunting, and duck-eating friends. Into it are incorporated many "top secret" ingredients and treasured procedures garnered over a period of more than fifteen years of never-to-be-forgotten duck hunting in the coastal marshes of Texas and Louisiana.

The assembling, preparing, marinating, and blending of the ingredients (and the guests!); the ritualistic sniffing, tasting and final corrective seasoning of the aromatic sauce during the final steps of cooking; and at long last the belly, palate and soul-satisfied but never too silent "slurrping" of this nimrod's dish of dishes comes close to the very pinnacle of culinary, gastronomical and social experience.

The ingredients, *modus operandi,* and so forth follow, just as Phil wrote them. I am quite sure that no other recipe has ever been presented in just this manner, at least not in any cookbook that I have ever seen. So, if you should have the urge to prepare this masterpiece, and wonder what ingredients you will need, just run your eyes down the two left-hand columns.

PHIL JUSTICE'S ORIGINAL RECIPE FOR GULF COAST WILD DUCK SPAGHETTI

(For Twelve Good Trenchermen)

Assemble, prepare, and make proper use of the various listed ingredients in the manner indicated:

Quantity	Ingredient	Modus Operandi	Remarks
11	Guests	Assemble at least 3 hours before time scheduled for eating	Guests should be free from ulcers
1	Chef		
2 qts.	Bonded Bourbon	Pour one jigger Bourbon into chef	
2 qts.	Best Scotch	Pour one jigger of guests' choice into each guest. Have guests engage in friendly games of chance, such as gin rummy, dominoes, checkers, pinochle, canasta, bridge or penny ante, or just let them shoot the bull	Place ice and soda where guests can help themselves
½ case	Sparkling water		
50 lbs.	Crushed ice		
12	Wild ducks	Clean and prepare for roasting whole (reserve gizzards, hearts and livers)	Mallards or Pintails preferred, but even Spoonies or Blackjacks will be good in this
12	White onions (medium sized)	Peel and insert one in each duck	
12	Garlic cloves	Peel and insert one in each duck	
1 cup	Cognac brandy	Rub ducks inside and out with brandy	
1 cup	Peanut oil	Mix oil, salt and pepper and brush over ducks	
6 tsp.	Salt	Roast in large pans 30 min. at 450°F., basting 3 times with remaining oil and brandy	
12 tsp.	Black pepper		
		Pour jigger of Bourbon into chef	Guests to pour their own at will
		Remove breasts; cut each into 2 pieces	
		Remove wing and leg joints	
		Remove onions and garlic cloves and cut up finely and reserve	
		Discard carcasses; reserve pan drippings	

Sauce:

Quantity	Ingredient	Modus Operandi	Remarks
½ cup	Butter	Place in large kettle or pot and heat	
½ cup	Olive oil		
1 cup	Celery, finely cut	Add these, also reserved onions and garlic, cook at low heat slowly 20 min. until soft, not brown	Check on guests' needs
1 cup	Green pepper, finely cut		
¼ cup	Parsley, finely cut		
1 lb.	Round steak, ground	Dredge in seasoned flour and sauté lightly in above mixture for 10 min.	
12	Gizzards, chopped		
12	Hearts, chopped		
½ cup	Flour		
½ tsp.	Black pepper		
½ tsp.	Salt		
		Pour jigger of Bourbon into chef	

Quantity	Ingredient	Modus Operandi	Remarks
1 #2 can	Solid packed tomatoes or equiv. fresh tomatoes		
2 6-oz. cans	Tomato paste or purée	Add all to contents of pot or kettle with mushroom liquid	Substitute for guests in turn
1 cup	Catsup	Reserve mushrooms	while they search
1 8-oz. can	Campbell's consommé	Simmer 30 min.	for flying saucers
1 Tbsp.	Paprika		
3 Tbsp.	Chili powder		
1 Tbsp.	Black pepper		
2 tsp.	Oregano		
½ tsp.	Basil	Grind leaves together in mortar	
½ tsp.	Thyme		
½ tsp.	Rosemary		
2 Tbsp.	Lee & Perrins		
1 cup	Good dry red wine		
1 Tbsp.	Celery salt (or 2 tsp. plain salt)		
½ tsp.	Mace		
1 Tbsp.	Peychaud's bitters		
1 tsp.	Tabasco		
		Pour one jigger Bourbon into chef	
2 8-oz. cans	Mushroom buttons		
		Add duck meat, livers, mushrooms and simmer entire mixture slowly while preparing spaghetti —20 to 30 min.	
6 qts.	Salted water	Place in large pot and bring to	
2 8-oz. cans	Consommé	fast boil	
3 lbs.	Finest long Semolina spaghetti or nearest thing available thereto	Add to above Breaking may be sacrilegious, unethical, unaesthetic and unconstitutional but does *not* affect taste Boil rapidly until done (12 to 20 min.) I prefer 15 min. for most brands Pour jigger Bourbon into chef Stir, smell and taste sauce, correct seasoning. Should be of a good consistency. Remove spaghetti, without rinsing, to large individual plates or large soup bowls (with or without overhead technique) Serve each guest 2 pieces duck breast, one leg, one wing and a generous ladling of sauce	
4 cups	Romano cheese or Parmesan cheese	Grate and add liberally to top of each serving	
4 qts.	Sparkling Burgundy (Great Western is excellent)	Have very cold and serve to guests as needed	
12 demitasse	Strong black coffee		
12 ponies	Authoritative brandy or liqueur of choice		
12 hours	Untroubled sleep		

There are many who will maintain that the duck is king of all game birds. But to my mind, for the bounty of its flesh and its exquisite flavor, the pheasant is supreme. I believe that this majestic bird had its origin in China, or rather Mongolia, and it is said that recipes for its preparation date back to the ancient Chinese dynasties.

As with duck, the pheasant connoisseur prefers his bird roasted, and my old and dear friend, Maurice Ross, Jr., of Chicago, has a marvelous recipe for roast pheasant.

Maury Ross, incidentally, started me on my food writing career. Otis and Lee, one of the leading wine merchants of Chicago, published an elaborate monthly brochure which was called *Wining and Dining*. It was sent gratis to customers and to the leading executives of Chicago firms. One day Maury, who is president of Otis and Lee, asked me if I would do a monthly column on cooking for *Wining and Dining*. I protested that I couldn't do such a column, but Maury insisted.

"You have a profound knowledge of food and wine, and you can prepare gourmet food better than anyone I know."

"But I've never written about it," I demurred.

"You can," Maury persisted. "I can't pay you what you're worth, but if you'll do a cooking column once a month for *Wining and Dining,* I'll give you a case of bonded bourbon for every column."

That did it. Maury Ross bought himself a boy!

About six months later, my boss at the Chicago *Tribune,* Mike Kennedy, asked me if I could do a once a week cooking column for the newspaper. This time I didn't protest, and so my column, "For Men Only!" was born—ten years ago.

Maury is a wonderful cook in his own right, and, in addition to this pheasant recipe, he has given me one or two others that I shall detail later on. The late Crosby Gaige thought so much of Maury's pheasant recipe that he included it in his last book, *Dining with My Friends.*

ROAST PHEASANT

1 *plump pheasant*	2 *onions, sliced*
Lemon juice	7 *tbsp. butter*
Brandy	½ *cup dry Madeira*
Fat bacon slices	1 *apple*
Salt and pepper	*Dry red wine*
4 *celery stalks*	2 *tbsp. flour*
4 *carrots*	1 *cup ruby port wine*

Clean the pheasant, and rub inside and out with lemon juice. Then sprinkle the bird generously, inside and out, with a good California brandy. Lard thoroughly with fat bacon slices, and sprinkle with salt and freshly ground pepper.

In a heavy skillet, sauté the celery stalks, cut up, the carrots, cut up, and the onions, sliced, in about 3 tablespoons of butter. When the vegetables are lightly browned, add the dry Madeira wine, and let the whole cook for 2 minutes. Then transfer the vegetables and their juices to the bottom of a large roasting pan.

Place a peeled apple, cut in quarters, inside the pheasant, and place the pheasant on the bed of vegetables in the roasting pan. Place in a 350-degree oven and roast for ½ hour. Then baste the pheasant with a good dry red wine, and continue basting frequently with additional wine and the pan juices until the bird is thoroughly cooked, about 1½ hours.

Remove the pheasant from the roaster and place on a hot platter, keeping the pheasant warm while the gravy is made.

Skim off any grease from the juices in the roaster. Add a *roux* of 2 tablespoons of flour and 4 tablespoons of butter. Stir this *roux* into the juices of the roaster, blending well until smooth. Let the gravy cook for about 5 minutes. Season the gravy with salt and pepper to taste, and then add the ruby port, stirring all the while.

Serve the pheasant on the platter, and just before carving, throw over it a good 2 or 3 ounces of brandy, set it alight, and let it burn out. The gravy should be served separately.

The Camellia Room of the Drake Hotel in Chicago has an excellent pheasant recipe, which has a bit of showmanship about it.

ROAST PHEASANT À LA CAMELLIA HOUSE

1 *pheasant*	½ *oz. sherry wine*
Stalks celery	3 *oz. lard*
3 *tsp. pâté de fois gras*	4 *oz. flour*
2 *oz. gravy*	2 *oz. milk*
2 *diced mushrooms*	3 *oz. water*

Pinch salt

Clean the pheasant thoroughly, and stuff with crisp uncut stalks of celery. Roast in a 400-degree oven for 30 minutes. At the end of that time, remove the celery from the pheasant and place the bird in an ovenproof casserole. Add to the casserole the *pâté de fois gras* (the original recipe calls for 2 teaspoons of goose liver and ½ teaspoon of truffles, but the *pâté de fois gras* will give the same flavor),

2 ounces of the gravy from roasting the pheasant, the diced mushrooms, and the sherry wine.

Make a bread dough by cutting the lard into the flour. Then combine with the milk, water, and salt. Knead and roll out into a rope about ¾ inch in diameter and the circumference of the casserole. Pack this dough rope around the edge where the cover and the casserole meet, so that no air can escape. Place the sealed casserole in the oven and bake for 20 minutes.

Serve from the casserole with the cover on. The unsealing of the casserole at the table causes a flood of aroma that whets the appetite and increases the enjoyment of the pheasant. This recipe will serve 2, or possibly 3.

The fall of the year, in nature, is somewhat symbolic of decline and deterioration. But, gastronomically, it seems to me to be a period of awakening to new pleasures of the palate that have been dormant throughout the summer. During the warm to hot, humid days of summer our appetites are inclined to lag, and, by and large, it is the lighter foods that seem to have the most appeal. But come late fall, the thought of the rich and succulent duck, pheasant, quail, and venison stirs our imagination and whips our taste buds to pleasurable anticipation.

When it comes to hunting and fishing, I am a complete dud. Therefore, the happy hunter will argue that I cannot possibly get as much enjoyment out of eating game birds as he does. Arising at dawn, crouching in a blind on the edge of some reedy lake or pond, or tramping miles across the countryside on a frosty morning, waiting for the moment when coveys rise and whirl away, adds a zest to your appetite for the bag of game as nothing else can. Well, that I will dispute. No nimrod can possibly get any more enjoyment out of eating ducks, quail, partridges, or pheasants than I do. When hunter friends promise me a bird or two on their return from hunting, my mouth begins to water, and by the time the birds arrive I am drooling.

One of my friends is fortunate, financially and in a business way, in that he can travel about the country and hunt wherever hunting is best. Not long ago he came back from South Dakota with three plump pheasants for me, and a recipe for cooking them that had been given him out there.

This dish is an unusual one. The true pheasant lover might object to the last ingredient, claiming that it masks the flavor of the pheasant. To some extent I will agree, but, on the other hand, it is very fine eating.

PHEASANT AND SWEETBREADS

3 *pheasants, disjointed*	4 *oz. brandy*
Flour	1½ *cups sweet cream*
Salt and pepper	½ *cup dry white wine*
9 *oz. butter*	¾ *cup chopped onions*
3 *sweetbreads*	1 *cup grated Parmesan cheese*

Clean and singe the pheasants, wipe them with a cloth soaked in brandy, and then disjoint, and shake the pieces well in a bag containing seasoned flour.

In a heavy skillet, melt ½ pound (8 ounces) butter, and when hot add the pheasant pieces, and brown them on all sides.

Wash and blanch 3 sweetbreads in boiling water for 3 minutes. Then, in a saucepan, melt 1 ounce of butter, and when it is hot sauté the sweetbreads until light brown, about 10 minutes. Then add the sweetbreads to the pheasant pieces in the skillet.

Remove the skillet containing the pheasant pieces and the sweetbreads from the fire, pour over them 4 ounces of brandy, which has been warmed, and set alight. When the flames begin to die down, extinguish them by adding the sweet cream and the dry white wine. Place the skillet in a 450-degree oven until the mixture bubbles, then add the finely chopped onions. Return the skillet to the oven and reduce the heat to 325 degrees, and bake until the pheasants are tender, about 1 to 1½ hours.

Now, the dish can be served as it comes out of the oven, or it can be removed from the oven, the top sprinkled with the grated Parmesan cheese, and placed under the broiler until the cheese begins to bubble. Serve either way very hot.

Geese are much more popular in Europe than in America. In this country, geese are usually only seen on the market during the holidays, when they substitute for turkeys on Christmas, or for a New Year's dinner. Back in the nineties, they were quite prolific on American farms, but sixty years later most people had forgotten about them. However, I read an article in *Newsweek Magazine* a couple of years back where a New Mexican rancher was going in for raising geese in a big way.

Nearly every country in Europe has its particular way of preparing and cooking geese. In Ireland, geese are stuffed with potatoes (natch!) and onions. The Hungarians stuff theirs with mashed potatoes and onions. In old Russia, the favorite stuffing was buckwheat groats, and the goose was served surrounded with roasted apples. The Germans use apples or sauerkraut for the stuffing; the English, apples and raisins; and the Dutch, pears, onions, and cider. The Flemish method is to use chopped ham, onions, celery, and a little gin to moisten the stuffing.

I thought of calling the following recipe Roast Goose United Nations, but as some individuals are "agin" that world organization, I shall call it Roast Goose International. There's a hint of many countries among the ingredients, even Iraq.

ROAST GOOSE INTERNATIONAL

1 10- to 12-lb. goose	2 medium onions
Applejack	½ cup chopped celery
Salt and pepper	1 bay leaf
3 cups ryebread crumbs	¼ tsp. fennel seeds
½ lb. dried prunes	¼ tsp. ground nutmeg
Dry white wine	¼ tsp. dried tarragon
3 tbsp. butter	1 tbsp. chopped parsley
1 tsp. lemon juice	¼ lb. diced cooked ham
3 pears	⅓ cup ground almonds
3 apples	Powdered ginger

1 tbsp. currant jelly

Clean and singe a 10- to 12-lb. young goose, and rub it inside and out with applejack which has been seasoned with salt and pepper.

Crumble 6 to 8 slices of ryebread with caraway seeds in it, or enough to make 3 cups of breadcrumbs.

Soak ½ lb. of prunes in water overnight, then cook until tender in enough dry white wine to cover. When the prunes are cool, pit them and reserve, also reserving the wine they were cooked in.

In a large skillet, melt the butter, and when it is hot, add the lemon juice, the chopped apples, pears, onions, and celery. Sauté this for about 6 minutes. Then add the crumbled bay leaf, fennel seeds, ground nutmeg, dried tarragon, chopped parsley, salt and pepper to taste, and a total of 1 cup of applejack (utilize any of the seasoned applejack that remains after anointing the goose). Cook until the apples and pears are tender, stirring the whole occasionally. Then put the contents of the skillet through a fine sieve, rubbing the solids through, into a large bowl.

To the contents of the bowl, add the breadcrumbs, diced cooked ham, the ground almonds, and the cooked prunes. Mix everything well. If the stuffing seems too dry, moisten with applejack. The stuffing should be fluffy, not too moist. Stuff the goose with it.

Sew up or skewer the vent, truss the goose, and brush it with melted butter seasoned with a little powdered ginger. Prick the skin in several places to allow the fat to run out. Place the goose in a covered roaster, breast side down, and roast in a 400-degree oven for 1 hour. Drain off all the grease, and add the wine the prunes were cooked in (and enough more, if necessary, to make 1 cup) and 1 cup of water. Place the goose breast side up, and cook until done, about 3 hours (allow 20 minutes to the pound total roasting time), basting frequently.

When goose is done, remove to a hot platter. Skim off any fat, and measure remaining liquid. If necessary, add enough dry wine to make 3 cups. Add a tablespoon each of applejack and currant jelly. Blend in enough flour and butter *roux* to make the gravy a good consistency. Heat, and serve in a gravy boat.

The Fort Sumter Hotel, out on the Battery in Charlestown, South Carolina, is noted for its superb food, and there one finds Southern cooking at its best. I detailed two or three of their most succulent dishes in my *With a Jug of Wine,* notably their She-Crab Stew in a Cup and their Native Crab Meat Deep-Dish Pie. One of their most luscious dishes is squab, after the style in which it was cooked on the great plantations, where gracious living and dining was the rule, rather than the exception.

POTTED SQUAB ON WILD RICE
PLANTATION STYLE

4 *young squabs* (¾ *to* 1 *lb.* each)	*celery tops*
	collards
1 *cup dry red wine*	*kale*
1 *cup dry sherry wine*	*spinach*
2 *bay leaves*	*Salt*
6 *black peppercorns*	*Freshly ground pepper*
Small bunch soup greens	*Flour*
beet greens	1 *cup consommé*
mustard greens	½ *lb. wild rice*
turnip greens	*Water*
dandelion greens	*Butter*
1 *tbsp. cranberry jelly*	

Split the freshly killed, cleaned squabs and remove the breastbone.

Make a marinade of the dry red wine, the dry sherry, the bay leaves, peppercorns, a small bunch of soup greens cut in small pieces (a suggested list is given above; use what you can obtain), and 1 teaspoon of salt. Place the squabs in this marinade and allow to remain overnight.

When ready to cook, remove the squabs from the marinade and dry. Then shake them in a paper bag containing seasoned flour.

In a large skillet, melt 2 ounces of butter and allow it to brown. Then sauté the squabs until lightly browned, and add the chopped greens strained from the marinade. Let these brown, then add 1 tablespoon of flour, and blend it in. Next add the hot consommé, and let all simmer until the squabs are almost done. Then add the wine marinade, and let simmer until the squabs are tender.

Water-boil the wild rice until tender and fluffy, about 30 to 40 minutes. Drain, sauté lightly in a little butter, then place in a casserole, salt and pepper it to taste, and place the squabs on top. Add to the gravy the cranberry jelly, and let it melt. Simmer for a moment, then strain the gravy over the squabs and rice, and serve piping hot.

The Oxford English Dictionary defines frog as "a tailless amphibious animal of the genus *Rana*." In some cookbooks, frogs' legs are classed as fish, in others as mollusks, and in still others as game. But, however they may be classified, they are delicious eating. Iles Brody, in his fascinating book, *On the Tip of My Tongue,* describes the taste of them as "an amalgamation of the finest filet of sole, the most delicate veal, the wing of a spring chicken; and its whiteness surpasses any of them." To this, I will most heartily agree.

Frogs' legs vary in size from the very small ones that live near creeks (if you've ever lived in the country when you were young, you probably delighted in going frogging) to the very large, which are usually called bullfrogs. The frogs' legs one gets in the finer restaurants are usually medium in size. I have eaten jumbo frogs' legs in the Chicago Athletic Club that were as big as chicken legs. In the frozen food departments of the better stores, one can find jumbo frogs' legs from Cuba. Incidentally, I have it on good authority that frogs' legs are not classified as meat, and can therefore be eaten on Fridays and during Lent.

Probably the best known dish of frogs' legs is Frogs' Legs Provençal, which is, and should be, redolent with garlic. It is one of my very favorite dishes. Running it a close second is Frogs' Legs Poulette.

FROGS' LEGS POULETTE

18 *pairs medium-sized frogs'* *legs (about 2 lbs.)*	½ *cup dry white wine*
Cold milk	½ *cup chicken broth*
Brandy	1 *tsp. lemon juice*
3 *tbsp. butter*	1 *tbsp. chopped parsley*
4 *chopped shallots*	*Few grains cayenne pepper*
¾ *lb. fresh mushrooms*	1 *cup medium cream sauce*
Salt and pepper	2 *eggs yolks*
1 *tbsp. flour*	⅓ *cup cream*
	1 *tbsp. sweet butter*

Marinate the frogs' legs (the medium-sized are the best) in enough cold milk to cover (about 1½ to 2 cups) to which 1 ounce of brandy to each cup has been added. Allow the legs to stand in the brandied milk bath for at least 2 hours.

In a saucepan, put the butter, and when it is hot add the chopped shallots (or 2 little green onions, tops and bulbs chopped), and the mushrooms, sliced. After about 7 minutes, add the drained frogs' legs, and salt and pepper to taste, and continue to sauté, for 5 minutes, stirring constantly or shaking the pan so that the legs won't stick. Then sprinkle with a generous tablespoon of flour, blend it in well, and then add the dry white wine, the chicken broth, the lemon juice, the chopped parsley, and the few grains of cayenne pepper. Bring to a boil, then simmer gently for about 15 minutes, or until the frogs' legs are tender.

Remove the legs to a warm platter, and to the sauce in the pan add the medium cream sauce. Bring to a boil, then take off the fire and add the egg yolks, lightly beaten with the cream. Reheat, but do not boil, and stir in 1 tablespoon of sweet (unsalted) butter. Return the legs to the sauce, and serve as is on toast. If desired, serve in pastry shells. In such a case, remove the meat from the cooked frogs' legs and add the meat to the sauce.

I cannot understand why many people dislike, or will not eat, rabbit. Gastronomically speaking, rabbit is one of the most versatile of edible animals. The tender, delicately flavored meat of domestic rabbits (which are dressed with the same care afforded chickens) takes wonderfully to a variety of sauces and seasonings and methods of cooking. The wild rabbit is most plentiful, and therefore the least popular of all our game, yet it may be cooked in any of the ways suitable for the domestic rabbit. Furthermore—and this is important in our present economy—rabbit is inexpensive and may be used in as many ways as poultry, and in the same ways.

One of the classic British dishes is jugged hare. In an 1803 edition of a famous British cookbook (*The Art of Cooking Made Plain and Easy,* by Mrs. Glasse) there is a recipe for jugged hare (so-called because it was really cooked in an earthenware jug set in a pot of boiling water), which shows that its popularity has endured for more than 150 years. One of the specialties of the Savoy Hotel in London has always been jugged hare. If you went to the Coronation and stopped at the Savoy, you may have eaten it. If you didn't, you can certainly make it in your own home.

JUGGED HARE

1 *young rabbit, disjointed*	4 *slices bacon*
4 *tbsp. brandy*	1 *lemon rind, grated*
4 *tbsp. olive oil*	3 *tbsp. chopped parsley*
Salt	1 *tsp. dried thyme*
Freshly ground pepper	2 *bay leaves, minced*
1 *onion, sliced*	*Pinch powdered cloves*
2 *bay leaves*	8 *small onions*
Pinch dried thyme	1 *tbsp. mushroom catsup*
1 *clove garlic*	*Beef bouillon*
3 *whole cloves*	*Liver of rabbit*
Dry red wine	1 *tbsp. butter*
Flour	½ *cup port wine*

1 *tbsp. currant jelly*

Have your rabbit or hare cut into serving pieces by cutting the back into 2 pieces, and severing every joint. And be sure to get out the liver, which should be freed from the gall bladder and those portions touching it, washed, and reserved.

(If any of the male members of the family have gone out on a rabbit hunt, and returned with a young, plump wild rabbit or hare, it should be skinned and cleaned thoroughly, the blood collected, and the rabbit disjointed as directed above. The blood is used in making the sauce, which adds to its flavor. But if you are using a domestic rabbit, the blood is not necessary.)

Place the rabbit pieces in a crock, and add the brandy, olive oil, salt and freshly ground pepper to taste, the sliced onion, the bay leaves, dried thyme, the crushed clove of garlic, the cloves, and enough dry red wine to cover. Mix everything well, cover the crock, and let the rabbit pieces marinate for about 6 hours.

Remove the rabbit pieces from the crock, drain, and flour. In the bottom of a casserole lay the bacon slices, then put in a layer of rabbit pieces. Sprinkle with a mixture of seasonings (the grated lemon rind, the chopped parsley, the dried thyme, the minced bay leaves, and a pinch of powdered cloves) which have previously been made up. Then put in the casserole layer of the quartered small onions. Repeat the layers in the order above given, until all the pieces of rabbit have been used.

Next pour over the contents of the casserole the marinade, to which you have added the mushroom catsup (this is sometimes a little hard to come by, but Crosse & Blackwell's bottled Mushroom Sauce can be substituted) and enough beef bouillon so that the marinade will barely cover the contents of the casserole. Cover the casserole, and seal with a flour and water paste, so that no steam will escape. Put the casserole in a 300-degree oven for about 1½ hours.

At the end of the cooking time, unseal the casserole and take up the rabbit pieces and onions, and keep them hot. Strain the remaining liquid into a saucepan, bring it to a quick boil, then reduce the flame. Put the liver, which has been previously sautéed in 1 tablespoon of butter, through a sieve into the sauce.

(At this point, if you have used a wild rabbit and collected the blood, slowly heat the blood, mix it with 3 or 4 tablespoons of sauce, and then stir it into the sauce.)

Add to the sauce the port wine and the currant jelly, blend well, and pour the sauce over the rabbit and onions. This is really a magnificent dish. This serves 3 to 4.

From 1950 through 1954, the Amino Products Division of the International Minerals and Chemical Corporation, producers of Ac'cent, a pure monosodium glutamate, published a delightful little booklet each month called *New Notes in Cooking*. Its editors were Joan Rock, from the East, and Emily Chase Leistner, from the West. Each month the eight-page booklet brought a medley of new and interesting ideas about food to food writers, and I seldom failed to find an unusual recipe or two in the issues.

One of the recipes which I tried featured rabbit in a wine- and herb-flavored sauce, which I believe was a creation of Emily Chase Leistner, and it was out of this world.

BAKED RABBIT BURGUNDY

2 2½- to 3-lb. rabbits	1 tbsp. chopped parsley
Flour	1½ cups beef bouillon
Salt and pepper	1 cup dry red wine
½ lb. salt pork	1 bay leaf
2 cups diced carrots	Small pinch dried thyme
1 cup diced onion	Small pinch dried marjoram

1½ tsp. Ac'cent

Have the rabbits disjointed, and shake the pieces in a bag containing seasoned flour.

In a large heavy skillet or Dutch oven cook the salt pork, cut into tiny dice, until crisp and golden brown. Then remove the salt pork bits and reserve. In the salt pork drippings brown the rabbit pieces nicely, and then remove them to a casserole, preferably an earthenware one. To the browned rabbit pieces in the casserole, add the diced carrots, the diced onion, the chopped parsley, and the salt pork bits.

To the drippings in the skillet add ¼ cup of flour, and blend well. Then add to the skillet the beef bouillon and the dry red wine (preferably a Burgundy). Cook, stirring constantly, until the mixture boils and thickens. Then add the bay leaf, finely crushed, the dried thyme and marjoram, salt and pepper to taste, and the Ac'cent. When this is all well blended, pour the sauce over the rabbit pieces and vegetables in the casserole, cover, and bake in a 350-degree oven for 1½ to 2 hours, or until the rabbit meat is tender. Baste occasionally, and add a little more wine during the cooking if necessary to thin down the gravy. Serve from the casserole, to 6 or 8.

Another very simple and delicious recipe for rabbit uses white wine.

RABBIT IN WHITE WINE

1 *young rabbit*	¼ *tsp. dried thyme*
2 *cups dry white wine*	1 *tbsp. chopped parsley*
4 *tbsp. butter*	*Pinch dried chervil*
1 *clove garlic*	*Dash nutmeg*
2 *onions*	*Salt*
½ *cup sliced fresh mushrooms*	*Freshly ground pepper*

Disjoint the rabbit and cut into serving pieces. Place in a crock or bowl, and cover with the dry white wine, and let stand overnight.

In a heavy skillet or Dutch oven melt the butter, and add to it the clove of garlic, minced. Drain the rabbit pieces and put them in the skillet with the onions, diced, and sauté until the rabbit pieces are browned on all sides. This should take about 20 to 25 minutes. Then add the sliced fresh mushrooms, the dried thyme, chopped parsley, the dried chervil, the nutmeg, salt and freshly ground pepper to taste, and the wine the rabbit was marinated in. Cover and let simmer for 1½ to 2 hours, or until the rabbit is tender, and the meat comes easily away from the bones.

RABBIT À LA CACCIATORA

1 3- *to 4-lb. rabbit*	3 *tbsp. butter*
Salt and pepper	2 *tbsp. olive oil*
1 *onion, sliced*	1 *clove garlic*
1 *small bay leaf*	2 *oz. brandy*
1 *carrot, sliced*	½ *lb. fresh mushrooms*
1 *stalk celery, chopped*	2 *cups canned tomatoes*
1½ *cups dry red wine*	1 *tbsp. tomato paste*
Seasoned flour	¼ *tsp. dried oregano*

1 *tbsp. chopped parsley*

Cut up the rabbit, which has been cleaned, into about 8 pieces (2 shoulders, 2 legs, and 4 pieces of the back and breast). Place the rabbit pieces in a deep bowl or crock, sprinkle with salt and freshly ground pepper, and add to the rabbit pieces the sliced onion, the bay leaf, crumbled, the thinly sliced carrot, and the chopped celery. Pour over all the dry red wine, and let the rabbit pieces marinate in this mixture for at least 6 hours.

When ready to cook, remove the rabbit pieces from the marinade, drain, and shake in a bag of seasoned flour.

In a heavy skillet heat the butter and olive oil together, adding the clove of garlic, minced. When the fat is hot, add the floured rabbit pieces and brown on all sides—about 10 minutes. Then pour over the rabbit pieces in the skillet the brandy, warmed, and set alight. After the flame has died out, remove the rabbit pieces and keep warm.

In the same skillet add the vegetables drained from the marinade, and the mushrooms, sliced. Cook for about 7 minutes, then add the canned tomatoes, the tomato paste, the dried oregano, the chopped parsley, and the wine marinade. Simmer gently for about 10 minutes, then return the rabbit pieces to the skillet, cover, and simmer over a low flame for about 45 minutes to 1 hour, or until the rabbit is tender. Correct seasoning, if necessary, and serve very hot with boiled rice, wild rice, noodles, or spaghetti. This serves about 4.

(7) POULTRY

Have you ever pondered the chicken? Probably not, for one seldom meditates upon things that are habitual, or frequently met with. Yet chicken is, in many respects, an astonishing comestible. For instance, consider the following:

There is probably no country on the face of the globe whose people do not prepare and eat chicken. I have come across chicken recipes from every continent, even from remote Pacific and Indonesian islands.

Chicken is adaptable to every possible method of cooking.

Chicken is at home in every milieu—for company dinners or everyday economical meals; for gourmet palates, or for peasants in the fields; for dainty appetizers, or for lunch boxes that go to school or work; for elaborate buffets, or for picnic baskets; for schoolroom lunches or for swank weddings.

And who are chicken's customers? Let me make a parable.

Are you familiar with Shakespeare's *As You Like It*? Whether or no, Jacques, brother of Orlando, in the Forest of Arden, philosophizes on man's part in life to the banished Duke, Rosalind's father. He begins, "All the world's a stage, and all the men and women merely players . . . and one man in his time plays many parts, his acts being seven ages."

This will probably strike you as being incongruous as hell, but as I read the passage, the thought came to me: "At every stage of man's life, chicken is an appropriate and desirable food." So I set out to paraphrase Jacques' speech, and here are my notes.
"At first the infant . . ."
(Chicken is among the first solid foods a baby is given.)
"And then the whining schoolboy, with his satchel . . ."
A piece of fried chicken is a jewel among jewels in the school lunch box.)
"And then the lover . . ."
(The daintiest, most delectable food to order for your beloved on a first dinner date is breast of chicken under glass.)

"Then a soldier . . . seeking the bubble reputation even in the cannon's mouth."

> (Napoleon, during his campaigns, had roast chicken served to him nearly every night.)

"And then the Justice, in fair round belly with good capon lin'd."

> (Self-explanatory)

"The sixth age shifts into the lean and slippered pantaloon . . ."

> (Chicken is an integral part of the diet of elderly people, because it not only is a ready source of nutrition, but because its flavor stimulates dwindling appetites.)

"Last scene of all, that ends this strange, eventful history is second childishness . . . mere oblivion, sans teeth . . ."

> (And so what could be more nourishing than a good cup of chicken broth?)

I wouldn't venture to guess what way of cooking chicken is the most popular, at least throughout the world. In America, the Southerner would probably say fried; gourmets from the Far East might say curried; in the Baltic regions, natives could say stewed. But this I do know—there is no easier way of cooking delectable chicken dishes than in a casserole.

In these days of homes without servants, and the all-too-often astronomical cost of food, even the most informal entertaining can be a headache. Of course, if you can afford to, and can get help, there isn't much of a problem. But when you have to get the dinner yourself; fix a few simple appetizers; make the predinner libations; greet your guests; serve the libations and drink your own while trotting back and forth between the kitchen and the living room to watch dinner; serve the dinner; and clean up and wash the dishes (after maybe having dropped a few bucks at bridge or canasta), life is not exactly a bowl of cherries.

Frankly, there isn't an easy way to entertain without help, no matter how much you enjoy having friends in for dinner and an evening of cards, records, or just chitchat. But you can keep things simple, and plan your dinner so that most of it is virtually cooked by the time the guests have arrived, by having a casserole dish. Then you can serve the libations and appetizers, and enjoy them with your guests, and when everyone is down to the last couple of swallows, you can go into the kitchen and serve dinner in a few minutes.

We have used the following chicken dish frequently for informal entertaining, and it always rates raves. It was devised by an old and dear friend who lives in Walnut Creek, in California, Orleanne Harvey, and I have named it Chicken Orleanne. It is a grand entree for a party of four, and can be prepared in advance.

CHICKEN ORLEANNE

3 *large chicken legs*   *Parsley, chopped*
3 *large chicken thighs*   *Rosemary seasoning powder*
2 *large chicken breasts*   1 *stalk celery*
Fresh lime juice   3 *medium-sized carrots*
Salt   5 *small white onions*
Freshly ground pepper   ½ *cup dry white wine*
Seasoned flour   1 *15½-oz. can cream of*
4 *oz. butter*   *mushroom soup*
½ *clove garlic*   *Paprika*

Get 3 large chicken legs and thighs and two large breasts, dividing the legs and thighs, and halving the breasts. Brush the pieces with fresh lime juice, season with salt and freshly ground pepper, and shake in a bag of seasoned flour. Sauté the chicken pieces in a heavy skillet in the butter until they are a golden brown (about 20 minutes).

Next, place a layer of chicken pieces in a casserole, and sprinkle the layer with ½ clove of garlic, minced, a generous pinch of parsley, and 2 light sprinkles of rosemary seasoning powder. Then add a second layer of chicken pieces, and repeat the seasonings on that layer. Then sprinkle over the chicken pieces the stalk of celery, chopped, and lay over and around the top the medium-sized carrots, sliced in half lengthwise, and the little white onions.

In the skillet the chicken was sautéed in pour the dry white wine, and blend it well with the butter remaining in the skillet. Then add the cream of mushroom soup, and again blend the contents of the skillet. Then pour this sauce over the contents of the casserole, sprinkle the top lightly with freshly ground pepper and paprika, put into a moderate oven (285-300 degrees) and bake for 2 hours. Serve from the casserole.

On a recent motor trip through the South I was filled, as always, with a great nostalgia for those days "Befo' the Wah." They were the days of the great plantations, stately and spacious houses; of gracious living, unstinted hospitality, and fine food; of great kitchens peopled by portly, bandanna-headed cooks who created fabulous dishes just for the sheer joy of bringing pleasure to others. As I drove through the countryside, I was not in a 1955 automobile, but mounted on a spirited bay. I'm on my way over to call on Marse Henry Calvert, who will have a tall, frosted mint julep waiting for me. And then I'll be off to Green Acres for a dinner such as only Evalina, General Buford's cook, can prepare— a freshly killed, succulent chicken, spoonbread, corn pudding, candied yams, and eggnog pie. And who knows . . . maybe later in the evening Scarlett O'Hara will gesture imperiously, and . . .

"Better pull over to the curb, Mister," a voice cuts in. "You've been doing forty-five in a twenty-five-mile-an-hour zone." And so I'm jerked back to the present.

But later, at the home of friends in Alabama, the past sort of lived again when we did have a wonderful Southern dinner, complete with spoonbread, corn pudding, and a wonderful sherried chicken in a casserole. (Sure, we had mint juleps to start with!)

SHERRIED CHICKEN IN A CASSEROLE

1 3- to 4-lb. frying chicken	1 cup diced celery
Salt	2 tbsp. minced onions
Freshly ground pepper	1 tbsp. flour
Flour	¼ cup dry sherry
⅓ cup butter	1 cup thin cream

Cut up the frying chicken, sprinkle with salt and pepper, flour lightly, and fry slowly in the butter. Then transfer to a casserole. Add to the butter in the skillet the diced celery, minced onion, and flour. Stir over a low flame for 2 minutes, season lightly with salt and pepper, and add this mixture to the chicken in the casserole. Add the dry sherry wine and thin cream, cover, and bake in a moderate (350 degree) oven for 30 to 40 minutes. Serves 3 to 4.

Lilla Deeley, in her charming little book, *Hungarian Cookery*, speaks of the tradition amongst Hungarians for a warm midday meal, which, wherever possible, is the chief meal of the day. So strong is this tradition that even farm and industrial workers insist upon it. Mrs. Deeley says that it is the usual sight in the country to see the female members of the family carrying the midday meal to the fields in a specially constructed carrier, which keeps the courses warm. The same applies to town workers; the midday pause finds wives in long queues waiting outside factories with warm meals for their husbands.

Because casserole dishes keep hot for quite a period of time, they are very popular. I strongly suspect that the following dish has a Hungarian origin, not only because of its name, but because of the presence of sour cream, paprika, and white wine. The recipe came from Emily Chase Leistner, in *New Notes in Cooking,* whom I have mentioned before.

BAKED CHICKEN CZARDAS

1 3- *to* 3½-*lb. frying chicken*	1 *cup thick sour cream*
1½ *tsp. Ac'cent*	1 *tsp. paprika*
4 *tbsp. butter*	½ *tsp. grated lemon rind*
1 *small onion*	*Salt and pepper*
3 *tbsp. flour*	2 *tbsp. dry sherry*
1 *cup dry white wine*	2 *tbsp. chopped parsley*

Cut the chicken in serving pieces, sprinkle them with 1 teaspoon of Ac'cent, and let them stand 15 to 20 minutes.

Melt the butter in a large, heavy skillet, and brown the chicken pieces in it slowly on all sides. Then transfer the chicken pieces to a casserole.

To the fat in the skillet add the onion, minced, and sauté gently for 5 minutes. Then blend in the flour, add the dry white wine and the sour cream, and cook, stirring constantly until the mixture boils and thickens. Next add the paprika, grated lemon rind, ½ teaspoon of Ac'cent, and salt and pepper to taste.

Pour the gravy over the chicken in the casserole, cover, and bake in a 350-degree oven for 1 hour, or until the chicken is tender.

Place the chicken on a hot platter, and to the gravy add the sherry and parsley. Blend, let heat, and pour the gravy over the chicken. This serves 3 or 4.

The French word *ménagère* means an "economical housewife; thrifty, saving, frugal." I think the word applies to a large majority of French housewives, urban and provincial, particularly the latter group. Certainly, French cuisine abounds with thrifty dishes, such as "one-dish meals" as Americans have come to call them. Such classics as *Pot au Feu, Beef en Daube,* Brittany Beef en Casserole, *Cassaulet,* and Short Ribs of Beef Burgundy, where the meat, vegetables, and sometimes potatoes are all cooked together in the same pot or casserole, are typical examples.

This next savory chicken dish, named after the thrifty housewife, combines chicken, vegetables, and potatoes in a casserole, along with other delectable items.

CHICKEN À LA MÉNAGÈRE

2 *young chickens* (1½ *lbs.*   2 *little green onions*
    each)   10 *small mushroom caps*
Salt and pepper   4 *oz. brandy*
Dried chervil   1 *cup dry white wine*
¼ *lb. bacon*   2 *medium carrots*
1 *clove garlic*   1 *white turnip*
¼ *lb. raw ham*   2 *medium potatoes*
      1 *cup fresh or frozen peas*

Disjoint two young and tender chickens (about 1½ pounds each). Season the pieces with salt and pepper to taste, and sprinkle sparingly with dried chervil.

In a heavy skillet fry the bacon, diced. When the bacon is crisp, remove the pieces, and in the bacon drippings brown the clove of garlic, sliced. When the garlic is brown, remove it. Then add to the skillet the raw ham, diced, little green onions (bulbs and tops), minced, the small mushroom caps, and the chicken pieces.

When the chicken pieces are browned, pour over the contents of the skillet the warm brandy, set it alight, and as the flames die down, add to the skillet the dry white wine. Turn up the flame under the skillet, and let the liquid come to a boil. Boil for 1 minute, then remove the skillet from the fire.

In the meantime, parboil the carrots, white turnip, and peeled potatoes, for about 10 minutes. Then drain the vegetables, and when cool enough to handle, mince the carrots and turnips, and cut the potatoes in medium dice.

In the bottom of a casserole make a bed of the parboiled, minced vegetables, and sprinkle with salt and pepper to taste. Lay the chicken pieces on the bed of vegetables, and add to the casserole the fresh (or thawed frozen) peas. Now empty the remaining contents of the skillet (the diced ham, little green onions, the mushroom caps, and the liquid) into the casserole, and sprinkle the diced, cooked bacon over all. Cover the casserole, and cook in a 325-degree oven for about an hour, or until the chicken is tender. Serve from the casserole. This should serve 6.

Have you ever had the experience of enjoying a particularly delicious dish, and then racking your brain, or your memory of taste sensations, to try and determine what it was that gave the dish its wonderfully subtle and elusive flavor? I have, many times, and always I knew that I had partaken of something prepared by a master cook, even though he, or she, was far from being a professional.

I think the famed Oscar of the Waldorf has succinctly summed up the whole matter of flavoring and seasoning food. He said:

The art of seasoning food is essential in good cooking, as certain seasonings lift up certain foods. In using them, however, the homemaker must be careful not to over-season or under-season, but rather to obtain a delicious blend which will bring out the flavor of the predominant ingredient in the dish and add that elusive aroma, so subtle that even the gourmet hesitates to name it.

In culinary combinations of food, the spices and other stimulants are used not merely for the purpose of imparting their own flavor but with the aim of exciting the organ of taste to a heightened perception of the flavor of the meat, soup, poultry, game, vegetables, sauces, etc.

The perfection of the art of making culinary combinations is the production of a happy combination, in which the elementary flavors are all lost and indistinguishable in the new one created by their combined effect on the palate.

Chicken lends itself particularly to delicate nuances of flavor as in this Chicken à l'Estragon, which utilizes the intriguing flavor of the herb tarragon.

CHICKEN À L'ESTRAGON

1 2- to 3-lb. chicken
1½ tsp. dried tarragon
4 oz. dry white wine
Salt

Freshly ground pepper
2 oz. butter
½ lb. small mushrooms
½ cup chicken broth

First you put about 1½ teaspoons of dried tarragon leaves into the dry white wine, and allow this to stand for at least 3 hours.

Cut the chicken into serving pieces, and season with salt and freshly ground pepper. Then melt the butter in a heavy skillet, and when the butter is hot, but not brown, add the chicken pieces and brown them well on all sides. Then transfer the chicken to a casserole, and add the small mushrooms, stems and caps separated, to the skillet and cook for 6 to 7 minutes. Then add the clear chicken broth to the skillet, along with the wine and tarragon leaves that have been standing, and stir the whole over a medium flame, loosening any particles in the pan, for about 5 minutes. Then pour the contents of the skillet over the chicken in the casserole, cover, and cook for about 45 minutes in a 325-degree oven, or until the chicken is tender. Serve the same wine that was used in the cooking, only of course chilled. Serves 3 to 4.

I don't think there is any place on earth where the sky is so blue, the rocks so red, and the sea so iridescent blue-green as along the fabulous Côte d'Azur—the French Riviera. From Saint-Raphael to Monaco there are towns that well might have come out of a fairy tale—Cannes, Antibes, Nice, and Monte Carlo.

Riviera cooking is a combination of French Provençal and Italian. One of the most famous Riviera dishes is *Pissaladiera,* a tart in bread dough covered with sautéed onions, leeks, garlic, black olives, and anchovy filets. Another very elegant and thoroughly delicious dish is Chicken à la Riviera.

CHICKEN À LA RIVIERA

1 3-*lb. frying chicken*   12 *ripe olives, pitted*
2 *tbsp. butter*   3 *tbsp. dry sherry*
2 *tbsp. olive oil*   1½ *tbsp. consommé*
6 *small new potatoes*   ½ *tbsp. lemon juice*
3 *artichoke bottoms*   Salt
Freshly ground pepper

Cut up the chicken into serving pieces.

In a large skillet heat the butter and olive oil. Add the chicken pieces, the new potatoes (about the size of walnuts), and the artichoke bottoms. Sauté for 15 minutes. Then cover the skillet and put in a 350-degree oven for about 10 minutes.

Transfer the chicken pieces, potatoes and artichoke bottoms and pan juices to a casserole, and add the ripe olives, sherry, consommé, lemon juice, and salt and freshly ground pepper to taste. Cover the casserole, place in a 300-degree oven, and cook about 15 minutes more, or until the chicken and potatoes are tender. This recipe serves 3.

Along about April, in bygone days, young and tender broilers made their appearance on the market, and everyone craved "spring chicken." But for some years now, thanks to a progressive poultry industry, young, tender, flavorful, and meaty chickens are available the year round. Throughout the year, in modern poultry markets, you'll see fryers, broilers, roasters, stewing hens, and capons displayed in abundance.

Fried chicken, particularly in the South, means just what it says —just plain fried, in butter or oil. But, actually, fried chicken can be richly embellished. There are a great many dishes where the chicken starts out as plain fried, but ends up in wondrous ways. For instance:

FRIED CHICKEN BAKED IN CREAM

2 *frying chickens*	¾ *lb. fresh mushrooms*
Milk	2 *cups cream*
Seasoned flour	*Salt and pepper*
4 *oz. butter*	2 *oz. brandy*
	Watercress

Disjoint the chickens, and put them in a shallow glass baking dish. Cover them with milk, and let stand for about 30 minutes. Then remove them from the milk, drain, and shake the pieces in a bag of seasoned flour.

In a skillet melt the butter, and when hot, put in the chicken pieces and sauté them until they are golden brown on all sides. Then remove them from the skillet, and drain on paper toweling.

In the same skillet, sauté the mushrooms, sliced, for about 6 to 7 minutes. Then add to the mushrooms, the cream, and salt and pepper to taste. Turn up the flame and let the mixture come to a boil, then remove the fire.

Arrange the chicken pieces in a casserole, and sprinkle them with the brandy. Then pour the cream and mushrooms over the chicken pieces, and bake in a 325-degree oven for about 40 minutes, or until the chicken pieces are tender, and the cream has thickened. Garnish with sprigs of watercress, and serve from the casserole. This will serve 4 to 6, depending upon the size of the chickens, and the appetites.

Two of the great Spanish chicken dishes are *Arroz con Pollo* and *Paella*. The first is chicken cooked with rice, and the second is chicken and shellfish cooked with rice. There are recipes for both in my *With a Jug of Wine,* but I would like to detail here another version of *Paella*.

The ancient dish takes its name from the vessel in which it is cooked, *Paella,* which is the Spanish word for an iron pot. Somerset Maugham knew *Paella* as *Arroz à la Valenciana,* and he described it as being composed of chicken, clams, mussels, prawns, saffron, red peppers, rice, and "I know not what else." The late Crosby Gaige, gourmet extraordinary, tells of his improvisation on the dish in his last fascinating book, *Footlights and Highlights*. His version utilized chicken, clams, and rice, and a sprinkling of grated Parmesan cheese. Louis Diat, the celebrated chef of the Ritz, in New York, gives his version of *Arroz à la Valenciana* in his book, *Cooking à la Ritz,* and he substitutes lobster for shrimps and clams.

Well, who am I to be left out of the parade! So here is my version of *Arroz à la Valenciana* with not only chicken and clams, but lobster, and savory vegetables. It may sound a little formidable, and it is work, but I don't believe anyone who makes and eats it will say that it wasn't worth the trouble.

ARROZ À LA VALENCIANA

2 *broiling chickens, quartered*
Salt and pepper
Paprika
Powdered ginger
½ *cup olive oil*
½ *lb. bacon*
2 *lobsters* (1½ *to* 2 *lbs each*)
2 *onions*
2 *green peppers*
3 *tomatoes*

1 #2 *can artichoke hearts*
2 *cups long-grain rice*
Hot chicken broth (*about* 4 *cups in all*)
24 *small clams*
12 1-*inch pieces of Italian sausage*
3 *cloves garlic*
1 *tsp. saffron powder*
½ *cup dry white wine*

Quarter the broilers, and rub them with salt, pepper, paprika, and powdered ginger.

In a heavy iron pot, or Dutch oven, or casserole, put the olive oil, and the bacon, diced. When sizzling, add the chicken pieces, and sauté until they are golden brown on all sides. Remove them and keep warm, and to the pot add the lobsters, cut in pieces, and when they are well sautéed, remove them and keep warm.

To the pot add the onions, chopped, and the green peppers, chopped. When the onions begin to brown, add the tomatoes, cut in pieces, and the artichoke hearts, drained. Cook for about 5 minutes, then add to the pot 2 cups of long-grain rice, well washed. Stir from time to time to keep the rice from burning, and cook until the rice begins to take on color and dry out a little.

Return the chicken pieces and the lobster pieces to the pot, and pour in 1 cup of hot chicken broth. When this is absorbed, add another cup of hot chicken broth. Simmer until the chicken and rice are nearly tender.

Now add to the pot 24 small clams in their shells, which have been well scrubbed, and about 12 1-inch pieces of Italian sausage. If necessary, add more hot chicken broth, depending on the state of the rice.

In a mortar (or heavy bowl) put the 3 cloves of garlic, sliced, the teaspoon of saffron, and about 6 ounces of hot chicken broth. With a pestle (or a muddler) grind the garlic and mix well, until the broth is thoroughly impregnated with the garlic and saffron. Then strain the broth into the pot, and add the dry white wine, and correct the seasoning with salt and pepper.

When the rice is properly cooked (enough of the hot chicken broth having been added to complete the cooking), each kernel of rice should be separate, and not of a mushy consistency. The clams will have opened their shells, and the chicken and lobster will be tender to the fork. Serve from the pot or casserole in which the dish has been cooked to 6 or 8.

In nearly all cookery, particularly in the cooking of meats and chicken, there are two terms used which engender confusion in the minds of many cooks—fry and sauté.

As far as I am concerned, the two words mean the same thing, and within this book, they are interchangeable. Frying in deep fat is another thing (such as cooking French-fried potatoes, dough-nuts, fishballs, etc.) and will always be so designated.

Well, enough of such pedantry. Let's get on with our succulent barnyard friend, who has captivated the palate of men for centuries.

Here is a sautéed chicken done in an exciting new way. The sauce has a flavor and texture that is beyond compare. It is called Chicken Celeste, and it is truly celestial.

CHICKEN CELESTE

1 *frying chicken (about 3½*
   lbs. cut in serving pieces)
Flour
Salt and pepper
2 *tbsp. butter*
2 *tbsp. olive oil*

1 *medium onion, chopped*
1 *cup dry sherry wine*
½ *tsp. Ac'cent*
1 *cup mayonnaise*
2 *tbsp. chopped parsley*
Generous dash paprika

Shake chicken pieces in bag containing seasoned flour. Heat the butter and oil in a large skillet or Dutch oven, and brown chicken pieces nicely on all sides. Then add the chopped onion, sherry, and Ac'cent to the skillet, cover, and simmer gently 45 minutes to 1 hour, or until chicken is tender, turning and basting chicken occasionally.

Remove chicken pieces to platter and keep warm. Add the mayonnaise to the juices in skillet and blend well (use rotary beater, if necessary, to achieve perfect smoothness). If gravy seems too thick, thin it with a little more sherry.

Add the chopped parsley and paprika. Correct seasoning if necessary. Pour gravy over chicken. Serves 3 or 4.

Chicken takes unto itself with gastronomical profit a wide variety of seasonings, herbs, wines, spirits, and cordials. I have even heard of two chicken recipes calling for beer, one calling for stout, and one using ale.

Chicken takes on a completely new personality when it is prepared with brandy or cognac. This spirit makes even the most tender bird more toothsome and flavorful, and it adds zest without detracting from or overpowering the other ingredients included in the recipe.

The first delightful chicken dish using brandy is called Chicken

Charente, named after the small department of France which produces the great brandies.

CHICKEN CHARENTE

1 *2-lb. chicken*
1½ *tbsp. butter*
½ *lb. fresh mushrooms*

4 *tbsp. heavy sweet cream*
1 *lemon (juice of)*
2 *tbsp. cognac*

Salt and pepper

Cut a small (2-pound) chicken into serving pieces. Melt the butter in a skillet, and when it is hot sauté the chicken pieces and the mushrooms, sliced very thin. When the chicken pieces are golden brown, add the cognac, the sweet cream, and the lemon juice, and let the whole simmer until the chicken is tender. Salt and pepper to taste, and serve very hot. This serves 2 or 3. Peas in butter and riced potatoes are pleasant accompaniments.

The second chicken dish cooked with brandy is named after the district of Paris called Montparnasse, but I'm not quite sure why. This district was, for a long time, inhabited by such leading artists as Picasso and Rousseau, but now it is inhabited by raucous and penniless artists from the numerous "Art Academies" that infest the section. But, in spite of its name, Chicken Montparnasse is neither undistinguished nor commonplace.

CHICKEN MONTPARNASSE

1 *capon (about 4 lbs.)*
Seasoned flour
4 *oz. butter*

3 *little green onions*
4 *oz. brandy*
1 *cup chicken bouillon*

Quarter the capon and shake the pieces in a bag of seasoned flour. Heat the butter in a heavy skillet, and when it is bubbling, put in the chicken pieces and lightly brown them on all sides. Then add the finely chopped little green onions.

Warm the brandy in a ladle, and set fire to it. Pour the burning brandy over the chicken, let it burn for a few seconds, and then add the chicken bouillon. Let the whole simmer until the chicken is tender. This will serve 3 to 4, and is at its best served on a bed of fluffy rice which has been cooked in chicken stock and mixed with sautéed mushrooms.

I told about that small and select circle of gourmets in Chicago called the Streeterville and Sanitary Canal Gourmet and Study

Society in *With a Jug of Wine*. It is composed of a group of men who are dedicated to the art of eating and drinking well. Once a month the members gather for dinner at the home of the man selected as the host-chef, who plans and prepares the meal, and who is assisted in the selection and serving of the wines by a designated cellarer.

A really noteworthy dinner was served at the opening of a recent season by Walter Drennan, who is a real estate operator in Chicago by day, and a gourmet cook by night. The hors d'oeuvre was imported caviar served on a block of ice, accompanied by champagne. The entree was Chicken Legs à la Drennan, served with wild rice. The salad was a chilled limestone lettuce with a sharp Cheddar cheese dressing, and the dessert was Cherries Jubilee. A California Sauvignon Blanc was served with the dinner and champagne accompanied the dessert. Coffee and a fine champagne brandy closed the meal.

The chicken dish was a work of art, and one of the most delicious I have ever tasted, yet simple to prepare. I made it a couple of week ends later for guests, and everybody was tremendously enthusiastic over the dish. I later prepared it on my Chicago television cooking show, and hundreds of requests came in for the recipe.

CHICKEN LEGS À LA DRENNAN

4 *complete chicken legs*	*Pinch finely chopped leaf sage*
Seasoned flour	½ *tsp. chili powder*
3 *oz. butter*	*Paprika*
Pinch dried marjoram	1 *cup chopped parsley*
Pinch dried thyme	½ *cup dry white wine*

In a heavy and rather deep iron skillet, melt the butter. Then add a pinch each of marjoram, thyme, and finely chopped leaf sage, the chili powder, and a generous sprinkling of paprika. Blend all these ingredients thoroughly with the melted butter, stirring with a fork.

Toss the chicken legs (legs and thighs separated) in a bag of seasoned flour* and then put them in the skillet with the seasoned

---

* To make seasoned flour, put 1 cup of flour in a medium-sized strong paper bag and add 1 teaspoon of salt, 1 teaspoon of pepper, and ½ teaspoon of paprika. Shake it up and it is ready for use. It can be reused as long as there is any left. Just fold up the bag and keep it in the flour cannister.

butter and brown them on both sides over a fairly brisk flame or medium high heat. Then turn the flame or heat down to the lowest point, cover the skillet, and let the chicken legs slowly simmer for anywhere from 45 minutes to an hour, or until tender. Then remove the chicken legs to a platter and put them in a warm oven.

To the juices in the skillet add the chopped parsley and very dry American white wine. Stir and blend everything well, and when hot pour over the chicken legs and serve.

One of the finest restaurants in San Francisco is Bardelli's on O'Farrel Street. For a great many years it has been one of the favorite eating places of San Francisco's *bon vivants* and gourmets, and the luster of its cuisine has never dimmed. Rather, since the personable Charles Bardelli took it over, its reputation for superb food has been enhanced.

To me, Charles is the typical Gallic master chef. He is always in his white uniform, with a tall white chef's hat set at a rakish angle on his head. He is unforgettable, with his little pointed beard, his twinkling blue eyes, his expressive hands, and his beaming countenance when anyone praises some special dish he has prepared.

And Bardelli's has another asset in addition to exquisite food and a magnificent chef. It is the host, Stu Adams, who is Bardelli's son-in-law. Stu has a sparkling wit, and a fund of excellent, albeit spicy, stories. I have a particular fondness in my heart for Stu, since he witnessed, with a flourish, the signing of my contract with the publishers of my *Fisherman's Wharf Cook Book.*

If you were to question habitual patrons of Bardelli's and ask them their favorite dish, you might get a number of different answers. But I am sure that all would agree that Chicken Jerusalem, an original creation of Charles Bardelli's, is one of the most outstanding and luscious chicken dishes in the world. I believe that this is the first cookbook that the recipe has ever appeared in.

BARDELLI'S CHICKEN JERUSALEM

1 2-*lb. chicken*	*Nutmeg*
Flour	1 *lb. sliced mushrooms*
2 *oz. butter* (4 *tbsp.*)	6 *artichoke bottoms*
Salt	¾ *cup dry sherry*
White pepper	2 *cups hot cream*
	Chopped parsley

Cut the chicken into 8 pieces and roll the pieces in flour. In a skillet, melt the butter, and when hot brown the chicken pieces on all sides. Season with salt, pepper, and a little nutmeg to taste.

Add to the skillet the sliced fresh mushrooms. Cut the artichoke bottoms into quarters and add them to the skillet. Add the dry sherry, cover the skillet, and simmer the whole for 25 minutes, or until the chicken is cooked through and tender. Then stir in the hot cream. Sprinkle with finely chopped parsley before serving. This recipe serves 2 to 3.

I think *Vichyssoise* is the most elegant of all soups. It is made with potatoes, leeks, chicken broth, white wine, cream, and other vegetables, and it is at its best cold. Here, however, is an adaptation of the *Vichyssoise* principle to a tender young chicken braised with potatoes, onion, wine, and sour cream, which gives the chicken the richness and suavity of the famous soup.

CHICKEN VICHYSSOISE

1 *frying chicken*
Seasoned flour
¼ *cup butter*
¼ *cup lard*
2 *cups thinly sliced potatoes*

¾ *cup sliced little green onions*
Salt and pepper
½ *cup consommé*
½ *cup dry white wine*
1 *cup commercial sour cream*

Cut the chicken into serving pieces, and shake them in a bag of seasoned flour.

Melt the butter and lard in a large skillet, and sauté the chicken pieces in this until golden brown on all sides. Pour off any excess fat, and push the chicken pieces to the center of the skillet. Arrange the thinly sliced potatoes in a circle around the chicken pieces, salting and peppering the potatoes lightly. Sprinkle the sliced little green onions (bulbs and tops) over all, and add to the contents of the skillet the consommé and the dry white wine. Cover the skillet and simmer about 30 minutes, or until the chicken pieces are tender. Remove the cover, pour the sour cream over all, and continue to cook over a low flame for about 5 minutes, or until the mixture is heated through. This serves 4 deliciously.

Sans souci, in English, means "without care." So I think this next chicken dish is aptly named, because it is so simple to prepare, and so felicitous in flavor.

CHICKEN SANS SOUCI

3 tbsp. olive oil

3 tbsp. butter

2 2½-lb. frying chickens,
 halved

3 tbsp. flour

1 can condensed chicken
 consommé

½ cup dry white wine

1 4-oz. can mushroom stems
 and pieces, undrained

2 tbsp. chopped parsley

2 tbsp. chopped onions

Salt and pepper

1 tsp. Ac'cent

Heat the oil and butter in a large, heavy skillet (or divide the amount of oil and butter in two skillets if you haven't a very large one) and brown the halved chickens nicely on all sides. Then remove the chicken halves to a large casserole (or a medium-sized roasting pan).

To the butter and oil in the skillet add the flour, and blend it in well until the *roux* is smooth. Then add the chicken consommé and the ½ cup dry white wine and cook, stirring constantly, until the mixture boils and thickens. Then add the undrained mushroom stems and pieces, the chopped parsley and onions, salt, pepper and Ac'cent. When well blended, pour the sauce over the chicken halves, cover the casserole (or roaster), and bake in a 350-degree oven for about an hour, or until the chicken is tender, turning and basting the chicken halves occasionally. This recipe serves 4, but it is easily multiplied for larger servings.

In previous chapters I have spoken of Lawry's Spaghetti Sauce Mix. While it was originally intended to be used with *pastas,* its versatility is amazing. I have detailed its use as an appetizer and a sauce for shrimps, and now here is a chicken dish utilizing it. It is called Chicken Supreme, and I think it is well named, for it has supreme lusciousness.

CHICKEN SUPREME

1 3-lb. frying chicken

Lawry's seasoned salt

1 pkg. Lawry's Spaghetti Sauce
 Mix

½ cup fine breadcrumbs

⅓ cup vegetable shortening

½ cup dry white wine

Cut the chicken into serving pieces, and sprinkle with Lawry's seasoned salt. Also blend the package of the spaghetti sauce mix with the breadcrumbs. Then roll the chicken pieces slowly and carefully in the seasoned crumb mixture.

Melt the vegetable shortening (or butter, if you prefer) in a heavy skillet, and when it is medium hot, sauté the prepared chicken pieces until they are golden brown. Then remove the browned chicken pieces to a casserole, or shallow baking dish, add the dry white wine and whatever is left of the seasoned crumb mixture, cover, and bake in a 350-degree oven for about 45 minutes, or until the chicken is tender. This serves 3 to 4.

If you have ever motored through the White Mountains in New Hampshire, you've probably run across the Mount Adams Inn in North Woodstock. If you have, and have eaten there, I don't need to tell you about the wonderful food that the proprietors, Fred and Helen Kershner, serve. One of their most sought-after specialties is Potato Soup, the recipe for which I detailed in *With a Jug of Wine*. Another delectable dish which Fred and Helen devised is Baked Fried Chicken, Holland Style. Surprisingly enough, I have been told, chicken fixed this way will stay fresh almost indefinitely. Personally, I've never had an opportunity to test this theory, because it is so delicious that there is never any left when I have made it.

BAKED FRIED CHICKEN, HOLLAND STYLE

1 *chicken* (*breasts, legs and thighs only*)
Seasoned flour
2 *tbsp. bacon drippings*

1 *medium onion*
1 *clove garlic*
⅔ *cup chicken broth*
⅓ *cup dry sherry*

Dredge the chicken pieces in seasoned flour. In a heavy skillet heat the bacon drippings, and add the chopped onion and the crushed clove of garlic. Then put the chicken pieces in the skillet, brown them on all sides, and remove them to a baking dish, or casserole.

To the fat and onions in the skillet add the chicken broth and sherry. Stir until well blended, and then pour the contents of the skillet over the chicken pieces in the baking dish. Cover, and bake in a 375-degree oven for about ¾ hour, or until the chicken is tender. Serve as it comes out of the baking dish, or, if you wish, thicken the gravy with a flour and butter *roux*.

How many will this recipe serve? Well, Mrs. Wood and I, who are very fond of chicken regardless of how it is fixed, get away with every smidget. So that makes it serve 2. If junior, or another third party, is fond of drumsticks, it's a cinch. But, otherwise, to make it serve 3 is your problem.

A wonderful chicken dish that one sometimes encounters on the menus of fine restaurants is Chicken *Sauté Sec* (*sec* being French for "dry"). But, strangely enough, the recipe is almost impossible to find in cookbooks. But fortunately I found an excellent recipe in a brochure put out by the Wine Advisory Board in San Francisco, and I am delighted to herewith present it.

CHICKEN SAUTÉ SEC

1 3½-lb. frying chicken cut in pieces
Flour
Salt and pepper
4 tbsp. butter
2 shallots (or little green onions)

2 tbsp. chopped parsley
Pinch dried thyme
Pinch dried basil
½ cup California dry white wine
1 4-oz. can sliced mushrooms

Dust the chicken pieces with flour and season with salt and pepper. Melt the butter in a large heavy skillet, add the chicken pieces, and sauté until they are golden brown on all sides. If necessary, add a little more butter to the skillet. Next add the finely chopped shallots (or little green onions, bulbs and tops), chopped parsley, the dried thyme and basil, and the dry white wine (a good California sauterne, Chablis, or White Pinot). Cover the skillet tightly and simmer gently for 30 minutes. Then uncover and add the drained sliced mushrooms (or ¼ pound of sliced fresh mushrooms which have been sautéed in a tablespoon or so of butter for about 6 minutes). Continue cooking for about 15 minutes, or until the chicken is tender and no liquid remains in the pan. This recipe serves 3 to 4.

Just plain old broiled chicken is pretty terrific in any language. Salt and pepper chicken halves, dot them with butter, and broil. That's all there is to it for a taste thrill to even a jaded appetite. But not long ago I dared to gild the lily, so to speak, and darned if I didn't come up with a topper for that plain old, delicious broiled chicken!

, young, tender broiler	Salt
1 clove garlic	Freshly ground pepper
Lime juice, fresh	Dried tarragon
Butter	3 oz. French (dry) vermouth

Have your butcher clean and split a young and tender broiling chicken, weighing about 1½ to 2 pounds. Rub halves of chicken all over with a cut clove of garlic. Place the halves in a shallow broiling pan, skin side down, sprinkle with fresh lime juice, salt and freshly ground pepper, dot liberally with butter, and pour into the broiling pan about 2 ounces of dry (French) vermouth. Place about 4 inches below a medium broiler flame. As the chicken begins to brown, baste it with the vermouth, turn the halves skin side up, sprinkle with fresh lime juice, salt and freshly ground pepper, dried tarragon, and dot liberally with butter. When the skin side begins to brown, baste with the vermouth, and turn again. As the chicken cooks, continue to baste, adding more vermouth as is necessary, and turning to prevent over-browning. When the chicken is done, about 50 minutes to an hour, depending upon size of chicken, the halves should be nicely browned all over, and the juice practically cooked away. Remove the chicken halves to hot plates. Add a little more vermouth to the pan, stir it around to absorb any brownness, and pour the juices over each chicken half. This recipe serves 2. To my mind, this is broiled chicken at the peak of perfection, with a flavor that is indescribable.

The Coahoma Woman's Club of Coahoma, Mississippi, is composed of women from towns throughout Coahoma County, in the heart of what is known as the "Delta"; a section of low, flat land of rich fertility stretching from Memphis, Tennessee, to Vicksburg, Mississippi. It is bounded on one side by the Mississippi River, and on the other by a series of small waterways emptying into the Yazoo River. There are no cities of any size, but the towns are connected by cotton plantations, so the region is, in spirit, one large community. Consequently the people are closely related in interests and modes of living. The Deltans have two aims in life: a comfortable, pleasureful existence, and raising cotton. To them the epitome of pleasure is a gathering of good friends, good liquor, good food, and hours of conversation, all in an atmosphere of leisurely informality. It has been so ever since their forebears, planters from Virginia, the Carolinas, and Georgia first settled great tracts of the fever-ridden swampland and turned them into productive plantations. The Coahoma Woman's Club published a cookbook in 1949, and it was sent to me.

There were a number of luscious recipes contained in the book, many of which had been "handed down" in families for generations. One that struck my fancy was the entree in Miss Blanche's Favorite Garden Supper—Charcoal Broiled Chicken.

CHARCOAL BROILED CHICKEN

3 *tender chickens*	½ *cup dry sherry*
Olive oil	*Salt and pepper*
1 *cup butter*	½ *cup cream*
1 *lb. fresh mushrooms*	*Beaten egg yolk*
1 *tsp. cracked black peppercorns*	*Lemon slices and parsley*

Prepare 3 chickens for broiling in the usual way (splitting in half), brush with olive oil, and lay on a barbecue grill over low coals.

In the meantime, prepare the barbecue sauce. Put the butter in a saucepan and heat. Slice the fresh mushrooms thin, and broil in the butter for 5 minutes. Add the cracked black peppercorns and dry sherry. Allow to boil up, then remove the mushrooms and set both the mushrooms and the sherry-butter aside to keep hot. As the chickens cook, turn frequently, basting with the sherry-butter mixture. When the chickens are thoroughly done, salt and pepper them, and arrange on a hot platter. Add to the sauce the cream and thicken with the beaten egg yolk. When heated, pour the mushrooms and the sauce over the chicken, and garnish the dish with lemon slices and parsley.

For the past two years I have been acting as a food consultant for the Table Products Company (a division of Safeway Stores, Inc.), among whose products is Nu Made mayonnaise. Originally, I did not accept the assignment until I had satisfied myself by numerous tests that their mayonnaise was a fine, top-quality product in every way. However, it did not take me long to discover that Nu Made mayonnaise is delicately flavored, dependably fresh, and has a richness and a creaminess that I had previously thought that only a homemade mayonnaise could have.

Over a period of many months I have been experimenting with the use of mayonnaise far beyond its usual use in salads, dressings, and so forth. For instance, I found that I could make what I have called a "mock" Hollandaise with Nu Made mayonnaise that was foolproof, and which could be kept and reheated again without losing one bit of its deliciousness. I also found many uses for mayonnaise as a shortening; as an added "plus" in sauces and gravies and egg dishes; and as a wonderful ingredient in preparing seafood dishes, meat dishes, vegetable dishes, appetizers, and chicken dishes.

About a year ago I was asked what I could do with a barbecue sauce for chicken using mayonnaise. I experimented, and after a number of tries I developed something that was really intriguing. I tried it out on my wife, and she loved it. And to me, her approval is the highest accolade I can strive for, because her praise is not given lightly.

BARBECUED CHICKEN

2 *plump broilers*
1 *cup mayonnaise*
3 *oz. dry white wine*
2 *cloves garlic, minced*
1 *tsp. dry mustard*
1 *tsp. paprika*
1 *tsp. celery salt*
½ *tsp. dried rosemary* (*or rosemary seasoning powder*)
½ *tsp. poultry seasoning*
½ *tsp. hickory smoked salt*
½ *tsp. sugar*
2 *tbsp. Worcestershire sauce*
2 *tsp. A-1 sauce*
1 *tsp. white wine tarragon vinegar*
½ *tsp. Angostura bitters*
¼ *tsp. Tabasco sauce*

Mix all the ingredients (except the broilers!) thoroughly until the sauce is well blended and very smooth.

Split the broilers, lay them in a large shallow pan, and pour the sauce over them. Let them marinate in the sauce for a couple of hours (this is not absolutely necessary, but it does improve the flavor of the final product).

If you are going to broil the chickens on an outdoor grill, or an indoors rotisserie, brush the sauce from the chickens with a dry basting brush, place them on a spit over coals, and brush them well with the sauce. As they cook, baste them with the sauce about every 5 minutes until the chickens are done.

The chickens can be cooked under a range broiler. In this method, place the brushed-off chicken halves on the broiler rack at least 3 inches from the flame or heat, which should be rather low, and brush them with the sauce. Turn them about every 5 or 6 minutes, brushing well with the sauce each time. Watch them to see that they don't scorch—if they brown too quickly, lower them, or turn down the flame. They should broil for about 50 minutes. This serves 4, unless you apportion a quarter of a chicken to each person. But that would be for the birds, and I'm not kidding!

Latin America, contrary to accepted American thinking, has a heritage of fine European cuisine. To their gourmets, the eating of fine food and the service of fine wines is truly one of the fine arts.

During one of the conferences of food editors in Chicago at the Drake Hotel, the Pan American Coffee Bureau gave a Latin American dinner for those attending the conference. It was not only unusual, but delicious beyond words. From start to finish it was typically Latin American, starting with *Crema de Esparragos* (cream of asparagus soup) and ending with *Helado Mocca con Nueces del Brazil* (coffee ice cream topped with Brazil nuts). The entree was *Pollo al Vino,* which is chicken in wine with a chestnut and shrimp stuffing.

But you don't have to make a trip to South America to enjoy this wonderful chicken dish. Here's how you can make it right in your own home.

POLLO AL VINO

1 4- to 5-lb. roasting chicken	½ cup chopped mushrooms
¾ cup port wine	1½ cups raw shelled shrimp
¼ lb. butter	½ tsp. dried tarragon
⅓ cup grated onion pulp	¼ cup golden raisins
¼ tsp. garlic salt	¼ cup seedless raisins
¼ tsp. freshly ground pepper	1 can chicken broth
3 tbsp. minced celery	Fine breadcrumbs
3 tbsp. chopped chestnuts	Flour and butter roux

Clean one 4- to 5-pound roasting chicken carefully, and pat with a dry towel. Moisten thoroughly inside and out with the port wine, season lightly, and allow it to remain in the refrigerator overnight.

To make the stuffing, heat ¼ pound of butter in a skillet, then add the grated onion pulp (scrape an onion with a teaspoon to get onion pulp), garlic salt, and freshly ground black pepper. Sauté this lightly, then add the minced celery, the coarsely chopped roasted chestnuts, coarsely chopped mushrooms, raw shelled small shrimp, and the chopped tarragon (or dried tarragon). Sauté the whole for about 10 minutes until the shrimps are lightly colored (you can substitute crab meat or lobster for the shrimp). Now add the golden raisins and seedless raisins, and enough fine dry bread-crumbs to make a stuffing that is not too moist. Stuff the chicken with this mixture, and truss the chicken. Place the chicken in a pot and cover with the chicken stock, diluted according to directions, which should cover the chicken. Simmer gently until almost tender. Then remove the chicken to a roasting pan and roast in a 375-degree oven, until lightly browned, basting occasionally with the remaining stock. Serve with saffron rice and gravy made from the stock, which can be thickened slightly with a flour and butter *roux*.

Russians, of course, are great users of sour cream, and it is found in a great many of their recipes. One of their famous sauces is Smitane, composed of sour cream, white wine, and onions. This sauce is particularly good on game and chicken. One of the most delightful and delicate chicken dishes I know of is Breast of Chicken Smitane.

BREAST OF CHICKEN SMITANE

6 *half chicken breasts*	3 *small onions*
Brandy	4 *mushrooms*
Salt	*Cayenne pepper*
Freshly ground pepper	1 *cup dry white wine*
Powdered rosemary	2 *cups sour cream*
5 *oz. butter*	1 *tbsp. lemon juice*
	Dash Worcestershire sauce

Halve 3 full chicken breasts (or buy 6 halves) and rub them with brandy. Let them stand for about an hour, then rub them with a mixture of salt and pepper, to which a generous pinch of powdered rosemary has been added.

Heat 3 ounces of butter in a skillet, and when it is foaming, sauté the chicken breasts over a gentle flame until they are nicely browned and tender. Remove the breasts to a heated platter, or keep hot in a warm oven.

In a saucepan melt 2 ounces of butter, and when hot, add the onions, chopped, the mushrooms, chopped, and a dash each of salt and cayenne pepper. Sauté until the onions and mushrooms are tender. Then add the dry white wine, the sour cream, the lemon juice, and a dash of Worcestershire sauce. Simmer gently, un-covered, for about 20 minutes, or until the sauce is reduced to the consistency of heavy cream. Correct the seasoning of salt and cay-enne pepper if necessary. Put the sauce through a sieve, and pour over the chicken breasts.

The classic chicken dish of old Russia is Chicken Kiev, or *Côte-lettes Kiev* (*côtelettes* is French for cutlets), or Breast of Chicken, Kiev. It is a very swank dish, usually found only on the menus of expensive restaurants.

In its original form, I believe, Chicken Kiev is simply boned chicken breasts flattened out, and rolled around a piece of sweet butter. It is then rolled in beaten eggs, breadcrumbs, and fried in butter or oil. Of course, different chefs have different versions of the dish, but I think the following recipe, which I devised, is the most savory of any I have ever tasted. I know that sounds immodest, but then, it's only my opinion, plus, however, the opinion of gourmet friends who have tasted it.

BREAST OF CHICKEN KIEV

3 *large chicken breasts*	2 *tbsp. chopped parsley*
6 *mushrooms, finely chopped*	*Salt and pepper*
Butter	2 *eggs*
½ *lb. sweet butter*	1 *tbsp. vodka*
1 *clove garlic*	*Fine breadcrumbs*

Remove the bones and skin from 3 large chicken breasts and cut away all gristle (or have the butcher do this for you). Separate the 2 halves of each breast, making 6 half breasts. Place each half breast between 2 sheets of waxed paper, and flatten with the flat side of a cleaver or a wooden mallet. They should somewhat re-semble thin pancakes.

Sauté the finely chopped mushrooms in 1 tablespoon of butter for about 5 minutes, or until tender.

Let ½ pound of sweet (unsalted) butter come to about room temperature. Then cream together the sweet butter, the clove of garlic, finely minced, the chopped parsley, and the sautéed chopped mushrooms until smooth. Chill in the refrigerator until firm enough to handle, then shape the seasoned butter into 6 oval rolls about 2½ to 3 inches long and ¾ to 1 inch wide at the thickest part. Place these rolls into water with ice, and let them remain until hard.

Sprinkle a very little salt and pepper on each flattened half breast of chicken. Remove the butter rolls from the water and ice, quickly dry each, and place 1 roll on each of the flattened chicken breasts. Roll the chicken around the butter roll, folding the ends in so that the butter rolls are completely encased. Watch this carefully, because if the rolls are not completely encased, the butter will leak out as it melts, and all your work has gone for naught. Secure the rolled chicken breasts with wooden toothpicks.

Lightly beat 2 eggs with the vodka. Roll the rolled-up chicken breasts in fine breadcrumbs, then in the beaten eggs, and again in breadcrumbs. Fry in plenty of butter until the rolls are golden brown, making certain that the butter they are fried in is not too hot, as if it is, the outside of the rolls will brown before the chicken has a chance to cook thoroughly. When the rolls are golden brown, drain them on paper toweling, and place in a hot oven for about 5 minutes. Serve at once.

My good friend and culinary confrere, Emily Chase Leistner, of Stockton, California, is not only a brilliant home economist and foods consultant, but is also a raconteur. During her career she has had many amusing experiences, but I think the one that tops them all is the following.

Emily and her husband were invited to dinner with friends. "Come to dinner Saturday night at seven," they were told. When they arrived on schedule, the house was practically dark! Many rings of the doorbell finally brought the host and hostess . . . in full bedtime regalia, obviously unprepared for company.

"You're a week early," the Leistners were informed, and, to put it mildly, they felt pretty foolish. But nothing would do but the Leistners must come in anyway, which they finally did. However, in a matter of minutes two more couples arrived, and the Leistners began to be suspicious rather than uncomfortable. It looked like a put-up job. The fact that a tour of the kitchen produced no evidence of anything resembling a dinner added to their confusion. And then, as someone suggested scrambled eggs all around, the mystery was solved. A sumptuous Scalloped Chicken Casserole was produced from the refrigerator, along with a jug of previously mixed dry martinis. The casserole was whisked into the oven, and by the time the libations were consumed, it was ready for the table, which had been quietly set by the teenage daughter. The Leistners said they had never enjoyed an evening more.

Perhaps this little anecdote will give you an idea for a similar surprise party. Here's the recipe for the dish, which may be assembled
ahead of time, and baked just before serving.

SCALLOPED CHICKEN CASSEROLE

Chicken

1 4- to 5-lb. stewing chicken	2 onions, quartered
Boiling water	2 stalks celery
2 tsp. Ac'cent	2 tbsp. chopped parsley
1 tbsp. salt	1 tbsp. peppercorns

Stuffing

¼ cup chopped onion	½ tsp. Ac'cent
¼ cup chopped celery	¾ tsp. salt
¼ cup chicken fat or butter	¼ tsp. pepper
6 cups soft breadcrumbs	1½ tsp. poultry seasoning
¼ cup chicken broth	

Sauce

½ cup chicken fat or butter	⅓ cup dry sherry
½ cup flour	Salt and pepper
2¼ cups chicken broth	Celery salt
2 eggs, lightly beaten	Paprika

Place the stewing chicken, including the giblets, in a large kettle and
barely cover with boiling water. Add the Ac'cent, salt, onions, celery, parsley, and peppercorns. Bring to a boil, then cover and simmer for 2½ to 3 hours, or until chicken is tender. Let the chicken
cool in the broth, then separate the meat from the bones and remove
skin. Cut the meat in good-sized pieces; grind the skin or cut fine
with scissors; and grind or chop the giblets. Strain the broth, and
skim off fat.

To make the stuffing, sauté the onion and celery gently in chicken
fat or butter for 5 minutes in a saucepan. Add the mixture to the
breadcrumbs (use at least day-old bread), then add the Ac'cent,
salt, pepper, poultry seasoning, and chicken broth. Toss gently until
well mixed.

To make the sauce, melt the chicken fat or butter in a saucepan
and blend in the flour. Then add the chicken broth and cook, stirring constantly, until the mixture boils and thickens. Remove from

the heat. Stir a little of the hot sauce into the lightly beaten eggs, then stir this mixture back into the remaining sauce. Add the dry sherry and ground chicken skin, and season to taste with the salt, celery salt and pepper.

To assemble the dish, spread all but 1 cup of the stuffing over the bottom of a greased shallow baking dish (12 x 8 x 2 inches). Over the stuffing arrange the pieces of chicken. Pour the sauce over the chicken, and then sprinkle the reserved cup of stuffing over the top and dust with paprika. Bake in a 375-degree oven for 30 minutes. This will serve 6 to 8.

As mentioned, this dish may be assembled ahead of time, and when cool placed in the refrigerator. In such a case allow about 35 to 40 minutes for it to bake in the oven before serving.

By and large, I'm not overly fond of stewed chicken, or chicken fricassee, unless it is made at home. I guess I was spoiled when I was a youngster—I can still remember Sunday down on Grandmother's farm, when the standard dinner was tender, succulent chicken swimming in rich fricassee gravy, and gobs of fluffy baking-powder biscuits. And if there wasn't quite enough chicken for second helpings, there was plenty of the gravy to ladle over the biscuits. That was eating!

In the Baltic countries they used to make a chicken stew that was unusual, and very delicious. The original of the following recipe came from Riga, Latvia.

BALTIC CHICKEN STEW

1 4-lb. chicken	Salt
Seasoned flour	Pepper
3 oz. butter	Chicken liver, finely chopped
1 carrot, diced	1 tbsp. drained capers
1 onion, diced	3 cups condensed consommé
1 parsnip, diced	1 cup dry red wine
Pinch dried basil	½ lb. mushrooms, sliced
Pinch dried thyme	Flour
Pinch dried marjoram	Butter

Cut the chicken up as for fricassee, and shake the pieces in a paper bag containing seasoned flour. In an iron skillet melt 3 ounces of butter, and when the butter is hot put the chicken pieces in and sauté them to a golden brown on all sides, about 15 minutes. Then remove the chicken pieces and keep them warm. In the same skillet put the diced carrot, diced onion, and diced parsnip, and sauté these vegetables for about 15 minutes. If necessary, add a little more butter to the skillet.

Now put the chicken pieces and the vegetables in a stewing pot or pan, add dried basil, thyme, and marjoram, salt and pepper to taste, the chicken liver (finely chopped), the drained capers, condensed consommé, and dry red wine. Cook gently for about 45 minutes, then add the sliced fresh mushrooms. Let the whole cook for about 15 minutes more, then remove the chicken pieces to a hot platter, and keep warm. Slightly thicken the sauce with a little flour blended with soft butter (equal amounts of each), boil the sauce up, and then pour it over the chicken. Plain buttered noodles make an excellent companion.

Every once in a while, through my syndicated column, "For Men Only!" I am fortunate in receiving a wonderful recipe from my readers. Gilbert E. Coble, of Garrett, Indiana, sent me a recipe for what he called just plain chicken with rice. In his letter accompanying the recipe he said:

I welcome this opportunity to tell you that I look forward to each of your articles, and I enjoy trying the dishes you give the directions for making. There is nothing I enjoy more than experimenting with foods, and "springing" the results on my friends. The enclosed recipe has received a great deal of praise.

CHICKEN WITH RICE

1 4-*lb. roasting chicken*	3 *cups chicken broth*
⅔ *cup olive oil*	1 *cup dry white wine*
1 *green pepper*	1½ *tsp. salt*
1 *Spanish onion*	⅛ *tsp. pepper*
2 *cloves garlic*	1½ *tsp. paprika*
2 *whole canned tomatoes*	1 *cup raw rice*
1 *slice cured ham, cut ½ inch*	½ *cup pimiento*
thick	*Stuffed olives, sliced*

Clean and disjoint the roasting chicken. Slowly brown in the olive oil. Remove the chicken. Cut the green pepper and Spanish onion in eighths, and sauté in the olive oil with 2 cloves of chopped garlic. When the onions and pepper are tender, add the tomatoes and 1 slice of cured ham (½ inch thick) which has been cut in cubes.

Cook 10 minutes, then add the chicken, and 4 cups of boiling water. (At this point I deviated, and added 3 cups of chicken consommé and 1 cup of dry American white wine.) Bring to the boiling point, cover, and simmer for 35 minutes. Then add the salt, pepper, and paprika. Cook 20 minutes longer, or until the chicken can be boned. Remove the chicken, add the rice, and cook 30 minutes, stirring occasionally. Then add the pimientos, and the chicken meat. Let this simmer very slowly for about 10 minutes, then place on a hot serving platter or dish, and garnish with sliced stuffed olives.

Chicken pie is not a dish that I would order in a restaurant, no matter how excellent the cuisine happened to be. I am very, very fond of chicken pie, and one of my favorite "in a hurry" dishes is a frozen chicken pie. There are a few brands on the market today that are most appetizing, although I have found Swanson's Frozen Chicken (and Beef) Pies to be the best. I usually keep about four of each in the freezer, and when you want a simple meal without any bother or fuss, it is so easy to take one out of the freezer, stick it in the oven, and in 40 minutes or so it is ready to eat.

But a real, old-fashioned chicken pie is a work of art, and nothing can touch it to my way of thinking. Somehow, it sort of takes me back to my grandmother's farm, where it was a frequently served dish, made with freshly killed chickens, garden fresh vegetables, and thick cream. If you've ever eaten the dish out in the country, I think this version will have a nostalgic effect on you.

OLD FASHIONED CHICKEN PIE

1 4- to 5-lb. stewing hen
1 cup dry white wine
Water
1 large onion
3 stalks celery
1 sprig parsley
1 bay leaf
6 peppercorns
Pinch dried marjoram
12 small white onions
6 small carrots

1 pkg. frozen baby lima beans
½ lb. fresh mushrooms
2 tbsp. butter
2 tbsp. flour
1 tsp. Worcestershire sauce
1 tsp. grated lemon rind
2 egg yolks
½ cup cream
Rich pastry crust
1 egg
2 tbsp. cream

Salt and pepper

Cut the stewing hen into pieces. Put into a pot, add the dry white wine and enough water to cover. Also add 1 large onion, peeled and cut in quarters, stalks of celery (and leaves), sprig of parsley, bay leaf, peppercorns, pinch of dried marjoram, and 2 teaspoons of salt. Bring to a boil, then lower the flame and simmer for about 2 hours, or until the chicken is tender. Let the chicken cool in the broth. Then take the chicken pieces out, remove the skin, and separate the meat from the bones, cutting it in fairly good-sized pieces. Then strain the broth and reserve, discarding the solids.

Boil the whole tiny white onions and small carrots in a little salted water for about 15 to 20 minutes, or until just tender. Also cook a package of frozen baby lima beans according to directions on package.

In a saucepan sauté the sliced fresh mushrooms in the butter for about 6 minutes. Then blend in the flour, and add 2 cups of the strained chicken broth, the Worcestershire sauce, and grated lemon rind. Cook, stirring constantly, until it thickens. Beat the egg yolks with the cream, take the saucepan off the fire, add salt and pepper to taste if necessary, and stir this into the mushroom sauce.

Arrange the tiny onions, the carrots (cut in 1-inch pieces), the baby lima beans, and the chicken meat in a casserole or baking dish, and pour the mushroom sauce over all. Cover the casserole with a rich pie crust, slitting the top of the dough before baking to allow the steam to escape. Brush the dough with a mixture of 1 egg slightly beaten with 2 tablespoons of cream to give the crust a rich color when done. Place in a 425-degree oven until crust is golden brown, about 25 minutes. This recipe will serve about 6.

To most people the word curry brings to mind India and the Far East. Actually, curry is a condiment compounded from several spicy ingredients, such as coriander seeds, ground turmeric, cumin seed, ground ginger, black pepper, ground fenugreek, ground chilies, and other spices. It is so commonly used that it has been called the "salt of the Orient."

Today, in America, curry powder may be obtained in almost any grocery store, but many of the brands are a far cry from genuine Indian curry powder. In India and the Far East curry powder is prepared as needed from day to day from fresh ingredients. However, genuine curry powder may be obtained in high-class specialty food shops, but the cost is high. One of the best domestic curry powders is put out by the Spice Islands Company and, like all of their herbs and spices, it is excellent.

The curries most frequently encountered in the Far East are shellfish curries, chicken curries, and vegetable curries. Incidentally, curries should always be served in separate dishes, and never with rice as a border, but as a separate dish. They are usually eaten with a dessert spoon and a fork, and a well-prepared curry will never need a knife.

In my *With a Jug of Wine* I have detailed three delicious curries —an East Indian Shrimp Curry, a Lamb Curry, and a Capon and Lobster Curry. In this volume I have added one or two others, among them, a real Chicken Curry. In devising this curry, I have deviated from a true Indian curry in that I have used wine, which is, of course, forbidden to Moslems.

CHICKEN CURRY

1 4- to 5-lb. chicken	2 onions
Water	1 tomato
1 large onion, quartered	4 tbsp. flour
4 cloves	2 tbsp. curry powder
1 carrot, large	¼ tsp. ground cardamom
3 stalks celery	½ tsp. ground ginger
2 tbsp. chopped parsley	½ tsp. salt
8 peppercorns	½ tsp. freshly ground pepper
1 bay leaf	4 cups chicken broth
1 tsp. salt	1 lime (juice and grated rind)
Dry white wine	¼ cup seedless raisins
4 oz. butter	½ cup grated coconut
1 clove garlic	2 tbsp. Major Gray's chutney
1 apple, green	(chopped)
½ cup cream	

Cut up the chicken into serving pieces and put into a pot. Cover with water, and add the large onion, quartered, sticking into each quarter a whole clove, the carrot cut in 1-inch pieces, the stalks of celery with their leaves, the chopped parsley, peppercorns, bay leaf, and 1 teaspoon of salt. Cook, but do not boil, closely covered, until the chicken is tender, 2 hours or more depending upon the age of your bird. Then, when cool, discard the chicken skin and remove the meat from the bones, cutting the meat in medium-sized pieces. Strain the broth, and reserve. You will need about 4 cups. If necessary, add enough dry white wine to the broth to make up the 4 cups.

Melt the butter in a large skillet, adding the minced clove of garlic. When the butter is hot add the green apple, peeled and chopped, 2 onions, sliced, and the tomato, seeded and chopped. Cover, and smother this mixture about 10 to 15 minutes, or until the vegetables are soft, but not browned.

Mix together the flour, curry powder, ground cardamom, ground ginger, ½ teaspoon of salt, and the freshly ground pepper. Sprinkle this dry mixture over the sautéed vegetables in the skillet, mixing well, and cook for about 5 minutes, stirring constantly until all is well blended. Then slowly add the chicken broth, the juice and grated rind of 1 fresh lime, and the seedless raisins. Let all this simmer for 20 to 30 minutes.

To the sauce add the chicken meat, the grated coconut, the cream, and the chutney. Mix gently and let this heat thoroughly for about 15 minutes over a very low flame. The sauce should be thick and rich.

Serve with a big bowl of fluffy rice, and accompany with any or all of the following curry adjuncts—crisp chopped bacon, chopped hard-cooked eggs, chopped peanuts, chopped cashew nuts, chutney sauce, chopped little green onions, finely chopped orange peel, Bombay duck (a small dried salted fish, which is packed in tins), freshly grated coconut, and oven-heated raisins.

A word as to serving. After you have distributed the curry over the rice, sprinkle the curry and rice with a teaspoon of whichever the condiments you desire. Mix all together with your spoon and fork, and fall to with a will!

This may sound strange, but it is nevertheless true. In the Far East, where the weather is very hot, the natives dress in the sheerest of clothes and eat hot dishes to cool off. And believe me, Far Eastern curries are really hot.

So, taking a tip from the Far East, try a Bombay curry in a chafing dish on some hot summer day or evening. This recipe is much simpler than the preceding chicken curry, but most delightful.

BOMBAY CHICKEN CURRY IN A CHAFING DISH

½ roasted chicken

2 oz. butter

½ clove garlic, minced

½ apple, chopped

1 tsp. chopped onion

1 tbsp. shredded coconut

¼ tsp. English mustard

1 tbsp. curry powder

1 heaping tsp. flour

1 cup chicken broth

Pinch ground cardamom

Pinch ground ginger

3 tbsp. sour cream

¼ tsp. lemon juice

Remove the skin and remove the meat from the bones of half a roasted chicken, and cut the meat in small pieces (you can use a medium-sized can of boned chicken).

In the blazer of your chafing dish melt the butter and add the minced garlic. When the butter is hot, add the chopped apple and chopped onion. Fry for a few minutes, and then add the coconut and the English mustard, the curry powder mixed with the flour. Mix well, and cook for about 3 or 4 minutes, stirring constantly to blend well. Then add the chicken broth and a small pinch each of powdered ginger and powdered cardamom. Stir well, and when it boils, remove the blazer from the fire and add the chicken.

Put the water jacket, with boiling water in it, over the flame, and put the blazer and its contents in the water jacket, and simmer the curry for about 10 to 15 minutes, or until it is thoroughly heated. Add the sour cream and ¼ teaspoon of lemon juice, blend, let heat, and then serve.

I have previously mentioned Max I. Mori, the accomplished chef of the Kona Inn on the island of Hawaii. He also appreciates a fine curry, and in his little book of famous recipes, he includes Chicken Currie à la Mori, which is delicious.

CHICKEN CURRIE À LA MORI

1 plump chicken, 4 lbs.

Salted water

2 coconuts (meat)

1½ cups milk

¼ lb. butter

2 large onions

1 clove garlic

½ cup flour

2 tbsp. curry powder

1 tsp. salt

2 cups chicken broth

2 cups heavy cream

1 cup drained mushrooms

Chicken liver

Chicken gizzard

1 tsp. Ac'cent

¼ cup dry white wine

Cut the chicken into serving pieces, place in a pot, cover with slightly salted water, and cook until the chicken is tender, about 2 hours. When cool, remove the chicken pieces, discard the skin, and remove the meat from the bones. Reserve the chicken meat, broth, and chicken liver and the chicken gizzard, both of which should be chopped.

Prepare 2 cups of fresh coconut milk by grating the meat from 2 fresh coconuts, and soak the grated coconut meat in the milk for about an hour. Then strain the coconut milk through a cheesecloth, and squeeze the grated coconut into the coconut milk until all the liquid has been extracted. Reserve the coconut milk.

Melt the butter, and in it sauté the chopped onions and chopped garlic until onions are limp, but not browned. Then add the flour which has been thoroughly mixed with the curry powder and the salt. Cook, stirring constantly, for about 5 minutes. Then slowly add 2 cups of the chicken broth, the heavy cream, and the 2 cups of coconut milk, previously prepared. Cook, stirring constantly for about 10 minutes, or until the sauce is smooth and free from lumps.

Remove the sauce from the heat and place in the top of a double boiler. Add the chicken meat, the drained mushrooms, the chopped liver and gizzard. Let this simmer for 2 hours.

Before serving, add the Ac'cent (Chef Mori uses the Japanese Ajinomoto powder, which is the same as Ac'cent) and the dry white wine. When all is hot, serve with flaky rice.

When I was in New York a few years ago, I discovered the Divan Parisien Restaurant, which was then on East Forty-fifth Street. They had a specialty that is worth the price of a trip to New York, Chicken Divan. I was so taken with the dish that I finally persuaded John Paffrath, one of the proprietors, to give me the recipe.

On my last trip to New York I found that the Divan Parisien had moved from its old address, and is now located in the Chatham Hotel, at Forty-eighth and Vanderbilt.

CHICKEN DIVAN

1 *boiled chicken*	½ *tsp. Worcestershire sauce*
Broccoli	*Grated Parmesan cheese*
½ *cup melted butter*	*Salt*
½ *cup flour*	*Freshly ground pepper*
2 *cups chicken broth*	*Dry sherry wine*
1 *cup whipped cream*	1 *cup Hollandaise sauce*

Boil a fairly large chicken in slightly salted water until tender. Discard skin, remove the meat from bones, and slice.

Cook about 3 large bunches of broccoli in salted water until tender, drain, and keep warm.

Next, prepare the sauce. Melt the butter in a saucepan, or top of a double boiler, and blend in the flour. When smooth, slowly add the chicken broth, and cook, stirring constantly, until thick and smooth. Then fold in the whipped cream, and add the Worcestershire sauce, 2 tablespoons of grated Parmesan cheese, 2 ounces of sherry, and salt and freshly ground pepper to taste. Last of all, add 1 cup of Hollandaise (or mock Hollandaise) sauce.

Cover a large ovenproof platter with a layer of the cooked broccoli. Then cover the broccoli with slices of the cooked chicken meat. Next, pour over all the sauce. Sprinkle the whole liberally with grated Parmesan cheese, and place under the broiler until the cheese is nicely browned. Before serving, dash dry sherry liberally over the top.

A somewhat similar dish is Chicken à l'Almonde. This is prepared with diced cooked chicken and asparagus, but with the addition of chopped almonds. It is at its delicate best if fresh asparagus is used, and freshly cooked chicken. But it can still be delicious if canned boned chicken is used, and frozen asparagus instead of the fresh.

CHICKEN À L'ALMONDE

1½ lbs. fresh asparagus or 2 pkgs. frozen	4 tbsp. flour
2 cups diced cooked chicken	½ tsp. Ac'cent
4 tbsp. butter	1 tsp. salt
½ cup chopped blanched almonds	Dash white pepper
	1 cup chicken stock
	1 cup milk
Paprika	

Cook and drain the fresh asparagus, or cook the frozen asparagus according to directions on the package. Cut the asparagus in 1-inch pieces, and arrange on the bottom of a shallow baking dish. On top of the layer of asparagus, place the diced cooked chicken.

Prepare the sauce. Heat the butter in a saucepan and add the finely chopped blanched almonds. Simmer for 3 minutes, and then add the flour, the Ac'cent, the salt, and the white pepper. Stir until well blended, then remove from the heat. Add slowly, stirring carefully to keep smooth, the chicken broth and the milk. Cook over moderate heat, stirring constantly, until the mixture thickens and comes to a boil. Boil gently for ½ minute.

Pour the sauce over the chicken and asparagus, sprinkle with paprika, and bake in a 375-degree oven for about 25 minutes. This should serve 6.

The Chinese also have a delightfully delicate-flavored dish with almonds, chicken, Chinese vegetables, and rice. It makes an attractive "one main dish type meal," and is easily served to a crowd. All the ingredients are available in almost any grocery store.

CHINESE CHICKEN ALMOND WITH RICE

1 *cup uncooked rice*
½ *cup blanched almonds*
3 *tbsp. salad oil*
1 *clove garlic, cut in half*
1 *tsp. salt*
1 *cup diced cooked chicken*
1 *cup canned bamboo shoots*

½ *cup sliced fresh mushrooms*
1 *tbsp. liquid from bamboo*
   shoots
1 *tbsp. liquid from water*
   chestnuts
½ *cup canned water chestnuts,*
   sliced

½ *cup thinly sliced celery*

Gravy
2 *tsp. cornstarch*
½ *tsp. sugar*
Salt

4 *tbsp. water*
4 *tsp. soy sauce*
½ *cup sliced green onion*

Cook the rice according to your favorite method.

Brown the blanched almonds in 1 tablespoon of oil, and set aside.

With a fork mash the halved garlic into the salt in a skillet. Then add 1 tablespoon of oil, and the chicken. Brown the chicken lightly. Then add 1 tablespoon of oil, and the bamboo shoots and mushrooms. Brown these lightly, then add the liquid from the bamboo shoots and water chestnuts. Cover tightly, and cook over a low heat for 5 minutes. Uncover, and add the water chestnuts, thinly sliced, the celery, and ¼ cup of browned almonds. Just heat through, as the celery and water chestnuts should remain crisp.

For the gravy, shake up in a small jar the cornstarch, salt, sugar, water, and soy sauce. Stir this into the above mixture, and cook until the liquid thickens and is smooth. Sprinkle over the dish the green onions and the rest of the browned almonds. Serve with hot, fluffy cooked rice. This will serve 4 persons.

That leftover part of a Virginia ham, the remains of Sunday's roast chicken, and other leftovers often have a way of staying in a refrigerator for days—and finally being thrown away.

Here's a recipe to end THAT particular annoyance for all time. It is equally helpful to the bachelor girl whose culinary efforts are confined to the kitchenette unit of a city apartment. A slice of ham, a small can or a few pieces of roast chicken, picked up at her neighborhood delicatessen, will provide the basis for a delectable Sunday night supper or an emergency meal for last-minute guests.

CHICKEN TRAFALGAR

2 *thin slices cooked ham*	1½ *cups cream or evaporated*
6 *slices stewed or roast chicken*	*milk*
18 *mushroom caps*	1 *tsp. Angostura aromatic*
¼ *cup butter*	*bitters*
1 *tbsp. flour*	*Buttered toast*

The ham should be sliced rather thin. Use left over cooked ham or buy the sliced boiled ham sold in grocery stores. Cut each slice into three pieces and sauté with chicken and mushroom caps in the butter. Arrange buttered toast on serving dish. Place pieces of ham on toast, then a slice of chicken (preferably white meat). Remove mushrooms from pan. To butter remaining, add one tablespoon flour, blend well, then add cream or evaporated milk. Bring slowly to a boil, stirring constantly. Cook to thicken slightly, then add Angostura and pour over the chicken. Top with the mushrooms. This recipe will make 6 individual servings.

I don't suppose there are many people who have not savored the deliciousness of Fritos. In the Wood household we always have a supply on hand to munch on at cocktail time, along with salted nuts, or snacks of cheese.

But somehow I had never thought of using them for cooking, until Emily Chase Leistner passed on (via *New Notes in Cooking*) a recipe that had been sent to her by Nell Morris, the director of Fritos Consumer Service, in Dallas, Texas. I tried it, and it is really out of this world.

FRITOS CHICKEN PATTIES

3 *tbsp. butter*	¼ *tsp. garlic salt*
6 *tbsp. flour*	1 *cup diced cooked chicken*
1 *cup milk*	2 *cups finely crushed Fritos*
½ *tsp. salt*	(*measured after crushing*)
½ *tsp. Ac'cent*	2 *eggs, beaten*
	Butter

Make a white sauce of the butter, flour, and milk, then add the salt, Ac'cent, garlic salt, the finely chopped cooked chicken, and ¾ cup of crushed Fritos. Cool, then form into flat cakes. Dip the cakes into the beaten eggs, and then roll in the remaining Fritos. Dip into the beaten eggs again, and again roll in the crushed Fritos. Then fry in butter until brown. Serves 4.

Hash has been debased in so many restaurants and homes that the average individual is very skittish about it. Books on humor are full of jokes about hash, such as the following:

Two men sat down at the counter of a restaurant. The first man said to the waiter, "Bring me a plate of hash."

The waiter called out to the kitchen, "Gent wants to take a chance."

The second man said, "I'll have some hash too."

This time the waiter called out, "Another sport!"

But hash can be a very elegant dish. If I am not mistaken, hash went high hat when chicken hash became one of Walter Winchell's favorite dishes in the Stork Club in New York.

Certainly Chicken Hash Parmentier is a tantalizing delicacy. It gets its name from the man who introduced the potato to France in 1786, Parmentier. All dishes bearing his name denote that potatoes have been embodied in the dish.

CHICKEN HASH PARMENTIER

2 *oz. butter*	*Salt and pepper*
1 *onion, chopped*	*Paprika*
½ *cup sliced mushrooms*	1 *cup cream*
2 *cups diced cooked chicken*	½ *cup cream sauce*
Duchesse Potatoes	*Mornay sauce*	*Grated Parmesan cheese*

Melt the butter in a saucepan, and when hot add the finely chopped onion and the thinly sliced mushrooms. Sauté for about 7 minutes, or until the onions are limp, but not browned. Then add the diced chicken, salt and pepper to taste, a sprinkling of paprika, and the cream. Simmer until the cream is reduced to half the original quantity, and then add the cream sauce, and blend everything well.

On a heatproof serving platter, make a border of Duchesse Potatoes with a pastry bag, and lightly brown under the broiler. Then place the chicken hash in the center, and cover with a Mornay sauce. Sprinkle grated Parmesan cheese over all, and brown under a hot broiler. This serves 4.

Duchesse Potatoes are riced boiled potatoes to which eggs and butter are added rather than milk, as in ordinary mashed potatoes. The recipe will be found in the chapter on potatoes.

Mornay sauce is a cream sauce to which cheese has been added. The recipe will be found in any basic cookbook.

If you've ever visited any of the Dutch communities in Pennsylvania, you may have partaken of Chicken Bott Boi, which is Pennsylvania Dutch for chicken pot pie. It is somewhat similar to American pot pie, but it has no crust. It is a one-dish meal that is not only easy to prepare, but inexpensive and unbelievably delicious.

Pennsylvania Dutch are divided into several sects or faiths, the more interesting being known as Amish, Mennonites, and Dunkards. The Amish came into prominence fairly recently through that delightful musical, *Plain and Fancy*.

These sects refuse to yield to such modern conveniences as telephone, electric lights, electric ranges, refrigerators, plumbing, automobiles, and so forth. However, one thing that is typical of the Pennsylvania Dutch is delicious food and plenty of it. They work hard, play their quaint games enthusiastically, and eat heartily. In fact, eating is one of their greatest pleasures, and any occasion—work, play, funeral, wedding, or barn-raising—is an excuse for a sumptuous meal.

Of the hundreds of main dishes placed on the table by the Pennsylvania Dutch, Chicken Bott Boi is probably the most popular. Noodles are one of the main ingredients of this dish, but they are different from the long, narrow noodles most people are familiar with. They are slightly thicker, each measures about 2 by 2½ inches, and are made from durum flour and egg yolks.

CHICKEN BOTT BOI

½ lb. Dutch noodles
1 tbsp. salt
3 quarts boiling water
3 tbsp. bacon drippings
1 cup chopped celery
½ cup diced green pepper
1 10½-oz. can cream of
 mushroom soup

¼ cup diced pimento
6 oz. chicken broth
2 oz. dry white wine
3 dashes Worcestershire sauce
4 oz. sharp Cheddar cheese
2 5½-oz. cans boned chicken
1 tsp. salt
Freshly ground pepper

Grated Parmesan cheese

Add 1 tablespoon of salt to 3 quarts of rapidly boiling water. Gradually add ½ pound noodles so that the water continues to boil. Cook uncovered, stirring occasionally, until tender—about 30 minutes.

While the noodles are boiling, melt the bacon grease in a large heavy skillet. When hot, add the chopped celery and diced green pepper, and cook until they are soft. Then add the cream of mushroom soup, diced pimento, clear chicken stock (or canned chicken bouillon), dry white wine, the Worcestershire sauce, and the grated sharp Cheddar cheese. Cook over a low heat, stirring occasionally, until the cheese is melted. Then add the boned chicken or turkey, or one of each, shredding the meat as it comes out of the can with a fork. (If you have left over cooked chicken or turkey, use that in the amount of 1½ or 2 cups.) Drain the noodles and add them to the mixture in the skillet. Sprinkle over the whole 1 teaspoon of salt and freshly ground pepper to taste.

When the noodles and the meat-vegetable mixture is well blended, pour it into a casserole or glass baking dish. Sprinkle the top generously with grated Parmesan cheese, and bake in a moderate oven (350 degrees) for about 25 minutes. Serves 4 to 6.

Here is a dish you can assemble fairly quickly, utilizing ingredients mostly that might be on your pantry shelves. The use of the dry white wine may call down upon my head the wrath of the Pennsylvania Dutch, but the flavor is worth it. With this meal I served slices of avocado on watercress, with a sharp French dressing. The dessert was pumpkin pie, topped by a rum-flavored whipped cream. The same dry white wine used in the Bott Boi was served with the meal.

The chicken is a priceless bird, not only because of its succulent meat and the many different ways of cooking it, but also because of its luscious livers. I sometimes wonder if there could be an appetite so jaded that it wouldn't rear up in keen anticipation at the smell and sight of delicately cooked chicken livers.

Chicken livers can be served at breakfast, either plain or made into an omelet, or scrambled with eggs. Chicken livers make an ideal light luncheon dish, and they can be made into a savory main course dinner dish.

The following dish is an ideal one for a Sunday brunch, along with scrambled eggs, grilled link sausages, and hot biscuits.

CHICKEN LIVERS IN SOUR CREAM

1 *lb. chicken livers*
2 *oz. butter* (4 *tbsp.*)
1 *green pepper, minced*
2 *tbsp. flour*
½ *pint sour cream*
¼ *cup chicken broth*

1 4-*oz. can mushroom stems and pieces, drained*
2 *tbsp. chopped parsley*
1 *tbsp. grated onion*
Salt and pepper
½ *tsp. Ac'cent*

Cut the chicken livers in half, and gently sauté them in a large skillet with the butter, turning frequently for about 5 minutes. Remove livers. Sauté the minced green pepper in same pan for 5 minutes. Sprinkle the flour over green pepper and stir well. Add commercial sour cream and chicken broth. Cook, stirring constantly, until mixture boils and thickens. Then add the mushroom stems and pieces, drained, chopped parsley, grated onion, salt and pepper to taste, and the Ac'cent. Just before serving, add livers to sauce and heat gently, but thoroughly. Serves 4 to 6.

The late Ernest Byfield, one of the great restaurateurs of America, had a way of doing unusual things with food. One of the meals he liked best was breakfast down on his farm, and one of his favorite breakfast dishes was chicken livers. The magic touch to this dish was soaking the livers from about 10-week-old White Rocks in milk and Madeira wine overnight. So I have adapted this trick to these chicken livers with a Madeira sauce.

CHICKEN LIVERS SAUCE MADEIRA

1 *lb. chicken livers*	3 *tbsp. butter*
Milk	2 *tbsp. flour*
4 *oz. Madeira wine*	¾ *cup consommé*
Salt and pepper	½ *tbsp. chopped parsley*
	1 *tsp. grated lemon rind*

Cut the chicken livers in half and place in a shallow dish. Add enough milk mixed with 2 ounces of Madeira wine to just cover the livers, and allow to stand overnight.

When ready to cook, drain the livers on paper toweling, sprinkle with salt and pepper to taste, and sauté them in a saucepan with the butter for about 6 to 7 minutes, or until their red-juiced look has disappeared. Then transfer them to a warm platter.

To the juices in the pan add the flour, and blend well. Then slowly add the consommé mixed with 2 ounces of Madeira, the chopped parsley, and the grated lemon rind. Cook, stirring constantly until the sauce is smooth and thickened. Then return the sautéed chicken livers to the sauce, and when heated serve on toast points. Serves 2 to 3.

One of the favorite dinner dishes at our home is curried chicken livers served with rice. It is very simple to prepare, and inexpensive

CURRIED CHICKEN LIVERS

2 *oz. butter*	1½ *tbsp. flour*
1 *lb. fresh chicken livers*	1 *tbsp. curry powder*
Small clove garlic	¾ *cup beef bouillon*
	2 *oz. Madeira wine*

In a heavy iron skillet melt the butter, and when the butter is sizzling hot put in the fresh chicken livers. Sauté for about 7 minutes, or until their red-juiced look disappears and they are delicately colored on all sides. Remove from the skillet and put into a hot dish to keep warm.

Crush the garlic into the butter and juices in the pan, and then sprinkle in the flour and curry powder. When the dry ingredients are well blended with the butter and juices, add the condensed beef bouillon and dry Madeira wine, stir in well, and allow to simmer gently until slightly thickened. Then return the chicken livers to the skillet, stir the whole gently, and serve the livers and their sauce over rice.

I wouldn't attempt to guess how many people in this land of ours are familiar with the name Duncan Hines. For a great many years he and his wife have been traveling back and forth, and up and down, America, familiarizing themselves with hotels, motels, and restaurants. The results of their investigations have been summed up in such books as *Lodging for a Night, Adventures in Good Eating,* and *Adventures in Good Cooking.*

I am very fond of Duncan and Clara Hines, and I always look forward to seeing them. While I was writing this book, they came to San Francisco and I had luncheon with them. Clara told me of a wonderful recipe she had for chicken livers, so I asked her for it. She promptly sent it to me, and it is so good that I am sharing it with the readers of this book.

CHICKEN LIVERS SAUTÉ À LA MARSALA

4 *tbsp. butter*
1 *lb. chicken livers*
Salt and pepper
Flour

1 *clove garlic*
3 *tbsp. chopped parsley*
1½ *cups chicken broth*
½ *cup Florio Dry Marsala Wine*

Season the chicken livers and dredge them in a little flour. Brown them over a low heat in a skillet with the butter.

Chop the garlic and parsley fine and add to the chicken livers along with the chicken stock. Let simmer over a low flame for about 15 minutes.

Add the Florio Dry Marsala Wine and let cook 5 minutes. If the sauce should be too thin for your taste, thicken with a little arrowroot, or cornstarch. Serve over rice, toast, waffles, or an omelet, to 4 persons.

While the regal turkey is truly an American bird, it is surprising to learn that a great many of the peoples in countries all over the world have come to appreciate its succulent supremacy, and consider it, as we do in America, a festive dish.

In most countries, turkey is roasted, but in Mexico they usually parboil the disjointed turkey, and serve it in a peppery sauce. *Mole de Guajolte* is a national dish of Mexico, along with *Mole Poblano*. This latter dish is turkey in a chocolate sauce, also well spiced with three different kinds of chilies, and four or five different herb seeds.

However, I am old-fashioned enough to want my turkey stuffed and roasted. The sight of a golden-brown bird on a platter is part of its delight, and the carving of it is a momentous occasion. Stuffings are varied from year to year at our house, bringing the anticipation of a new taste thrill.

Stuffed fowls are exceedingly popular among the people of the Near East. In "The Book of the Thousand Nights and a Night" (*The Arabian Nights*) mention is frequently made of fowls stuffed with pistachio nuts, and modern Near East cooks still use this delicate nut for flavoring. So suppose we call the following dish Turkey Scheherazade, in honor of the heroine of the Arabian Nights!

TURKEY SCHEHERAZADE

1 10- *to* 12-*lb. turkey*   *Olive oil*
                         ¼ *tsp. powdered ginger*

Stuffing

½ *cup raw rice*   *Chopped giblets*
2 *tbsp. butter*   ½ *cup seedless raisins*
1 *large onion*   ½ *tsp. dried thyme*
2 *stalks celery*   ¼ *tsp. dried sage*
6 *cups breadcrumbs*   1 *tbsp. chopped parsley*
Dry sherry wine   *Salt*
1 *cup pistachio nuts*   *Freshly ground pepper*
                    1 *beaten egg*

Gravy

¼ *cup pan drippings*   1 *cup water*
¼ *cup flour*   1 *cup dry white wine*
                    Salt and pepper

Rub the inside and out of the turkey with olive oil, then rub the inside with about ¼ teaspoon of powdered ginger. Boil the giblets in water (except the liver) about 1 hour, or until tender. Add the liver to the boiling giblets about 8 minutes before the cooking time is up. Also cook the rice in your favorite manner, so that it will be fluffy and tender.

In a saucepan melt the butter, and when hot add the sliced onion and chopped celery. Sauté these until the onion takes on a little color.

In a large bowl combine the day-old bread, cubed, which has previously been moistened with dry sherry wine, the sautéed onions and celery, the pistachio nuts, the boiled rice, the chopped giblets, the seedless raisins, dried thyme, dried sage, chopped parsley, salt and freshly ground pepper to taste, and the beaten egg. Mix gently but thoroughly, and stuff the turkey with it, closing the opening, of course, either with skewers, or sewing (I always put the heel of a loaf of bread over the opening, and then sew the skin together over it).

You may have your own favorite way of roasting the turkey. I prefer to use a low temperature, because it assures better flavor and appearance, less shrinkage, and less loss of juices, 325 degrees for 3½ to 4½ hours. A splendid idea is to dip cheesecloth in melted butter, and drape it over the turkey so that it covers the entire bird. Then brush it with melted butter throughout the baking time.

To make a luscious gravy, skim off the fat and pour into a bowl. Put ¼ cup of drippings back into the pan, and blend in thoroughly the flour. Cook until bubbly, stirring constantly. Then add the water and dry white wine, and salt and pepper to taste. Cook, stirring constantly, until the gravy is thickened, about 5 minutes.

Probably the first country of the Old World to take the turkey to its heart was Spain. This was probably the Mexican turkey (which had undoubtedly been domesticated in Mexico for a long time), and was brought back to Spain around the year 1530. Some of these Mexican turkeys reached England about ten years later. The Spaniards have devised a very special and flavorsome stuffing for Señor Turkey, and they call this stuffed turkey *El Pavo Relleno à la Catalana,* or Stuffed Turkey à la Catalane.

EL PAVO RELLENO À LA CATALANA
(Stuffed Turkey à la Catalane)

1 15-*lb. turkey*	3 *cups water*
Melted butter	1 *cup dry sherry*

Stuffing

1 tbsp. bacon drippings	2 large mushrooms
½ lb. lean ham	Pinch dried thyme
Turkey liver	Pinch dried marjoram
8 pork sausages	Pinch dried basil
½ lb. dried prunes	1 tbsp. chopped parsley
½ lb. dried peaches	1 bay leaf
6 oz. pine nuts	Salt and pepper
1 lb. cooked chestnuts	½ cup dry sherry

In a frying pan melt the bacon drippings (or lard) and put in the minced lean ham and the turkey liver cut in small dice. When browned, add the pork sausages, and the following ingredients: dried prunes, dried peaches, which have previously been soaked for 12 hours in water, drained, and coarsely chopped, pine nuts, and cooked chestnuts, both coarsely chopped. Next sprinkle in a pinch each of thyme, marjoram, basil, and chopped parsley, crumbled bay leaf, and salt and pepper to taste. Moisten the whole with the dry sherry, and mix well. When the mixture is partially cooked, remove it from the fire and add the large mushrooms, sliced. Cut the pork sausages into little pieces, again mix well, and stuff the turkey with the mixture. It is best to do this the day before the turkey is cooked, so the bird can absorb all the flavors. But be sure the stuffing is chilled, and the stuffed bird is refrigerated. Before the turkey goes into the oven, brush it with a little melted butter, and pour about 3 cups of water and 1 cup of sherry into the bottom of the roaster. Baste frequently, adding more water and sherry in the above proportions as necessary. Roast, allowing 20 to 25 minutes per pound.

There was a time when the turkey made his first annual appearance on the gastronomical stage at Thanksgiving. He was a perennial hit, and almost always was called back for an encore at Christmas time. He then went into limbo for about eleven months, gone but not forgotten.

Those turkeys of yesteryear were no pygmies, either. I have read of one in Vermont that weighed fifty-six pounds, and twenty- to twenty-five pound birds were quite common when the whole family journeyed to Grandmother's house for a Thanksgiving feast. For years growers schemed and struggled to grow bigger and bigger turkeys, by selecting only the biggest for breeding stock.

But things are different now! Instead of trying to grow turkeys bigger and bigger, they are trying to get them smaller and smaller, and they have now gotten them down to about the weight of a large capon, or even less. But don't despair, kiddies. They're still growing them man-sized, from ten and twelve pounds up to twenty-five pounds—of course for roasting. But why should such a succulent bird be good only for roasting? And that's where the five- and six-pound turkeys come in. Try this recipe for size and taste appeal.

SMOTHERED JUNIOR TURKEY

1 5-*lb. turkey* (*cut up*)	*Salt*
Seasoned flour	*Freshly ground pepper*
3 *medium onions, quartered*	¼ *lb. butter*
½ *tsp. dried marjoram*	6 *stalks celery*
½ *tsp. dried thyme*	1 *cup consommé*
1 *tbsp. chopped parsley*	1 *cup dry white wine*

Gravy

Turkey neck	1 *bay leaf*
Turkey gizzard	*Pinch dried marjoram*
2 *turkey backs*	*Pinch dried thyme*
2½ *cups water*	½ *cup dry white wine*
1 *small onion*	*Flour and butter* roux

First, dredge the turkey pieces in seasoned flour. Lay the pieces in the bottom of a roaster. Around the pieces place the fair-sized onions, peeled and cut in quarters. Sprinkle the pieces with dried marjoram and thyme, 1 tablespoon chopped parsley, and salt and freshly ground pepper to taste. Liberally dot the turkey pieces with pieces of butter about the size of grapes (I use ¼ pound of butter). Then lay the stalks of celery, leaves and all, across the turkey pieces and onions. Then pour around the sides of the roaster the consommé and not too dry white wine (an ordinary dry wine can be used). Then cover the roaster and put it into a hot oven (450-500 degrees) for ½ hour. At the end of that time baste the turkey pieces, and turn the oven down to 300 degrees, cover the roaster, and let the whole thing cook for about 2 hours, basting every ½ hour.

After the turkey pieces are put in the oven for the first time, put the neck, the gizzard, and the two backs (each one broken in half) into a saucepan in 2½ cups of water, to which have been added a small chopped onion, a bay leaf, crumbled, and a small pinch each of dried marjoram and thyme. Let this simmer until the giblets are tender. Remove the giblets and backs, cutting the giblets and the meat from the backs into small pieces. Strain the broth, and add the dry white wine to it, along with the chopped giblets and pieces of meat.

When the turkey pieces are tender, uncover the roaster and turn the oven up for a quick browning, and then remove the turkey pieces, onions, and celery to a hot platter. Put the roaster on top of the stove over a medium flame, add the wine broth to the gravy in the roaster, add a little flour and butter *roux,* and when the gravy has thickened, pour it over the turkey pieces. And what a dish!

Some time ago some enterprising individual or firm decided that if chicken parts could be sold, turkey parts could also be marketed. So huge frozen breasts, legs, and thighs of turkeys made their appearance in stores. I never was enthusiastic about them, but now that these junior turkeys are on the market, whole or cut up, there is a new opportunity for exciting dishes. The junior turkey breasts have the full flavor and succulence of turkey meat, and they are plump and tender. Take this recipe, for instance.

BREAST OF TURKEY

1 *breast from 5½-lb. turkey*	*Pinch paprika*
3 *oz. butter*	3 *oz. cream*
1 *large mushroom cap*	1 *oz. milk*
1 *heaping tbsp. cooked ham*	*Pinch arrowroot*

Melt the butter in a skillet, and sauté the turkey breast (cut in half) on each side for about 15 minutes. Then add the mushroom cap, cut in matchstick-size strips, and the ham, cut the same way (julienne). Cover the skillet and smother this for about 10 minutes. Add a pinch of paprika, and shake the pan to make certain the flavor is well distributed.

Remove the two halved turkey breasts to a warm platter, and with the mixture in the skillet combine the cream and milk. Bring the mixture to the boiling point, and then return the halved turkey breast to the skillet. Thicken the sauce to the desired consistency with the arrowroot (or a little flour creamed with butter), and then serve. This will make 2 servings.

During the post-Thanksgiving days, I can eat cold turkey right off the carcass until there isn't a smidget left. Then a wonderful turkey soup is made from the carcass, the recipe for which is in *With a Jug of Wine*. However, I am inordinately fond of turkey, and I realize that there are many people who become a little tired of it without additions. So, let's talk cold turkey, dressed up a little bit, for a few pages.

Usually Junior and/or Dad have dibs on the drumsticks. But if there are two legs left, try deviling them. Of course, the tendons should have been drawn before the turkey was roasted.

DEVILED DRUMSTICKS

2 *turkey drumsticks*
1½ *tsp. Escoffier Sauce Diable*
1 *tsp. butter*

1 *tsp. dry mustard*
½ *tsp. curry powder*
Butter

With a sharp knife cut slits in the drumsticks down to the bone, and parallel with the bone, and stuff the pockets with the following paste: Blend together the Escoffier Sauce Diable, the softened butter, the dry mustard, and the curry powder. Heat the 2 stuffed drumsticks in plenty of butter, and serve. The flavor of the sauce cooks all through the drumsticks, and you will really have a new taste thrill.

Poultry, of course, combines beautifully with ham, and particularly turkey. So here is way number 2 to use up leftover turkey.

CREAMED TURKEY AND HAM GOURMET

¼ *cup butter*
¼ *cup flour*
1¼ *cups rich milk*
½ *cup turkey stock*
¼ *cup dry sauterne*
½ *tsp. Ac'cent*

Dash powdered mace
Salt and pepper
1 *cup diced cooked turkey*
1 *cup diced cooked ham*
1 *4-oz. can sliced canned mush-
rooms, drained*

Melt the butter in a saucepan, and stir in the flour. When well mixed, slowly add the milk and turkey stock (you can use canned chicken broth or bouillon), and cook, stirring constantly, until the mixture boils and thickens. Then gradually stir in the dry sauterne. When blended in, add the Ac'cent, dash of mace, salt and pepper to taste, the diced cooked turkey and the diced cooked ham, and the mushrooms (if you wish, you can use sliced fresh mushrooms which have been sautéed in a little butter for about 7 minutes). When all is blended and heated through, serve in patty shells, or in rice or noodle rings. This recipe serves 4 to 6. Green beans and a mixed green salad go perfectly with this dish, and of course the beverage should be chilled dry sauterne wine.

I imagine there are mighty few homes in this country of ours that do not celebrate New Year's Eve with some sort of a party. Most of the parties will range from very large ones, with elaborate buffets and libations, to very small and simple family affairs.

If your gathering to welcome the New Year is to be a small one, and you don't want to go in for multiple courses, either sitdown or buffet (which, of course, entails a lot of preparation), I don't know of a more delightful combination than Turkey à la King (which can use up the leftover turkey from Christmas) and Crêpes Monte Carlo.

The Turkey à la King, which I will guarantee will be different from any other you have ever tasted, can be made in the morning, and reheated to serve in a casserole or chafing dish.

TURKEY À LA KING

3 *tbsp. butter*	4 *tbsp. cream*
2 *tbsp. flour*	3 *cups diced cooked turkey*
½ *small bay leaf*	3 *tbsp. butter*
½ *tsp. salt*	1 *cup chopped green pepper*
Pinch *freshly ground pepper*	1½ *cups sliced fresh mush-*
Dash *powdered nutmeg*	*rooms*
1 *cup rich milk*	3 *tbsp. chopped pimento*
¾ *cup mayonnaise*	3 *oz. dry Madeira wine*

Melt 3 tablespoons of butter in a saucepan over a medium flame. Then blend in the flour, the small bay leaf, salt, a pinch of freshly ground pepper, and a dash of nutmeg. Remove the saucepan from the fire, and stir in the rich milk very slowly. Return the saucepan to the heat and stir constantly while cooking for about 10 minutes— or until the sauce is thickened to the consistency of heavy cream. Remove the saucepan from the heat, take out the bay leaf, and gently mix in the mayonnaise, stirring constantly. Then add the cream, and stir until the mixture is well blended. Next add the cooked, diced turkey meat. Incidentally, the foregoing recipe, up to the adding of the turkey, makes a superb rich cream sauce, or white sauce.

In a frying pan melt 3 tablespoons of butter, and in it lightly sauté the chopped green pepper and sliced fresh mushrooms until tender—about 10 minutes. Then add these to the cream sauce and turkey, and let simmer gently over a low flame for about 10 minutes, stirring constantly. Remove from the heat and add the chopped pimento and dry Madeira wine (if you haven't the Madeira, use 2 ounces of sweet [cream] sherry and 1 ounce of dry sherry). Blend well, and serve. If you make this ahead for serving later, be sure to let the mixture cool thoroughly without a cover until time to reheat. The recipe serves 6 generously.

Stuffings for turkey are almost as important as the bird itself. Yet all too often turkeys are stuffed with the same old breadcrumb-sausage-sage stuffing. To my mind, and for my taste, two of the finest and most delectable stuffings are a brandied chestnut stuffing, and a pecan and cornbread stuffing. In the six years during which my book, *With a Jug of Wine,* has been on the market, I couldn't begin to tell you how many readers of the book have raved, either in person or by letter, about those two stuffings.

The original Thanksgiving Turkey was, of course, a wild turkey, and I guess everybody, except the diaper set, recalls the pictures of a wide-hatted Pilgrim, his blunderbuss over his shoulder, bringing home the ceremonial gobbler, while a lurking Indian or two leered from behind trees.

Nowadays, most of us "shoot" our turkeys off the counter of the market, while a lurking butcher leers at your pocketbook from behind his scales. But we can re-create at least the illusion of a wild turkey to a farm-raised bird with this wild rice stuffing, for it gives a suggestion of a wild turkey flavor.

WILD RICE STUFFING FOR TURKEY

2 *cups raw wild rice*   ½ *cup dry sherry wine*
Tepid water   1 *cup sliced fresh mushrooms*
½ *cup olive oil*   ½ *cup chopped green pepper*
1 *cup finely diced celery*   1 *tbsp. chopped parsley*
1 *cup chopped onion*   2 *tsp. salt*
1 *can condensed beef consommé*   1 *tsp. Angostura bitters*

Wash the uncooked wild rice, and soak for an hour in tepid water. Heat the olive oil in a heavy skillet and then, stirring constantly, add the drained wild rice and the finely diced celery and chopped onion. When blended, add the condensed beef consommé and dry sherry. Then stir in the sliced fresh mushrooms, chopped green pepper, chopped parsley, salt, and Angostura bitters. Cover tightly, and allow to simmer for ½ hour, or until rice is done.

This dressing is best, and the flavor is improved, if the mixture is cooled in a bowl, and kept overnight in the refrigerator.

For many years I have listened to arguments for and against oyster stuffing for turkey. People who are fond of oysters love it, and point out that oysters are as traditional to Thanksgiving as the turkey, and that the plump and tender oyster was present at the very first Thanksgiving Day celebration.

Well, if you like oyster dressing, here is an unusually delicious one. If you don't, forget it, and try something else.

OYSTER STUFFING FOR TURKEY

4 *pints oysters*   2¼ *tsp. salt*
Oyster liquor   ¾ *tsp. freshly ground pepper*
1½ *cups butter*   1½ *tsp. ground sage*
2 *cups finely chopped onions*   ¾ *tsp. dried thyme*
2 *cups chopped celery*   1 *lb. chestnuts*
3 *tbsp. chopped parsley*   *Water*
3 *tbsp. finely chopped green*   4 *quarts soft breadcrumbs*
    pepper   *Dry white wine*

Simmer the oysters in their own liquor until the edges curl. Then drain, and chop coarsely, reserving the liquor.

Melt the butter in a large skillet, and add the finely chopped onions, celery (leaves and stalks), chopped parsley, and finely chopped green pepper, salt, freshly ground pepper, ground sage, and dried thyme. Cook about 4 minutes over a low flame, stirring constantly.

Boil the chestnuts in water for about 20 minutes, then, when cool enough to handle, remove the shells and skin, and chop coarsely.

Now combine the sautéed vegetables, the chopped chestnuts, the chopped and drained oysters with the soft breadcrumbs. Mix thoroughly, and moisten with equal parts of dry white wine and the oyster liquor, if the dressing is too dry. It should be of a medium consistency. Thoroughly cool if the stuffed turkey is to be refrigerated overnight, and stuff the bird.

The above amount of dressing should fill both cavities of about a 16-pound turkey. If there is any dressing left over, place it in a greased casserole and put in the oven during the last 30 minutes the turkey is being roasted. If the casserole stuffing seems too dry, moisten it with some of the juices of the roasting bird.

I feel that a chapter on poultry would not be complete without mentioning a relatively new bird which has been developed to grace the tables of epicures, gourmets, or anyone who wants something new in unusual and delicious dishes. I am referring to the Rock Cornish game hen.

This tiny bird is a cross, having the strains of the domestic Rock Cornish hen and the Malayan gamecock of India. These squab-sized birds weigh about 1 pound each, which makes them ideal for individual servings, and their flavor combines the subtle sweetness of the grouse and the succulence of the finest young milk-fed chickens. As a matter of fact, the taste of the Rock Cornish game hen and the White African guinea hen is very similar. However, the meat of the game hen is all white.

These birds were developed by Jacques Makowsky, and are raised on his farm in Pomfret Center, Connecticut. From that point they are shipped to distributors in the major cities of America, and the distributors in turn supply retail outlets.

Rather recently, they have been deep frozen and packaged, not only in a ready-to-cook state, but also stuffed and oven-ready for roasting.

The Rock Cornish game hen can be cooked in almost any way that a guinea hen or chicken can be cooked, but they are at their best roasted, or split and broiled. Personally, I think it is a shame to split them, for their appearance, whole and roasted, has an eye appeal that will augment their taste appeal.

The easiest way of cooking these dainty birds is roasting them. Season them with salt and pepper inside and out, and place a piece of salt pork on the breast of each. Put in a roaster and roast about 30 minutes. At the last minute add equal parts of consommé and dry white wine to the drippings in the roaster to make the gravy.

These squab-sized birds can be stuffed with great taste profit.

STUFFED ROAST ROCK CORNISH GAME HEN

4 *Cornish game hens*	3 *oz. Madeira wine*
Thinly sliced bacon	*Salt*
3 *oz. consommé*	*Pinch nutmeg*
	2 *tbsp. currant jelly*

Stuffing

½ *lb. sausage meat*	*Freshly ground pepper*
4 *chicken livers*	*Pinch ground allspice*
1 *tbsp. butter*	*Pinch ground rosemary*
1 *cup toasted breadcrumbs*	*Pinch ground marjoram*
	3 *oz. Madeira wine*

Make a dressing of sausage meat, slightly cooked to fry out the fat (and, of course, the sausage meat should be stirred with a fork to break up the meat). Sauté the chicken livers, coarsely chopped in the butter. Mix the sausage meat and the chicken livers with the toasted breadcrumbs, and season the whole with salt and freshly ground pepper to taste, the ground allspice, ground rosemary, thyme, and marjoram. Mix the whole well together, then add the Madeira wine and enough cream to bind the dressing together.

Stuff the 4 birds, but do not sew them up, as the quick heat must penetrate the stuffing. Wrap the birds with strips of thinly sliced bacon, and put them into a baking dish. Add the consommé and Madeira wine, salt, and a pinch of nutmeg.

Cook the birds about 30 minutes in a 375- to 400-degree oven, basting frequently. Ten minutes before they are done, remove the bacon. Skin off some of the fat in the basting sauce, and add to it a little more Madeira and the currant jelly. This recipe serves 4.

(8) VEGETABLES

If you have ever seen any of the earliest art forms of prehistoric times which have been unearthed, you may recall that most of them depicted giant animals with men killing them. But I have never seen, or heard of, any crude drawings showing men pulling a carrot out of the earth, or digging potatoes, or tearing a head of cabbage apart.

Of course, there is a reason for this. For nearly three quarters of a million years from the time man first emerged as a human animal, the basis of his subsistence was the flesh of such beasts as the Brontosaurus, the woolly mammoth, the Brontops, the Uintatherium, and such like. (Don't get me wrong—I'm no "Bridey Murphy" who lived during that period—I've just read books and looked at pictures!)

Vegetables, per se, probably started out as a substitute food when good red meat was not available. It is said that the art of cooking vegetables didn't come into being until earthenware or iron pots that could stand the heat were invented. And even after that forward step had been made, the vegetables that were eaten were few, such as beans, turnips, parsnips, mallows, and cabbage. In Greece, vegetables were the lowly fare of the poor, or of the Spartans.

But regardless of their origins (it is claimed by some that they came down via witch doctors and medicine men) vegetables became an important part of the *haute cuisine* of Europe, and only after having mastered the art of making soups, cooking roasts, devising sauces and entrees, does the apprentice chef pass on to the intricacies of preparing vegetables for the table.

The basic rules for the cooking of vegetables are very few and simple. Use only the freshest, preferably the young and small ones. They should be cooked in a minimum of water and time; steaming is ideal. When cooked in water, it should be salted. But never—oh, NEVER, PLEASE, use soda to preserve the color. The addition of a little monosodium glutamate (I always use Ac'cent) points up the flavor of vegetables. And don't allow vegetables to stand after they are cooked. And, finally, don't overcook. Serve your vegetables slightly crisp (as those past masters of the art of vegetable cookery, the Chinese, do) and not reduced to a pulpy, colorless mass.

From the point of view of nutrition, vegetables should be a must at least once a day. As a matter of fact, most meals are not complete without at least one vegetable, although in Grandmother's time usually three or four were called for. Maybe that's why people were healthier in the old days.

There are at least forty different vegetables available to cooks in America today, and there are almost countless ways of preparing them so that they are not only appetizing, but have eye appeal. Yet the majority of cooks find it difficult to dream up new and different ways of serving vegetables. Not that the standard ways are not good—corn on the cob, fresh peas in butter, spinach, either plain or creamed, boiled onions in cream, green beans in butter, stewed tomatoes, etc. But it is easy to tire of them, and the smart host or hostess is ever on the lookout for intriguing variations on the main theme. So I would like to offer a few delectable preparations which have merited praise from all who ate them.

Before passing on to the preparation of some vegetable dishes, I'd like to insert here a gratuitous plug for the frozen food industry. While there are many excellent frozen comestibles on the market, to my mind the industry has surpassed itself in the vegetable field. Peas, beans, broccoli, Brussels sprouts, lima beans, asparagus, and a few other vegetables have practically as fine a flavor frozen as fresh, and a lot less work in the preparation of them is involved. I have never yet gone wrong using frozen vegetables from reputable packers or processors.

Twenty-five years ago artichokes definitely graced only the tables of the elite or were on the menus of only the very top eating places in large metropolitan cities. I very well remember the time I was served my first artichoke. I hadn't yet reached high school age, but I was passionately devoted to a young lady two years my junior.

One Sunday evening Dream Girl's mother invited me to join the family for dinner at an exclusive club. The dinner had been ordered in advance and after the entree had been served, the waiter placed an amazing object at my place. It was dark green and had funny-looking spear-shaped leaves sticking out. I thought, "What the heck is this and how do you eat it?" I waited patiently to see how the other people attacked this queer-looking object and suddenly, to my amazement, the hostess began picking the leaves off, dipping them in melted butter and drawing them through her teeth. So I followed suit. But I must confess I was very disappointed in the result. It was not until many years later that I appreciated the delicate nutty flavor of the artichoke. I will admit eating an artichoke is a lot of work, but I think it is worth it.

There are two different forms of artichokes—the globe artichoke, which might look like a cross between a small cabbage and a pine cone, and the Jerusalem artichoke, which is a root vegetable resembling a small potato or a yam. This latter is dismissed from consideration forthwith.

Globe artichokes are usually served whole. The stems are cut off close to the base, the large outside leaves are stripped off, the ends of the remaining leaves are snipped off, and they are boiled, for 15 to 20 minutes, or rather simmered, in water, olive oil, and a clove or two of garlic. Then they are drained, and served with melted butter, mayonnaise, or Hollandaise sauce. Artichokes are also popular stuffed.

Thanks to America's very progressive canning industry, excellent artichoke hearts and artichoke bottoms can be bought in almost every grocery store. The latter are more often used in salads, but my favorite preparation of the hearts is to sauté them in olive oil, and sprinkle them with grated Parmesan cheese.

SAUTÉED ARTICHOKE HEARTS

1 #1 *tall can small-size hearts of artichokes*	*Small pinch ground sage*
	Salt
Flour	*Freshly ground pepper*
1 *egg, beaten*	4 *tbsp. olive oil*
Small pinch dried thyme	2 *cloves garlic*
Grated Parmesan cheese	

The #1 tall can size of artichoke hearts (net weight, 1 pound) contains approximately 9 to 12 whole hearts. Drain them on paper toweling, and then flour them.

To the whole beaten egg add the dried thyme, ground sage, and salt and freshly ground pepper to taste. Mix this well, and then dip the floured artichoke hearts in the mixture.

In a heavy skillet heat the olive oil to which has been added the cloves of garlic, minced. When the oil is hot, add the floured and egg-dipped artichoke hearts. When they have nicely browned on one side, turn them, and sprinkle the browned side with grated Parmesan cheese. When the other side has browned, serve them, very hot. This will serve 3.

One of the first signs of spring is the appearance on the markets of asparagus, and people who are very fond of it will eat it almost every day throughout its short season. It is a very old vegetable, having been a favorite of the ancient Romans. Their way of cooking it cannot be improved upon. Even before I knew of their method I used it, so maybe in another life I was an ancient Roman cook!

Break off the tough ends of asparagus at a point where they will snap off when you break them. Then peel the ends with a patent peeler (also known as a floating blade vegetable knife). Then tie them in a bundle. In the bottom part of a double boiler put about 1½ cups of water, add salt, and when the water is boiling *stand* the bundle of asparagus in the vessel. Then invert the top of the double boiler and place it over the bottom part. Cook for about 15 to 20 minutes. In this way, the tougher parts of the asparagus are cooked in the boiling water, but the top parts are steamed, and when served the whole stalk of asparagus is properly cooked, and the delicate tips are not mushy. Hollandaise sauce or melted butter is the best accompaniment.

Frozen asparagus is very near the fresh in appearance and flavor, but, to my way of thinking, asparagus is one of the few vegetables that loses a great deal of its subtle flavor in canning. It's probably at its best steamed and served with drawn butter.

Asparagus stalks cut into 1-inch pieces and cooked in cream is mighty fine eating. But I think the following recipe is one of the most unusual and zestful of asparagus dishes.

DEVILED ASPARAGUS

1 pkg. frozen asparagus   ½ cup dry sherry
1 cup evaporated milk   2½ tsp. Angostura bitters
½ tsp. salt   ¾ cup grated Parmesan
Dash of pepper   cheese
2 well-beaten eggs

Defrost 1 package of frozen asparagus pieces and place them in a buttered baking dish. Mix together the evaporated milk, the salt and pepper, the beaten eggs, the dry sherry, the Angostura bitters, and the ¾ cup of grated Parmesan cheese, less 2 tablespoons. Pour this sauce over the asparagus, sprinkle the top with the 2 tablespoons of grated Parmesan cheese, set the baking dish in a pan of hot water, and bake in a 350-degree oven for 50 minutes.

Bananas are really a fruit, and are so classified. Yet among many peoples of the West Indies and Central Africa, bananas are a staple food. Banana bread is considered quite a delicacy, and banana flour is highly nutritious and digestible. And very often, particularly in the Latin American countries, bananas serve as an accompaniment (sort of a vegetable) to entrees.

An instance of this was illustrated in the dinner of the Pan American Coffee Bureau for food editors at the Drake Hotel a few years ago. The entree was *Pollo al Vino,* which has been detailed in the chapter on chicken, and the two accompaniments were *Habichuelas Tiernas* (green beans Latin American style) and *Frituras de Banano al Ron* (Rum Banana Fritters). And are they luscious!

FRITURAS DE BANANO AL RON
(Rum Banana Fritters)

3 *bananas*	½ *cup dark rum*
Powdered sugar	¾ *cup brown sugar*
½ *lime (juice of)*	*Flour*
Powdered cloves	*Fritter batter*
Powdered cinnamon	*Fat*

Fritter Batter

1 *egg yolk*	½ *cup milk*
1 *tbsp. butter*	½ *cup sifted flour*
¼ *tsp. salt*	1 *tbsp. sugar*
	1 *egg white*

Split the bananas lengthwise, and cut each into 4 cross sections. Dust with powdered sugar. Sprinkle with the lime juice, a little powdered clove, and a generous amount of cinnamon. Add to them the dark rum, cover, and let stand for at least an hour. Then drain them, roll in the brown sugar, and then in flour. Dip in the sweet fritter batter, and fry in shallow fat (2 inches deep in a heavy skillet) heated to 375 degrees. Drain on paper toweling, dust with sugar and cinnamon, and serve immediately.

To make the fritter batter, beat one egg yolk. Then add the butter, salt, and ¼ cup of milk. When blended, add the flour and the sugar. Stir until smooth, and then add the other ¼ cup of milk. Finally, fold in the stiffly beaten egg white.

Thicken the rum marinade with a little arrowroot, heat, and pour over the fritters.

The broad term "beans" covers a multitude of culinary delights. There are about 15 different varieties of beans, some of the most common being green beans, string beans, wax beans, lima beans, kidney beans, soy beans, and the numerous dried beans.

Beans, I believe, are among the oldest known vegetables. Soy beans have been used for thousands of years by the people of the Orient. An interesting culinary footnote to history is the fact that the ancient Greeks and Romans made use of beans in gathering the votes of the people, and for the election of magistrates. A white bean signified "yes," and a black bean meant "no."

Green beans (or string beans) is one of the most popular of vegetables. One of the favorite dishes of France is *Haricots Verts,* and it is to be found on almost any French menu. It is so highly regarded that it is often served as a separate course.

By and large, I don't think that there is any other nation that cooks green beans as well as the French. One of the specialties of the Pre Catalane Restaurant in the Bois de Boulogne in Paris is *Haricots Verts Parisienne,* which is young green beans cut diagonally and simmered in butter and white wine with a touch of lime juice.

What a place the Pre Catalane was! It was probably the most spectacular and exquisitely laid out restaurant in Paris. You dined on a terrace skirting a lake on which swans swam about, and colored lanterns danced in the breeze. There was soft music, gloriously beautiful women, oftentimes accompanied by regal French poodles who sat in chairs beside their mistresses. On a moonlit spring night, what a place for dinner, dancing and romance!

Let's see, where was I? Oh yes, talking about green beans. For no particular reason I got on an experimental binge not long ago with string or green beans. One that I devised I called String Beans

Smitane, and it is really a de luxe vegetable dish, which will go with almost any entree.

GREEN BEANS SMITANE

2 *lbs. fresh string beans*	4 *tbsp. flour*
(*or* 3 *pkgs. frozen*)	1 *cup mayonnaise*
Boiling salted water	¾ *cup sour cream*
1 *cup finely chopped onion*	¼ *cup dry white wine*
2 *oz. butter*	*Salt and pepper*

Cut the fresh string beans diagonally, or get 3 packages of French-style frozen string beans (these latter are just as good as the fresh, and a whole lot less work). Cook the beans in a small amount of boiling salted water until just tender (or follow the directions on the frozen packages), and then drain. Sauté the finely chopped onion in the butter until the onions are limp. Then stir in the flour, and blend it well with the butter and the onions. Then add the mayonnaise, the sour cream, the dry white wine, and salt and pepper to taste, stirring constantly while the mixture cooks until it is creamy—just a few minutes. Then add the drained beans to the sauce, heat through, and serve.

Mushrooms marry beautifully with a number of comestibles, but they mate succulently with string beans. Try the following combination at your next dinner party, and I can assure you that it will rate raves.

STRING BEANS WITH MUSHROOM SAUCE

1 *lb. fresh mushrooms*	1 *tsp. salt*
2½ *oz. butter*	1 *lb. fresh string beans*
1 *tbsp. flour*	*Slightly salted water*
3 *oz. dry Madeira wine*	½ *tsp. granulated sugar*
2 *cups cream*	*Pinch dried savory*

In a saucepan sauté the fresh mushrooms, sliced thin, in 1½ ounces of butter until the mushrooms are tender—about 8 to 10 minutes. Then sprinkle in the flour, blending it with the butter in the pan. Then blend in the dry Madeira (sercial). Next add the cream and ½ teaspoon of salt. Stir over a low flame until smooth and thickened, and keep hot.

Cook the small green string beans in slightly salted water for about 10 to 15 minutes, or until tender. (Frozen string beans can be used, and if so, follow directions on the package for cooking.) Drain off the water, add ½ teaspoon of salt, the fine granulated sugar, a pinch of savory, and 1 ounce of butter. Stir over a very low flame to heat thoroughly.

Place the string beans in the center of a dish, and pour the mushroom sauce around them.

Herbs give a particularly interesting flavor to vegetables—make them something different. But the next green bean recipe has an added touch of piquancy—bacon.

HERBED STRING BEANS

4 slices bacon	2 tbsp. chopped parsley
1 small onion, sliced	⅛ tsp. dried marjoram
2 tbsp. chopped green pepper	Tiny pinch dried rosemary
1 #2 can string beans, or	¼ tsp. Ac'cent
2½ cups cooked beans	Salt and pepper

Dice the bacon slices, fry slowly until crisp, and then remove the bacon bits and reserve them.

Add the thinly sliced onion and the chopped green pepper to the bacon drippings in the pan, and sauté them gently for about 5 minutes. Then add the beans (if you use the canned, drain them), the parsley, marjoram, rosemary, Ac'cent, and salt and pepper to taste, cover, and simmer gently for 5 minutes. Turn the beans into a heated serving dish, and sprinkle the bacon bits over the top.

I think my favorite among all vegetables is lima beans. Hot or cold, plain or fancy, or in combinations, I never get enough of them. My preference is the Fordhook lima beans, which are the large ones. And to me they are equally good either fresh or frozen.

Lima beans are, of course, highly nutritious. In Brazil, they are to the population what potatoes are to the people of Ireland.

Being so fond of lima beans, I have experimented several times with them. I have devised two inexpensive but delicious entrees, which appear under the chapter on meat, and the following recipe can either be a Lenten entree, a luncheon dish, or a vegetable.

SHERRIED LIMA BEANS

1¼ *cups chopped onions*
¾ *cup chopped green pepper*
1 *clove garlic*
¼ *cup olive oil*
2 *cups cooked lima beans*
½ *cup dry sherry*

1 *cup chopped ripe olives*
½ *cup grated Parmesan cheese*
1 *tsp. salt*
1 *tbsp. chili powder*
1 *6-oz. can tomato paste*
4-5 *bacon slices*

Sauté the chopped onions and chopped green pepper and 1 clove of garlic, minced, in the olive oil in a skillet until tender. Then add the cooked lima beans (the frozen ones do very nicely, but undercook them a little), the dry sherry, the chopped ripe olives (with a little of their liquid), ¼ cup of grated Parmesan cheese, the salt, good chili powder, and the tomato paste (or tomato sauce). Mix gently, but well, and place the whole into a casserole (2-quart size). Sprinkle ¼ cup of grated Parmesan cheese over the top, and bake in a 350-degree oven for about 20 minutes. Garnish with crisp bacon strips (about 4 or 5), unless you are serving this as a Lenten dish. This should serve 6.

Plain cooked lima beans can be delightfully enhanced by creaming ⅓ cup of butter until it is soft, then blending in 1 teaspoon each of onion powder and paprika, and combining this seasoned butter with the hot cooked lima beans, shaking until the butter mixture and the beans are thoroughly mixed.

Television has certainly thrown a monkey wrench into the eating habits of many homes. Sometimes two programs are scheduled that you don't want to miss, and either they run concurrently, or there is a time lapse of half an hour or three-quarters of an hour between them. This results in (a) you have to eat too early or too late, or (b) you have to plan on something that can be prepared and cooked in the above-mentioned half or three-quarters of an hour. Of course, there are several frozen plate television dinners that can be popped in the oven and served on TV trays, but by and large they don't bear repeating too often.

At our house we enjoy baked beans occasionally when television interferes with the dinner hour (or two). We dress them up with onions, cheese, and red wine.

DRESSED UP BAKED BEANS

4 *medium onions*   1 *cup grated sharp Cheddar*
3 *tbsp. butter*   *cheese*
2 *jars baked beans*   4 *tbsp. dry red wine*

Peel and slice the onions, and sauté them in a large saucepan in the butter until they are tender. Then add the contents of a glass jar of baked beans, the grated cheese, and the dry red wine. Mix gently but well, and transfer the mixture into an ovenproof glass baking dish and bake in a 350-degree oven for 30 minutes. Serve with steamed canned brown bread, and the same wine that went into the beans.

One of the vegetables that is not too well appreciated is the beet. Mention beets to a New Englander and he'll think of red flannel hash; to a Russian or Pole, he'll think of *borsch*. Beets are one vegetable that are just about as good canned as they are fresh. If you like beets, I think you'll enjoy them cooked in port wine.

BEETS IN PORT WINE

2 *cups* (1 #2 *can*) *diced beets*   2 *tsp. cornstarch*
½ *cup beet liquid*   1 *tsp. butter*
½ *cup port wine*   *Salt and pepper*

Drain the liquid from a #2 can of diced beets. Heat ½ cup of the beet liquid and the port wine in a saucepan. Add the cornstarch, and cook, stirring, until transparent. Now add the diced beets, the butter, salt and pepper to taste, and heat thoroughly. This serves 4 quite happily.

A rather well-known recipe for beets is called Harvard Beets. I can't imagine why they should be named after one of America's oldest colleges, unless they originated there. If, however, you are a Yale man, call them Yale Beets. But whatever you call them, they're good.

HARVARD BEETS

3 *cups cooked beets, diced*   ¼ *tsp. pepper*
1 *tbsp. flour*   2 *tbsp. vinegar*
2 *tbsp. sugar*   1 *tbsp. lemon juice*
½ *tsp. salt*   ½ *cup dry red wine*
                2 *tbsp. butter*

Mix together the flour, sugar, salt and pepper. Add to these the vinegar, lemon juice, and dry red wine. Cook this mixture slowly until thick, stirring constantly. Then mix in the diced, cooked beets, and heat thoroughly. Then add the butter, stir it in, and serve.

Among the pre-teenage set, broccoli is about as popular as spinach. I've always gotten a kick out of the story about those two famous characters, Topsy and Eva. They were eating their lunch together, and got to talking about vegetables. Topsy observed:

"You know, Miss Eva, of all the vegetables I like, I love carrots the bestest."

"I love green peas the best, Topsy, but I really do hate spinach," Eva admitted. Then she leaned over to get a closer look at what Topsy was eating. "Topsy, what's that funny-looking stuff you're eating?" she asked.

"Dat's broccoli, Miss Eva."

"Is it good?" Eva asked.

"Well, Miss Eva," Topsy answered, "if'fn all you had to eat for dinner was broccoli, you'd be dyin' for a little spinach just fo' dessert."

Broccoli is really a very delicious vegetable, but it is usually subjected to mighty rough treatment in many kitchens. Too often, boiled for a long time, it comes out wilted and a muddy green color, and practically unfit for human consumption.

Broccoli can well be cooked as asparagus is cooked—in the bottom of a double boiler with the top inverted over it. I like it served with melted butter, or Hollandaise sauce, but it is at its delectable best served with an almond sauce.

BROCCOLI, ALMOND SAUCE

3 10-*oz. pkgs. frozen broccoli spears*
3 *egg yolks*
1 *tsp. cornstarch*
½ *cup dry white wine*
1 *tbsp. lemon juice*
¼ *cup melted butter*
¼ *tsp. Ac'cent*
Salt and cayenne pepper
½ *cup slivered almonds*

Cook the broccoli according to directions on the package.

Beat the egg yolks slightly in the top of a double boiler, then blend in the cornstarch, and add the dry white wine, lemon juice, and melted butter. Cook over boiling water in the bottom of the double boiler, stirring constantly for 2 or 3 minutes, or until thickened. Add the Ac'cent, salt and cayenne pepper to taste, and the slivered almonds. When heated, pour the sauce over the cooked broccoli. This serves 6.

Cabbage is definitely "other side of the tracks." Yet one of the most popular American dishes is corned beef and cabbage. Jiggs's love of this dish is one of the central themes of George McManus' comic strip *Bringing Up Father*. Rich and poor alike flock to Dinty Moore's in New York for corned beef and cabbage.

Cabbage is one of the mainstays of Russian menus, and their Russian Cabbage Soup S'chee is popular throughout Russia.

I personally prefer red cabbage, and when it is cooked with apples and red wine, it makes a very pleasing change from the usual run of fresh vegetables.

RED CABBAGE WITH APPLES
AND RED WINE

1 *medium-sized head red cabbage*	*Pepper*
	¼ *tsp. caraway seeds*
3 *medium-sized green apples*	1 *cup beef bouillon*
½ *lb. salt pork, diced*	½ *cup dry red wine*
Salt	4 *tbsp. brandy*

Wash the head of red cabbage, and shred rather fine.

Peel, core, and slice the medium-sized tart green apples.

Arrange the cabbage in a saucepan with alternating layers of apple slices and the salt pork, diced. Add salt and pepper to taste, and sprinkle over the caraway seeds. Add the beef bouillon and dry red wine. Cook rapidly, uncovered, for 10 minutes. Then transfer to a greased baking dish, and sprinkle over the contents the brandy. Cover, and cook in a moderate oven for 1 hour, making sure there is enough moisture. If too dry, add a little more red wine.

One of the horrors on menus in a great many restaurants is a dish that appears all too frequently—creamed carrots and peas. Don't get me wrong; I'm not against any one of these vegetables singly or in combination. But when they're set before you intermingled with a sometimes gray glutinous mass which is called cream sauce, they're pretty dreadful. I've known people who completely eschew carrots and/or peas just because their first experience with them was the above-mentioned atrocity.

Carrots are not, as I once heard a man say, "damn bunny food." They are a very ancient vegetable, and, in our modern world, can be prepared in many exciting ways. Cut in slivers and iced, raw carrots combined with celery and olives are excellent appetizers. And, in addition, they are good for you, inasmuch as they are an excellent source of Vitamin A. When properly cooked, they're tender and delicious.

Why this method of cooking them is called California style, I don't know. But I do know they're good.

CARROTS CALIFORNIA STYLE

6 *to* 8 *medium carrots*	1 *onion*
2 *tbsp. butter*	*Salt*
½ *clove garlic*	*Pepper*
½ *cup dry white wine*	

Shred 6 to 8 medium carrots (you should have about 4 cups).

In a heavy saucepan melt the butter and add the garlic, crushed and minced. When butter is hot add the onion, peeled and minced, and let cook until soft. Then add the carrots, salt and pepper lightly, and add the dry white wine. Cook gently for 10 to 15 minutes, or until the carrots are tender.

Tender baby carrots are particularly delicious. One evening I was in an experimental mood. I had had a sidecar cocktail, which I'm very fond of, so I concocted a glaze for baby carrots in which the ingredients for a sidecar are a base, and this is what resulted.

CARROTS À LA SIDECAR

24 *baby carrots*	3 *oz. lemon juice*
Butter	2 *oz. brandy*
1 *oz. Cointreau*	2 *oz. honey*
Parsley	

Put about 24 baby carrots in cold, salted water, bring to a boil, and cook until just tender, about 15 minutes. Then remove them from the water, drain, and lay in a single layer in a buttered baking dish.

Make a syrup of the Cointreau, lemon juice, brandy, and honey. Pour this over the carrots and bake in a moderate oven (350 degrees) for about 15 minutes, basting occasionally with the syrup.

Sprinkle with parsley, and serve.

By the way, to preserve the delicate flavor and precious vitamins of young carrots, just scrub them with a good hard vegetable brush and cook them.

CARROTS FRANÇAISE

2 *lbs. young carrots*   *Dash cayenne pepper*
Salted water   1 *tsp. sugar*
2 *cups consommé*   2 *tbsp. butter*
1 *tsp. salt*   ¼ *cup dry white wine*

Parboil the carrots in enough salted boiling water to cover for 5 minutes, then drain.

Heat the consommé, add the salt, cayenne pepper, and the sugar, and then add the carrots, and cook until they are tender. Drain off the broth (reserving it) and add the butter to the carrots, and keep them warm.

Reduce the reserved consommé broth in a saucepan to ¼ cup, then add the dry white wine. Place the carrots in this wine broth, and simmer until most of the liquid is absorbed. Serve very hot.

Carrots have a reputation of being very beneficial to those who suffer from liver complaints, and of course Vichy, France, is a mecca for such sufferers. So I suppose that is where Carrots Vichy got its name. Incidentally, when you see "à la Vichy" on a menu, you may be sure that the dish has a garnishing of carrots.

There are a number of recipes for Carrots Vichy, but most of them are merely young and tender carrots cooked in a little water, seasoned with butter, salt and pepper, and sprinkled with chopped parsley. But this recipe will give you a new taste thrill.

CARROTS VICHY

3 *cups sliced carrots*   3 *oz. water*
3 *tbsp. butter*   3 *oz. cream sherry* (*sweet*)
¼ *tsp. salt*   ½ *tsp. meat extract*
                  Chopped parsley

Slice enough young carrots (don't peel or scrape them, for the flavor and precious vitamins and salts are in and close to the outer skin) to give you 3 cups. Put them in a heavy skillet with the butter, salt, water, and cream sherry (or Madeira). Bring to a brisk boil, and stir in the meat extract (if the meat extract is very salty, reduce the amount of salt). After the meat extract has been stirred in, cover tightly and let the whole boil for about 10 minutes, or until just tender. Then uncover, and reduce the flame a little, letting the broth in which the carrots are cooking evaporate until they fry a golden color in the remaining butter. Then sprinkle with chopped parsley, and serve. In the latter stages of cooking, watch the carrots carefully, because they scorch very easily. Shaking the pan occasionally avoids this.

Did you know that cauliflower, along with broccoli, is a member of the cabbage family? I didn't, for a long time. But I did and do know that cauliflower, properly cooked, is one of the most delicious members of its family, and marries beautifully with a number of sauces.

The English say that cauliflower should never be boiled, but should be steamed for 30 to 45 minutes. I believe the favored American way of cooking cauliflower is to cook it, closely covered, in a small amount of water, to which lemon juice has been added so as to keep the flowerets white. Cooked this way, only salt and pepper and melted butter are needed. But try Cauliflower Diplomatique sometime. I know it will delight you.

CAULIFLOWER DIPLOMATIQUE

1 2-lb. head cauliflower	2 cups dry white wine
Salt	1½ oz. olive oil
Hot water	1 clove garlic
Small pinch dried basil	½ cup grated Parmesan cheese

Get a prime, solid 2-pound head of cauliflower, remove the leaves and stalks, separate into flowerets, and place in a deep saucepan. Salt it lightly, and pour in barely enough hot water, to which a small pinch of basil has been added, to cover the bottom of the saucepan. Cover, and let steam slowly for about 10 to 15 minutes, or until just barely tender. Then drain and place in a bowl, and cover with the dry white wine. Allow to marinate for 1 hour, then remove the cauliflower from the wine and drain.

In a heavy saucepan put the olive oil, and when hot add the clove of garlic, crushed. When the garlic browns, remove it, and add the drained cauliflower flowerets. Sprinkle over them the grated Parmesan cheese, and shake the pan gently until the flowerets are well coated. Then place them in a casserole.

Add the wine marinade to the saucepan, and bring to a boil, and continue to boil until the liquid is reduced to ½ to ¾ cup. Then pour the liquid over the flowerets in the casserole and place in a 400-degree oven, uncovered, until the top is lightly browned. This should serve about 4 appreciative people.

By the way, don't throw away the outside leaves from the cauliflower. Trim off the leafy part from the large center ribs, cut into 2-inch pieces, crisp in the refrigerator, and serve like celery, sprinkling with salt, pepper, and fresh lemon juice.

Corn is one vegetable that I will only eat in its fresh state. Perhaps I have been unfortunate, but to me frozen corn on the cob is pretty dreadful.

The most succulent fresh corn on the cob I have ever eaten was prepared by Maury Ross, Jr., at one of his outdoor barbecue parties. To duplicate it, take as many ears of corn as you need and put them in boiling salted water for 2 minutes. Remove the ears, drain them, and coat them with peanut butter. Then place them over a charcoal fire and roast them until they are nicely browned. To fix them that way in the kitchen, wrap each ear spiralwise with a slice of bacon after spreading on the peanut butter. Then put them under the broiler, and take out when the bacon is broiled. Man, that's eating!

For some strange reason, eggplant is not a very popular vegetable in America, yet, probably more than any other vegetable, it lends itself to a wide variety of preparations. It goes beautifully with almost any seasoning or herb; it can be boiled, baked, fried, or broiled; it can be prepared as an entree, as a meat substitute, as an appetizer, or as a vegetable dish.

In the Near East, eggplant is baked or stewed in oil or broth. It is also combined frequently with lamb or mutton. One of the great dishes of the Near East is *Iman Bayeldi*—stuffed eggplant.

IMAN BAYELDI
Baked Stuffed Eggplant

1 *medium-sized eggplant*
5 *to* 6 *onions, sliced*
2 *to* 3 *green peppers, chopped*
4 *cloves garlic*
½ *cup seedless raisins*
½ *cup pine nuts*

½ *cup chopped parsley*
¼ *cup chopped fresh mint*
¼ *cup raw rice*
1 *cup olive oil*
2 *to* 3 *fresh tomatoes, sliced*
Salt and pepper

½ *cup dry vermouth*

Peel and slice about 5 or 6 onions, chop 2 or 3 seeded green peppers and about 4 cloves of garlic. Combine them with the seedless raisins, chopped, and pine nuts, chopped, the chopped parsley, chopped fresh mint (or 1 teaspoon of dried mint). Mix well, then add the well-washed raw rice. Into this mixture stir the olive oil.

In a 2-quart casserole place a layer of eggplant slices, then a layer of the above mixture, and repeat the layers until all are used. Slice 2 or 3 fresh tomatoes over the top layer (or use an equivalent amount of canned tomatoes), season with salt and pepper, and pour over all a scant ½ cup of dry vermouth. Cover, and cook in a 300-degree oven for 2 hours. Serve from the casserole, or chill and serve. It is better if this dish is prepared 24 hours ahead of time, and reheated. Serves 4.

Italian cooking is all too often thought of in terms of spaghetti—and spaghetti only—but many other delicious dishes developed in Italy can be adapted to American kitchen methods.

When the principal ingredient, in this case eggplant, is in fairly good supply, such dishes can save money for the budget-conscious housewife and give her family a pleasing variation.

In this Americanized version of Italian Eggplant, canned tomatoes are substituted for the Italian tomato paste, and American cheese for the "Mozzarella" and "Parmigiana" of the original.

ITALIAN EGGPLANT ANGOSTURA

1 *small eggplant*
1 *large onion, sliced* (1 *cup*)
1 # 2½ *can tomatoes* (3½ *cups*)
½ *tsp. nutmeg*

1½ *tsp. salt*
⅛ *tsp. pepper*
1 *tbsp. Angostura bitters*
¼ *lb. American cheese*

Bacon drippings

Peel and cut eggplant in ¼-inch slices. Sauté eggplant and onion slices in drippings until tender. Mash tomatoes and cook 10 minutes with nutmeg, salt, and pepper, remove from fire and add Angostura. Put layer of eggplant in buttered casserole, layer of onion rings, layer of cheese sliced thin, and pour on some of the sauce. Repeat till all ingredients are used. Bake in a moderate oven of 375 degrees F. for ½ hour. A little grated garlic will improve the flavor of the dish—if it's not overdone. Serves 6.

Eggplant, plain or breaded and fried in olive oil, is mighty toothsome. But with a walnut dressing, it is out of this world.

FRIED EGGPLANT, WALNUT DRESSING

1 *eggplant*	½ *cup cider vinegar*
Salt and pepper	½ *cup dry sherry wine*
Ac'cent	¼ *clove garlic, grated*
Olive oil	1 *tbsp. sugar*
1 *cup walnut meats*	¼ *tsp. Ac'cent*

Cut an unpeeled eggplant crosswise in slices ⅜-inch thick. Sprinkle with salt and pepper to taste, and Ac'cent. Pan fry in olive oil until eggplant is tender, turning to brown on both sides.

In the meantime, put the walnut meats through a food grinder, using next to finest blade. Then combine the walnuts with the cider vinegar, dry sherry, garlic, sugar, and Ac'cent.

Serve the eggplant hot, and pass the walnut dressing in a separate bowl.

Here is another baked eggplant dish, this time with a Hungarian touch.

BAKED EGGPLANT WITH SOUR CREAM

2 *lbs. eggplant*	*Salt and pepper*
Boiling salted water	¼ *tsp. Ac'cent*
1 *cup sour cream*	2 *tbsp. grated Parmesan cheese*
1 *tsp. Worcestershire sauce*	*Paprika*

Peel and dice about 2 pounds of eggplant. Cook, covered, in boiling salted water for 10 minutes, or until just tender. Drain thoroughly, then mix the eggplant with the sour cream, Worcestershire sauce, salt and pepper to taste, and the Ac'cent. Then turn into a greased casserole, sprinkle with the grated Parmesan cheese, dust with paprika, and bake in a 375-degree oven, for about 25 minutes, or until bubbly. This serves 4 or 5.

Onions are one of the greatest flavoring agents, and almost indispensable in a great many dishes. There is probably no better known soup throughout the world than onion soup.

However, as a vegetable, the lowly onion was, for a great many years, favored only by those who lived "on the wrong side of the tracks." But through the ingenuity of many chefs, they have become a gourmet dish. Take, for instance, smothered onions with black walnuts and sherry!

GOURMET ONIONS

3 *dozen small onions*   *Flour*
Condensed consommé   ⅓ *cup butter*
Dry sherry wine   1 *cup broken black walnuts*

Wash and peel the onions, put them in a heatproof baking dish, cover them halfway with equal parts of condensed consommé and dry sherry, cover, and bake in a 350-degree oven for ½ hour. Then uncover, turn the onions, dredge them with flour, add the butter, and sprinkle over them the broken-up black walnuts. Re-cover, and continue baking for about 15 minutes, or until the onions are tender.

The sweetest and most flavorsome of all onions is the Bermuda onion. They're large and sweet and are ideal for stuffing. If you've never tried onions stuffed, you've got a new taste thrill out of Baked Stuffed Onions.

BAKED STUFFED ONIONS

6 *large Bermuda onions*   1 *cup breadcrumbs*
Freshly ground pepper   *Pinch thyme*
Cayenne pepper   *Salt*
1 *cup fresh mushrooms*   ⅓ *cup sherry*
½ *cup chopped cooked ham*   *Melted butter*

Peel and wash the Bermuda onions, then parboil in boiling salted water for about 20 or 25 minutes. Then drain, and scoop out the centers, being careful not to break the onions. Dust the insides with freshly ground pepper mixed with a tiny pinch of cayenne pepper.

Chop the scooped-out portion together with the fresh mushrooms. Mix in the chopped cooked ham, breadcrumbs, thyme, salt to taste, and the sherry.

Fill the onions with this mixture, and put them in a shallow, generously buttered baking dish. Brush melted butter over them, top and sides. Cover, and place in a moderate oven (350 degrees) and bake for about 40 minutes, or until tender. During the last 10 minutes, remove the cover.

Parsnips are one of the least appreciated vegetables known to man, and I don't doubt but that this is due to the fact that they are seldom cooked properly.

Actually, parsnips have a delicious, nutty flavor. They were a great delicacy in ancient Rome. Apicius, a Roman gourmet during the beginning of the Christian Era, and the author of a famous cookbook, had eight or nine recipes for cooking parsnips, including one with a wine sauce. The following recipe is very similar to one of his.

HERB SEASONED PARSNIPS

12 *young parsnips*	⅛ *tsp. dried thyme*
Boiling water	⅛ *tsp. dried marjoram*
4 *tbsp. butter*	*Salt*
1 *tbsp. sauterne wine*	*Freshly ground pepper*
	Minced parsley

Wash, rinse, and scrape 12 medium-sized young parsnips, or 6 large ones. Cut the large ones in halves lengthwise, or leave the small ones whole. Cover with boiling water, and simmer them until tender, anywhere from 30 minutes to an hour. In a heavy frying pan, melt the butter and add the sauterne. Also, add the dried thyme and marjoram. Now, brown the drained and cooked parsnips in this, sprinkle with a little salt and freshly ground pepper to taste and minced parsley, and serve very hot.

I guess peas are the most popular of all summer vegetables, and, from what I can discover, they have been around for a very long time. It is said that they have been traced back to prehistoric times. Peas have been found in the Swiss lake dwellings of the Bronze Age; and dried peas were uncovered among the ruins of ancient

Troy where they had been buried in pottery jars for over thirty centuries. I must confess that there have been times when I was sure that I had been served some of these ancient ones.

Petits Pois à la Française is the French vegetable de luxe, but somehow it rarely tastes the same outside of France. Probably because you can't get the tiny fresh French peas in America. However, here is the French recipe, and it can be superb.

PETITS POIS À LA FRANÇAISE
(French Green Peas)

3 *lbs. peas in pod*	*Freshly ground pepper*
5 *green lettuce leaves*	1 *tbsp. chopped parsley*
4 *small white onions*	*Pinch thyme*
1 *tsp. sugar*	2 *tbsp. butter*
Salt	1 *oz. chicken broth*
1 *oz. dry white wine*	

Shell about 3 pounds of fresh peas.

In a heavy saucepan make a bed of 3 or 4 green lettuce leaves, and place the shelled peas on the lettuce. Add the small white onions, peeled, the sugar, a pinch of thyme, the chopped parsley, salt and freshly ground pepper to taste, 2 rounded tablespoons of butter, the chicken broth, and dry white wine. Cover tightly, and cook over a low flame until the peas are done, and there is little or no liquid left in the saucepan. This should be anywhere between 15 to 30 minutes, depending on the age of the peas.

Serve immediately.

But French housewives combine peas and lettuce in a dish called Green Peas *Bonne Femme,* which means "housewife style." It is at its best using fresh peas.

GREEN PEAS BONNE FEMME

4 *lbs. fresh peas*	6 *oz. condensed consommé*
1 *head romaine lettuce*	6 *oz. dry white wine*
3 *tbsp. butter*	*Pinch dried marjoram*
2 *slices bacon*	1 *tbsp. chopped parsley*
12 *little green onions*	1 *tbsp. chopped celery leaves*
1 *tbsp. flour*	*Salt and pepper*

Shell 4 pounds of peas and cut a head of romaine lettuce into shreds. In a casserole melt the butter and lightly brown in it the thin slices of bacon and sliced little green onions (bulbs only). Then add the flour, and blend well until smooth, and the lettuce. Pour into the casserole the canned condensed consommé and dry white wine, bring to a boil, stirring constantly. Let it simmer for a few minutes, then add a pinch of dried marjoram, the chopped parsley and chopped celery leaves, and the shelled peas. Salt and pepper to taste, and cook gently for about ½ hour, stirring frequently. Serve from the casserole.

Within the past few years, the frozen food industry has perfected the freezing of peas to the point where they are practically comparable to choice peas fresh-picked from the vine. I fancy myself as a connoisseur of peas (in my salad days I have been known to eat as many as six dishes of peas at a meal!), and I am being perfectly frank when I say that a great deal of the time we use frozen peas.

Emily Chase Leistner, who has a magic touch with nearly all foods, has a couple of recipes using frozen peas that are delicious. The first she calls Paris Peas.

PARIS PEAS

1 12-oz. pkg. frozen peas	1 small onion
¼ tsp. Ac'cent	½ cup cream
4 slices bacon	Dash of freshly ground pepper

Cook the peas according to the directions on the package, adding the Ac'cent when the peas are partially thawed. When peas are tender, drain.

Dice the bacon slices and mince the onion. Fry the onion and bacon dice together until bacon is crisp. Then add the cooked peas, the cream, and the pepper. Serve piping hot in sauce dishes. This serves 4, but not generously.

I've tampered with Emily's second recipe, Peas and Mushrooms, by adding a little dry white wine instead of water. I think the change gives an added fillip to the dish.

PEAS AND MUSHROOMS

2 12-*oz. pkgs. frozen peas*	*Mushroom liquid*
1 4-*oz. can sliced mushrooms*	*Dry white wine*
2 *tbsp. butter*	1 *chicken bouillon cube*
2 *tbsp. flour*	¼ *tsp. Ac'cent*

Salt and pepper

Cook the peas according to the directions on the package, then drain. Also drain the mushrooms, and add to the mushroom liquid enough dry white wine to make ¾ cup.

Sauté the mushrooms in the butter for 5 minutes; blend in the flour; add the diluted mushroom liquid and cook, stirring constantly, until the mixture boils and thickens. Add the bouillon cube, and stir until dissolved. Then add the Ac'cent, and salt and pepper. Combine the peas, mushrooms, and sauce, and heat gently before serving. This serves 6.

Stuffed vegetables may often take the place of an entree, particularly during the Lenten season. A delicious and inexpensive main course may be concocted by stuffing green peppers with leftover meat. But here's a Lenten variation of the stuffed green pepper using cooked macaroni and Roquefort cheese flavored with dry white wine.

MACARONI STUFFED GREEN PEPPERS

4 *large green peppers*	*Cayenne pepper*
1½ *cups cooked macaroni*	⅓ *cup fine bread or cracker*
(*short length*)	*crumbs*
⅔ *cup Roquefort cheese*	1 *small onion*
⅔ *cup diced fresh tomatoes*	½ *tsp. sugar*
Generous pinch paprika	¼ *cup dry white wine*

Salt and pepper

Remove the seed cores from the green peppers, cover with boiling salted water, and boil 5 minutes. Drain and place in a baking pan. In the meantime, mix together the cooked short-length macaroni, the crumbled Roquefort cheese, the diced fresh tomatoes, salt and pepper to taste, a generous pinch of paprika, a shake of cayenne pepper, the fine bread or cracker crumbs, the onion, peeled and minced, the sugar, and dry white wine. Pack this stuffing into the peppers, pour boiling water ½ inch deep around the peppers, and bake in a moderate oven for 30 minutes. When you partake of this dish, you'll forget all about meat.

Some people enjoy sitting in a comfortable armchair with a travel book or folders, and dream of taking in the sights of the fabulous countries and cities of the far-off world. But I like to sit at my desk with books about distant lands and ruminate on the mouth-watering delicacies which are indigenous to the various countries.

I have just been reading about that most interesting French province of Alsace, which for decades has had a highly troubled existence, being alternately torn between German and French rule. But its cooking has gone serenely on, regardless of politics, and one cannot help but drool over its gastronomic splendor. The pig and the goose and sauerkraut seem to form the backbone of Alsatian cooking, and in such comestibles, where could one find more succulence?

I have chronicled in *With a Jug of Wine* that epicurean masterpiece, *Choucroute Alsacienne,* which is sauerkraut cooked with champagne, smoked ham, and bacon. Sauerkraut, as one might well think, is not exclusively identified with Germany. Belgian gourmets serve fried oysters bedded on sauerkraut simmered in champagne, which is a taste-captivating delicacy. In Hungary they vary their *Magyar Gulyas* (Hungarian goulash) by adding sauerkraut instead of beef stock and potatoes, and call it *Szegdi Gulyas*. But to most food lovers *Choucroute Garni* is the finest of all sauerkraut dishes.

In Alsace, cooks believe that three days of preparation are required to bring *Choucroute Garni* to its greatest deliciousness. But it can be prepared in a few hours, and with ingredients that are easily obtainable. It is even better if it is made a day ahead, and reheated for serving. By the way, the next time you are in Paris, visit Brasserie Lipp, on the Boulevard St. Germain, for an authentic *Choucroute Garni.*

CHOUCROUTE GARNI
(Sauerkraut)

3 *lbs. sauerkraut*	½ *cup thinly sliced onions*
8 *slices bacon*	¼ *cup thinly sliced carrots*
12 *peppercorns*	¾ *lb. garlic sausage*
¼ *tsp. caraway seeds*	1 *lb. smoked ham butt*
3 *juniper berries*	1 *lb. loin of pork*
1½ *tbsp. goose fat* (*or lard*)	*Dry white wine*

Condensed beef bouillon

Wash the sauerkraut in water, drain, and pull apart. Place one-third of it in a deep earthenware casserole or kettle, the bottom of which has been lined with about 8 slices of bacon. Then add the peppercorns, slightly bruised, caraway seeds, juniper berries, 1½ tablespoons of goose fat (or lard), the thinly sliced white onions, and thinly sliced carrots.

In the center of the casserole or kettle, on top of the seasoned sauerkraut, place the garlic sausage, smoked ham butt, and loin of pork. Next repeat the layers of sauerkraut, seasonings, and meat and sausage, and then top with a final layer of sauerkraut. Finally, pour over the contents of the casserole or kettle enough dry white wine (a Chablis is best) and beef bouillon in equal parts to cover the contents (about 1 pint of each). Cover the casserole or kettle and place in a 350-degree oven, and cook for 4 hours.

To serve, arrange the sauerkraut on a platter, slice the ham, pork, and sausages over the sauerkraut, and serve with boiled potatoes. The Chablis wine is the perfect accompaniment.

If you are fond of boiled beef with horseradish sauce, the next time you have it serve sauerkraut with mushrooms as your vegetable.

SAUERKRAUT WITH MUSHROOMS

4 *cups sauerkraut*	1 *tbsp. flour*
Boiling water	1 *tbsp. butter*
½ *lb. fresh mushrooms*	1 *cup sour cream*
1 *oz. butter*	*Salt and pepper*

Scald the sauerkraut in boiling water, then drain and place in a heavy saucepan. In a skillet sauté the fresh mushrooms in about an ounce of butter until the mushrooms are tender. When cool enough to handle, slice them very thin, and add them to the sauerkraut, and let this simmer for about 20 minutes. In the meantime, brown the flour in the skillet the mushrooms were sautéed in with 1 tablespoon of butter, then add the commercial sour cream, salt and pepper to taste, and let it come to a boil. Then add that mixture to the sauerkraut and mushrooms, and continue simmering for about 20 minutes, stirring from time to time.

The beginnings of spinach seem to be a matter of dispute. One source said it was probably of Persian origin, and was introduced into Europe in the fifteenth century. Another source claims that spinach is a native of the Far East, and was introduced into Europe by the Dutch in the sixteenth century. Another source claims that Spaniards, in the twelfth century, considered spinach the prince of vegetables. But there is no conflicting opinion about spinach among pre-teenagers—they dislike it intensely, and have reputedly said, "To hell with it!"

Well, I'll say to hell with spinach the way it is usually cooked and served—a sorry-looking mess nine times out of ten. Spinach is supposed to be very good for one (although lately there has been some dispute about that among nutritionists), but it doesn't make any difference to me whether spinach, or any other comestible, is good for you or not. If it isn't cooked and served in an appetizing way, I say to hell with it.

French cooks consider spinach (which is called *épinard* in French) a very palatable vegetable, and they serve it in a number of ways. Because Mrs. Wood is very fond of it, we have it in our home quite frequently, sometimes just plain with butter and salt and pepper, and sometimes fancied up. Here are two of our favorite spinach specialties.

MUSHROOM CREAMED SPINACH

3 *tbsp. butter*
4 *tbsp. flour*
1 *can cream of mushroom soup*
1 *14-oz. package frozen spinach*

2 *tbsp. dry sherry*
½ *tsp. grated onion*
Dash nutmeg
Salt and pepper

Melt the butter in the top of a double boiler over direct heat, then blend in the flour. Add the condensed cream of mushroom soup and cook slowly, until the mixture boils. Then place over boiling water in the bottom of the double boiler.

With a very sharp knife, cut the unthawed block of frozen spinach into 6 or 8 chunks, and add to the mixture in the top of the double boiler. Cover, and cook over boiling water 25 to 30 minutes, stirring occasionally. Then add the dry sherry, grated onion, the nutmeg, and salt and pepper to taste. Mix well, heat, and serve to 4.

SPINACH AND SOUR CREAM

1 14-oz. package frozen chopped spinach	½ cup sour cream ½ tsp. minced onion
1 tbsp. butter	¼ tsp. Ac'cent
1 tbsp. flour	Salt and pepper

Cook the frozen chopped spinach according to directions on the package, and then drain thoroughly.

In a saucepan melt the butter, and then blend in the flour. Add the sour cream and cook, stirring constantly, until the mixture boils and thickens. Then stir in the cooked spinach. Add the Ac'cent, the minced onion, and salt and pepper to taste. Heat gently but thoroughly, and serve to 3 or 4.

When we were living in Chicago, Bourke Corcoran (the deviser of Chipped Beef and Cream à la Corcoran, page 131) gave a small dinner party for a couple of visiting firemen from Boston.

Arthur Bent and Raymond Burgess, members of the exclusive L.F.L.G. Society of Boston, volunteered to make the first course themselves. The preparations started in the afternoon, in secret session. But when their course made its appearance on the table there were exclamations of surprise, and after the first taste, practically salvos of praise. It was Cold Tomatoes Cobb.

I immediately pressed them for the recipe, which they very graciously gave. Later, I learned that the recipe was from Edith Key Haines's book, *Wonderful Ways to Cook,* published by Rinehart in 1937, and revised and republished in 1951. The boys sent me a copy of the book, and I was delighted with it, for it contains more than six hundred pages of wonderful recipes, not only for everyday people, but for gourmets.

COLD TOMATOES COBB

7 large ripe tomatoes	¼ tsp. freshly ground pepper
1 small white onion	5 tbsp. mayonnaise
1½ tsp. salt	1 heaping tbsp. minced parsley
1 tsp. fine curry powder	

First mix the mayonnaise, minced parsley, and curry powder together, and when well blended place in the refrigerator to chill.

Peel and scrape or grate the white onion. Scald and skin the large ripe tomatoes, and then chop them into small but firm pieces, seeds included. Combine the tomatoes and the scraped onion with the salt and freshly ground black pepper, and when well mixed, place in the freezing tray of the refrigerator. Keep them there until they are thoroughly chilled, but not frosty. To serve, place the tomatoes in bouillon cups or small Chinese bowls. Then in the center of each serving place about 2 teaspoons of the mayonnaise mixture. The flavor of this combination is really indescribable, and the coldness adds to its deliciousness.

I think tomatoes are mostly thought of as salad fare, outside of being stewed. But broiled tomatoes make a superb vegetable accompaniment with steak, *filet mignons,* hamburgers, and also fish. Here are two or three outstanding recipes for broiling tomatoes.

SHERRIED BROILED TOMATOES: Cut fresh tomatoes in half and prick the cut surfaces with a fork. Drizzle dry sherry over the cut surfaces, then sprinkle with salt, pepper, and dried oregano, and top with bacon slices. Broil 5 to 7 minutes. Then top with mayonnaise, sprinkle with grated Parmesan cheese, and lightly brown under the broiler.

CURRIED BROILED TOMATOES: Sprinkle curry powder lightly over tomato slices that have been buttered, and broil them until heated through.

EPICURE'S BROILED TOMATOES: Make a cheese mix of one 8-ounce package of cream cheese, 4 ounces of Blue cheese (or Roquefort), 1 tablespoon each of dry sherry wine and cream, 2 tablespoons of chopped parsley, ½ teaspoon each of grated onion and Worcestershire sauce, salt to taste, and ¼ teaspoon of Ac'cent. (This makes about 1 cup.) Cut tomatoes in half crosswise and liberally spread the cut sides with the cheese mix. Sprinkle with fine dry breadcrumbs and dust with paprika. Broil slowly until the crumbs are nicely browned and the tomatoes are piping hot.

I first became acquainted with zucchini at the home of an Italian friend of mine, and it was a case of love at first taste. This first dish was a very plain one, *Zucchini Fritti*—zucchinis cut in ½-inch slices, fried in hot peanut oil for about 3 minutes, and then sprinkled with salt and pepper, grated Parmesan cheese, and chopped parsley. Man, was that super!

Zucchini is, of course, a variety of summer squash, and, I believe, the Italian name for the green, cucumber-shaped squash, which is a great favorite among the people of Italy.

Without further ado, I would like to offer four zucchini recipes, any one of which should make you a zucchini addict. The first two utilize zucchini sliced; the next stuffed; and the fourth is sort of a zucchini pie.

ZUCCHINI WITH PIMENTO CHEESE

2 *lbs. zucchini*	1 *8-oz. can tomato sauce*
1 *medium onion*	1 *cup pimento cheese*
1 *clove garlic*	*Salt and pepper*
2 *tbsp. olive oil*	½ *tsp. Ac'cent*

Wash the zucchini, trim off the end but do not peel, and slice crosswise paper thin.

Mince the onion and garlic, and sauté slowly for 5 minutes in the hot olive oil. Then add the sliced zucchini, cover, and cook gently for about 10 minutes, or until the zucchini is barely tender, stirring gently frequently. Then add the tomato paste, the shredded processed pimento cheese, salt and pepper to taste, and the Ac'cent. Cover and cook *slowly* 5 minutes, gently stirring occasionally. Serve in sauce dishes to 6.

ZUCCHINI LAWRY'S

1 *pkg. Lawry's Spaghetti Sauce Mix*	2 *tbsp. olive oil*
	½ *tsp. Lawry's seasoned salt*
1 #2 *can tomatoes*	4 *cups sliced zucchini*
¼ *cup grated Parmesan cheese*	

Place the spaghetti sauce mix, the tomatoes, and the olive oil in a large skillet and stir until blended. Bring to a boil, then cover and simmer for 15 minutes.

Wash and slice the zucchini (about 6 to 8). Add the sliced zucchini to the sauce, cover, and continue to simmer for about 15 minutes, or until the zucchini is tender. Sprinkle with the grated Parmesan cheese, and serve hot to 4 to 6, depending upon appetites.

STUFFED ZUCCHINI

1½ *lbs. small-sized zucchini* (6 *to* 8)	2 *eggs, slightly beaten*
	2 *tbsp. olive oil*
1 *cup fine soft breadcrumbs*	¼ *tsp. dried thyme*
½ *cup finely chopped cooked spinach*	¼ *tsp. Ac'cent*
	Salt and pepper
½ *cup grated Parmesan cheese*	*Garlic salt*
1 *tsp. minced onion*	*Paprika*

Wash the zucchini and trim off the ends. Parboil whole in boiling salted water for 15 minutes, then drain. When cool enough to handle, cut the zucchinis lengthwise in halves and scoop out the insides with a teaspoon, leaving the shell clean.

Drain the scooped-out pulp of the zucchinis thoroughly. Mix this pulp with the breadcrumbs, spinach, ¼ cup of the grated Parmesan cheese, the minced onion, the slightly beaten eggs, the olive oil, dried thyme, Ac'cent, and salt, garlic salt, and pepper to taste.

Fill the zucchini shells with this mixture. Arrange the stuffed shells in a greased shallow baking pan. Sprinkle with the remaining ¼ cup of grated Parmesan cheese, and dust with paprika. Bake in a 350-degree oven for 30 minutes. Serves 6.

ZUCCHINI AND SAUSAGE

2 lbs. zucchini	½ cup grated Parmesan cheese
½ lb. sausage meat	Pinch dried thyme
¼ cup chopped onion	Pinch dried rosemary
½ cup fine cracker crumbs	Garlic salt
2 eggs, slightly beaten	Salt and pepper
½ tsp. Ac'cent	

Wash the zucchini and trim off the ends, but do not peel. Cook the zucchini whole in boiling salted water for 15 to 20 minutes, or until just tender. Then drain *thoroughly,* and chop coarsely.

Cook the sausage meat and the onion together until the sausage meat begins to brown, stirring it with a fork to break the sausage into bits. Then add the coarsely chopped zucchini to the sausage and onion, together with the cracker crumbs, the slightly beaten eggs, the Parmesan cheese (less 2 tablespoons), the dried thyme and rosemary, the Ac'cent, and the garlic salt and salt and pepper to taste. Mix everything well, and then turn into a 9-inch greased pie plate, sprinkle with the remaining 2 tablespoons of grated Parmesan cheese. Bake in a 350-degree oven for about 45 minutes, or until firm and delicately browned. To serve, cut in wedges. This will serve 4.

(9) POTATOES, PASTAS, AND RICE

Does your mouth water at the sight of a crackly brown-skinned baked potato, with its mealy whiteness bursting through the top? Do you cast a longing eye on steaming boiled potatoes, snow-white and flaky, with a butter glaze, and flecked with bits of green parsley? And then do you resolutely turn your eyes away, and reach for a slice of unbuttered whole-wheat toast, because you just can't afford to put on any extra pounds?

Well, take heart, ladies and gentlemen! The tasty tuber has been grossly maligned. While potatoes do contain starch, they contain less of it than rice or peas. And, furthermore, potato starch is more digestible than many other starches. Nutrition experts say that a medium-sized potato is no more fattening than a large orange or apple, a medium-sized piece of meat or a baking powder biscuit, or a thin slice of bread.

I imagine that the baked potato is the most popular method of cooking potatoes. The French call them *pommes de terre en robe de chambre* (potatoes baked in their jacket). The potatoes should be scrubbed and dried, then anointed with bacon drippings, and baked for an hour in a moderate (350 degrees) oven. Then they should be slit lengthwise with a sharp knife, and the sides pressed to make the slit gape. A generous piece of butter is placed in the opening before serving, or a tablespoon of sour cream can be inserted, and the top sprinkled with chopped chives. Or, for a little fancier preparation, try these stuffed baked potatoes.

BAKED STUFFED POTATOES

4 *large baking potatoes*
¼ *cup soft butter*
1 *cup chive cottage cheese*
2 *tbsp. mayonnaise*

Salt and pepper
½ *tsp. Ac'cent*
½ *cup grated Parmesan cheese*
Paprika

Scrub and bake the potatoes as usual. When they are done, cut a thin lengthwise slice from the top of each, and scoop out the insides into a mixing bowl. Mash the potatoes well with a fork, then beat in the soft butter, the chive cottage cheese, the mayonnaise, salt and pepper to taste, and the Ac′cent. When thoroughly blended and smooth, pile the mixture into the shells, but do not smooth the tops. Sprinkle the tops with the grated Parmesan cheese, dust with paprika, and bake in a 450-degree oven for 8 to 10 minutes, or until the cheese on top melts and the potatoes are piping hot. This serves 4.

If you should ever celebrate St. Patrick's Day in Dublin on March 17, you would really have a time for yourself, for the Feast of St. Patrick is a great celebration for all of those who are a-wearing o' the green, not only in Ireland, but wherever loyal Irish foregather.

There are many fine dishes that might be served to you in Ireland, such as Cockie-leekie soup, a delectable dish made from chicken, rice, and leeks; stewed beefsteak with savory balls; Irish roast goose with potato stuffing; flummery, which is particularly Irish, and is made from cold oatmeal porridge with raisins, sugar, and almonds stirred into it before being put in a mold. And of course you would have colcannon and Irish soda bread, both of which are delicious.

Since the Irish believe that "a day without potatoes is a day without nourishment," you'll always find potatoes on an Irish menu. And their favorite is colcannon, in which the mingling of fluffy white mashed potatoes with the delicate green of onions and cabbage makes it inviting as well as tasty. Here's the way they make it in Ireland:

COLCANNON

Tender green cabbage leaves	*3 tbsp. butter*
Water	*1¾ lbs. new potatoes*
15 little green onions	*1 quart water*
1½ cups milk	*½ tsp. salt*
½ tsp. salt	*¼ tsp. dried basil*
	Melted butter

Boil tender green cabbage leaves (enough to make about 2 cups when chopped) in water for about 5 minutes. Then drain and chop finely. Also chop about 15 good-sized spring, or little green, onions (utilizing the bulbs and tops) and put them to soak in the milk to which the salt has been added. Then put them on to boil in the milk, adding the butter, and simmer slowly until tender.

Peel and slice about 1¾ pounds of new, or red, potatoes, put them in a pan, cover with 1 quart of water to which ½ teaspoon of salt and ¼ teaspoon of dried basil has been added, and boil until the potatoes are tender. When they are, drain them and begin mashing. Gradually add the chopped onion and milk, and the chopped cabbage leaves, pounding them into the potatoes. Keep mashing and stirring until the potatoes become fluffy, and the onion and cabbage leaves are entirely absorbed. In Ireland they use a wooden masher, or pestle, and call this "beetling." Pepper and salt to taste. To keep the potatoes in the pan hot while mashing, put the pan in a larger pan with boiling water.

Serve colcannon hot on individual plates. Make a depression in the center of each portion and fill the cavity with melted butter. Eat with a spoon, from the outside in, dipping a spoonful of colcannon into the melted butter.

Mashed potatoes can be a delight or an abomination. To be made to perfection, firm potatoes should be used; they should be boiled or steamed, then dried over a low flame to evaporate the moisture; they are at their creamy best, in my opinion, when they are put through a ricer, then rich milk, butter, salt, and white pepper added, and they are beaten until they are fluffy. Too much milk added makes them too creamy, not enough milk added leaves them too stiff. But one of the greatest culinary abominations is watery, lumpy mashed potatoes.

There are many variations of mashed potatoes. One of the best known is Duchesse Potatoes. It is really glorified mashed potatoes, having egg yolks added, and a little cream. If used as a garnish, such as on a planked entree, the potatoes are put through a pastry tube and worked into a border. Or they may be shaped with a pastry tube into various forms for individual servings, then browned under the broiler on a cookie sheet.

DUCHESSE POTATOES

2 *lbs. potatoes, boiled*	*White pepper*
2 *tbsp. butter*	*Dash nutmeg*
1 *tsp. salt*	3 *egg yolks*
	Hot cream or milk

Boil the potatoes, which have been peeled, in salted water, or steam them until tender. Drain thoroughly, and if they have been boiled, empty the water from the pan and dry them out by shaking them in the pan over the fire until all moisture has been evaporated. Then put the potatoes through a ricer, and whip them with a wooden spoon until they are very smooth. Then add the butter, salt, pepper, and nutmeg, and the egg yolks, and enough hot milk or cream to moisten. Beat the mixture until it is very fluffy.

A most unusual and delectable potato dish is *Pommes Dauphin,* which were served at the Golden Era Dinner of the American Spice Trade Association in New York.

POMMES DAUPHIN

2½ *lbs. potatoes*	4 *eggs*
½ *cup butter*	1 *tsp. nutmeg*
1 *cup dry white wine*	1 *tsp. salt*
½ *tsp. salt*	1 *pinch black pepper*
1 *cup sifted flour*	*Deep fat for frying*

Peel the potatoes and boil in salted water until tender. While the potatoes are boiling, put the butter, dry white wine, and salt in a saucepan, and bring to a boil. Then add the flour and cook over a low flame, stirring constantly, until the mixture leaves the side of the pan and forms a ball (about 1 minute). Cool slightly and beat in the eggs, one at a time, beating until smooth after each addition.

Drain the potatoes and press them through a ricer. Add the salt, pepper, and nutmeg, and then blend in the above mixture well.

Drop by tablespoonfuls into hot deep fat (375 degrees) and fry to a light golden brown. Drain on paper toweling and keep warm until ready to serve. Serves 5 to 6.

Croquettes is the culinary name of balls of any and every kind of food, free from bones, gristle, fibers, and such. But I never order croquettes of any kind in a restaurant because they, like hash, may contain a multitude of sins. Meat croquettes can be very dreadful in restaurants, but very luscious at home.

In very fine restaurants you probably take no chances when ordering potato croquettes, for fine chefs can turn out marvelous ones.

I am very fond of them, so much so, in fact, that I have experimented, and here is one of the results.

POTATO CROQUETTES, NOIX D'ACAJOU
(Potato Croquettes with Cashew Nuts)

4 *cups hot mashed potatoes*	*Pinch dried rosemary*
1 *egg, beaten*	*Cashew nuts*
2 *tbsp. dry sherry*	*Deep fat for frying*

Add a generous pinch of dried rosemary to the hot mashed potatoes and shape into croquettes about the size of an egg, and cool (the mashed potatoes should not be too creamy).

Beat an egg together with the sherry, and dip the croquettes into the egg mixture. Then roll the croquettes in cashew nuts which have been ground and crushed until very fine. Then fry in deep fat, drain on paper toweling, and serve at once. This will serve about 6.

French peasants are a thrifty lot, and throughout southern France potatoes cooked in white wine often compose a meal's main dish. This combination may sound strange, but I can assure you it is delicious.

POTATOES IN WHITE WINE

1 *lb. raw potatoes*	*Pinch thyme*
8 *slices lean bacon*	*Pinch marjoram*
1 *tbsp. butter*	*Salt*
6 *small onions*	*Pepper*
1 *bay leaf*	*American dry sauterne*
1 *tbsp. chopped parsley*	*Flour*

Dice the bacon slices (as lean as you can obtain) and simmer them until golden brown in a skillet with the butter and onions. Then add the raw potatoes, peeled and cut in pieces about the size of English walnuts. Add the bay leaf, chopped parsley, pinch each of thyme and marjoram, and salt and pepper to taste, and enough dry American sauterne to reach to the top of the potatoes. Cook very slowly for at least an hour, or until the potatoes can be pierced easily with a fork. When they are done, lift them out of the pan with the onions and diced bacon and put them at the back of the stove in a hot dish. Then boil up the wine gravy for a few minutes. If you like your sauce thickened, sprinkle in a little flour. After the sauce is of a consistency to your liking, pour it over the potatoes and onions and bacon and serve piping hot.

One of the most tempting potato dishes to me is Potatoes au Gratin. I can't think of an entree that doesn't team up felicitously with cheese and potatoes, and this combination has an added taste appeal.

POTATOES AU GRATIN WITH SHERRY

4 cups diced cooked potatoes   *1⅓ cup grated American or*
2 tbsp. butter   *Cheddar cheese*
2 tbsp. flour   *¼ cup dry sherry wine*
1 cup milk   *Salt and pepper*
                       Paprika

Melt the butter in a saucepan, and stir in the flour. When well blended, add the milk and cook, stirring constantly, until the mixture is thickened and smooth. Then add 1 cup of grated American or Cheddar cheese, and stir over a low heat until the cheese is melted. Remove from the heat, add the medium dry sherry wine, and salt and pepper to taste. Blend the whole, then add 4 cups of diced, cooked potatoes. Turn the whole into a greased casserole, and sprinkle the top with ⅓ cup of the same grated cheese that was used in the cooking, and a generous sprinkling of paprika. Bake in a hot oven (400 degrees) for about 20 minutes, or until bubbly and delicately browned.

Some night, when you have leftover boiled potatoes, or leftover browned potatoes which have been cooked with a roast, try sherried potatoes with mushrooms. This is a simple yet savory dish, adaptable to whatever number of people you want to serve. I am purposely leaving out the amount of ingredients, because you can measure them according to your needs.

SHERRIED POTATOES WITH MUSHROOMS

Sliced cooked potatoes   *Salt and pepper*
Condensed cream of mushroom   *Dry sherry*
     soup   *Fine breadcrumbs*
          Grated Parmesan cheese

Place a layer of sliced cooked potatoes in the bottom of a casserole, salt and pepper them to taste, and cover with condensed cream of mushroom soup. Then add another layer of the sliced cooked potatoes, salt and pepper them, and add another layer of the cream of mushroom soup. Continue layers until the casserole is nearly full. Then sprinkle over the contents of the casserole some dry sherry wine, cover the top with fine breadcrumbs, sprinkle with grated Parmesan cheese, and bake in a moderate (350 degrees) oven until hot.

To a German, *Sauerbraten* or pot roast without potato pancakes is like eggs without salt. And although I am not German, I am in full accord.

I have eaten potato pancakes in a number of fine German restaurants such as Lüchow's, in New York (one of the finest in America), the Red Star Inn in Chicago, Mader's in Milwaukee, and Schroeder's Café in San Francisco. But the finest potato pancakes I have ever eaten I had in the Flamingo Hotel in Las Vegas, believe it or not.

I went to Las Vegas to get material for a story on the food served at the fabulous hotels on the "Strip." We stopped at the Flamingo, and I used that delightful hotel as a base for operations. I might say, parenthetically, that Mrs. Wood and I have never had more perfect accommodations and service than we had at the Flamingo.

I had the pleasure of having luncheon the day after our arrival with Jack Denison, the suave and handsome maître d', and John Kohler, the chef. The latter was born in the Black Forest in Germany, and had been a chef at the old Waldorf in New York and at many of the most famous restaurants in South America and America. We spent two hours happily talking about food and wine, and I had a potato pancake that Kohler made for me. It was so wonderful that I asked for the recipe. Here it is.

POTATO PANCAKE FLAMINGO

2 *large raw potatoes*	2 *eggs, lightly beaten*
1 *tbsp. flour*	1 *tbsp. baking powder*
1 *tbsp. matzoth meal*	*Salt and pepper*
1 *tbsp. sour cream*	*Chicken fat (or butter)*

Peel and grate the raw potatoes, and to them add the flour, matzoth meal, sour cream, the lightly beaten eggs, the baking powder, and salt and pepper to taste. Mix everything well.

Melt hot chicken fat (or butter) in a pan, and when it is hot, use a large tablespoon to put the mixture into the pan. Fry on both sides until crisp and brown. This will make enough pancackes for two people.

O'Brien Potatoes is a tasty dish in which cooked potatoes are diced, and fried with the addition of onions, green peppers, and pimento. But Emily Chase Leistner came up with an adaptation which is called Potato Pancakes O'Brien, and they are mighty gratifying.

POTATO PANCAKES O'BRIEN

1 *egg, slightly beaten*	2 *tbsp. minced green peppers*
3 *tbsp. flour*	2 *tbsp. minced pimento*
¼ *cup milk*	¼ *tsp. Ac'cent*
2 *tbsp. minced onion*	*Salt and pepper*

2 *cups* (*firmly packed*) *grated raw potatoes*

Mix the egg and flour until smooth, then stir in the milk. When well blended, add the minced onion, green pepper, pimento, Ac'cent, salt and pepper to taste, and the grated raw potatoes (the potatoes should be peeled and grated just before adding to the batter to prevent darkening).

Drop the mixture in circles (¼ cup each) on a well-greased griddle. Cook over medium heat about 5 minutes on each side, or until potatoes are tender. This recipe makes 8 pancakes, and they are delicious with pot roast, or for a Sunday brunch with ham or bacon and eggs.

Oddly enough, I have found a number of people who do not know the difference between sweet potatoes and yams. In one sense of the word they are very similar, in that they are sweet to the taste and look something alike. But the yam, when cooked, has a much higher moisture content, and is sweeter than the sweet potato. The sweet potato is pale yellowish in color, but the yam is usually a reddish brown. Too, the yam is apt to be much larger than the sweet potato. I have read where true yams in the South Sea Islands grow up to eight feet in length and eighty pounds in weight!

Regardless of their differences, they are both mighty fine eating, particularly with pork dishes. The following recipe I have called Baked Yams Tahiti, and has a South Seas touch.

BAKED YAMS TAHITI

2 *lbs. cooked yams* (*or* 2 1-*lb.*   ½ *cup dry sherry*
      canned yams)   ½ *tsp. salt*
1 *cup crushed pineapple*   ¼ *tsp. pepper*
2 *ripe bananas*   *Butter*
                    Miniature marshmallows

Drain the crushed pineapple, and combine it with the cooked, peeled yams (or two 1-pound cans of yams which have been drained) and the ripe bananas. Mash these all together well, then add the dry sherry, salt, and pepper. Whip everything together until the mixture is smooth, then place it in a buttered baking dish or a casserole. Dot the top with butter and miniature marshmallows. Bake in a 350-degree oven for 45 minutes, or until the mixture bubbles slightly and the marshmallows are lightly browned.

In this recipe, sweet potatoes are better for baking and stuffing than yams.

BAKED STUFFED SWEET POTATOES

6 *sweet potatoes*   ¼ *tsp. salt*
1 *lime, juice of*   *Pinch pepper*
Grated rind of lime   *Dash Angostura bitters*
2 *oz. Cointreau*   *Butter*

Bake the sweet potatoes, then cut in half, and carefully scoop out the centers, being careful not to damage the shells. Place the scooped-out potatoes in a bowl, and add to them the lime juice and the grated rind of the lime, and 2 ounces of Cointreau or orange curaçao, about ¼ teaspoon of salt, a pinch of pepper, and a dash of Angostura bitters. Mash the potatoes and their seasonings, and put them back into their shells. Dot the tops with butter, and bake in a 300-degree oven, covered, for about 30 minutes. If you wish, they can be browned under the broiler before serving.

Crunchy walnuts and sweet potatoes go hand in hand for a glamorous extra on a party menu.

CANDIED SWEET POTATOES AND WALNUTS

Sliced cooked sweet potatoes   *2 oz. orange juice*
Broken walnuts   *2 oz. orange curaçao*
1 cup brown sugar   *¼ cup butter*
1 tbsp. cornstarch

Arrange layers of sliced, cooled sweet potatoes and broken walnuts in a shallow baking dish.

Make a sauce of the brown sugar, orange juice, orange curaçao, and butter, and thicken with the cornstarch. Pour this sauce over the potato and walnuts, and bake in a 375-degree oven for about ½ hour.

Common and often overlooked flavorings, or an unusual ingredient, will do the same thing for an over-familiar dish that a new hat, purse, and gloves will do for a last season's dress—make it new and exciting.

The addition of a secret blend of tropical spices, which is Angostura bitters, and whiskey, gives an exciting, exotic flavor and aroma to the low-priced, highly nutritious—and sometimes very dull—sweet potato.

TIPSY SWEET POTATOES

4 cooked sweet potatoes   *¼ tsp. salt*
¾ cup brown sugar   *2 tbsp. butter*
½ cup bourbon whiskey   *1 tsp. Angostura bitters*

Cut the sweet potatoes, which have been peeled, in half lengthwise, and arrange in a greased baking dish.

Combine the brown sugar, whiskey, salt, and butter, and cook for 3 minutes over a low heat. Then stir in the Angostura bitters, and pour the mixture over the potatoes. Bake in a 375-degree oven for about 30 minutes, basting with the syrup while cooking.

Coming up last, but not least, in the sweet potato parade is a recipe from the Islands.

SWEET POTATOES HAWAIIAN

Cooked sweet potatoes   *Sliced lemons*
Sliced canned pineapple   *Light rum*
Sliced oranges   *Butter*

Boil sweet potatoes with their skins on in salted water until soft, about 20 to 30 minutes. Remove, peel, and slice to about ¼-inch thickness.

In a well-buttered casserole place a layer of sliced sweet potatoes, then cover with a layer of sliced canned pineapple, also cut about ¼ inch in thickness. Add another layer of the sliced sweet potatoes, and top them with a layer of thin orange slices. Add another layer of the sliced sweet potatoes, and top this layer with a layer of thin lemon slices. Pour over all light rum, dot generously with butter, and bake in a moderate oven (350 degrees) until a rich golden brown, or about 30 minutes.

As a chapter, or section, of any general or specialty cookbook, it is impossible to do justice to the fascinating subject of the Italian *pastas.* I have two particular cookbooks which are devoted exclusively to *pastas,* and anyone who is fond of spaghetti, macaroni, *et al,* should possess them. One is Crosby Gaige's *Macaroni Manual,* which has little history but hundreds of wonderful recipes; and the other is *Spaghetti Dinner,* by Giuseppe Prezzolini, which is about equally filled with history and recipes.

Many cookbooks credit Marco Polo with bringing spaghetti to Italy from China. But this is just a legend, and is not true. As Giuseppe Prezzolini points out, Marco Polo lived from 1254 to 1323, yet by the year 1200 the food was well known in Italy and was mentioned in an historical document, *The Life of the Blessed Hermit William.*

But if you want to go in for legends, you'll get a kick out of one sponsored by the National Macaroni Institute, which is entitled "A Legend of Love," and I quote:

One day, hundreds of years ago, a young Chinese maiden was busy preparing her daily batch of bread dough. Becoming engrossed in conversation with an ardent Italian sailor, she forgot her task.

Presently dough overflowed from the pan and dripped in strings that quickly dried in the sun. When he observed what had happened, the young Italian, hoping to hide the evidence of his loved one's carelessness, gathered the strings of dried dough and took them to his ship. The ship's cook boiled them in a broth. He was pleased to find that the dish was appetizing and savory. Upon the ship's return to Italy, word of the delicious new dish spread rapidly, and soon it was popular throughout the land.

I guess there must be hundreds of different forms of *pastas*. Macaroni is, of course, tubular in shape, and varies in size from thin macaroni (*bucatini*) to extra large macaroni (*tufoli*), which is usually cut in 2½- to 3½-inch lengths. These large forms of macaroni are usually stuffed.

Spaghetti varies in size from fine strings, known as "Angel's Hair" (*fidelini*) to regular spaghetti. Spaghetti is sometimes hollow.

There are flat types of macaroni, such as *fettuccelle,* a medium-size noodle type of plain macaroni; fancy shapes of macaroni, such as bow ties (*farfalle*), small shells (*maruzzelle*), large shells (*maruzze*), and spirals (*rotelle*). And there is cut macaroni, either in the form of elbows or straight (*ditali*).

There are Italian fluffy egg noodles, classed as fine, medium, and broad. (This latter is better known as *lasagne.*)

And lastly there are various tiny macaroni shapes for soups (the best known are probably alphabets) and *pastina,* which are an ideal baby food cut in tiny stars and rings.

An old friend of mine is Ted Sills, of New York, Chicago, and very lately of California. Ted is the head of a very fine public relations firm, and, among other products, he beats the drums for the National Macaroni Institute. Through him I became a member of the Macaroni-of-the-Month Club, and, because I don't believe in wasting comestibles, I have eaten more *pasta* products than any three Italians you can gather together. But don't get me wrong, I love spaghetti and macaroni, and I am an avid collector of *pasta* recipes, particularly those that can't be found in the usual run of cookbooks, magazines, and newspaper columns.

On Italian freighters, spaghetti is a staple food. Because ships' stores always contain olive oil, garlic, canned tomatoes, onions and tinned anchovies, a favorite sailor dish is Spaghetti Marinara.

SPAGHETTI MARINARA

8 oz. spaghetti
3 quarts boiling water
1 tbsp. salt
4 tbsp. olive oil
2 cloves garlic
2 medium-sized onions
1 large can tomatoes

10 canned anchovy filets,
    chopped
2 oz. dry white wine
Freshly ground pepper
¼ tsp. dried oregano
Grated Parmesan cheese

Add the salt to the rapidly boiling water, and then gradually add the spaghetti so that the water continues to boil. Cook, uncovered, until tender, about 10 to 12 minutes.

Put the olive oil in a heavy saucepan, and when it is hot add the garlic, crushed, and the onions, sliced. Sauté for 5 to 10 minutes, or until the onions are soft. Then add the tomatoes, and cook rapidly for about 5 minutes. Add the chopped anchovy filets, the dry white wine, freshly ground pepper, and the dried oregano. Lower the flame, and simmer for about 45 minutes.

Drain the spaghetti, and pour the sauce over it. Sprinkle with grated Parmesan cheese, and serve immediately. This will serve 3.

The Italian *pastas* offer a number of opportunities for Lenten dishes, or other meatless meals. They team up flavorfully with eggs, cheese, fish, and shellfish. The following dish, utilizing shrimp, is most unusual and appetizing.

SPAGHETTI-SHRIMP CASSEROLE

8 oz. spaghetti
3 quarts boiling water
1 tbsp. salt
¼ cup butter
½ lb. fresh mushrooms, sliced
2 tsp. grated onion
¼ cup flour
1½ cups milk
½ cup dry white wine

1 tsp. salt
¼ tsp. freshly ground pepper
½ lb. cooked fresh shrimps
½ cup thinly sliced celery
3 hard-cooked eggs, sliced
3 cups diced cooked carrots
1 tbsp. hot milk
Salt
Nutmeg

First, cook your spaghetti. Add 1 tablespoon of salt to 3 quarts of rapidly boiling water. Gradually add 8 ounces of spaghetti so that the water continues to boil. Cook, uncovered, stirring occasionally, until tender, about 12 minutes if you like it *al dente* (when there is a slight resistance to biting), or up to 15 minutes if you like it softer. When the spaghetti is done, drain it in a colander.

In a saucepan, melt the butter over low heat, then add the fresh mushrooms, sliced, and the grated onion. Sauté these for about 5 minutes, then add the flour, and blend well. Then gradually stir in the milk and dry white wine (which have been previously mixed together), and continue cooking until thickened, stirring constantly. Add 1 teaspoon of salt and the freshly ground pepper.

In a bowl, combine the mushroom sauce, the cooked fresh shrimp, shelled and deveined, the thinly sliced celery, the hard-cooked eggs, sliced, and the cooked spaghetti. Mix all these together well, but gently, and turn into a greased 2-quart casserole.

Mash 3 cups of diced cooked carrots with 1 tablespoon of hot milk, adding a little salt and nutmeg to taste. Arrange the mashed carrots in a ring on top of the casserole. Bake in a moderate (350 degrees) oven for about 25 minutes, or until the carrots are lightly browned. This should make 6 servings.

The repertoire of entrees which the average housewife presents to her family (and how often it is exhausted and then repeated) seems to me to be of great importance where the well-being of a family is concerned. Eating is, of course, one of the most essential phases of our daily existence.

If it becomes a habit—fish on Friday, a roast on Saturday, chicken on Sunday, chops on Tuesday, steaks on Thursday, leftovers on Monday and maybe Wednesday—a good deal of zest is taken out of the approach to the dinner table. But if, instead of the same thing every six or seven days, the main dishes are varied, and surprise dishes crop up every once in a while, dinner can be looked forward to with enthusiasm.

The *pastas* and the almost endless combinations of comestibles that go with them offer great opportunities for varying menus, not only deliciously but inexpensively. Take this one, for instance, that Mrs. Wood and I were delighted with.

MACARONI AND LUNCHEON MEAT CASSEROLE

8 oz. macaroni, cut
3 quarts boiling water
1 tbsp. salt
1 12-oz. can luncheon meat
¼ lb. sharp Cheddar cheese
1 #2 can tomatoes

1 bay leaf
½ tsp. salt
Generous pinch dried basil
Freshly ground pepper
Dash Worcestershire sauce
4 oz. dry white wine

Add 1 tablespoon of salt to 3 quarts of rapidly boiling water. Gradually add the cut macaroni, so that the water continues to boil. Cook, uncovered, stirring occasionally, until tender (about 12 to 15 minutes, depending on how well done you like your macaroni). Drain the macaroni in a colander.

In a 2-quart casserole, place three alternate layers of cooked macaroni, sliced luncheon meat, and thinly sliced sharp Cheddar cheese. In a bowl, combine the canned tomatoes, bay leaf, ½ teaspoon of salt, a generous pinch of dried basil, freshly ground pepper to taste, a dash of Worcestershire sauce, and the dry white wine. Blend these, and pour the mixture over the ingredients in the casserole. Cover, and bake in a moderate (375 degrees) oven for 30 minutes. Serve piping hot to from 4 to 6 and accompany with a tossed green salad, and the same wine (chilled) as was used in the cooking.

Gastronomically, Lent is a difficult season for many people, and particularly for cooks. *"Repas maigres,"* as the French people call fish meals, may well tax the ingenuity of anyone in the kitchen when they become the rule rather than the exception during the forty days preceding Easter. But when one realizes that there are a vast number of dishes which can be made without recourse to flesh or fowl, then cooking during Lent can be a pleasurable experiment.

That old meatless stand-by, macaroni and cheese, can become a little tiresome. But when it is fancied up, it can be an epicurean dish. The following is something really special.

OYSTER-MACARONI SUPPER

2 cups elbow macaroni	2 cups grated Cheddar cheese
3 quarts boiling water	¼ cup grated Parmesan cheese
1 tbsp. salt	½ cup milk
2 tbsp. butter	1 tsp. celery seed
1 medium onion, chopped	1 tsp. salt

1 pint undrained oysters

Add 1 tablespoon of salt to the rapidly boiling water, and then gradually add the elbow macaroni so that the water continues to boil. Cook uncovered, stirring occasionally, until tender. Drain in a colander.

Meanwhile, melt the butter in a saucepan. Add the onion, finely chopped, and sauté until tender, about 7 to 10 minutes. Then add the two cheeses, milk, celery seed, 1 teaspoon of salt, and the oysters. Cook over a low flame, stirring occasionally, until the cheeses are melted. Then add the macaroni, mix well, and serve. Serves 4 to 6.

Here is a macaroni and cheese casserole that is really fancy pants. I am told it is a favorite among Southern cooks, so we'll call it:

MACARONI CASSEROLE, SOUTHERN STYLE

8 oz. elbow macaroni	2 tbsp. grated onion
3 quarts boiling water	1 10½-oz. can cream of mush-
1 tbsp. salt	room soup
½ lb. ground raw smoked ham	1 cup dry sherry
2 cups grated Cheddar cheese	1 tsp. salt
½ cup chopped green pepper	Freshly ground pepper

Cook the macaroni in the usual way, and drain in a colander.

In a large bowl combine the ground ham, cheese, green pepper, grated onion, cream of mushroom soup, dry sherry, salt, and freshly ground pepper to taste. When the ingredients are well mixed, add the cooked macaroni, and mix lightly but thoroughly. Pour the mixture into a 2-quart casserole, cover, and bake in a 350-degree oven for 1 hour. Serve piping hot to 4 to 6.

One of the great Italian *pasta* dishes, usually served in a baking dish, is *lasagne*. It is named after the Italian broad noodles.

I had a rather interesting and amusing experience in the detailing of the recipe in my syndicated column, "For Men Only!" The recipe I told about and printed came from an Italian family, and happened to be authentic. However, I substituted Lawry's Spaghetti Sauce Mix, which simplified it. But a week or so later I received an anonymous letter from a young Italian lady in Chicago, who took me to task for a recipe she said was "strictly for the birds."

Well, here is the recipe for Lasagne, which I think is pretty fine. And following it, I will reprint her letter in full, and her recipe.

LASAGNE

1 *lb. ground chuck beef*	1 *pkg. Lawry's Spaghetti*
2 *tbsp. olive oil*	*Sauce Mix*
2 *cloves garlic, minced*	½ *lb. lasagne*
Seasoned salt	*Salted water*
Pepper	½ *lb. Mozzarella cheese*
1 *8-oz. can tomato paste*	¾ *lb. Ricotta cheese*
1 #2 *can tomatoes*	½ *cup grated Parmesan cheese*

Brown the ground chuck beef in the olive oil in a large skillet, adding the minced garlic to the beef, and seasoned salt, and pepper to taste. Simmer slowly for about 10 minutes. Then add the tomato sauce or paste, the canned tomatoes, and the package of spaghetti sauce mix. Stir everything thoroughly, cover, and simmer for 30 minutes.

Meanwhile, boil ½ pound of *lasagne* in salted water until tender (about 20 to 25 minutes) stirring frequently to prevent *lasagne* sticking together. When just barely tender, drain the *lasagne* well, and rinse.

Arrange a layer of the meat sauce in the bottom of a large casserole. Cover this with a layer of *lasagne*. Then make a layer of Mozzarella cheese (a soft Italian cheese, usually sold in balls at Italian grocery stores) over the *lasagne*. Dot the slices of Mozzarella cheese with Ricotta cheese (an Italian cottage cheese). Repeat the layers, ending up with a layer of *lasagne* and sauce. Sprinkle generously with grated Parmesan cheese, and bake in a 375-degree oven for about 20 minutes. The total amounts of the cheeses needed are ½ pound of Mozzarella, ¾ pound of Ricotta, and ½ cup of Parmesan, grated. This recipe will serve about 6. Of course, an Italian-type wine, such as Barbera or Chianti, is a must.

And now for the letter and recipe from Madam X. I do wish she had signed her name so I could have called on her, for she sounded quite intriguing. Perhaps if she ever reads this, she will break down and reveal her identity.

Chicago Tribune
435 N. Michigan
Chicago 11, Ill.

Attention: Mr. Morrison Wood ("For Men Only!")

Dear Sir:

Your recipe for Lasagne and Italian sauce is *strictly for* the birds.

Recipe: Step #1
Sauté 1 lb. ground round steak, (3 T. olive oil), 1 good-size garlic clove chopped very fine, 1 small onion chopped fine, 1 t.-spoon oregano (this is what makes your sauce), cook all this until everything is brown.

Step #2
Open a small can of tomato paste, with same can of water, cook with ingredients above until well blended, then open a #2 can of tomatoes to a half can of water and stir very well with a tablespoon of salt (more or less if desired). Cook this on a very low flame for about 3 hours and if you want a thinner sauce, just add more water, thick sauce leave as is. (You will certainly see the difference if you follow this recipe from an Italian herself—me). *Try it sometime.*

Let's get another thing straight. Lasagne is not an Italian paste. *It is a filling*—in fact very rich *if it is made right.* Not the way you have printed.

For four people—3 lbs. Ricotta, 1 egg, 3 T. sugar, ½ t. salt, chopped parsley. Mix these all together and keep until ready in a refrigerator. Cook 1 lb. wide noodles to taste, (soft, hard, or med.) After noodles are cooked, let water run on noodles a few seconds so noodles won't stick together. Then drain on/in colander. Now you are ready to prepare casserole.

Have a large casserole length of noodles. Have grated *Italian Cheese* prepared ready to sprinkle.

Step #1—Grated cheese sprinkled at bottom of casserole to start, layer of gravy (plenty at bottom). Then you put a layer of noodles, layer of filling, etc., *along with gravy for each layer of noodles and filling.* On your last layer on top, make sure you have plenty of gravy and grated cheese. Now you are ready to put into oven.

Step #2—Oven should be 375 degrees and baked for ten minutes only because if it is baked too long, your Lasagne will be all dried out. Now you are ready to serve.

Hope you enjoy yourself. This is genuine LASAGNE. You will never taste Lasagne anywhere like this in your life. I guarantee it through experience. I never eat this out because there's not a restaurant that can compare with it.

I will close now hoping that you stuff yourself too much. (You probably can't even boil water.)

'Bye now. . . .

Madam X

Aren't I terrible?

Rice is the most important food in the world, and its cultivation is as old as civilization itself. Rice is today, as it has always been, the basic food of more than half of the world's population. In the Orient, rice is virtually the only food of millions of people—their means of sustaining life. Approximately 95 per cent of the world's rice crop is produced in the Asiatic orbit.

There seems to be some dispute as to where rice was first cultivated. The Encyclopaedia Britannica tells us that a ceremonial ordinance was established in China by the Emperor Chun-nung twenty-eight hundred years before Christ, in accordance with which the Emperor sows the rice himself, while the seeds of four other kinds may be sown by the princes of his family.

There is no trace of rice as a native plant in the early histories of Egypt, Persia, Greece, or Rome. It is not mentioned in the Bible; but its culture is alluded to in the Talmud. There is proof of its culture in the Euphrates Valley and in Syria, four hundred years before Christ.

Rice always has played an important part in the civil, social, and religious ceremonies and observances of many Oriental peoples. It was, and still is, the medium of exchange in many parts of the Orient.

The almost world-wide custom of throwing rice at newly married couples is believed to be a survival of the ancient religious practices of the Hindus and Chinese. In the Orient, rice is the emblem of fecundity and fertility, and throwing it at a newly wedded pair symbolizes the wish that they may be blessed with offspring.

The high nutritive value of rice as a daily diet is adequately attested by the survival of hundreds of Americans who fell prisoner to the Japanese during those grim days of 1942. Through more than three and a half years of imprisonment, these soldiers and sailors were subjected to Nipponese brutality, were worked unmercifully, and yet their diet consisted of no more than three, or sometimes as little as two small bowls of rice per day. Occasionally, it is true, this diet was augmented by a thin broth, and perhaps a little black bread—but, always, there was rice. And it was rice, even in incredibly small quantities, which sustained their strength under brutal, slave-work conditions.

It seems to me that there is almost as much disagreement over the proper method of cooking rice as there is over its origin, or the proper way to make a mint julep. I have tried many methods. My first success with cooking rice came from the directions in Charles H. Baker's *The Gentlemen's Companion,* and for many years that was the only method I followed. But not too long ago I was introduced to converted rice, and since then I have had great success with the least amount of trouble. I never use any other kind of rice than Uncle Ben's Converted Rice, and I merely follow directions on the package. I put a cup of raw rice in the top of a double boiler, and add to it 1 teaspoon of salt and 1 teaspoon of lemon juice. I put the top of the double boiler over boiling water in the lower half, then I pour in 2¼ cups of boiling water over the rice, cover, and let the rice cook until it has absorbed all the water— about 45 minutes. The result is that each grain is tender, fluffy, and separate. Also, this converted rice requires no washing, which is another asset.

Over a period of time, I have learned a few tricks about cooking rice, to give it an unusual flavor. One of these is to use ½ cup of dry white wine as part of the water called for. Another little trick is to use 1 cup of beef bouillon as part of the water called for, or 1 cup of chicken bouillon. Still another is to toss hot flaky cooked rice with sliced toasted almonds and sautéed fresh mushrooms which have been coarsely chopped.

An unusually flavorsome rice dish is baked rice with herbs. It goes wonderfully with many meat and chicken dishes.

BAKED RICE WITH HERBS

1½ *cups converted rice*
3 *tbsp. olive oil*
½ *cup chopped onion*
½ *cup chopped celery*
¼ *cup chopped parsley*
1 *chopped clove garlic*

2 *cups chicken bouillon*
1 *cup dry white wine*
Pinch dried thyme
Pinch dried rosemary
Salt and pepper
½ *tsp. Ac'cent*

Heat the olive oil in a heavy skillet, and sauté in it the rice, chopped onion, celery, and parsley and garlic slowly for 5 minutes, stirring frequently. Then add the chicken bouillon, dry white wine, dried thyme and rosemary, salt and pepper to taste, and the Ac'cent. Bring to a boil, and then pour into a 2-quart casserole. Cover, and bake in a 375-degree oven for 30 minutes. Uncover, stir gently with a fork, then cover, and continue baking for 10 minutes. This will serve 6.

I imagine that most people think that spaghetti and macaroni are eaten all over Italy. Yet in northern and central Italy there is a broad section where macaroni in any shape or form is rarely eaten. Through the length and breadth of the valley of the Po River, from Turin near the French border to Venice on the sea, rice and corn-meal dishes are the rule. The Italian *Rissoto* and *Polenta* are favorite dishes of those Italians. And they have many wonderful ways with rice. The following is the Italian version of baked rice.

ITALIAN BAKED RICE

4 *cups cooked converted rice*
½ *cup chopped pimento*
½ *cup finely diced onion*
¼ *cup diced green pepper*
2 *tsp. salt*
¼ *tsp. pepper*
Dash cayenne pepper
1 *tsp. Worcestershire sauce*
¾ *cup grated Parmesan cheese*
2½ *cups canned tomatoes*
2 *tbsp. butter*

Combine the rice, pimento, diced onion, diced green pepper, salt, pepper, cayenne, Worcestershire sauce, and one-half of the grated cheese. Stir to blend well, then turn into a 2-quart, well-buttered casserole. Add the tomatoes and their juice. Top with the remaining cheese and dot with the butter. Bake in a 350-degree oven for 30 minutes. This serves 6.

The talented and very charming Mabel Sherrill, director of Lawry's Home Economics Kitchen, devised a rice dish which she calls "Spanish Rice," in which Lawry's very versatile Spaghetti Sauce Mix is one of the principal ingredients. But with all due respect to Mabel Sherrill, I can't see why it was called Spanish. To me it's quite Italian, but I have added a touch to justify the "Spanish"! But Spanish or Italian, it is very, very delicious.

SPANISH RICE

⅓ cup olive oil   1 can tomato sauce
1 cup finely chopped onion   2 pkgs. Lawry's Spaghetti
1 cup finely chopped green pepper   Sauce Mix
1 #2 can tomatoes   1½ cups converted rice
Dry sherry wine   1 tsp. Lawry's garlic spread
                1 cup grated Parmesan cheese

Cook the finely chopped onion and finely chopped green pepper
in the olive oil for about 10 minutes. Then add the canned tomatoes
(drained) and an amount of dry sherry equal to the juice drained
from the tomatoes. Also add the tomato sauce, and 2 packages of
Lawry's Spaghetti Sauce Mix. Stir thoroughly, cover, and simmer
for 15 minutes, covered.

Cook the converted rice in salted boiling water until tender, then
drain, and add to the seasoned sauce. Place the whole in a 3-
quart casserole which has been rubbed with the garlic spread.
Sprinkle 1 cup of grated Parmesan cheese over the top, and bake in
a 350-degree oven for 30 minutes. This can be made ahead of time,
and reheated. It will serve 6, generously.

Fried rice is simply cooked rice fried in peanut oil with egg, salt
and pepper, finely chopped green onions, and soy sauce for about
7 to 8 minutes. This is the fried rice that accompanies Lobster
Cantonese, or any other substantial Cantonese dish. But it can be
practically a Hollywood production as a main dish. Butt-Chen
Chow-Fon is fried rice with "eight precious ingredients," which are
chicken, duck and sausage meat, ham, bacon, shrimps, lobster meat,
and crab meat, chopped lettuce, and soup stock. Needless to say,
that is a dish.

One of the courses that was served to us at Johnny Kan's wonderful restaurant in San Francisco's Chinatown was Fried Rice with
Ham (Foh Tuey Chow Fon). I have never tasted fried rice anywhere that could approach this dish.

FRIED RICE WITH HAM

3 *tbsp. peanut oil*   1 *tsp. Ac'cent*
¼ *tsp. salt*   2 *eggs, beaten*
1 *cup diced cooked ham*   4 *cups cold cooked rice*
¼ *cup thin slices dried onion*   3 *tbsp. soy sauce*
                 Finely cut green onions

Preheat a large 12- to 14-inch frying pan and put in the peanut oil
(or fat) and the salt. Then add the cooked ham, diced in small
pieces, and the slices of dried onions. Sauté over a moderate flame
for 3 to 4 minutes, stirring constantly.

Blend the Ac'cent with 2 eggs beaten, and add to the ham and
onion mixture. Then add the cold cooked rice. Cook over a moderate flame, stirring constantly, and pressing the rice down. Then add
the soy sauce, and continue to cook until the rice is fairly brown
and hot. Serve, garnishing the fried rice with finely cut little green
onions. This will serve 4 to 5.

Dear to the hearts (and tummies) of a great many people is rice
pudding. I will admit that it can be very captivating, but personally
I don't care for it. Or perhaps I should say that with me it doesn't
rate too high on the list of delectable desserts. But not too long ago
I had a delightful and frosty taste surprise which was called Frozen
Cherry Rice Delight. It is a "cheery" ending for any meal.

FROZEN CHERRY RICE DELIGHT

½ *cup raw converted rice*   2 *cups canned tart red cherries*
2 *cups milk*   1 *cup whipping cream*
2 *eggs*   1 *tsp. kirsch*
¾ *cup sugar*   ¼ *cup sugar*

Cook the rice and the milk in a double boiler until the milk has
cooked into the rice (about 35 minutes). Add the eggs and ¾ cup
of sugar. Mix well, and continue cooking for 5 minutes, stirring
occasionally. Remove from the heat and cool. Fold in the drained
canned cherries, and spread the mixture in a freezing tray.

Whip the cream and fold in the kirsch and ¼ cup of sugar.
Spread the whipped cream over the cherries and rice mixture. Place

in the freezing compartment long enough to set the whipped cream, but do not freeze hard. When the cream is set, place the dessert on a shelf in the refrigerator until serving time. This recipe makes 8 servings.

There seems to be a bit of confusion in the minds of a large number of people about wild rice. Many believe that wild rice is just what its name might imply—ordinary rice that grows wild, or is not cultivated. But, as a matter of fact, wild rice is not a true cereal, as rice is, but is the seed of a tall, broad aquatic grass, native to North America. It is found in fresh water and brackish swamps, in nearly all states east of the Rocky Mountains.

Minnesota is one of the greatest wild rice producers in the United States, and the privilege of harvesting it is given only to the Indians. Their method of harvesting has been rather primitive, but nonetheless effective. Two squaws went out in a canoe, and while one paddled the other bent the grass stalks over the canoe and struck them with a stick, throwing the grains into the canoe. Then the rice was taken ashore and dried in the sun or over a fire. It was later threshed by beating with sticks, and winnowed in birchbark trays, and then stored.

Some time ago, one of Duluth's best known gourmets, Dr. J. F. Robinson, a dentist, sent me down a package of Minnesota wild rice, which had been harvested by the Indians on the Nett Lake Reservation, about a hundred miles north of Duluth. With it he sent me a mouth-watering recipe for wild rice which was built by his friend, Mrs. Elrose Spehar. If you try it, I think you will agree with Dr. Robinson and myself that it is the best wild rice you have ever tasted.

WILD RICE WITH MUSHROOM SAUCE

2 cups wild rice
3 quarts boiling water
½ lb. bacon
½ cup butter
1 cup chopped celery
1 cup chopped onion

½ cup chopped green pepper
1 tsp. salt
½ tsp. pepper
1 cup chicken broth
2 cans cream of mushroom soup
1 can mushrooms

Soak the wild rice in warm water for 2 hours, washing it several times, and then drain. In a large saucepan, have 3 quarts of water boiling vigorously. Add the wild rice, and when the water boils again, turn off the heat, and let it stand, covered, for 10 minutes. Then drain it again. During this time chop the bacon and fry until crisp.

In a skillet or saucepan put in the butter, and when it is hot add the chopped celery, chopped onion, and the seeded, chopped green pepper, the salt and pepper. Sauté until celery, green pepper, and onion are about half done. Then mix the rice, the bacon, the sautéed celery, onion, and green pepper, and the chicken broth, place in a greased baking dish, cover, and let bake in a 375-degree oven for ½ hour. While this is baking, mix together the cream of mushroom soup and a can of mushrooms with their juice, and heat thoroughly. Serve the rice with the mushroom sauce poured over it.

My old friend Walter Drennan, of Chicago, who is a gourmet extraordinary and a cook *par excellence,* recently introduced me to a dish new to me, and gave me about a pound of the main ingredient, processed wheat kernels, called by the Armenians, *Bulghour.*

George Mardikian, the famous San Francisco restaurateur, enthuses about *Bulghour* in his excellent Armenian cookbook, *Dinner at Omar Khayyam's,* and one of the specialties of his restaurant is Bulghour Pilaf. *Bulghour* is processed from wheat, and, to my way of thinking, is far superior to rice. It is cooked in the same way, but has much more taste. It can be obtained in any Armenian or Greek store, but I understand that it is processed only in California.

Here is Walter Drennan's recipe for cooking it. It is very simple.

BULGHOUR

2 *tbsp. butter*   1 *cup* Bulghour
1 *small onion, chopped*   2 *cups chicken broth*

You merely melt the butter in a heavy kettle, and add the small onion, chopped very fine. Simmer the onion for a few minutes (be careful not to brown the onion) and then add the *Bulghour.* Stir and mix, and then add the boiling chicken broth. Mix well with a wooden spoon, and bring to a fast boil. Then cover tightly, reduce the flame to the lowest possible point, and let simmer for 20 minutes. The liquid should be entirely absorbed. This serves 4 people.

Bulghour goes with practically any meat dish, but it is particularly delicious with lamb.

(10) SALADS, SALAD DRESSINGS, AND SAUCES

Many well-known men in times past have written on salads, and one, the Canon of St. Paul's Cathedral in London, Sidney Smith, wrote a poem on making a salad dressing. But to my mind the wittiest comment on salads was written by Oscar Wilde.

"To make a good salad is to be a brilliant diplomatist; the problem is entirely the same in both cases—to know exactly how much oil one must put with one's vinegar."

Salads, as we know them today, are "Johnny-come-latelys" in the field of gastronomy. In very early times only the poor ate salads, and they consisted of greens dipped in salt. It wasn't until the latter part of the seventeenth century that such things as chicken, lobster, and fish were added to greens in a salad. John Evelyn, the English diarist, botanist, and epicure, wrote a treatise which was called *Acetaria, or A Discourse on Salats,* and was published near the close of the seventeenth century. As the late Arnold Shircliffe said in his wonderful book on salads, *The Edgewater Salad Book:* Evelyn's work imparts order to chaos, and furnished the cooks with intelligent rules and wholesome precepts, and gave precise limits to an art whose special followers had hitherto been the champions of gastronomic license and the illustrators of gastronomic caprice."

I wonder how many people stop to think that salads are almost as necessary to a meal as meat and potatoes and vegetables; not only healthwise, but tastewise? They not only serve as an equalizer to rich entrees, but they help the taste buds to prepare for the rich desserts.

At elaborate dinners salads are usually served as a separate course. To serve their function as a bridge between the entree and the dessert, they should be simple, cold, and crisp, with a tart dressing. In California, salads are almost always served as a first course. Some people are enthusiastic about this idea, others are not. However, first-course salads, if they include seafood, are an appetite whet, and very pleasing.

One of the outstanding salads, in my opinion, is a Caesar Salad. It serves admirably as a first-course salad, or a separate course salad. In my *With a Jug of Wine,* I gave a recipe for a Caesar Salad, but since then I have devised what I think is a much better recipe.

CAESAR SALAD

6 *slices French bread*
Olive oil
4 *cloves garlic*
1 *tsp. salt*
6 *tbsp. olive oil*
2 *tbsp. red wine vinegar*
1 *tbsp. fresh lemon juice*

½ *tsp. Worcestershire sauce*
½ *tsp. salt*
1 *tsp. dry mustard*
1 *tsp. freshly ground pepper*
4 *filets anchovies*
1 *tbsp. grated Parmesan cheese*
1 *lb. romaine lettuce*

1 *raw egg*

First, prepare the croutons, which can (and should be) fixed hours in advance. Cut 6 slices of French (or Italian) bread ½ inch thick, and then cut each slice into 6 pieces. In a heavy skillet put about 4 tablespoons of olive oil and 2 small cloves of garlic which have been cut in slivers. When the oil is hot add the pieces of bread, and sauté until they are golden brown on all sides. Then set them aside until ready to use.

In a large wooden salad bowl place 2 medium-sized cloves of garlic which have been cut in half, and sprinkle them with 1 teaspoon of salt. Crush the cloves of garlic with a fork, mixing the crushed cloves and salt around in the bowl. This takes about 2 minutes. If you are very fond of garlic, leave the crushed pieces and the salt in the bowl. Or, if you prefer, discard both the garlic and the salt.

Put 6 tablespoons of the best olive oil (I never use any olive oil except the Old Monk brand, both for salads and cooking) in the salad bowl and beat with a fork for about 1 minute, or until thick. Then add 2 tablespoons of red wine vinegar (again I make bold to recommend the Spice Islands vinegars) and 1 tablespoon of fresh lemon juice, and beat well with the fork until thoroughly blended with the olive oil. Next add the Worcestershire sauce, the dry mustard, ½ teaspoon of salt, the freshly ground pepper, the filets of anchovies cut into small pieces, and the grated Parmesan cheese. Again beat the whole with the fork until well blended.

Now add the romaine lettuce, which has been washed, thoroughly dried, and well chilled, and broken into medium-sized pieces. Toss well with a wooden salad fork and spoon until the lettuce pieces are well marinated, but not so vigorously as to bruise the lettuce. Next add a whole raw egg (if you desire, you can coddle the egg by placing it in a bowl of very hot water for 5 minutes) broken over the lettuce, and again mix well, but gently. Last, add the croutons (which have been previously sautéed) and toss with the salad. However, don't toss so much that the croutons become soggy. They should be crisp and crunchy. Serve the salads at once on salad plates or in wooden salad bowls.

Another excellent first-course salad is Celery Victor, which utilizes celery hearts. If fresh celery hearts are used, they should first be braised in boiling chicken bouillon until they are tender, and then chilled. But the easiest way is to use canned celery hearts, which require no cooking.

CELERY VICTOR

2 *tbsp. red wine vinegar*	6 *tbsp. olive oil*
1 *tbsp. well-drained India relish*	1 #2 *can celery hearts, well drained*
½ *tsp. salt*	*Lettuce, chilled*
¼ *tsp. coarse black pepper*	1 *hard-cooked egg, chopped*
¼ *tsp. Ac'cent*	1 *2-oz. can anchovy filets*

Mix together the red wine vinegar, the India relish, salt, coarsely ground pepper, Ac'cent, and the olive oil, and blend well.

Arrange the well-drained celery hearts in a shallow dish, pour the dressing over them, and chill for at least 2 hours.

At serving time place the celery hearts on 4 lettuce-lined salad plates, pour any dressing remaining in the dish over them, and sprinkle with the finely chopped (or grated) hard-cooked egg. Top each salad with 2 or 3 anchovy filets. Serves 4.

One of San Francisco's delightful and unusual restaurants is the Paris Louvre, on Pacific Street. It is sort of a corner of Paris in San Francisco, and is known as the "House of *Crêpes Suzettes.*" These are a specialty of the restaurant, and André, one of the maître d's, takes great pride in preparing them at your table. At just the right moment the lights in the restaurant go out, and the eerie flames of the ignited cordials dance about the *crêpe* cart.

The Paris Louvre is now owned by Edmond Gallicano, who has been the master chef there for twelve years. Mrs. Wood and I had dinner there not long ago, and I had the finest Frogs' Legs Provençale that can be had outside of France.

Adolphe Motta used to be one of the owners, and he was quite a guy. He has invented a martini cocktail that has won several international awards, and tops any martini cocktail I have ever tasted. But don't begin to drool, Martini Fanciers. Adolphe's recipe is a closely guarded secret, and I'm sorry I can't divulge it in this book.

Adolphe also invented a salad which is a conversation piece. He calls it Adolphe's Bird's Nest Salad. When it is placed before you it looks exactly like a bird's nest, and beside it is placed a napkin, folded and twisted, which looks just like a bird sitting beside its nest. I can't tell you how to concoct the napkin bird, but I can tell you how to make the salad.

ADOLPHE'S BIRD'S NEST SALAD

Fluffy Boston lettuce	*Filets of anchovy*
Small head lettuce	*Pure olive oil*
Sprigs watercress	*Tarragon wine vinegar*
Shredded red cabbage	*1 canned pear tomato*
Cream cheese	*Salt*
Chopped chives	*Freshly ground pepper*

On a salad plate make a bed of fluffy Boston lettuce. Next, take a small, firm head of lettuce, cut it in half, and scoop out the center. Place this half of the lettuce head on the Boston lettuce, and around the edges place sprigs of watercress, to give the effect of a nest. Then place in the bottom of the scooped-out lettuce head a little bit of shredded red cabbage.

Mix cream cheese with chopped chives, and mold the resultant mixture into the form of small bird's eggs. Place about 3 eggs in the nest.

For the dressing mince very fine a small amount of anchovies, and add 3 parts of pure olive oil and 1 part of tarragon wine vinegar, and 1 pear tomato (canned) with the juice and seeds squeezed out (1 for each person), salt and freshly ground pepper to taste.

Mix this well, chill thoroughly, and pour over the bird's nest and the eggs in the nest, which have also been chilled.

Mexican cuisine is noted for its lack of salads, rather than distinctive ones. A first-course salad is practically unknown in Mexico, and when the Mexicans do serve a salad, it is served with the entree, usually in a large bowl. However, once a year a salad becomes a main dish. After midnight mass on Christmas Eve, the traditional dish is *Ensalada de Noche Buena,* which is a salad made up of beets, fruits, peanuts, and pomegranate seeds.

I am not at all sure of the derivation of *Ensalada Verde,* which is Green Salad. In spite of its Mexican name, I doubt that it came from Mexico. But I do know that it is a captivating and piquant dish. It is one of my favorite salads, and I have served it most profitably as a first-course salad.

ENSALADA VERDE

½ cup green pepper, chopped
¼ cup sweet red pepper, chopped
2 tsp. chopped parsley
Generous pinch dried basil
Generous pinch dried mint
1 tsp. chopped anchovies
2 tbsp. capers, drained

½ cup fresh tomato (pulp only) chopped
2 tbsp. chopped celery
1 tbsp. chopped little green onions
6 radishes, chopped
½ cup olive oil
½ tsp. salt

⅛ tsp. pepper

Toss the vegetables lightly with a wooden salad fork. Then add the herbs, seasonings and anchovies, and again toss lightly. Last, gradually add the olive oil, tossing the salad while adding. Chill thoroughly, and serve in individual wooden salad bowls.

The most popular salad food in Mexico is the avocado. The Mexicans were, I believe, the first to combine avocados with seafood as salads. But one of the best-known Mexican salads is guacamole, which, of course, is made with avocados.

I have eaten a number of versions of Guacamole Salad, but the one I think is tops is to make a guacamole dunk (see chapter on Hors d'Oeuvres, page 33), and spread this on tomato slices which have been bedded on shredded lettuce. Pour over all a good French dressing, and serve, chilled.

Every once in a while I read articles in the public prints on cooking which get my dander up. They are written by males, and they are all variations on the theme that women just can't properly or decently prepare and/or cook certain kinds of food. From their lofty ivory towers (complete, no doubt, with the latest and most expensive kitchen gadgets and equipment) these superior males pontificate that the cooking of game should never be entrusted to a woman; that if you want a steak ruined, let a woman cook it; and that only men can make a decent and edible salad.

In my opinion, that's hokum, pure and simple. One of the most delicious duck dishes I ever ate was devised by a woman; a woman taught me a trick in cooking steaks that gave it an out-of-this-world flavor; and my wife makes the most delectable (as well as gorgeous) tossed salad I have ever tasted.

Don't get me wrong—I am no traitor to my sex! But I am an ardent disciple of the art of preparing fine food, and I hate to see it befuddled with balderdash.

In the matter of salads I will freely admit that many women have perverted the art of salad making and turned out some of the most impossible and atrocious salads of which the mind can conceive. On the other hand, I have known a great many women who were literally magicians when it came to whipping up salads.

From Phoenix, Arizona, comes a he-man salad with an old-fashioned tang, concocted by a woman.

ONION AND CUCUMBER SALAD

Garlic	¾ cup chilled sour cream
Slices sweet onion	¼ tsp. dry mustard
Sliced unpeeled cucumber	2 tbsp. tarragon wine vinegar
Red radishes, sliced	Pinch sugar
White radishes, sliced	Salt and pepper

Rub a salad bowl with garlic, and then line the bowl with slices of sweet onion separated into rings. Then fill with crisp, thin, and unpeeled cucumber slices, and crisp, thin slices of both red and white radishes. Mix the chilled sour cream, dry mustard, tarragon wine vinegar, a pinch of sugar, and salt and pepper to taste. Pour this dressing over all, chill well, and serve.

In my work of devising recipes for Nu Made mayonnaise, I am frequently called upon to work out a specific dish. One that was asked for was an out-of-the-ordinary salad that could be prepared quickly, and that would have eye appeal.

It was summertime, and all I could think of was something that was cold and tart. So I went to work, and finally came up with an intriguing combination of jellied mayonnaise and tomato slices. Here it is.

TOMATO SLICES WITH JELLIED MAYONNAISE

1 *envelope unflavored gelatin*
¼ *cup cold water*
1½ *cups boiling water*
1½ *cups Nu Made mayon-*
    naise
2 *tbsp. wine vinegar*
1 *tbsp. Worcestershire sauce*

1 *tbsp. chopped drained capers*
2 *tbsp. fine chopped onion*
10 *drops Tabasco sauce*
Dash cayenne pepper
Salt to taste
Tomato slices
Dried oregano

Soften the envelope of unflavored gelatin in the cold water. Then add the boiling water and mix well, and set in refrigerator to chill.

Blend the mayonnaise well with the wine vinegar, Worcestershire sauce, and drained, chopped capers, the finely minced onion, the Tabasco sauce, cayenne pepper, and salt to taste. When gelatin begins to firm, blend in mayonnaise mixture and spoon into a shallow baking dish about 8 by 8 inches. Mixture should be about ¾ inch thick. Refrigerate until well set and firm.

Peel and slice tomatoes, sprinkle lightly with dried oregano, and chill. To serve, place tomato slices on bed of greens. Unmold jellied mayonnaise, cut into circles with cookie cutter, and place on top of tomato slices.

I think that those two succulent members of the bean family—kidneys and limas—make wonderful salads. One that is particularly intriguing comes from the little cookbook that I have mentioned before, *Favorite Recipes of the Coahoma Woman's Club of Coahoma, Mississippi.* It is a kidney bean salad with a Mexican hot sauce.

KIDNEY BEAN SALAD WITH MEXICAN HOT SAUCE

1 *can tomato sauce*
¼ *cup chili sauce*
3 *tsp. Bahamian mustard*
2 *tsp. onion juice*
¼ *cup prepared horseradish*
1 *tsp. chili powder*
¼ *cup tart vinegar*
½ *tsp. sugar*

1 *tsp. salt*
1 *tsp. dried basil*
2 *cloves garlic, sliced*
Dash cayenne pepper
Cold mayonnaise
1 *can red kindey beans,*
    drained
Lettuce

Grated Parmesan cheese

First, make the Mexican hot sauce. Combine the first 12 ingredients and simmer them in a saucepan gently until thickened slightly. Then strain through a coarse sieve, and dilute to desired consistency with very cold mayonnaise. This is very "hot stuff," to quote the recipe, so use very carefully.

Open, drain, and chill the kidney beans. Spoon them onto crisp lettuce leaves and sprinkle with the grated Parmesan cheese. Top with the Mexican hot sauce diluted with cold mayonnaise. If desired, garnish the salad with hot pickled peppers.

The above recipe should serve 6.

Of all the varieties of lettuce, my favorite is Bibb, or Kentucky Limestone, lettuce. The heads are small, but the deep green leaves have a delicious flavor and unique crispness. It was developed by Jack Bibb, of Frankfort, Kentucky, I believe. It is expensive, but if you can get it, it is well worth the extra cost.

The Sherman Hotel in Chicago has developed a very delectable salad using Bibb lettuce, which they call Ambassador Salad.

AMBASSADOR SALAD

6 *heads Bibb lettuce*
1 *avocado pear*
1 *medium tomato*
6 *artichoke hearts*
¾ *cup olive oil*

¼ *cup tarragon wine vinegar*
1 *clove garlic*
¼ *tsp. dry English mustard*
½ *tsp. Worcestershire sauce*
Salt and freshly ground pepper

Wash the vegetables thoroughly. Cut the heads of lettuce in half lengthwise, using 3 halves per person. Peel the avocado, cut in half lengthwise, and remove the stone. Then cut crosswise. Quarter the tomato. Cut artichoke hearts in half lengthwise.

Combine the olive oil and vinegar. Add the garlic, mustard, Worcestershire sauce and salt and freshly ground pepper to taste. Stir and blend well.

To serve, pour the dressing over the salad ingredients in a large wooden bowl. Or, on individual salad plates arrange the lettuce halves with avocado, tomato quarters, and artichoke hearts, and then pour the dressing over each serving. This will serve 4.

I guess the recipes for a potato salad are legion. They can be plain, they can be fancy, they can be hot or cold, and they can utilize almost any type of salad dressing.

One that I think is a little different, and a little tastier, is one that I devised which seems to have a particular appeal to men. But it apparently appeals to women and children, too, because after the recipe had appeared in my column, my next-door neighbor told me she and her twelve-year-old daughter had really gone to town with it.

CURRIED POTATO SALAD

4 *cups diced raw potatoes*	1¾ *tsp. salt*
1 *tsp. salt*	⅛ *tsp. ground black pepper*
1 *tsp. curry powder*	⅛ *tsp. garlic powder*
Boiling water	¼ *tsp. curry powder*
3 *tbsp. French dressing*	1½ *cups diced celery*
2 *tbsp. fresh lemon juice*	½ *cup diced green pepper*
1 *tbsp. grated onion*	2 *diced hard-cooked eggs*

¼ *cup mayonnaise*

Cook the diced raw potatoes in a saucepan, adding 1 teaspoon of salt and 1 teaspoon of curry powder to boiling water to cover the potatoes. Do not overcook the potatoes.

Drain the potatoes, and add to them the French dressing, fresh lemon juice, grated onion, 1¾ teaspoons salt, the ground black pepper and garlic powder, and ¼ teaspoon of curry powder. Marinate for 30 minutes, or until the potatoes are cold. Then blend in the diced celery, diced green pepper, diced hard-cooked eggs, and the mayonnaise.

When serving, put lettuce leaves on plates, heap with potato salad, and sprinkle a little paprika over each serving. This will serve 6. You can make it the night before and keep it in the refrigerator.

Another unusual potato salad is this one that combines meat, potatoes, and vegetables into one delicious dish—an ideal main dish for a hot night.

POTATO SALAD DE LUXE

1½ cups sliced mushrooms	¼ cup shredded raw carrots
6 tbsp. olive oil	½ cup chopped celery
4 tsp. fresh lemon juice	2 cups diced cooked meat
¼ cup minced onion	(ham, chicken, tongue,
1 tsp. salt	lamb, beef)
⅛ tsp. pepper	Crisp lettuce
2 cups sliced cooked potatoes	French or mayonnaise dressing

Sauté the sliced fresh mushrooms in the olive oil until tender. Let cool slightly, then add the fresh lemon juice, minced onion, salt and pepper. Let stand until cold. Combine the sliced cooked potatoes, shredded raw carrots, chopped celery, diced cooked tongue (or ham, chicken, beef, or lamb). Pour mushroom mixture over all and marinate at least 1 hour. Serve on bed of crisp lettuce. A French or mayonnaise dressing may be served if desired.

Coleslaw goes perfectly with broiled fish or spareribs. As far as I am concerned, it is a must. Yet it is very difficult, if not impossible, to (a) be served a palatable coleslaw in the average restaurant, (b) buy a decent coleslaw in delicatessens, or (c) find a worthwhile recipe in cookbooks, newspapers, and magazines. Only in two restaurants have I ever found a super coleslaw. The finest I have ever tasted is served in the Pit Restaurant in Chicago (they have recently moved from Rush Street to 1139 North Dearborn Street). For years I have tried to wangle the recipe out of Florence Simmons, the very charming owner, but it's been no dice, and I can't say that I blame her. The other restaurant that served excellent coleslaw was Phil Schmidt's seafood restaurant on the southern outskirts of Chicago.

So what have I done? I've devised a coleslaw of my own, in cooperation with the Nu Made mayonnaise people. I won't rate it above or below the coleslaw at the Pit, but I do think it is damn good.

PIQUANT COLESLAW

1 *head cabbage*
Ice water
⅓ *cup tarragon white wine*
    vinegar
2 *tbsp. sugar*
½ *tsp. salt*
¼ *tsp. pepper*
Paprika
½ *cup chopped green pepper*

2 *tbsp. chopped pimiento*
1 *tbsp. chopped little green*
    onions
¼ *tsp. celery seed*
¼ *tsp. dried dill weed*
¼ *tsp. caraway seeds*
½ *cup Nu Made mayonnaise*
½ *cup sour cream*
1 *tbsp. horseradish*

Shred the cabbage, and then soak in ice water for about 30 minutes. Drain, and dry thoroughly.

To the shredded cabbage add the white wine tarragon vinegar, sugar, salt, pepper, and a sprinkling of paprika. Toss and let marinate for 1 hour. Then drain (reserving the liquid) and lightly squeeze the cabbage to remove any excess liquid.

Add to the cabbage the green pepper, chopped pimiento, little green onions, celery seed, dried dill weed, and caraway seed. Again toss lightly.

Mix together the Nu Made mayonnaise, sour cream, horseradish, and the reserved seasoned vinegar. Pour over the cabbage mixture, and toss lightly.

June is traditionally a month in which boys and girls get married, although I don't know why (not why they get married, but why June in particular). If I were a bride (this, of course, is a purely rhetorical supposition), I would choose the winter months, because there would be no outside interests, like golf, or swimming, or tennis, to possibly lure Dreamboat away from the cozy little nest which he has provided. And cold winter nights are ideal to indoctrinate a doting husband into the gentle art of cooking.

And now back to June, and brides, and salads. My very dear and old friend, the late Arnold Shircliffe, devised a very colorful and exceedingly tasty salad, which he called the Bride's, or Sweetheart, Salad. I always thought it was a perfect salad for a bridal breakfast (which is usually a very hearty meal).

BRIDE'S SALAD

Lettuce	1 *large blueberry*
Large half fresh pear	6 *blueberries (or red or black*
Vegetable coloring	*raspberries, or black-*
Cream cheese	*berries)*
Cream	*Green pepper*
	French dressing

Make a bed of lettuce on a cold plate, pulling it apart so it will lie flat. Place a large peeled half of a fresh pear (or a canned pear) on the lettuce. Dip your finger in a little vegetable coloring and rub it over the pear half. This gives it a red coloring. Mix some cream cheese with a little cream, put it in a pastry bag, and squeeze it out around the pear in the shape of a heart. At the cleft of the heart place a large blueberry, and at equal intervals around the sides of the heart place 6 more large blueberries, or red raspberries, black raspberries, or blackberries. Next, cut some small diamond-shaped pieces from a green pepper, and place these between the berries. Make 2 larger diamond-shaped pieces of green pepper, and place them on either side of the berry at the cleft of the heart. Pour over the salad French dressing, which will give a glaze effect. Thus you have a delicious salad, and quite appropriate for a bride—the white representing purity, the red representing love, and there is green for a little jealousy!

As a rule, I am not very keen about fruit salads, and I think most men feel the same way. To my way of thinking, the trouble with the majority of them is that they are covered with an excessively sweet and gooey dressing. However, a fruit salad laced with a real French dressing can be delightful with certain entrees. And I would like to offer for your approval an orange salad, with a most unusual dressing, that I have found to be most intriguing.

ORANGE SALAD

½ *cup mayonnaise*	¼ *tsp. salt*
2 *tbsp. Roquefort cheese*	*Pinch powdered ginger*
1 *small clove garlic, minced*	*Pinch fine granulated sugar*
2 *tsp. chopped ripe olives*	*Oranges*
2 *tsp. drained capers*	*Lettuce*

First of all, the dressing. Cream together the mayonnaise with the Roquefort (or Danish blue) cheese, until the mixture is smooth. Then add the minced garlic, chopped ripe olives, the drained and chopped capers, salt, and a pinch each of powdered Jamaica ginger and fine granulated sugar. Blend everything thoroughly, and then chill.

Peel an orange, separate the segments, and peel them. Place them in the refrigerator, and chill them thoroughly. When ready to serve, place the chilled orange segments on a bed of crisp lettuce, and cover them with the dressing.

I might as well confess that I don't care for salads as a main course (or only course) luncheon dish. Women, of course, love them. And there are many men who eat a salad for luncheon. About the only salad I ever eat in the middle of the day is a Green Goddess Salad (with either tiny bay shrimps or crab meat mixed with limestone lettuce). The recipe for the Palace Hotel's famous Green Goddess dressing is in my *With a Jug of Wine,* so I won't repeat it here.

Most of the chicken salads I have ever eaten have been far too bland to suit my taste. But here is one that has a lot of umph!

CURRIED CHICKEN SALAD

2 *cups diced cooked chicken* ⅛ *tsp. ground black pepper*
1 *cup diced celery* ½ *tsp. curry powder*
¾ *tsp. salt* 1 *tbsp. fresh lemon juice*
   3 *tbsp. mayonnaise*

Combine the diced cooked chicken with the diced celery, salt, ground black pepper, curry powder, fresh lemon juice, and mayonnaise. This can be served on your picnic plates over a bed of crisp lettuce, and garnished with radishes or stuffed green olives.

Thelma Stephenson, of Duluth, Minnesota, is what I call a gourmette. I have never had the pleasure of meeting her, but through a mutual friend, Dr. Robinson, I have had a number of her recipes, and every one has been excellent. Not long ago she sent me her recipe for a luncheon salad via Franklyn Kohler of Chicago, who also conducts a syndicated food column, "The Skillet Club for Men," and who is a practicing gourmet extraordinary.

ARTICHOKE AND CRAB MEAT SALAD

1 *cup diced artichoke hearts*	½ *cup tomato catsup*
(cooked or canned)	½ *tsp. Worcestershire sauce*
1 *cup crab meat*	*Salt*
½ *cup heavy cream*	*Freshly ground pepper*
1 *cup mayonnaise*	¼ *cup chopped olives*

Mix the diced cooked artichoke hearts and crab meat, and chill. Whip the heavy cream and combine with the mayonnaise, tomato catsup, Worcestershire sauce, and salt and freshly ground pepper to taste, and chill. When ready to serve, combine the sauce with the artichoke and crab-meat mixture, tossing gently to mix well. Serve on lettuce cups. If desired, ¼ cup of chopped or ripe green olives may be added to the sauce.

SALAD DRESSINGS

The number of salad dressings is limited only by the ingenuity of the millions of people who concoct them. *The Edgewater Beach Hotel Salad Book,* by the late Arnold Shircliffe, lists 211 different recipes for salad dressings. Mary Dahnke's excellent *Salad Book* lists ninety-two. And if I were to go through my several hundred cook books and pick out recipes for salad dressings, the total might well run over a thousand.

Actually, there are only five basic salad dressings—French, sour cream, mayonnaise, animal fat, and cooked. So all other salad dressings are variations on those basic five.

In my *With a Jug of Wine* I have given the authentic recipes for the five basic dressings, and nineteen outstanding variations on them. The six salad dressings that follow I think are also outstanding.

One of the most memorable meals I have ever had in my whole life was a luncheon in a garden two thousand feet above the floor of the Santa Clara Valley, near the crest of the Santa Cruz Mountains, in California.

Mr. Alfred Fromm, owner of the Domain of Paul Masson, had invited Mrs. Wood and me to visit the vineyards and winery, and have luncheon with him. We started our ascent to the vineyards about eleven o'clock on a beautiful Sunday morning, thinking it would only take a few minutes to reach our destination. But I had not counted on the road. It started out innocently enough, but after a few yards, it took on a terrifying aspect. Wisely shifting into low gear, we started climbing the steep, narrow, twisting gravel road, which had hairpin turns all the way. With almost every breath my wife oh'd and ah'd at the breath-taking view, but I was so panicky that I didn't lift my eyes from the road for as much as a single peek. I guess I must have held my breath all the way, for when we reached the winery I let out one long shuddering sigh of relief, and collapsed weakly over the wheel.

After a most interesting tour of the cool, fragrant winery, we joined our host at his hilltop house, located on a level bit of ground several feet above the winery. Great trees shaded the house and garden from the hot sun, and the view was the most fabulous I have ever seen. Hillside vineyards, the majestic Santa Cruz Mountains, the rolling, brilliantly green fields of the valley, and huge trees stretched before our eyes for untold miles in three directions.

And then came luncheon, which had been transported from town in big hampers. Seated at a colorfully decorated table in the garden under the trees, Mr. Fromm's Chinese boy served us. There were great slices of tender, succulent roast beef, thin slices of baked ham, slices of corned beef, generous pieces of juicy white turkey, and slices of pungent salami. There was a big basket of crusty French bread, and with the cold meats a tossed green salad was served, with a dressing that was out of this world. Champagne was the beverage, and for dessert there were bowls of huge, luscious strawberries marinated in wine, and a wonderful blueberry pie. And after that, a large plate of assorted cheeses. The *pièce de résistance* was the Paul Masson Triple Red Champagne.

The salad dressing is a specialty of Mrs. Fromm, and Mr. Fromm was kind enough to send me the recipe. It is wonderful not only on greens, but on California crabs, and shrimps. It is called Salad Dressing with Watercress.

SALAD DRESSING WITH WATERCRESS

⅓ *cup dry red wine*   *Dash freshly ground pepper*
⅔ *cup olive oil*   ½ *cup chili sauce*
⅓ *cup red wine vinegar*   ½ *cup chopped watercress*
1 *tsp. salt*   ½ *cup chopped onion*

Mix well together the dry red wine, pure olive oil, wine vinegar, salt, a dash of freshly ground black pepper, and the chili sauce. The bowl all this is mixed in should be ice cold. Stir the ingredients until thoroughly mixed, then add the chopped watercress and chopped onions. For a salad, pour this on greens, toss, and serve.

About three years ago, a reader of my column in the Chicago *Tribune,* Alfred A. Greenlee, sent me some recipes which he said were really outstanding and worthy of trying. I am always on the lookout for new and unusual recipes, so I set to work one rainy Sunday. Two of the recipes were for salad dressings, and after having tried them, I thoroughly agreed with Mr. Greenlee. The first I shall call an Anchovy Dressing, although he called it merely Salad Dressing.

ANCHOVY DRESSING

3 *cloves garlic, chopped*	1 *tsp. dry mustard*
¼ *tsp. salt*	1½ *tsp. sugar*
1 *small tin anchovies*	3 *squirts Tabasco sauce*
1 *cup olive oil*	*Pinch dried basil*
1 *tsp. salt*	2 *dashes Worcestershire sauce*
1 *tsp. paprika*	1 *cup white wine vinegar*

½ *cup dry sherry wine*

In a heavy measuring cup I put the finely chopped cloves of garlic and added about ¼ teaspoon salt. With a muddler (that implement so necessary to old-fashioned cocktails) I mashed the garlic until it was almost a paste. Then I added the contents of a small tin of filets of anchovies, with their oil, and mashed those into the garlic, until the whole was a somewhat moist paste. Then I filled the cup full with the finest olive oil, and let it stand.

In a heavy bartender's mixing glass, I put 1 teaspoon each of salt, paprika, and dry mustard, the sugar, 3 squirts of Tabasco sauce, a pinch of dried sweet basil, and a couple of dashes of Worcestershire sauce (this was an addition of my own). Then I added the white wine vinegar and sherry wine. This was stirred and mixed well; then the oil, garlic, and anchovies were added. Again the whole was thoroughly mixed and stirred, and then put into a glass jar, which was sealed with its cap, and put into the refrigerator to chill. At dinner the dressing was poured over a green salad of Bibb lettuce and watercress, the whole was sprinkled with coarsely ground peppercorns, and eaten. Mr. Greenlee was right. It was outstandingly delicious. I will say this, however; if you like a dressing in which the oil predominates, you will want to add more olive oil, perhaps another cup. But I am not in that class—the dressing as I made it was perfect for me.

The second of Mr. Greenlee's submitted recipes was for a sour cream dressing. He called it "out of this world," and he said it was devised by his sister-in-law, who sent it in to *Good Housekeeping Magazine,* and received an award for it.

SOUR CREAM DRESSING

1 *cup commercial sour cream*
⅓ *cup commercial salad dressing*
⅓ *cup chili sauce*
½ *green pepper, chopped*
½ *onion, minced fine*
1 *tsp. salt*

Combine all ingredients, and stir together lightly until well blended. This dressing is unusually good with fresh boiled shrimps.

Here are a duo of French dressings, each with an unusual taste appeal.

BOHEMIAN FRENCH DRESSING

1 *hard-cooked egg*
¼ *tsp. prepared mustard*
½ *tsp. Worcestershire sauce*
3 *tbsp. red wine vinegar*
½ *cup olive oil*
2 *tbsp. grated Parmesan cheese*
2 *tbsp. chopped parsley*
1 *tbsp. grated onion*
¾ *tsp. salt*
¼ *tsp. Ac'cent*
¼ *tsp. garlic salt*
¼ *tsp. coarse pepper*
¼ *tsp. paprika*

Mash the egg yolk to a paste with the mustard and Worcestershire sauce, then blend in the vinegar. Add the remaining ingredients, and mix thoroughly. Rice the egg white, and sprinkle over the salad. This makes a scant cup of dressing.

Use this dressing for mixed greens, chilled, cooked green beans, broccoli, or asparagus.

WALNUT FRENCH DRESSING

¾ *cup olive oil*
¼ *cup vinegar (or lemon juice)*
½ *tsp. Worcestershire sauce*
1 *tsp. salt*
½ *tsp. Ac'cent*
½ *tsp. dry mustard*
¼ *tsp. coarsely ground pepper*
¼ *tsp. paprika*
¼ *cup ground walnuts*

In a screw-top jar place all the ingredients, and shake vigorously until well blended. Makes 1 cup dressing, which is excellent with mixed green or vegetable salads.

And finally, here is a unique dressing for mixed green or vegetable salads.

CREAMY GREEN ONION DRESSING

2 *tbsp. mayonnaise*	¼ *tsp. Ac'cent*
¼ *cup lemon juice*	¼ *tsp. pepper*
1 *cup olive oil*	¼ *tsp. dry mustard*
1 *tsp. salt*	¼ *tsp. paprika*

1 *bunch little green onions*

Blend all the ingredients well, then add the bunch of little green onions which have been thinly sliced. This makes about 1⅓ cups of dressing.

SAUCES

While there are only five basic, or foundation, sauces (the French call them *Sauces Mères*—"Mother Sauces"), there are certainly well over a thousand other sauces. The *Codex Culinarius* lists 947 sauces, and such a modern cookbook as Escoffier gives recipes for 140; Jeanne Owen's *Book of Sauces* has 236 recipes, and Louis Diat's *Sauces French and Famous* has 218 recipes.

The two great master *sauciers* were Câreme and Escoffier, and their principles were radically different. Câreme's sauces were beautiful, delicious, and complicated, but more often than not they masked the flavor of meat, game, fish, and poultry rather than enhanced it.

Escoffier believed in simplicity. His sauces were designed to help rather than disguise the flavor of whatever dish they adorned. And today modern cooks take the same view—a fine sauce should enhance the flavor of a dish, or provide a flavor where one is lacking.

One of the most essential things to know about making a sauce is the thickening. The most common way is with a *roux,* which is a combination of flour and butter, either uncooked or cooked. Egg yolks are another thickening agent, usually for sauces containing milk or cream. But care is needed in adding egg yolks; because they can easily curdle the sauce. The best way is to mix the egg yolks with a little cream, then stir in some of the hot liquid, and finally turn the mixture back into the sauce. Butter can make a light delicate sauce a little thicker, and, of course, it adds flavor to a sauce. Many fine chefs "finish" a sauce by adding butter.

The French chefs have another trick in making sauces, which adds to the flavor and texture of a sauce. They use more liquid than other chefs, and then let the liquid cook down, or "reduce," to the desired consistency. Very often in recipes you will find the directions, "add 1 cup of wine, and cook until it is reduced by half." This "reduction" gives each ingredient in the saucepan an opportunity to release its full flavor.

The five basic sauces are Béchemel and Velouté (which are white), Sauce Espagnol, or brown sauce, mayonnaise, and Hollandaise. I have given the recipes for these basic sauces in my *With a Jug of Wine,* along with a few of the best-known sauces.

Hollandaise sauce is a *bête noir* to most home cooks. It can (and too often does) go wrong (curdle) in the wink of an eye. The water in the bottom of a double boiler must be kept just under the boiling point during the preparation and the butter must be added to the sauce in the top just a little at a time so that each addition is thoroughly blended before adding the next, and the sauce must be stirred constantly until it is finished.

Knowing the hazards of making a Hollandaise sauce, I decided I would experiment, and see if I could devise a foolproof Hollandaise. I worked with a mayonnaise, and finally came up with something that is simple, easy, and very delicious.

MOCK HOLLANDAISE SAUCE

1 *cup Nu Made mayonnaise*	2 *tbsp. lemon juice*
2 *generous tbsp. butter*	¼ *tsp. salt*
¼ *tsp. paprika*	

In a double boiler, over hot (not boiling) water, let the mayonnaise become well warmed. Then add the butter, broken into small pieces, and stir with a wire whisk, or table fork, constantly until the butter is melted. Then add the lemon juice and the seasonings, and stir until all is well blended.

The beauty of this sauce is that it can be made ahead, kept refrigerated, and rewarmed just before serving. Use it wherever Hollandaise sauce is called for.

Both Béchemel and Velouté sauce are cream sauces. The difference between the two is that Velouté sauce uses fish, meat, game, chicken, or vegetable stock (depending upon the dish the sauce is used with) instead of milk.

An ordinary cream sauce is made with equal parts of butter and flour, salt, pepper, and cream. However, the following cream sauce is a little more flavorsome.

CREAM SAUCE

2 *tbsp. butter*   ¼ *tsp. white pepper*
2 *tbsp. flour*   Dash cayenne pepper
½ *tsp. salt*   1 *cup cream*
                   Dash Worcestershire sauce

Melt the butter in a saucepan, and then stir in the flour slowly until the mixture is smooth. Add salt, white pepper, cayenne and cream. Stir this constantly over a slow flame until the sauce is smooth and thickened. Finish by adding a dash of Worcestershire sauce and blending it well into the sauce.

This is a richer version of a cream sauce.

RICH CREAM SAUCE

4 *tbsp. butter*   1 *tsp. salt*
2 *tbsp. finely chopped onions*   ¼ *tsp. white pepper*
4 *tbsp. flour*   2 *cups cream*
                   2 *egg yolks*

Melt the butter in a saucepan and then add the finely chopped onions, and cook until the onions are soft, but not brown, over a gentle flame. Then add the flour, blend well, and cook slowly until the flour just starts to turn golden. Then add the salt and white pepper. Gradually, while stirring constantly, preferably with a wire whisk, stir in the cream. Keep stirring, over a low flame, until the mixture thickens and bubbles. Let bubble for about 3 minutes, then remove from the fire. Add a little of the hot sauce to the beaten egg yolks, and then stir them into the sauce, blending thoroughly. Strain through a fine sieve. This makes approximately 2 cups of sauce.

A sauce I developed in connection with Nu Made mayonnaise I called White Sauce Elegante. It is a super-rich cream sauce, and is very elegant.

WHITE SAUCE ELEGANTE

2 *tbsp. butter*	1 *cup warm milk*
2 *tbsp. flour*	*¾ *cup Nu Made mayonnaise*
5 *peppercorns*	4 *tbsp. cream*
½ *tsp. salt*	1 *tbsp. butter*
½ *small bay leaf*	*Pinch ground nutmeg*

Melt 2 tablespoons of butter in a saucepan. Add the peppercorns (or a pinch of ground pepper), the salt, the grated nutmeg, the bay leaf, crumbled, and the flour. Cook over a medium flame, blending butter and flour until perfectly smooth (about 3 or 4 minutes, stirring constantly). Then add the warm milk very slowly, stirring constantly with a wire whisk, or spoon. Cook slowly, stirring frequently, for about 10 minutes, or until the sauce is thickened to the consistency of heavy cream.

Strain the sauce into another saucepan, and add to it the ¾ cup of mayonnaise (*add 1 cup if the finished sauce is to be refrigerated for 4 hours or more before using), stirring constantly. When the mayonnaise is well blended in, add the cream, and 1 pat of butter (about 1 tablespoon), and stir the whole until well blended. If a thinner sauce is desired, stir in additional cream.

This recipe makes about 1 pint of sauce. It is at its delicate best if refrigerated for 4 hours or more, and then gently reheated.

In the chapter on Fish, I detailed the famous Filet of Sole Marguery, as it was prepared in the old Marguery Restaurant in Paris. In that recipe, the sauce was an integral part of the whole dish. However, here is a recipe for Sauce Marguery which is not quite so complicated, and yet perhaps more zestful.

SAUCE MARGUERY

¼ *cup butter*	1 *cup fish stock*
1 *cup sliced fresh mushrooms*	½ *cup milk*
5 *tbsp. flour*	½ *cup heavy cream*
½ *tsp. Ac'cent*	2 *tsp. drained capers*
1 *tsp. salt*	1 *cup cooked shrimp*
Dash white pepper	3 *tbsp. dry white wine*

Heat the butter in a saucepan and add the sliced fresh mushrooms. Simmer over a moderate flame for about 3 minutes and then add the flour, Ac'cent, salt, and white pepper. Stir until everything is well blended, and remove from heat. Then add slowly, stirring carefully and constantly to keep smooth, the fish stock and the milk.

Return to the moderate flame, stirring constantly, until the mixture thickens and comes to a boil. Boil gently for ½ minute. Then add the heavy cream, the capers, the cooked shrimp which have been cut in small pieces, and the white wine. Mix well and reheat. This recipe makes about 2½ cups of sauce. It is ideal with poached fish.

Marchand du Vin sauce is, as the name indicates, the sauce of the wine merchants. It is a brown sauce, and particularly delicious over steaks.

MARCHAND DU VIN SAUCE

1 *tbsp. butter*	5-6 *whole peppercorns*
1 *shallot, finely chopped*	2 *whole cloves*
1 *tsp. chopped chives*	*Pinch allspice*
1 *tbsp. flour*	1 *crushed clove garlic*
1 *cup dry red wine*	1 *tbsp. chopped parsley*
1 *cup consommé*	*Fresh lemon juice*

Melt the butter in a saucepan, and before the butter gets hot add a finely chopped shallot (or a little green onion), and 1 teaspoon finely chopped chives. Cook for a few minutes over a slow fire, but do not let boil. Next sprinkle with 1 tablespoon of flour, and let the mixture brown. Then add the dry red wine, consommé, the peppercorns, slightly bruised, the whole cloves, a pinch of allspice, and a crushed small clove of garlic. Raise the fire to a hot flame and bring to a boil. Lower flame and let cook about 15 minutes, stirring occasionally. When cooked, strain the mixture through a fine sieve into another saucepan, and add the chopped parsley, heat until sizzling hot, and just before serving, add a few drops of strained lemon juice. Pour this sauce over a broiled steak (well browned on the outside and pink and juicy in the center).

Another wonderful sauce for meats is Madeira, or Sauce Madère. This too is a brown sauce, and uses Sauce Espagnol as a base. In the opinion of many, this is one of the best wine sauces.

It can be made very simply and quickly by adding 4 tablespoons of meat essence to ¾ cup consommé, and then adding about 3 tablespoons of Madeira. But to get the full, rich flavor of this sauce, make it this way.

MADEIRA SAUCE

2 *tbsp. butter*	*Freshly ground pepper*
1 *cup chopped fresh*	¼ *cup tomato paste*
mushrooms	4 *oz. Madeira wine*
½ *tsp. salt*	1 *cup Espagnol Sauce*

1 *tsp. chopped parsley*

Melt the butter in a saucepan, and add the chopped fresh mushrooms, salt, freshly ground pepper to taste, and cook until the mushrooms are brown, about 10 minutes. Then add the tomato paste, Madeira wine, and 1 cup of Sauce Espagnol. Let this boil gently for about 6 to 8 minutes, then add 1 teaspoon of chopped parsley, and blend it in.

Probably the most popular sauce used with fish and shellfish is a tartar sauce. There are scores of recipes for tartar sauce, but I think you will like the intriguing tang of the following recipe.

TARTAR SAUCE

1 *cup mayonnaise*	1 *tbsp. chopped chives*
1 *tbsp. chopped capers*	½ *tsp. dried chervil*
1 *tbsp. chopped green olives*	½ *tsp. dried tarragon*
1 *tbsp. chopped parsley*	2 *tbsp. dry white wine*
1 *tbsp. chopped pickles*	1 *tbsp. chopped pimiento*

Dash paprika

Blend all of the ingredients together well. Serve as is, or well chilled for cold fish or seafoods.

Of all the aromas that can come out of the kitchen, I don't know of a more wonderful one than that of cooking relishes. I can remember, and smell, as though it was only yesterday, the heavenly scents of my grandmother's piccalilli, cucumber relish, pickled watermelon rind, and chili sauce, as they were being prepared in her large, old-fashioned kitchen.

What with the many excellent condiments that are put out commercially these days, the art of putting up one's own relishes is almost a forgotten one. In these days when time and effort are rationed commodities, it is much easier to buy one's relishes at the store. But if you have the time, and the facilities, and you want a real taste thrill, try your hand at a small batch of, say, chili sauce.

Carlyle Stevens, a writer and director with Radio Station WGN, and an accomplished amateur chef, brought me a small sample of some chili sauce he had made at his Lake Bluff, Michigan, home. I tasted it, and raved over it. He said the recipe was based on the way his Canadian grandmother made chili sauce, and he typed it out for me. It is not at all difficult, and you will be repaid a thousandfold for the time and effort you put into it.

CARLYLE STEVENS' CHILI SAUCE

36 *tomatoes*	1 *lb. brown sugar*
12 *green peppers*	2 *tbsp. celery seed*
3 *sweet red peppers*	¼ *tsp. ground black pepper*
8 *large onions*	1 *tsp. paprika*
⅓ *quart cider vinegar*	1 *tsp. powdered cloves*
⅓ *quart tarragon vinegar*	1 *tbsp. ground allspice*
⅓ *quart wine vinegar*	¼ *tsp. curry powder*
⅜ *cup salt*	3 *bay leaves, crumbled*

2 *tsp. Ac'cent*

Peel and cut into small chunks the tomatoes (scalding the whole tomatoes in boiling water makes the peeling easy—the skin slips right off). Grind, not too fine, the green peppers, the red (sweet) peppers. Chop fine, or grind up, the large peeled onions.

Put these into a large kettle with 1 quart of vinegar (equal parts of cider, tarragon, and wine vinegars), and let them settle down to a slow boiling. Also add the salt, brown sugar, celery seed, ground black pepper, paprika, powdered cloves, finely ground allspice, curry powder, the bay leaves, crumbled, and the Ac'cent. Boil the whole slowly for about 3½ hours, until thick as desired, and stir frequently to prevent burning.

In a note to me, Carlyle said: "All the seasonings may be varied to suit one's individual tastes. If you like your chili sauce sweet, add more brown sugar, but I think it is better if it is not too sweet. If you really like it tart, use even less sugar than the indicated pound. I would suggest extreme care in exceeding the indicated amounts of clove, allspice, and curry. Bay leaves, too, are a seasoning to be used with discretion. The recipe I have given you will make about 6 quarts."

(11) EGGS AND CHEESE

One of my favorite egg stories has to do with two traveling sales-men motoring through Georgia. They spent the night in a small rural hotel, and early the next morning they went into the dining room for breakfast. A sleepy-eyed waiter came to the table to take their order.

"I'll have sliced oranges," the first salesman said, "a rasher of bacon, two boiled eggs, toast and coffee."

The waiter turned to the second salesman, who said, "Bring me the same as my friend, but eliminate the eggs."

The waiter shuffled away, and then shortly appeared with the two orders of sliced oranges. Then he said to the second salesman, " 'Scuse me, suh, but what was yo' order again?"

"I'm having the same thing as my friend here," he answered, "but eliminate the eggs."

The waiter nodded, and took off for the kitchen. About five minutes later he reappeared. Addressing the second salesman, he said, " 'Scuse me again, suh, but would you mind having boiled eggs? De cook, he done say de 'liminator is busted."

I don't know of any comestible that can be as varied as eggs. While there are nine basic ways to cook eggs (soft-boiled, hard-cooked, fried, broiled, baked, poached, scrambled, and in omelets and in soufflés), I'd be willing to wager that I could serve eggs three hundred and sixty-five days running, and have a different dish every day.

Eggs can take their place on almost any menu, can be a part of almost any meal. Egg dishes are ideal, of course, with breakfast and luncheon, they may be had for dinner and supper, and for late snacks. I, personally, do not care for egg dishes as an entree for dinner, but I know lots of people who do, particularly during Lent, or on Fast Days. And on occasions when I have had a hearty lunch-eon, and have no appetite for dinner, a fried egg sandwich around nine o'clock in the evening is mighty appealing and enjoyable.

I always feel a little sorry for those unimaginative individuals who consume practically the same breakfasts year in and year out. Can you imagine eating boiled eggs, toast, and coffee 365 days a year? Well, I know a chap who has eaten that same breakfast, without variations, for twenty years!

Variety is the spice of breakfasts as well as life, and I don't know of any breakfast dish that can be as varied as scrambled eggs. Scrambling eggs with bacon bits is rather commonplace, but when you add fresh breadcrumbs mixed with fines herbes, you have something deliciously different, though quick and easy.

EGGS SCRAMBLED WITH CRUMBS AND BACON

2 *slices bacon*
¼ *cup fresh breadcrumbs*
¼ *tsp. dried* fines herbes
4 *eggs*

¼ *cup thin cream*
¼ *cup dry sherry wine*
Salt
Freshly ground pepper

Chop the bacon (the new extra thick slices if you can get them) fine, and sauté gently in a skillet. When the bacon is about half cooked, add the fresh breadcrumbs (broken up rather fine) which have been sprinkled with the dried *fines herbes*. Continue cooking until the bacon and crumbs are lightly browned.

Break the eggs into a bowl and add the thin cream and sherry wine, and salt and pepper to taste. Beat them lightly, and pour into the skillet with the bacon and crumbs. Scramble to the degree of doneness you prefer, and serve immediately.

Almost any kind of previously cooked food, meat or vegetables, goes well with scrambled eggs. I frequently scramble eggs with little soupçons of leftovers, such as chicken gravy (absolutely terrific!), spaghetti sauce, a diced cooked potato, salami, a little chili con carne, asparagus, peas, stewed tomatoes, corned beef hash, and so on. I scramble eggs with different grated cheeses, with an ounce or so of dry sherry or dry white wine, and with various herbs and aromatic herb seeds (anise is one of my favorites).

Not too long ago I found a little dab of sour cream left in the container. So I came up with another succulent combination.

SCRAMBLED EGGS WITH SOUR CREAM AND CARAWAY SEEDS

2 *tbsp. butter*	1 *tbsp. dry sherry*
6 *eggs*	¼ *tsp. Worcestershire sauce*
½ *tsp. salt*	¼ *cup sour cream*
Freshly ground pepper	1 *tbsp. caraway seeds*
	Parsley

Melt the butter in a heavy saucepan, and when bubbling hot add the eggs, lightly beaten together with the salt, freshly ground pepper, dry sherry, and Worcestershire sauce. Stir, and when the eggs begin to set, stir in the sour cream and the caraway seeds, and finish cooking. Garnish with parsley before serving. This will serve 3 or 4.

Anchovies go particularly well with scrambled eggs. One of my frequent breakfast (or luncheon) dishes is scrambled eggs garnished with strips of anchovies.

SCRAMBLED EGGS WITH ANCHOVY STRIPS

4 *eggs*	2 *oz. dry sherry wine*
Freshly ground pepper	1 *tbsp. cream*
Salt	2 *tbsp. butter*
	6-8 *filets of anchovies*

Break the eggs into a bowl, add the salt and freshly ground pepper to taste, the dry sherry, and the cream. Beat for a few moments, then turn the beaten eggs into a hot skillet in which the butter is bubbling. Stir with a fork until the eggs are done, but still moist. Turn onto hot plates, and across each serving lay 3 or 4 strips of anchovy filets. This serves 2.

The following combination of eggs and anchovies is very, very British, and very, very good. It is well suited to a luncheon.

SCRAMBLED EGGS ON ANCHOVY TOAST

6 *slices white bread*	⅛ *tsp. freshly ground pepper*
Butter	2 *oz. dry sherry wine*
Anchovy paste	2 *oz. cream*
6 *eggs*	1 *oz. butter*
½ *tsp. salt*	*Grated Parmesan cheese*

Remove the crusts from the bread slices, and toast. Butter the toast, then spread the buttered slices with anchovy paste, and keep warm.

Break the eggs into a bowl, add the salt, freshly ground pepper, dry sherry wine, and cream. Beat this thoroughly.

Melt 1 ounce of butter in a heavy skillet, and when the butter begins to brown, add the eggs. Scramble them until they are slightly on the underdone side, and then divide them over the slices of anchovy toast. Sprinkle the tops with the grated Parmesan cheese (about 3 tablespoons will do it) and put the egg-topped toast in a 450-degree oven for about 4 or 5 minutes, or until the cheese begins to melt. Serve immediately. A chilled dry white wine is a perfect accompaniment with this dish at luncheon.

The Pennsylvania Dutch have a great fondness for eggs, and a score or more legends about them. One of the most interesting is that eggshells should always be crushed before throwing them out, so that the witches couldn't use them as boats! The ancient Romans had a similar superstition, believing that evil spirits would lurk in uncrushed eggshells.

Of course, eggs are exceedingly good for one, and that is perhaps why Pennsylvania Dutch cooks are very lavish with them, particularly in cakes. They combine eggs in many ways, and, to strangers, some of those ways are odd. But while some of the recipes may seem strange, they are delicious. The following one makes for a mighty substantial breakfast—it will "stick to the ribs," as the saying goes.

DUTCH EGGS

4 eggs	2 tbsp. minced onion
2 tbsp. butter	Salt
1½ oz. beer	Pepper
4 cups diced cooked potatoes	½ tsp. celery salt

Melt the butter in a heavy iron skillet, and add to it the beer. When the mixture is hot, add the diced cooked potatoes and the minced onion, and fry until the potatoes are a light golden brown. Then break into the mixture the eggs, add salt and pepper to taste, and the celery salt. Stir the whole briskly until the eggs are set. Serve with hot, fresh-baked biscuits. This serves 4 (or probably only 2 Pennsylvania Dutch).

I think Sunday brunch always calls for something a little out of the ordinary in the way of a main dish, something different from morning breakfasts. An unusual egg dish that is ideal for a Sunday brunch is Eggs Miroton.

EGGS MIROTON

2 eggs
Salt and pepper
½ tsp. Worcestershire sauce

½ tsp. dry sherry
Grated Parmesan cheese
Sour cream

Use small individual casseroles or ramekins for each person to be served. Break 2 eggs into each, sprinkle with salt and pepper to taste, the Worcestershire sauce, and dry sherry, and then a generous sprinkling of grated Parmesan cheese. Cover the top with commercial sour cream and bake in a 350-degree oven for about 10 minutes. Then run under the broiler for another minute to brown the top slightly. The above recipe is for a single serving, so use your arithmetic for whatever number of servings you desire.

Little link sausages (I think Jones's are the best) and pecan rolls make a delectable accompaniment.

A somewhat similar dish, but with an added piquant flavor, is Eggs Dijon. To get the full benefit of the mustard flavor, use only the Dijon mustard, which is imported from France, and is made with white wine.

EGGS DIJON

1 tsp. prepared Dijon mustard
¼ tsp. salt
1 cup sour cream

3 tbsp. grated Gruyère cheese
1 tbsp. dry white wine
6 eggs
Buttered breadcrumbs

Mix together the Dijon mustard, salt, sour cream, grated cheese, and the dry white wine. This is the sauce.

Break the eggs into a greased shallow baking dish (or 2 eggs into each of three individual ramekins or casseroles). Cover the eggs with the sauce, and sprinkle buttered breadcrumbs over the top. Place the baking dish, or the individual dishes, in a pan of hot water, and bake in a 350-degree oven for about 15 minutes. This will serve 3.

Two of my favorite comestibles with eggs are chicken livers and mushrooms. I like to use them in scrambled eggs, and mushrooms go beautifully with this baked egg dish, which is perfect for a Sunday brunch. Let's be fancy and give it its French name.

OEUFS AUX CHAMPIGNONS
(Eggs with Mushrooms)

6 *eggs*	3 *tbsp. mayonnaise*
3 *tbsp. butter*	1 *little green onion, chopped*
½ *lb. fresh mushrooms*	1 *tbsp. chopped parsley*
2 *tbsp. flour*	*Salt*
1 *cup dry white wine*	*Freshly ground pepper*
1 *cup chicken broth*	2 *tbsp. melted butter*

Grated Gruyère cheese

Sauté the sliced fresh mushrooms in the butter in a saucepan. When they are lightly browned (about 8 minutes), stir in the flour, and blend well. Then add the dry white wine, chicken broth, mayonnaise, the chopped little green onion (bulb and top), and the chopped parsley. Season to taste with salt and freshly ground pepper, and cook, stirring, until the sauce is smooth.

Pour the sauce in a shallow baking dish, distributing it evenly. Then, carefully break the eggs over the sauce, distributing them evenly. Pour over all the melted butter, and sprinkle generously with the grated Gruyère (Parmesan can be used) cheese. Bake in a 350-degree oven until eggs are cooked. This will serve 3 or 6, depending upon how many eggs per person.

Throughout the Christian world, Easter is one of the most important festivals of the year. In all of Europe it is a day of great feasting, and each country has its special Easter dish. In Old Russia there would be a roasted pig and sausages and ham, and *Pashka* and *Kulitch* (Easter desserts). In Italy, *Agnellino* (roasted baby lamb) and *Carciofi Arrostiti* (roasted artichokes) are the traditional dishes. In Finland, a porridge is an indispensable dish on every table. In Greece, lamb is the favorite meat course, together with a special bread called Bread of Christ. And in nearly every country a traditional article of food is the Easter egg.

Going way back into antiquity, the coloring of eggs was an ancient custom, even antedating Christianity. Today our eggs may not have the vivid colorings that were customary in Europe and in early American times, but they should still be a delightful treat to the palate after they have served their purpose as a decorative symbol of Eastertime. So let's see to what gastronomic use they can be put.

The Balsams, a summer resort hotel at Dixville Notch, New Hampshire, boasts of an international kitchen, presided over by chef Hans Letsch. One of his outstanding egg dishes is Eggs Serenade, and by serving it at an Easter brunch, you can utilize some of the colored Easter Eggs.

EGGS SERENADE

4 *hard-cooked eggs*
2 *tbsp. mayonnaise*
¼ *tsp. dry mustard*
Salt and pepper
¾ *cup chopped mushrooms*

1 *tbsp. butter*
3 *chicken livers*
3 *tbsp. chili sauce*
⅔ *cup canned tomato soup*
2 *tbsp. grated cheese*

Cut the hard-cooked eggs in half lengthwise, remove the yolks and press them through a sieve. Moisten the sieved yolks with the mayonnaise, and season with the mustard and salt and pepper to taste.

Sauté the mushrooms in the butter in a saucepan until they are tender (6 to 7 minutes) and then add the chicken livers, and cook fast for 1 minute. Remove from the flame, and cut the livers into tiny pieces. Add the chili sauce and return the saucepan to the fire until the chili sauce browns (about ½ minute). Combine the mashed egg yolk mixture with the mushroom-chicken-liver mixture.

Place the halved whites of the hard-cooked eggs in a greased baking dish, and heap them with the combined mixtures. Spoon the tomato soup over the tops, sprinkle with grated cheese, and bake in a 425-degree oven for 10 to 15 minutes, or until heated through. This recipe serves 4.

I have spoken before of the products of the Spice Islands Company, and I gave the recipe for their delightful appetizer, Nuts and Bolts, in the first chapter. A few days ago Mr. Fredric H. Johnson, the president, sent me samples of three of their newest products: White Minced Onions (1 tablespoon soaked in an equal amount of water for 5 minutes equals a small onion), Spice Parisienne (a blend of pepper with herbs and spices), and Powdered Mushrooms (1 tablespoon is the equivalent to 3 tablespoons of whole dried mushrooms). All three are excellent. I know, because I used them in a meat loaf the next day.

I was intrigued by a recipe that was included with the samples, Ham and Eggs Vegas. It is certainly a departure from that old standby, Ham and Eggs—in fact, there is no similarity between the two. But the Vegas version is delicious, with a somewhat Western flavor. You might gamble with your taste buds on it some time.

HAM AND EGGS VEGAS

¼ -lb. ham slice
1 tbsp. butter (if necessary)
¼ tsp. garlic powder
1½ tsp. arrowroot
1 tbsp. Spice Islands Powdered
    Mushrooms
1 tbsp. Spice Islands Minced
    White Onions
1 tbsp. water

1 can condensed consommé
½ cup dry red wine
½ tsp. Spice Islands Mei Yen
    seasoning
Pinch dried marjoram
Pinch dried thyme
⅛ tsp. black pepper
¼ tsp. Spice Islands Spice
    Parisienne

6 hard-cooked eggs

Cut a ¼-pound slice of ham in thin strips, and sauté lightly in a frying pan (if the ham is very lean, sauté it in the butter). Then stir in the garlic powder; add the arrowroot, powdered mushrooms, and the minced white onions which have been soaked in water for 5 minutes, then drained. Mix all this well, then add the consommé and dry red wine. Cook over a low flame, stirring constantly until thickened and smooth. Stir in Mei Yen seasoning powder (a seasoned monosodium glutamate), the dried marjoram and thyme, the pepper, and the Spice Parisienne. Blend everything well.

Quarter the hard-cooked eggs and add to the sauce. Heat, then serve over toast triangles, or, if used as a luncheon dish, serve over fluffy rice.

Another very delightful brunch dish is Devonshire Eggs, which is an old English dish, and brings back an old use of mint.

DEVONSHIRE EGGS

½ tsp. chopped fresh mint
½ cup dry white wine
½ tbsp. chopped little green
    onions
1 tbsp. chopped parsley
1 tbsp. butter

1 tbsp. flour
Salt and pepper
1 tbsp. lemon juice
4 very fresh eggs
3 tbsp. fine breadcrumbs
Butter

2 tbsp. grated Parmesan cheese

In a saucepan simmer the chopped fresh mint, little green onions
and parsley, and the dry white wine for 15 minutes. At the end of
the simmering time stir into the mixture a *roux* made with the
tablespoon of butter and the flour creamed together, adding salt
and pepper to taste and the lemon juice. Stir and blend until the
sauce is smooth. If it becomes too thick, add a little more dry white
wine.

Boil the *very fresh* eggs in water for 4 minutes. Remove from the
water quickly, and let them cool in cool water. Then remove the
shells (very carefully, lest the eggs break and spoil the dish) and
lay the whole eggs in a shallow baking dish. Pour the sauce over
them, and sprinkle with the breadcrumbs which have been lightly
sautéed in a little butter, and the grated Parmesan cheese. Heat the
whole well in a 325-degree oven, and serve.

One of the best known and most popular egg dishes is Eggs Benedict. As you probably know, this dish is made up of a slice of ham
placed on an English muffin half, a poached egg placed on top of
the ham slice, and Hollandaise sauce poured over all.

Not long ago one of my friends asked me if I couldn't devise an
Eggs Benedict for Lenten menus. So I worked the following recipe
out. Gone is the ham—at least for Lent—and in its place is smoked
salmon, a substitution so tasty that you may want to adopt it perma-
nently. And instead of Hollandaise, I used my Mock Hollandaise
(page 335 under sauces). The recipe is quick and easy, and makes
4 servings. And best of all, the sauce can be made ahead, kept refrigerated, and rewarmed just before serving.

EGGS BENEDICT À LA LENT

4 *eggs*	*Butter*
2 *English muffins*	4 *slices smoked salmon*

Mock Hollandaise sauce

Split, toast, and butter each English muffin half. Top each half first with a slice of smoked salmon, then a poached egg, and cover all with the Mock Hollandaise sauce. Serve to 4 at once.

I am of the opinion that there is too much hocus-pocus about omelets. The main thing is that the more the eggs are beaten (with a fork or wire whisk—not an egg beater), the lighter the omelet will be. I use a plain old cast-iron skillet which I reserve just for omelets. I never clean it with soap and water—just wipe it thoroughly after each use with absorbent paper toweling. This keeps the cooking surface slick, and helps to slide the omelet out of the pan. Also, in making an omelet, use plenty of butter, and have it bubbling hot when you pour in the eggs.

I recently devised an omelet which I call Cheese Omelet Supreme. The mayonnaise in it gives it an unusual richness and flavor, and the omelet turns out a beautiful golden brown.

CHEESE OMELET SUPREME

5 *eggs*	2 *tbsp. butter*
3 *tbsp. mayonnaise*	½ *cup grated sharp Cheddar*
½ *tsp. Worcestershire sauce*	*cheese*
1 *tsp. finely chopped chives*	

Beat together until foamy the eggs, mayonnaise, Worcestershire sauce, and the finely chopped chives (or finely chopped little green onion tops).

Place the butter in a hot skillet, and when the butter begins to brown and give off a nutty fragrance, pour the beaten egg mixture into the skillet. Stir briskly with a fork to heat the whole mass evenly, then press the edges back toward the center, so that the soft part will immediately run to fill the vacant spaces.

Spread the grated, sharp natural Cheddar cheese over half of the omelet, and let it melt. Then, if you are an expert, raise the handle of the pan upward and let half of the omelet slide onto the serving plate. Then give it a flip so that the other half folds over. Otherwise, do the folding with a broad spatula. Serve at once to 4.

Omelets, in our house, are usually reserved for Sunday morning breakfast which, to my mind, is one of the most delightful meals of the week. The type of omelet served varies with our moods. An *Omelet aux Fines Herbes* is delicately delicious. It is simple—you merely add ¼ teaspoon of dried *fines herbes* to the egg mixture before beating (*fines herbes* consists of a mixture of thyme, oregano, sage, rosemary, marjoram, and basil; these are in dried form, and can be purchased in bottled form in fine food shops and grocery stores. I have found Spice Islands *Fines Herbes* to be the best and freshest).

I think our favorite omelet is a chicken liver omelet, and this is the way we make it.

CHICKEN LIVER OMELET

½ lb. chicken livers	1 tbsp. flour
Seasoned flour	½ cup condensed consommé
3 tbsp. butter	¼ cup dry Madeira wine
1 tsp. finely minced little green onions	4 eggs
	Butter
¼ tsp. dried tarragon leaves	Salt and pepper

Clean the chicken livers and dredge them with seasoned flour. In a skillet put 2 tablespoons of butter, and when it is hot add the floured chicken livers and sauté them for about 7 minutes, or until their red-juiced look disappears and they are delicately colored on all sides. Then remove them to a hot dish and keep warm.

To the butter and juices in the skillet add another tablespoon of butter, the minced little green onions, and the dried tarragon. Sprinkle in 1 tablespoon of flour, and when well blended in stir in the condensed consommé and the dry Madeira wine. Simmer gently until the mixture thickens a little, then add the chicken livers, and let heat while making the omelet.

Prepare the omelet, using 4 eggs for 2 people. Remember, be generous with the butter (I use about 2 ounces) and heat it to bubbling in a heavy skillet. Pour in the well-beaten eggs, which have been seasoned with salt and pepper, and stir well until the eggs begin to set, then stop. When the eggs are done, but still a little moist on top, slide the omelet onto a hot platter, cover half of it with the chicken livers and sauce, fold the other half over, and pour the remaining chicken livers and sauce over, and serve. This is a generous serving for 2.

One of the finest magazines published, in my opinion, is *Sunset,* the Magazine of Western Living. While it can be subscribed to (at an extra dollar a year) by people living outside the area of the West Coast, its circulation is largely in the area it serves.

Every issue is packed with tremendously interesting and helpful articles on travel, building and remodeling, workshop projects, food and entertaining, landscaping and outdoor gardening, and home management.

Of particular interest to lovers of fine food are the departments "Kitchen Cabinet" and "Chefs of the West." This latter department, or section, is filled with recipes from men. Men submit unusual recipes; the recipes are made up in the *Sunset* kitchen, and the finished product is served to a panel of culinary experts. If the recipes are passed upon favorably by the panel, each recipe is printed in the "Chefs of the West" section of the magazine, and each lucky man receives a cherished *Sunset Chefs of the West* cap. If a man should be fortunate enough to have a second recipe printed, he receives a chef's apron.

The number of men out in the West who earnestly and seriously strive to win chef's caps and aprons is rather amazing. Professionally, they range all the way from bankers and professors to cabdrivers. Incidently, *Sunset Magazine* has published an exceedingly interesting cookbook, which contains 575 recipes from 474 men. The book is called *Chefs of the West,* and sells for $3.50. It is a well-worthwhile addition to any gourmet's library.

Not long ago I was asked to be a member of the panel which passed on a series of recipes. Although it was early in March, some twelve of us sat down to luncheon in the beautiful patio adjoining the kitchen in *Sunset's* lovely building. We tasted, made notes on each dish, and finally turned in our reports. At this writing I don't know the results of the tastings, but we were served one dish that I thought was notable. It was submitted by C. K. Shumate, of San Diego, California. It was called Coronado Sunrise, and with the permission of the publishers of *Sunset Magazine,* I am detailing the recipe herewith.

CORONADO SUNRISE

1 *small pinch coriander, ground*	*¼ tsp. onion salt*
⅛ tsp. curry powder	*4 tbsp. table cream*
¼ tsp. chili powder	*6 egg whites*
⅛ tsp. black pepper	*½ tbsp. cold bacon drippings*
¼ tsp. baking powder	*4 egg yolks*
	¼ tsp. paprika

Combine the first 6 ingredients, and then blend them well into the cream. Beat the egg whites lightly, then gradually add them to the spice-cream mixture.

Grease 4 individual shallow baking dishes (or casseroles) with the bacon drippings. Divide the egg white-spice-cream mixture equally among the 4 dishes or casseroles. Bake in a 375-degree oven for about 30 minutes, or until the egg white mixture has set.

About 2 or 3 minutes before the egg white mixture has set (say 27 minutes), remove the dishes from the oven, and float 1 egg yolk in the center of each. Sprinkle with paprika, and return to the oven for 2 or 3 minutes. Then serve immediately. Serves 4.

Mr. Shumate's egg dish was accompanied with special rolls, which would be indicated if the dish were a luncheon entree. I append the recipe herewith.

CORONADO SUNRISE ROLLS

2 *frankfurter rolls, split*	1 *tbsp. prepared English*
2 *slices canned ham*	*mustard*
4 *slices American process*	1 *tbsp. butter*
cheese	

Trim all the fat from the ham. Cut the ham and cheese into pieces slightly smaller than the tops of the split rolls. Sauté the ham in the butter until it is slightly browned. Sprinkle the rolls with some of the ham-butter drippings, and then coat lightly with the mustard. Lay the cheese slices on the split rolls, then the slices of ham. Brush with the rest of the ham-butter drippings. Place on a cookie sheet and bake in the oven the last 10 minutes of the egg-baking time.

After the eggs have been removed from the oven, turn the temperature up to 500 degrees, and bake the rolls until the cheese is well melted and the ham has browned around the edges.

CHEESE

Cheese is one of the oldest foods in the world, and just about the simplest. According to legend, an ancient sheepherder, carrying his milk in a sort of a thermos jug made from the dried stomach of a calf (as was the custom), stopped to take a drink, and found that he had a solid to eat instead of a liquid to drink. In this particular case the calf's stomach hadn't entirely dried, and still had some rennet in it. So the rennet curdled the milk, with a surprising result.

In its simplest form, cheese is still made just about the same way as it was four thousand years ago. Anybody with a cow to milk and a calf to provide the rennet could conceivably be in the cheese business today. But there would be terrific competition, for today, in the United State alone, there are over six hundred varieties and styles of cheeses.

All varieties of cheese can be grouped into about eighteen basic families. Within these families there are only the subtlest of differences. Plain Limburger, for example, is a pretty rugged cheese. It originated in Belgium. But there are many cheeses that are simply Limburger on "good behavior!" Some of them that you will recognize are Brick Cheese, Chantelle, Muenster, Oka, Pont l'Eveque, and Camembert. Or take Blue cheese. It is made from cow's milk in many parts of the world. Included in this blue mold type of cheese are Gorgonzola, from Italy; Stilton, from England; and Roquefort, from France. This last, however, is made from sheep's milk.

I am inordinately fond of cheese, and I always have at least a half-dozen kinds on hand. And there are usually a couple of cheese spreads in the refrigerator as cocktail accompaniments.

To my mind, the greatest cheese spread of all is Liptoi, a savory cheese from Hungary. It is perhaps better known by its German name, Liptauer.

Most recipes for this wonderful cheese omit two important ingredients, ale and mustard. The true Hungarian Liptoi is made from a cream cheese prepared from goat's milk, but a cream cheese will do very well.

LIPTOI CHEESE

½ lb. cream cheese

¼ cup sour cream

2 oz. softened butter

2 tsp. anchovy paste

2 tsp. drained capers

2 little green onions, chopped

⅛ tsp. salt

1 tbsp. paprika

2 tsp. caraway seeds

½ tsp. dry mustard

1 oz. ale

The best and easiest way to make Liptoi is in a blender. Into the detachable glass bowl of the blender put the cream cheese, broken up, the sour cream, the softened butter, the anchovy paste, the drained capers, the little green onions (shallots are even better if you can get them), the salt, the best paprika that you can obtain, the caraway seeds, the dry mustard, and the ale. Whip this mixture to a smooth blend. You may have to stop the blender a couple of times and stir the ingredients with a spatula, but when all is mixing well let the blender go until everything is smooth and creamy. Put the mixture into a bowl, and place in the refrigerator.

To serve, garnish with radishes, and accompany with thin slices of brown bread or pumpernickel. Dry sherry, chilled, or Dubonnet and dry vermouth, mixed half and half, and chilled, are the indicated libations.

In San Francisco there is a very unique society called the Lower Montgomery Street Olive or Onion Society. The members are naturally dedicated to martinis. At one of their early meetings they decided on the perfect martini. As a guest I attended a later meeting held in a San Francisco restaurant, where they selected a brand of olives and a brand of bottled onions which best complemented their perfect martini. At this meeting I encountered Floyd Buick, a well-known radio personality in the Bay area. We got to talking about appetite whets to go with martinis, and he gave me his recipe for crock cheese. It is marvelous, and can be used as a spread cheese with predinner libations, or an after-dinner cheese.

CROCK CHEESE FLOYD BUICK

1 lb. American or Danish
   blue cheese

1 lb. imported Roquefort cheese

½ lb. grated Parmesan cheese

½ pint of good cognac

3 oz. dry sherry wine

Mix together and blend well the three cheeses. Then add the brandy and about 3 ounces of the dry sherry (there should be enough liquid to make a good paste). Again mix well, place in a crock, cover, and keep in a cool place (not the refrigerator) for a few days, so that the flavors will "marry." If you use this recipe as a dip cheese, thin it out with additional dry sherry wine. Of course, to make smaller quantities, use half, or a quarter of the above quantities of the ingredients.

Speaking of crock cheese, I have been served Down East what is called a "cheese pot," or "melting pot" cheese. As far as I could determine, this is a combination of Roquefort and cream cheese, to which is added olive oil, mustard, curry powder, monosodium glutamate, garlic, and dry sherry. Later, this mix is laced with rum, port, or brandy. If any of you readers have an old and treasured recipe for this, I'd deeply appreciate receiving it.

Two or three years ago the Bismarck Hotel in Chicago decided to give cheese a "new look" so that it might become the center of attraction at any cocktail party. Chef Meyer unveiled his creation at a press party at the hotel, and it proved a welcome diversion as a substitute for those "celebrating" cakes with their cloying sweetness. Every guest went for it with practically both hands, and almost before the other very delicious hors d'oeuvres were even touched, the cheese masterpiece was consumed down to the last crumb.

BISMARCK "NEW LOOK" CHEESE

6 *oz. Herkimer cheese*   1 *oz. claret wine*
10 *oz. American cheese*   1 *pinch curry powder*
10 *oz. cream cheese*   2 *drops Worcestershire sauce*
5 *oz. butter*   2 *drops Tabasco sauce*

Put the Herkimer cheese (a sharp, aged New York cheese made in Herkimer County) and the American cheese through the meat grinder. Then add the cream cheese, the butter, the dry red wine, the curry powder, the Worcestershire sauce and the Tabasco sauce. Mix all together well until thoroughly blended, and then mold in the form of a cake.

The top can be decorated with any design with cream cheese in any color (add vegetable coloring to the cream cheese), put it in a pastry bag, and squeeze it out. Then letter it as you desire with anchovy paste squeezed out of a pastry tube. This recipe makes a 2-pound cake.

Another taste-teaser is French Fried Camembert Cheese. Moisten triangles of Camembert cheese with white wine, then roll them in very fine breadcrumbs. Drop these coated triangles in hot fat. When they are golden brown, take them out, and you'll discover a new taste thrill.

For more years than I would care to mention, Cheese Dreams have been one of my favorite snacks. I can well remember the first time I ever tasted them—after one of Mother and Dad's 500 parties. And I can still savor the odor of their preparation—slices of sharp Herkimer County cheese placed between 2 half slices of bread, and fried in plenty of butter in a heavy skillet.

The Italians have a version of Cheese Dreams, only they call it Mozzarella in Carrozza (in a carriage). Mozzarella cheese is a moist, smooth, white unsalted cheese, and can be obtained in almost any Italian grocery store.

MOZZARELLA IN CARROZZA

8 *slices white bread*
Mozzarella cheese
Flour
2 *beaten eggs*
¼ *tsp. salt*
1 *oz. dry white wine*
Dash of Worcestershire sauce
1 *cup olive oil*

Cut off the crust from 8 slices of white bread, cut thin, and, as in Cheese Dreams, cut each slice in half. On each half slice of bread place a slice of Mozzarella the same size as the bread. Flour the whole thing well, and then dip in the lightly beaten eggs to which have been added the salt, dry white wine, and Worcestershire sauce. Fry the slices gently in about 1 cup of lard or olive oil, and serve very hot. Believe me, these items will go like hot cakes among any crowd of football rooters.

Every once in a while you hear someone extolling the virtues of the "good old days," and wondering if people weren't happier with the simple pleasures and less complicated mode of living, say, in the Gay Nineties. Well, I, for one, am perfectly happy with things as they are. I like hot and cold running butlers, modern plumbing and heating, and I find even a vintage automobile much handier than a horse and buggy. But there is one gadget that was associated with the era of gaslight, hansom cabs, and Gibson girls that I'm happy to see has staged a comeback—the chafing dish.

Welsh Rabbit (and don't let an old-timer catch you calling it Welsh Rarebit) is the classic chafing dish recipe. My father was a past master at making it, and his recipe is in my *With a Jug of Wine*.

An English variation on the Welsh Rabbit theme that is tasty and tangy and easy is English Monkey.

ENGLISH MONKEY

½ cup beer
½ cup evaporated milk
1 cup stale breadcrumbs
1 cup grated sharp Cheddar
  cheese

½ tsp. salt
¼ tsp. paprika
⅛ tsp. dry mustard
½ tsp. Worcestershire sauce
1 egg, slightly beaten

4 slices hot buttered toast

Combine the beer with the evaporated milk and cook in the blazer pan of the chafing dish with the stale breadcrumbs and grated sharp Cheddar cheese over boiling water until the cheese is melted. Then add the salt, paprika, dry mustard, and Worcestershire sauce. Next stir in the lightly beaten egg, and cook for about 1 minute, stirring constantly. Pour over hot buttered toast. This recipe will serve 4.

Still another variation of the Welsh Rabbit theme is a mushroom rabbit.

MUSHROOM RABBIT

½ lb. butter
6 tbsp. flour
1 pint milk
½ lb. sharp Cheddar cheese
1 lb. mushrooms

Butter
½ cup condensed tomato soup
½ cup dry sherry
Salt and pepper
Paprika

Toasted English muffins

For a mushroom rabbit, use the chafing dish. In the blazer pan over the flame melt the butter, then add the flour and milk. Cook until smooth and thickened, stirring constantly.

Place the blazer over the water pan, and when the water is heated add the diced Cheddar cheese. Cook until the cheese is melted, then add the sliced mushrooms, sautéed previously in butter, soup, sherry, salt, pepper, and paprika to taste. When the mixture is thoroughly heated, serve on toast or toasted English muffins.

A few years ago, I had a letter from a reader that gave me quite a kick. She said, in part: "I am a woman, and I should believe in those big letters printed in black, 'For Men Only!' Nevertheless, I enjoy your articles and your unusual recipes. . . . Sometime, if you have a recipe for 'Pizza Pie,' I would like to see it in print."

While I have great enthusiasm for Italian food and cooking, I had never eaten pizza. I have listened to Italians and Americans praise it to the skies, but somehow I had the idea that it wouldn't appeal to me. But the above letter (and others requesting a pizza recipe) could not be ignored, so I hied me over to a friend of long standing, Ric Riccardo. For nearly twenty years Ric and I had eaten together off and on, and discussed cooking, along with literature, music, and art. I have sampled many of the finest Italian dishes prepared by him, and I knew that a pizza recipe from him would be absolutely authentic.

Ric did more than give me the recipe for pizza. He took me over to the place where pizzas are a specialty, and made one for me right before my eyes. Then we waited for it to cook, over a bottle of Chianti, and twenty minutes later I was rapidly surrounding one of the tastiest Italian dishes it has ever been my pleasure to eat. And here's how it was made.

PIZZA

2 cups flour
1 cup water
¼ cake yeast
Mozzarella cheese

Canned tomatoes
Grated Parmesan cheese
Dried oregano
Freshly ground pepper
Olive oil

Make a bread dough of the flour, water, and yeast and let this rise. (At his Pizzeria, of course, a very large quantity of bread dough is made up, but he said that the amounts just quoted would do for a family pizza.) Now, spread the dough out on a large greased pie tin (about 12 or 14 inches across), just as you would for a pie, and don't make it thin. Next, fill the plate with thin slices of Mozzarella cheese (you can buy this at any good Italian store). Cover the cheese with fresh or canned tomatoes passed through a colander, and be generous with the tomatoes. On top of the tomatoes sprinkle plenty of grated Parmesan cheese, a couple of generous pinches of oregano, some freshly ground pepper, and sprinkle a few drops of olive oil over all. Then place it in a hot oven (500 degrees) and bake for 20 minutes. Serve it immediately, because it must be piping hot to get the full flavor out of it. Chianti wine is the perfect accompaniment.

The above is a cheese pizza. In place of the Mozzarella cheese, you can use sausages, or anchovies. In such a case, omit the first step (the thin slices of cheese) and cover the dough with the tomatoes. Then place six fingers of sausage meat over the tomatoes (as if they were to be the spokes of a wheel), sprinkle the grated Parmesan cheese and oregano and olive oil over the top, and bake. Or you can use six anchovies in place of the sausage. Some day, when I'm very hungry, I'm going to try a pizza with the Mozzarella cheese, the sausage, and the anchovies. That should be something!

A mushroom and cheese pie is something of an American variation of pizza. It can be served as a light main dish, or it can be cut in wedges and served as an appetizer.

MUSHROOM AND CHEESE PIE

1 8-oz. can mushroom stems and pieces	3 eggs, lightly beaten
	½ tsp. Worcestershire sauce
1 cup shredded Cheddar cheese	¼ tsp. scraped onion
1 baked (9-inch) pie shell	Salt and pepper
1 cup cream	½ tsp. Ac'cent
½ cup milk	Paprika

Drain the mushrooms *thoroughly*. Scatter the mushrooms and cheese evenly over the bottom of the baked pie shell.

Mix the cream and milk in a saucepan and heat to scalding. Then add gradually to the lightly beaten eggs, mixing well. Add the

Worcestershire sauce, scraped onion, salt and pepper to taste, and the Ac'cent. Pour this mixture over the mushrooms and cheese, and sprinkle with paprika. Bake in a 425-degree oven 35 to 40 minutes, or until a knife inserted in the center comes out clean. Remove from oven and let stand for 10 minutes or so before serving. This serves 4 or 5. Crisp bacon is an excellent accompaniment if this is served as a main dish.

On a winter's Sunday night, Danish Cheese Soufflé is a supper dish with the right, light touch. It's a savory meal in itself—nothing more needed except a crisp, green salad, a generous brewing of coffee, and a bowl of fresh fruit for dessert.

You'll find that the aroma of toasting cheese and the fragrance of coffee blend in a way that will make you forget about wintry winds outside. Make plenty of soufflé, plenty of coffee, and settle down to a perfect evening at home.

DANISH CHEESE SOUFFLÉ

2 *cups milk*	*Salt and pepper to taste*
2 *tbsp. grated onion*	3 *cups grated sharp Cheddar*
3 *cups bread cubes*	*cheese*
Dash Tabasco	4 *eggs, separated*
½ *tsp. dry mustard*	1 *tbsp. melted butter*
1 *tsp. poppy seed*	

Combine milk and onion in saucepan; heat to scalding. Add 2 cups bread cubes, seasonings, and cheese. Stir until melted. Beat egg yolks slightly; stir in a little of cheese mixture; stir into remaining cheese mixture; cool slightly. Beat egg whites stiff; fold in. Turn into 1½-quart casserole. Toss remaining bread cubes with melted butter and poppy seed; scatter over top of casserole. Bake in moderate oven (350 degrees) 45 to 50 minutes.

I don't believe there are any better companions in the gastronomic world than wine and cheese. They "marry" beautifully in cooking, and in their natural state I think they reach the peak of their affinity at the close of the meal. To many, their deliciousness is enhanced when fresh fruit joins them, which makes the saying, "Two is company, but three's a crowd," old hat.

The kinship between cheese and wine is a natural one, as Ernest Oldmeadow points out in his introduction to André L. Simon's *A Catechism Concerning Cheeses.* Oldmeadow says: "Both wine and cheese represent man's efforts to transmute the Perishable into the Durable." He explains that grape juice and milk were originally perishable, tended to "go bad" quickly. But human skill finally learned to make them "go good" by processes which are fundamentally natural. "In each case the original material undergoes a change into something rich and strange."

Let's look at some of the ways to serve wine and cheese. At appetizer time, sherry goes with almost any type of cheese and crackers, or with the many cheese dips or spreads. At such time, I prefer a dry sherry, and chilled.

There are a great many delightful luncheon dishes made with cheese, the queen of which is a cheese soufflé. With cheese luncheon dishes the perfect accompaniment is a chilled, dry white wine.

For a dinner dessert, the combinations of wine and cheese and fruit are almost endless. The traditional dessert wines are a rich, full-bodied port, a Madeira, a sweet, or cream, sherry, a Tokay, or Muscatel. Almost any kind of cheese can be used. My preferences are Brie, Camembert, Gorgonzola, Provolone, Roquefort, or Stilton. Crisp fresh apples or juicy ripe pears give an added plus to the wines and cheese. If you are going to have crackers, I think the toasted Bent water crackers are by far the best. Also, don't forget that a full-bodied red wine, possibly served with the entree, goes wonderfully well with robust-flavored cheeses.

Try this connoisseur's dessert tray one of these evenings, and listen for raves.

In the center of a large silver or glass tray, place some galax or vine leaves. On the leaves arrange sections of cored pear petal fashion. Around them place cored apple rings which have been brushed with lemon juice, each ring overlapping a little to form a circle. On the outer rim of the plate or platter place individual wedges of Roquefort, or Blue cheese, Camembert, that wonderful California cheese, Monterey Jack, Gruyère, Bel Paese, and Gjetost, a sweetish Norwegian cheese. The fruits, of course, are used in place of crackers, and the wine should be port or Madeira.

(12) DESSERTS

There seem to be three schools of thought on desserts. The most popular is that a dessert rounds out and balances a meal, and that even an uninteresting meal, followed by an excellent dessert, is not a total loss.

The other extreme is that a dinner may very well end after the salad, because no one is hungry by the time dessert is served. A dessert is unnecessary, it is too filling, and leaves one with a stuffed feeling.

The middle-of-the-road belief is that the meal should end with cheese and/or fruit, with perhaps a glass of cordial with the coffee for those who have a sweet tooth.

Personally, I feel that a dinner is incomplete without the finale of a dessert, even though it may be only cheese and fruit, before the coffee. And, having a sweet tooth to a degree, I want a pony of fine cordial to savor with my coffee, such as a Grand Marnier, chartreuse, Benedictine, or that magnificent Italian cordial, Gallieno.

But I do feel this way about desserts: If one is to be served (a light dessert after a heavy meal, or a substantial one if the meal has been light), it should have glamor, it should create a stir of interest. In short, it should be spectacular.

To my way of thinking, there have always been two great desserts: English Trifle, which has glamor, and *Crêpes Suzettes,* which are spectacular. And both of them are captivatingly luscious. The recipes for both of these desserts are in my *With a Jug of Wine.*

Since coming to San Francisco, I have had a dessert which joins English Trifle and *Crêpes Suzettes* right at the top of all desserts. It is Jerusalem Pancakes, a creation of master chef Charles Bardelli, who is the owner of Bardelli's Restaurant on O'Farrel Street, and whose Chicken Jerusalem (no relation to Pancakes Jerusalem) I have detailed in the chapter on Poultry.

363

JERUSALEM PANCAKE

⅓ apple, thinly sliced
1 generous pinch orange rind,
    julienne cut
3 almonds, slivered
1 tbsp. orange juice

⅓ cup Crêpe Suzette batter
⅓ cup melted butter
Cinnamon
Sugar
2 oz. anisette

4 oz. brandy

Crêpes Suzette Batter

1½ cups sifted flour
¼ cup powdered sugar
Generous pinch salt
1 cup milk

¼ cup melted butter
2 tbsp. orange curaçao
1 tsp. grated lemon rind
5 eggs

Make your batter first. In a mixing bowl combine the sifted flour, powdered sugar, and salt. Stir in slowly the milk, melted butter, orange curaçao, and lemon rind. Then add the well-beaten whole eggs, and beat the mixture vigorously until it is very smooth and of about the consistency of cream. Cover, and let stand 1 hour.

Fry the peeled, thinly sliced ⅓ apple in a heavy frying pan with half of the melted butter, until the apples are brown. Then add the orange rind and the 3 almonds, which have been slivered. Now pour ⅓ cup of Crêpe Suzette batter into the skillet to cover all. When the pancake has browned, turn it over and sprinkle on powdered cinnamon and sugar. When brown, turn it over and place in a hot crêpe pan (the blazer of your chafing dish is ideal) and pour over it the rest of the melted butter.

To serve, pour over the pancake the orange juice, the anisette and the brandy, and flame. As the flames die out, cut the pancake in two and serve, spooning the liquid over each half. This recipe serves 2 generously.

As I have confessed a number of times in the public prints, I can get along without most cakes very well. Perhaps I indulged in cake too much and too often in my youth. Perhaps my tastes have changed. In any event, I rarely take more than a small bite or two when it is served to me, particularly after a satisfying meal.

But a chocolate icebox cake is another story. That I go for in a big way. Mrs. Wood and I made one not long ago when we had guests, and I came back for a second helping, in spite of the fact that the dinner, up to the dessert, had been epicurean.

Here's how this nectar of the gods is made.

CHOCOLATE ICEBOX CAKE

¾ lb. sweet chocolate   Ladyfingers
3 tbsp. sugar   Cream (sweet) sherry
3 tbsp. water   Slivered almonds
3 tbsp. Cointreau   1 cup whipping cream
6 egg yolks   Sugar
6 egg whites   Vanilla flavoring
              Maraschino cherries

Melt the sweet chocolate in the top of a double boiler, then add 3 tablespoons of sugar, the water, Cointreau (or orange curaçao), and the well-beaten egg yolks. Cook slowly until thick and smooth, stirring constantly. Then take the top out of the double boiler, and set it aside to allow the contents to cool. When it is cool, fold in the stiffly beaten whites of the eggs.

Line the sides and bottom of a medium-sized spring form cake-pan with ladyfingers which have been split in half lengthwise, putting the flat side of the split ladyfingers against the sides and bottom of the cakepan. Moisten the ladyfingers with cream (sweet) sherry. Then pour in half of the chocolate filling, and sprinkle the filling with slivered almonds (you can buy these in cellophane packages). Then add another layer of split ladyfingers (flat side down) over the filling. Moisten them with the cream sherry, and pour over them the balance of the chocolate filling. Again sprinkle the top of the filling with slivered almonds, and again cover the filling with the split ladyfingers (flat side down), moistening them with cream sherry. The total amount of cream sherry needed will be anywhere from ½ to 1 cup. The ladyfingers should not be moistened to the point where they become soggy. Now set the cake, still in the spring form cakepan, in the refrigerator for at least 12 hours (you can make this the day before, and leave it in the refrigerator until shortly before serving the next evening).

Shortly before serving time, remove the spring form from the cake, leaving the cake on the bottom of the pan. Cover the top generously with 1 cup of whipping cream, whipped with a little sugar and a little vanilla flavoring. Decorate the top with mara-schino cherries, and/or slivered almonds.

In one of the Pan American Coffee Bureau news letters, there was a recipe for a delectable concoction that really looks regal on a party dinner table, or a gala buffet board. It is both similar to my Chocolate Icebox Cake recipe, and yet entirely different. But both recipes have one thing in common—they are both out of this world, eye-wise and taste-wise.

COFFEE CORONET

2 *envelopes unflavored gelatine*
½ *cup strong cold coffee*
1½ *cups strong hot coffee*
1 *cup sugar*
½ *cup broken pecans*
24 *ladyfingers* (*about*)

½ *pkg.* (*3 oz.*) *semi-sweet chocolate pieces, melted*
2 *cups heavy cream*
⅓ *cup rum*
3 *tsp. sugar*
1 *tsp. very freshly ground coffee*

Sprinkle the gelatine on the cold coffee. Then add the hot coffee and sugar, and stir until the sugar and gelatine dissolve. Chill until the consistency of unbeaten egg white.

Meanwhile split 9 or 10 ladyfingers, and dip one end of each half into the melted chocolate.

Whip the chilled gelatine mixture until it is light and fluffy. Whip the cream and fold in with pecans and rum. Spoon into a spring form pan to a depth of about ½ inch. Stand the chocolate-tipped ladyfinger halves upright around the edge of the pan, chocolate tips uppermost.

Add about ⅓ gelatine mixture, and cover with a layer of plain split ladyfingers. Add another third of the gelatine mixture, another layer of plain split ladyfingers, and top with the remaining gelatine mixture. Chill until firm, then remove from the pan.

Just before serving, sprinkle the top with a mixture of 3 teaspoons of sugar and 1 teaspoon of very finely ground coffee. This recipe makes about 12 servings.

One morning my Borden's delivery man left a leaflet on top of a bottle of cream. The leaflet gave directions for making a No-Bake Cheese Cake. It sounded good, and it looked easy, so on the next delivery I ordered some creamed cottage cheese and ½ pint of heavy cream, and proceeded to follow directions. The result was ambrosial. However, I made one slight alteration in Borden's recipe; I substituted kirsch for the vanilla extract.

NO-BAKE CHEESE CAKE

2 *envelopes unflavored gelatine*   1 *tbsp. kirsch*
1 *cup sugar*   2 *tbsp. melted butter*
¼ *tsp. salt*   1 *tbsp. sugar*
2 *egg yolks*   ½ *cup graham cracker crumbs*
1 *cup milk*   ¼ *tsp. powdered cinnamon*
1 *tsp. grated lemon rind*   ¼ *tsp. grated nutmeg*
3 *cups creamed cottage cheese*   2 *egg whites*
1 *tbsp. lemon juice*   1 *cup heavy cream*

In the top of a double boiler mix together the gelatine, 1 cup of sugar, and the salt.

Beat together the egg yolks and the milk and add to the gelatine mixture. Cook over boiling water, stirring constantly until the gelatine is dissolved and the mixture thickens, about 10 minutes. Then remove from the heat, add the grated lemon rind, and cool.

Stir in the cottage cheese, sieved, the lemon juice, and the kirsch. Chill, stirring occasionally, until mixture mounds slightly when dropped from a spoon.

While the mixture is chilling, make the crumb topping as follows: mix the melted butter, 1 tablespoon of sugar, the graham cracker crumbs, the cinnamon, and the nutmeg, and set aside.

Fold the egg whites, stiffly beaten, and heavy cream, whipped, into the chilled gelatine mixture. Turn into an 8-inch spring form pan and sprinkle the top with the crumb mixture. Chill until firm.

One of the classic, and favorite, dishes in France is *Coeur à la Crème* (hearts of cream). It gets its name from the little heart-shaped wicker baskets in which it is made, and the French eat it surrounded by fresh fruits, such as strawberries and raspberries.

The French preparation is somewhat involved. A much easier method is to salt cottage cheese to taste, and, while beating the cottage cheese, heavy cream is added. Little heart-shaped wicker baskets are lined with cheesecloth, and the cottage-cheese-cream mixture is poured in. The "hearts" are placed in the refrigerator overnight, and the whey is allowed to drain off. To serve, the hearts are unmolded on a plate, the cheesecloth removed, and a garnish of fresh strawberries or raspberries placed around the hearts. Or *Coeur à la Crème* can be eaten with jams or jellies.

Most American versions combine cottage cheese, cream cheese, and cream (either sweet or sour), and the mixture is molded and chilled. However, here is a very simple American version, delicately flavored with Crème de Noyau.

COEUR À LA CRÈME

2 *tbsp. unflavored gelatine*	1 *cup whipping cream*
½ *cup cold milk*	¼ *cup granulated sugar, fine*
1 *lb. creamed cottage cheese*	1 *tsp. Crème de Noyau*

Whole unhulled strawberries

Soften the gelatine in the cold milk, and dissolve over hot, not boiling, water. Put the cottage cheese through a fine sieve, or put in an electric blender until smooth. Stir in the dissolved gelatine and mix well.

Whip the cream, and beat in the sugar, 1 tablespoon at a time. Add the Crème de Noyau, and fold into the cheese-gelatine mixture. Fill individual heart-shaped molds, and chill until firm. Serve surrounded by the hulled strawberries.

Crème de Noyau is made by Cusiener, and is distributed in America by Browne Vintners.

Fried Cream (no relation to *Coeur à la Crème!*) is a dessert one often sees on menus, but it is not often understood. And perhaps that is just as well, for I have had some horrible Fried Cream in very good restaurants. But here is a recipe that is very delicious, devised by Louis Crillo, famed delicatessen owner of San Francisco.

FRIED CREAM

1 *quart milk*	3 *tbsp. cornstarch*
Pinch salt	*Water*
Sugar	*Vanilla extract*
⅔ *cup Cream of Wheat*	*Cracker meal*
Butter	*Butter*
4 *eggs*	*Brandy*

To the milk add a pinch of salt, and sugar to taste (I like mine with a little more than a hint of sweetness). Heat to the boiling point, then add the Cream of Wheat, stirring constantly. Cook slowly for 10 minutes. Add a lump of butter the size of a walnut.

To the eggs add the cornstarch, and a small amount of water. Beat these ingredients slightly and combine them with the Cream of Wheat. Stir well, and cook for another 10 minutes. When nearly finished, add vanilla to taste.

Pour into a shallow pan and cool. When thoroughly cool, slice and bread with cracker meal. Fry in butter until brown. To serve, pour brandy over the slices of Fried Cream, and set alight. Or a sweet sauce of your own choosing can be poured over.

Chilled, molded desserts are wonderful in the summertime, and are excellent after a rather hearty dinner. This one is particularly gratifying.

CRÈME D'ORANGE

2 *envelopes unflavored gelatine*
1½ *cups cold water*
½ *cup boiling water*
1 *6-oz. can frozen orange juice concentrate*

½ *cup sugar*
Dash salt
1 *cup heavy cream, whipped*
1 *cup orange marmalade*
3 *tbsp. Cointreau*

Soften the gelatine in ½ cup of cold water, and dissolve in the boiling water. Add the remaining cold water, orange juice concentrate, sugar, and salt. Chill until the mixture begins to thicken, then fold in the whipped cream. Pour into a 1½-quart mold and chill until firm.

Mix the marmalade and the Cointreau thoroughly, cover, and let stand at room temperature for 1 hour or longer.

To serve, unmold the Crème d'Orange, and serve with the sauce. This recipe serves 6.

While the following dessert is not exactly a *crème,* it is a pretty terrific combination.

STRAWBERRY CREAM

1 *quart fresh strawberries*
½ *cup sugar*
2 *oz. kirsch*

2 *oz. Cointreau*
3 *oz. light rum*
1 *pint vanilla ice cream*
1 *pint whipped cream*

Clean and hull the strawberries, and crush them lightly for color. Add to them the sugar, kirsch, Cointreau, and the rum.

Mix the vanilla ice cream and the whipping cream to the consistency of heavy cream. Pour this into the berries, folding in carefully. Let stand for about ½ hour in the refrigerator, and serve.

The famous French-born Sarah Bernhardt, was considered the greatest dramatic actress in America from 1880 to 1911. Talented, beautiful, accomplished at painting and sculpture in addition to the theater, Miss Bernhardt was very much a part of the epicurean society of her day. She often frequented Rector's, along with other notable thespians, such as Lilly Langtry, Wilton Lackaye, and Anna Held, and her favorite dessert, which she had difficulty in resisting, was Charlotte Plombière, which is also known as Ginger Crème. This was the dessert that was served at the Golden Era Dinner of the American Spice Trade Association in New York.

CHARLOTTE PLOMBIÈRE

¾ *cup sugar*
⅛ *tsp. salt*
4 *egg yolks, beaten*
1½ *cups scalded top milk*

1½ *tsp. powdered ginger*
1½ *cups heavy cream*
3 *tsp. kirsch*
Ladyfingers

Combine the sugar, salt, and the beaten egg yolks. Then gradually stir in the scalded milk. Cook, over hot water, until of custard consistency, stirring constantly. Cool, and then stir in the powdered ginger. Turn into a freezing tray, and freeze until partially frozen, about 45 minutes. Turn into a chilled bowl, and beat quickly with a rotary beater until smooth. Fold in the whipped cream and the kirsch. Return to the freezing tray and freeze until partially frozen, stirring 2 or 3 times.

Line the bottom and sides of an 8-inch spring form pan with split ladyfingers. Spoon the partially frozen cream mixture into the pan. If you want to be real fancy, garnish the top with whipped cream put through a pastry tube. Place in the freezer compartment and freeze firm.

When ready to serve, remove the spring form pan. For an old-fashioned touch, the charlotte may be garnished with a red ribbon tied around the outside and a nosegay of flowers tucked into the bow! This recipe serves 8.

It is always a red-letter day on my gastronomical calendar when I have my first fresh peach, usually at breakfast. From then on until the last peach has disappeared from the stores, I revel in peaches—for breakfast, lunch, and dinner. And if I were a between-meals eater, I'd eat 'em then. I don't think there is any other fruit in the world that has quite the delicacy of flavor a peach has.

No one seems to know about the origin of the peach. Pliny, writing in the first century, said: "As touching peaches in general, the very name in Latine whereby they are called Persica, doth evidently show that they were brought out of Persia first." Yet the peach has long been cultivated in China, and was written about some two thousand years before its introduction to the Roman world.

Fresh peaches are the basis for a great many desserts. One of the greatest desserts is Peach Melba, which was created by Escoffier in honor of the celebrated diva, Madame Melba, at the Ritz-Carlton Hotel in London. He poached peeled, fresh peach halves in a vanilla-flavored sugar syrup for 3 minutes. Then he lifted them out with a perforated skimmer and laid each half on a bed of vanilla ice cream, and covered the peach halves with a raspberry purée.

I have worked out a variation of Peach Melba which I like much better than the original.

PEACH MELBA À LA WOOD

Fresh peach halves   *Fresh raspberries*
Powdered sugar   *Powdered sugar*
Vanilla ice cream   *Framboise*

Sprinkle fresh peach halves with powdered sugar, and allow to stand for about 30 minutes. Then, after draining off the juice, place the peach half on a bed of vanilla ice cream, and cover the peach with a raspberry purée, made by mashing fresh raspberries, rubbing them through a sieve, then adding powdered sugar to taste, and enough Framboise (a high-proof raspberry cordial) to moisten the raspberry purée. If you can't get Framboise, use kirsch.

Back in 1949 I met Oleg Tupine, who was a *premier danseur* with the Ballet Russe de Monte Carlo. Monsieur Tupine gave me an interesting recipe for Bulgarian Wild Duck, and also a delicious dessert recipe for peaches.

POACHED PEACHES OVER ICE CREAM

Sliced peaches	*Cointreau*
Raspberry jam	*Ice cream*

Combine raspberry jam and Cointreau, and heat in a saucepan. When hot, poach sliced fresh peaches in the sauce for about 5 minutes. Remove from the fire, cool, and serve over individual portions of ice cream.

Another luscious peach and ice-cream dessert has a topping of macaroons, marshmallows, and sherry wine.

PEACHES WITH MACAROON SAUCE

6 *almond macaroons*	½ *cup whipping cream*
8 *marshmallows*	*Fresh peach halves*
½ *cup medium dry sherry*	*Vanilla ice cream*

Crumble the macaroons into a bowl, then add the marshmallows, cut into small pieces. Stir in the dry sherry and the whipping cream. Chill this mixture several hours, or overnight.

When ready to serve, beat the macaroon-marshmallow mixture in an electric blender until it is smooth. Place fresh peach halves, cut side up, in a sherbet glass. Fill each cavity with a scoop of vanilla ice cream, and spoon the macaroon sauce over all. This will serve 6.

When fresh peaches are out of season, you can make a notable peach dessert with canned cling peaches.

PEACHES IN PINEAPPLE-BURGUNDY SAUCE

1 #2½ *can cling peach halves*	¾ *cup sugar*
¾ *cup peach syrup*	1 9-*oz. can crushed pineapple*
¾ *cup Burgundy wine*	2 3-*oz. pkgs. cream cheese*
3 *tbsp. peach brandy*	

Drain the can of peach halves, reserving the syrup. In a saucepan combine the ¾ cup of peach syrup with the Burgundy and the sugar. Bring to a boil, stirring until the sugar is dissolved. Then add the peach halves, and simmer, uncovered, for about 10 minutes. Then remove the peaches to a serving bowl.

Add the undrained crushed pineapple to the syrup, and boil rapidly until reduced about one half. Pour this mixture over the peaches, and chill.

Whip the cream cheese to a fluff with about 3 tablespoons of peach brandy, and serve as a topping. This recipe serves 5 to 6.

A few years ago in New York, during the Food Editors' Conference, the Borden Company gave a most delightful luncheon. Offhand, I don't recall the menu, but I shall never forget the dessert. It was called *Ananas d'Orientale Mignardise,* and it was the most unusual and luscious dessert I have ever tasted, before or since.

The name is French, and freely translated means pineapple cut in small pieces Oriental style. But that gives only a small inkling of the preparation, taste, and serving. Actually, a small pineapple had been hollowed out, the meat cut in small pieces and mixed with strawberries, ice cream, and kirsch, the resulting mixture was returned to the pineapple shell, and the whole thing was placed in a freezer, from which it was served. Here is the method of preparation.

ANANAS D'ORIENTALE MIGNARDISE
(Pineapple Oriental Style)

1 *small pineapple*	*Vanilla ice cream*
Frozen strawberries	2 *oz. kirsch*

Cut off the top of a sun-ripened pineapple, about 1½ inches from the top. Scoop out the meat, using a curved grapefruit knife that is sharp.

Discard the tough and pithy meat, and cut the rest into small cubes. Add to the pineapple cubes the frozen strawberries which have been slightly melted, soft vanilla ice cream, and the kirsch (rum can be used, or even champagne). Place this mixture back in the pineapple shell, put the top back on or not, as you wish, and place the stuffed pineapple in the freezer. When it is frozen, serve, again with the top on or off. This serves one person.

The amount of frozen strawberries and ice cream to be used depends upon the size of the pineapple, and the amount of edible pineapple meat removed. The sum total of pineapple meat, frozen strawberries, and ice cream should just fill the pineapple cavity.

Near Vacaville, California, on Route #40 between San Francisco and Sacramento, there is one of the most charming restaurants imaginable, the Nut Tree. It has a fascinating history, and the Powers family, who own and run the restaurant today, are descendants of one Joseph Allison, who settled on the location over a hundred years ago. The idea of catering to passing travelers started on July 4, 1921, when Mrs. Powers, the granddaughter of Joseph Allison, sat under the huge nut tree in a rocker behind a six-foot prune tray loaded with figs, which were offered for sale.

Today the Nut Tree Restaurant is a huge, rambling place where the finest of Western foods are served in the delightful atmospheres of the dining rooms and patios. One of the unique features of the Nut Tree is their little individual loaves of marvelous bread. When you order a sandwich, the filling is served to you along with one of these little loaves, and you slice it on a miniature breadboard for your sandwich.

One of the dessert delicacies of the Nut Tree is their freshly sliced pineapple with what they call a marshmallow dressing.

PINEAPPLE À LA NUT TREE

Slices fresh pineapple	*2 egg whites*
1 cup sugar	*Vanilla to taste*
½ cup hot water	*⅓ cup mayonnaise*
5 oz. light Karo syrup	*Orange rind grated*

First, make the dressing. Combine the Karo syrup, sugar, and hot water, and cook until the mixture registers 248 degrees, or will form a thread. Beat the egg whites stiff, then add the hot sugar syrup slowly to eggs while continuing to beat. Flavor with the vanilla to taste. When cool, add the mayonnaise and orange rind, blending well.

To serve, spread the dressing over chilled slices, or fingers, of fresh peeled pineapple.

There is nothing more spectacular and fascinating at the dinner table than food that is brought in flaming, or flambéed, at the table. The eerie dancing of blue flames above a dish (particularly if the room is darkened, or the table is illuminated only with candles) seems to sharpen one's anticipation of deliciousness, for some unknown reason. And, of course, brandy or rum or kirsch (the three best flaming agents) do contribute their own inimitable flavors.

This culinary trick of blazing food is very simple to perform. Before being brought to the table, a little warm brandy (or rum or kirsch) is poured over the prepared dish, and is ignited with a match. The classical example is the English plum pudding, which I imagine was the great-granddaddy of all flaming desserts. However, when a dish is prepared with a sauce, it is best to pour the warm brandy in a ladle, or large spoon, ignite it, and when it is burning nicely, pour it over the top of the dish.

Cherries Jubilee is a classic flambéed dish, consisting of flambéed Bing cherries, which have been marinated in cordials, ladled over ice cream. Another exciting dish is Baked Bing Cherries Flambéed.

BAKED BING CHERRIES FLAMBÉED

2 *cans pitted Bing cherries*	1 *grated lemon rind*
1 *tbsp. fresh lime juice*	1 *glass black currant jelly*
1 *grated orange rind*	*Slivered almonds*
	4 *oz. kirsch*

Drain the Bing cherries thoroughly and place in a glass casserole. Pour over them the fresh lime juice, and sprinkle over them the grated orange and lemon rind. Cover with the contents of a glass jar of black currant jelly, and sprinkle slivered almonds liberally over the dish. Bake in a 375-degree oven for 10 to 15 minutes.

On serving, pour the warmed kirsch over the dish, ignite, and serve, flaming.

A banana may be just a banana when it is eaten "as is." But dressed up in a tender batter and served with an intriguing sauce, it becomes a dessert to delight epicures.

The following recipe comes from Ellen Saltonstall, of the Pan American Coffee Bureau. She asserts that these banana fritters are not just plain-Jane, and she is quite right. This superlative recipe has two special features. One is that the batter retains its crispness for a reasonable time after the fritters are done, which is a virtue when you are making them for company. The other is the coffee rum sauce that not only brings out the flavor of these featherylight morsels, but imparts an ambrosial accent of its own

BANANA FRITTERS WITH COFFEE RUM SAUCE

1 *cup sifted enriched flour*	1 *egg, well beaten*
2 *tsp. baking powder*	⅓ *cup milk*
1¼ *tsp. salt*	2 *tsp. melted shortening*
¼ *cup sugar*	2-3 *firm bananas*

Flour

Coffee Rum Sauce

1 *cup sugar*	3 *tbsp. cold coffee*
1½ *cups strong coffee*	2 *tbsp. butter*
2 *tbsp. cornstarch*	2 *tbsp. rum*

Mix and sift the flour, baking powder, salt, and sugar. Combine the egg, milk, and melted shortening, and then add to the dry ingredients and mix until smooth. (This is a very stiff batter, *do not thin it down.* It will stay crisp after frying for 15 to 20 minutes.)

Cut each banana crosswise into 3 or 4 even pieces, roll in flour, and coat with the fritter batter. Fry in shallow fat (2 inches deep), 375 degrees, about 5 minutes, or until well browned, turning often to brown evenly. Drain on a rack. This yields 8 to 12 fritters.

For the coffee rum sauce, melt the sugar slowly in a heavy skillet, stirring often. Add the coffee slowly, stirring constantly. Blend the cornstarch and cold coffee, and then stir into coffee-sugar mixture. Continue to cook and stir until the sauce boils and thickens. Remove from the heat and add the butter and rum, stirring until the butter melts. This makes about 2 cups of sauce.

Serve the fritters hot with the coffee rum sauce. The best accompaniment with this is fresh, fragrant coffee. Natch!

Another mighty good dessert is baked bananas topped with coconut cream. Of course, bananas, coconut, and rum go together like a "horse and carriage," or "love and marriage," if I may borrow from a popular song hit.

BAKED BANANAS WITH COCONUT CREAM

6 *firm bananas*	1 *cup heavy cream*
Melted butter	2 *tbsp. sugar*
Brown sugar	1 *cup shredded coconut*
Rum	½ *tsp. kirsch*

Peel the bananas and arrange in a greased, shallow baking dish; brush with melted butter, sprinkle generously with brown sugar, and drizzle a light rum over. Bake in a 375-degree oven for 15 to 20 minutes, or until the bananas are tender.

For the coconut cream, whip the heavy cream, sweeten with the sugar, and fold in the shredded coconut, and the kirsch. Serve this with the warm bananas. It will serve 6 lightly.

In spite of the fact that a great many people consider baked apples and cream a very savory breakfast dish or dessert, I have never cared for it. Mrs. Wood is very fond of apples, either eaten as is, or baked. So, at her request, I devised a baked apple dish that even made me smack my lips. Here it is.

STUFFED BAKED APPLES

6 *tart apples*	1 *cup chopped mixed nuts*
½ *cup sugar*	*(peanuts, almonds, and*
¼ *cup soft butter*	*cashews)*
1 *tsp. powdered cinnamon*	½ *cup sweet sherry*
1 *oz. brandy*	1 *pint sour cream*
	Powdered sugar
	Applejack

First you core the tart apples, and cut a little off the top of each apple.

Cream together the sugar with the soft butter, the powdered cinnamon, brandy, and the finely chopped mixed nuts (peanuts, almonds, and cashews). When well blended fill the centers of the apples with this mixture. Place the filled apples in a baking dish, and pour over the sweet (cream) sherry around the apples. Cover, and bake in a 400-degree oven for about 25 minutes, or until the apples are tender, basting with the sherry, and adding more sherry if necessary.

While the apples are baking, make a sauce of commercial sour cream flavored to taste with powdered sugar and applejack. The sauce should not be too thick. To serve, pour the sauce over the apples.

A long time ago I learned a trick from the Italians on serving fresh fruit for dessert to accompany a good lusty cheese. Instead of serving Chianti wine in wineglasses, serve it in water or highball glasses. (This is heresy, I know, and will probably call down on my head maledictions from those who adhere strictly to protocol in the serving of wines.)

When the entree is served, pass slices of peeled pears and apples. Stuff your glass with them, and then pour in the Chianti. As you drink your wine and the glass empties, fill it up with more wine, leaving the fruit in the glass. Then, as a dessert, eat the wine-soaked fruit from your glass, and nibble on some Gorgonzola, Provolone, or Strachino de Milano cheese. Follow this with caffè espresso, and a pony of Galliano or Strega.

According to my taste, the noblest thing about apples is rich, flaky pie crust!

Of course, pie is one of my favorite desserts. I would be hard put to name my favorite pie. Mince pie, lime pie, pecan pie, berry pies, apple pie. . . . I just couldn't slight one for the other. But I think I can eat apple pie oftener than any other.

You have no doubt heard or seen the expression, "He (or it) is as American as apple pie." And while a great many of us believe that apple pie is indigenous to America, it is really an English dish, a species of tart. I recall an article entitled, "Do's and Don'ts for Doughboys," by H. W. Seaman in the English Manchester *Sunday Chronicle,* in which he said, "What you call an apple pie we should have to call an apple tart with a lid on it."

I believe I am safe in saying that apple pie is the favorite dessert of the majority of Americans. And certainly there is no place in the world where apple pie is made any better than it is in the United States. There are variations on the theme: apple pandowdy, apple pie carrousel, apple pie made with applesauce, and so on, but just plain old apple pie, to my way of thinking, can't be beat. And, although I may be a little prejudiced, I think my wife makes about the best apple pie that I have ever eaten.

Some time ago we concocted a plain old apple pie, but I added a touch to her apple pie recipe that raised it one notch to the best apple pie I will *ever* eat. Every time I tell anyone about it, the listener drools and demands (not requests) the recipe. I've chronicled it a couple of times in my syndicated newspaper column, "For Men Only!" and I always receive letters from readers who have tried it, praising it to the skies. Well, here is the recipe.

APPLEJACK APPLE PIE

Make your favorite pie crust, and put the bottom layer into an 8- or 9-inch pie pan or ovenproof pie plate. Meantime, have sliced fairly thin 5 cooking apples. Put a layer of sliced apples over the bottom crust, sprinkle over 3 tablespoons of sugar, a liberal sprinkling of ground cinnamon, and a liberal sprinkling of fresh lime juice.

Now comes the secret—sprinkle over the layer of apples ½ ounce of applejack, and liberally dot the whole with small pieces of butter. Then add another layer of apples, repeating the sprinklings of sugar, cinnamon, applejack, and butter, but omitting the lime juice. Then add another layer of apple slices, repeating with the sprinklings of sugar, cinnamon, applejack, lime juice, and butter. Put the top crust on, and bake in a 400-degree oven until the pie starts to cook. Then lower the temperature to 350-degrees, and continue to bake until the apples are tender, and the crust is brown (about 1 hour).

Applejack is another name for apple brandy, which the French call Calvados. It is one of the oldest distilled liquors known to mankind, and is strictly a natural liquor, with no other ingredient added —the distillation of the fermented juice of apples. So, naturally, it adds a piquancy to any apple dish.

There are some people who would no more think of eating apple pie without cheese than they would of eating eggs without salt. So here is an applejack apple pie with the cheese built right in.

APPLE CHEESE PIE

Pastry for 2-crust pie
¾ cup sugar
2 tbsp. flour
⅛ tsp. salt
⅔ cup grated sharp Cheddar
    cheese

¼ tsp. powdered cinnamon
2 tsp. grated orange rind
5 cups sliced apples
Lime juice, fresh
Sugar
Applejack

3 tbsp. heavy cream

First, make your own favorite pie crust for a two-crust pie. Roll one half the pastry to fit a 9-inch pie pan, and flute the edges.

Combine the sugar, flour, salt, grated sharp Cheddar cheese, cinnamon (powdered), and grated orange rind. Mix together well, and sprinkle half of this mixture over the bottom of the unbaked pie crust. Then add about 5 cups of peeled, cored, and sliced apples, sprinkling each layer of apples with a little sugar, lime juice, and applejack. Then cover the apple slices with the remaining half of the cheese and sugar mixture, and drizzle over the top about 3 tablespoons of heavy cream.

Roll out the other half of the pastry, and cut into ½-inch strips. You can either make a latticework crust, or a spiral-strip crust. For the latter roll the pastry into a long piece, and cut lengthwise strips about ½- to ¾-inch wide. Beginning at the center of the pie plate, place one end of a strip on top of the filling, and start a spiral. Attach strips by moistening the ends with cold water and pinching together.

Bake in a 425-degree oven for about 45 minutes, or until the apples are tender. This recipe makes a 9-inch pie, but don't try to serve more than 6.

Apple pandowdy is a celebrated Maine dish. It is a sort of cross between an apple pudding and a deep-dish apple pie. In fact, some veteran State-of-Mainers call it apple pudding. There is also a variation on the preparation and the serving of it. One school of thought believes that after the apples are tender and the crust is brown, the pandowdy should be taken from the oven, the crust and the apples should be chopped together thoroughly, and then put back in the oven. Another version is to bake the apples and other ingredients, and then put on a baking powder biscuit crust, and bake for 15 minutes more. The latter is served with hard sauce, or cream; the chopped method calls for butter, or rich cream, or both. So, to add to the confusion, I'm adding applejack! The following recipe is for the chopped version.

APPLE PANDOWDY

Pastry for 2-crust pie   ½ tsp. salt
8 apples, peeled and cored   ½ cup molasses
½ cup sugar   ¼ cup applejack
¼ tsp. ground cinnamon   2 oz. butter
¼ tsp. grated nutmeg   Rich cream
                    Butter

Line a deep pan with pie crust. Peel, core, and slice the apples, and distribute them evenly over the pie crust. Mix together the sugar, ground cinnamon, nutmeg, and salt. Cover the apples with this mixture, then add the molasses and applejack. Dot the top with the butter. Put pie crust on top, crimp the edges, and bake in a 400-degree oven for 45 minutes. When the apples are tender and crust lightly browned, remove from oven, chop crust and apples thoroughly together, and add more applejack and molasses if dry, and put back into a 325-degree oven for about an hour. Serve piping hot, accompanied by plenty of butter and rich cream.

There are a number of recipes for Lime Pie, but of all I have tried, I like the one which Mrs. Wood makes to perfection—her Florida Lime Pie, which is made with condensed milk, fresh lime juice, and eggs, and topped with sweetened whipped cream flavored with rum and cinnamon. The recipe is in my *With a Jug of Wine*.

Although the following recipe is called a lime pie, it isn't exactly. It doesn't call for pie crust, and it is a frozen dessert. But it is a refreshingly frosty dessert on a hot day or evening, and unbelievably delicious.

FROZEN LIME PIE

6 *egg yolks*
1 *cup sugar*
Grated rind of 2 *limes*
Juice of 3 *limes*
6 *beaten egg whites*

2 *cups heavy cream*
2 *tbsp. rum*
1½ *cups chocolate wafer*
  crumbs

Combine in the top of a double boiler the egg yolks, sugar, the grated rind of the limes, and the lime juice. Over hot water in the bottom of the double boiler cook the mixture, stirring constantly, until it is thickened slightly. Then set it aside to cool. When cool, fold in the stiffly beaten egg whites, then the cream, which has been whipped after the rum has been added to it.

Crumb the chocolate wafers until you have 1½ cups. Sprinkle half of the crumbs into 2 ice-cube trays (with dividers removed), then pour the lime mixture into the trays, dividing it equally between the 2 trays. Top the lime mixture with the remaining chocolate wafer crumbs (again divided equally among the 2 trays) and put the trays into the freezing unit. To serve, slice from the freezing trays and serve the slices on very cold plates.

Incidentally, this recipe will serve 10 to 12, but what remains makes a wonderful midafternoon snack with tall glasses of iced coffee.

I am all for simplicity in desserts as far as possible, desserts that can be made ahead of time. Just recently I saw an advertisement of the Carnation Company in one of the national magazines for a no-bake, no-cook orange pie. And it was as good as it was claimed. However, the Old Experimenter had to fiddle around, with the result that a slight change added an intriguing new flavor. Instead of using 1 cup of hot orange juice, as the original recipe called for, I changed it to ¾ cup of hot orange juice and ¼ cup of warmed Cointreau. I hope the Carnation Company will forgive me.

CARNATION ORANGE PIE

1 3-oz. pkg. orange gelatine
¼ cup sugar
¾ cup hot orange juice
¼ cup warmed Cointreau
1 tsp. grated orange rind
1 cup undiluted Carnation
    milk

2 tbsp. lemon juice
1½ cups graham cracker
    crumbs
¼ cup melted butter
2 tbsp. sugar

Dissolve the gelatine and ¼ cup of sugar in the hot orange juice and warmed Cointreau, and then add the grated orange rind. Chill until thickened (about 20 to 30 minutes). Chill the contents of the can of Carnation evaporated milk in a refrigerator tray until soft crystals form (about 15 to 20 minutes).

Whip the chilled Carnation until stiff (1 minute). Add the lemon juice, and whip *very* stiff (2 minutes). Then fold the whipped Carnation into the chilled gelatin. Pour into the crust, and chill until firm (about 1 to 2 hours).

For the 9-inch graham cracker crust, mix the graham cracker crumbs with the melted butter and 2 tablespoons of sugar. Line sides and bottom of the pie plate, and let set.

Those enterprising coffee people came up with what to me was a new wrinkle in pie crusts a couple of years ago. I particulary liked it, because I am no pie crust maker. When it comes to making pie crusts, my wife is a past master, and whenever we make a pie, I leave the crust entirely up to her. I have never eaten better pie crust than she turns out, nor any even as good. But graham cracker crusts, and the like, I can do. The following one is easy, and the whole pie is simply delicious, and deliciously simple.

ALMOND CREAM PIE WITH COFFEE COCONUT SHELL

1 *pkg. vanilla pudding mix*
½ *cup chopped toasted almonds*
½ *tsp. almond extract*

1 *moist-pack can shredded coconut*
Strong hot coffee
2 *tbsp. butter*

To make the crust, empty the can of moist-pack shredded coconut into a bowl, and add enough strong hot coffee to barely cover the shredded coconut. Let stand for 5 minutes, then drain. Pat the coconut dry between layers of absorbent paper toweling. Next rub the butter on the sides and bottom of a 9-inch pie pan, and press the coconut on the butter, distributing it evenly. Bake in a 350-degree oven for 10 minutes, then cool.

To make the filling, prepare the pudding mix as directed on the package. Then stir in the almonds, and add the almond extract. Cool slightly, stirring once or twice. Then pour into the coffee coconut shell, and chill well before serving.

Each year I am advised by the publicists that the latter part of October is National Honey Week. However, if I may make with a funny, every week is honey week with me, because I have my own Bee (i.e., my wife, Beatrice).

An extended dissertation could be written about honey, which is one of the oldest sweets known to mankind. The Book of Joshua, in the Old Testament, describes the ideal land as one of "milk and honey," and both the Greeks and the Romans considered honey as food fit for the gods. There are references to honey as a food in Aspicius, who wrote a classic cookbook, and in the *Diepnosophists* of Athenaeus, an early Greek book on wining and dining.

In urban communities honey is thought of as a sweet substance that is delicious poured over waffles or hot biscuits. But honey can be used in many ways in the preparation of delectable dishes, particularly desserts.

Down in the Deep South they make a pie of honey and nuts, and it really is something to write North about.

SOUTHERN HONEY AND NUT PIE

3 *tbsp. flour*	1 *cup milk*
½ *tsp. salt*	1 *cup chopped pecans*
¾ *cup honey*	2 *lightly beaten eggs*
¼ *cup orange curaçao*	1 *tbsp. melted butter*

Cooked pastry shells

Mix the flour, salt, honey, and orange curaçao, then add to this the milk and coarsely chopped pecans. Cook this in a double boiler until it is thick. Cool slightly, and add the lightly beaten eggs and the melted butter. Return the mixture to the double boiler and cook about 5 minutes, or until the egg is well blended and the mixture is not lumpy. Then pour into baked pastry shells, and bake in the oven long enough to reheat the pastry.

A variation of this honey pie is to put the filling into a 9-inch prebaked pie shell, and top with an apricot meringue. To make the apricot meringue, use 2 egg whites and ¼ cup of sugar, and 2 tablespoons of apricot brandy. Place in a moderate (350 degrees) oven to set, and delicately color the meringue.

When Aladdin wanted something special, he just rubbed his magic lamp and presto—it appeared! But you don't need a magic lamp to enjoy this authentic Near East treat, called Arabian Delight. It combines the subtle flavors of honey and almonds, and it will make a conversation piece for any dinner party. Of course, if you want to go all out, you will serve Turkish coffee with it.

ARABIAN DELIGHT

1¾ *cups boiling water*	½ *cup canned chopped*
¼ *cup Crème de Noyau*	*roasted almonds*
Juice 2 *lemons*	1 *cup honey*
16 *Zwieback*	*Frozen whipped cream*

Combine the boiling water, and lemon juice, and pour over the Zwieback. Let stand until the Zwieback is puffed and softened, and then drain off the liquid.

Sprinkle half of the almonds in the bottom of an 8-inch pie pan. Add half of the Zwieback and top with half the honey and half the Crème de Noyau. Add the remaining Zwieback, and top with the remaining honey, almonds and Crème de Noyau. Bake in a 325-degree oven for 45 minutes. Cool slightly, and serve warm with frozen whipped cream. This will serve 6 to 8.

I can't think of a dessert that is more satisfying, or capable of more variations, than ice cream. It was wonderful, and well worth the trouble, in those not too distant days when a lot of energy and time went into making homemade ice cream (remember the tragedy when some of the rock salt seeped into the container as you were cranking it?).

Today the home ice-cream freezer is run by electricity, and you can have any flavor, or combination of flavors, you desire by the flick of a switch. You can now store gallons of your favorite ice cream (homemade or boughten) in your deep freeze, and it will keep for weeks.

There are certain festive occasions when you want your dinner to reach its climax with an elaborate dessert—in a blaze of glory, if I may coin a phrase! In such an event, there is nothing that can top a Baked Alaska. It is a dessert that is always served with great pride and some important gestures in the finest hotels, restaurants, and on luxury liners.

One rarely encounters Baked Alaska in private homes, unless the home boasts of an expert staff of servants or cooks. People who have never had it sometimes refuse to believe that ice cream can be baked in the oven, and come out firm. But the ice cream is well insulated with sponge cake under it, and covered by a meringue. As a matter of fact, it is not at all difficult to prepare and serve at home, and it is much more fun than card tricks. You can get your sponge cake at your good neighborhood bakery, and your ice cream from your drugstore or the frozen food department of your favorite grocery store. All that you have to do is to make a meringue, assemble the various ingredients, pop it into an oven, and serve.

BAKED ALASKA

1 *quart brick ice cream*	*Pinch salt*
Sponge cake, 1 *inch thick*	½ *cup Madeira wine*
4 *to* 5 *egg whites*	*Finely chopped cashew nuts*
½ *cup powdered sugar*	4 *empty eggshell halves*
1 *tsp. orange curaçao*	*Warm brandy*

First get a hard-frozen brick of ice cream in any flavor you want. The most popular are tutti-frutti, vanilla, and strawberry. Tell your purveyor that you're going to make Baked Alaska, and you want it frozen especially hard, and packed in dry ice, so that it will remain hard-cold until you use it. Next you'll want a layer of sponge cake about 1 inch thick (or maybe 2 layers). This will be the base on which you'll put your ice-cream brick, and it should be an oblong piece that will project an inch all the way around the brick of ice cream. If 1 slice won't do, use 2, or trim to fit. You will also need a meat plank, or a small breadboard, and a sheet of heavy white paper.

Make the meringue, using 4 or 5 egg whites, about ½ cup of powdered sugar, 1 teaspoon of orange curaçao, or Cointreau, and a pinch of salt. Beat the egg whites in a chilled bowl until they are stiff enough to form peaks. Continue beating and add slowly the powdered sugar and the teaspoon of the curaçao or Cointreau. Set aside for a moment.

Now for the assembly job. Place the sheet of heavy white paper, trimmed to fit, over the plank or breadboard. On top of the paper place the platform of sponge cake. Sprinkle the sponge cake with Madeira wine, about ½ cup (the cake should not be soaked, merely moistened). On top of the cake place the brick of ice cream. Now, working fast, spread the meringue over the ice cream and cake, covering every bit of the ice cream and cake with at least a ½-inch layer of meringue, using a spatula. Sprinkle about a tablespoon of finely chopped cashew nuts over the meringue, and set in the top of the meringue 4 perfect eggshell halves. Now slide your masterpiece into a 450-degree oven (preheat the oven so that it is 450 degrees when you put the Alaska in) and let it brown lightly. It will take only a few minutes, and the meringue browns pretty fast. If you want to peek at the end of about 3 or 4 minutes, do so, but don't open the oven door wide, because a chill at the critical moment can collapse the meringue.

When browned, take the Alaska out of the oven, slide it onto a serving dish, fill the egg halves with warm brandy, set aflame, and serve quickly. And there you are!

I suppose ice cream and cake is one of the most frequently served desserts in the American home, particularly where there are children. However, if there should be some cake left over, and some ice cream, an ice-cream sandwich is a very happy and tasty variation. If you're going to buy ice cream to make it, the best bet is pistachio ice cream.

ICE CREAM SANDWICH

1 *cup brown sugar*   ¼ *cup milk*
½ *cup butter*   1 *oz. Grand Marnier*
1 *egg, beaten*   *Slices cake*
         Pistachio ice cream

Make the sauce first, melt the cup of brown sugar (firmly packed) and the butter together in the top of a double boiler. Beat the egg and the milk together until well blended, and stir gradually into the sugar and butter mixture. Cook, over boiling water, stirring frequently, for 10 minutes. Then add the Grand Marnier slowly, being careful that the mixture doesn't curdle. This makes about 1½ cups of sauce.

For each serving, put 2 thin slices of angelfood, sponge, or chiffon cake together with a layer of pistachio (or other) ice cream between. Pour the warm sauce over each serving.

A very grand and swanky dessert, yet simple to prepare, is a Champagne Parfait.

CHAMPAGNE PARFAIT

Fill tall parfait glasses ⅞ full with pineapple or lemon sherbet or ice. With a glass stirring stick, about ¼ inch in diameter, drill a hole down the center of the firmly packed ice. Fill this hole with green crème de menthe. Then fill the glass with a good domestic champagne, and serve at once.

A somewhat similar dessert, yet simpler, is to put a ball of vanilla ice cream in a sherbet glass, punch holes on the top of the ice cream, and pour Grand Marnier over, seeing that the Grand Marnier penetrates the holes in the ice cream.

A wonderful topping for fresh Bing cherries or any of the fresh berries in season is to allow a quart of vanilla ice cream to soften. Add 3 ounces of rum, and stir briskly with a fork.

Here are a trio of ice-cream desserts that are different, and have tantalizing flavors.

(1) Sprinkle drip grind coffee over chocolate ice cream and then spoon brandy over it.

(2) Sprinkle grated semi-sweet chocolate over vanilla ice cream and then spoon crème de cacao over it.

(3) Top lemon or vanilla ice cream with orange marmalade, then spoon Cointreau over it.

In the above three desserts, serve the ice cream in sherbet glasses or dessert dishes, and pass the topping and liqueurs separately.

Okay, take it on from there, adventurers!

INDEX

Cheese *(Continued)*
and Tongue, en Casserole, 173
and Vegetable Chowder, 60
Apple-Cheese Pie, 379-80
Bismarck "New Look," 356-57
Cake, No Bake, 366-67
Connoisseur's Dessert Tray, 362
Crock, Floyd Buick, 355-56
Danish Soufflé, 361
Delices d'Emmenthal (Cheese Croquettes), 41
Dreams, 357
English Monkey, 358
French Fried Camembert, 357
Individual Pizzas, 20-21
Liptoi, 354-55
Mozzarella in Carroza, 357
Mushroom Rabbit, 358-59
Omelet Supreme, 350-51
Pizza, 359-60
Quiche Lorraine, 39-40
Cherries
Baked Bing, Flambéed, 374-75
Frozen Cherry Rice Delight, 314-15
Chicken, 207-250
à l'Almonde, 242-43
à la Ménagère, 212-13
à la Riviera, 214-15
à l'Estragon, 213-14
Arroz à la Valenciana, 216-17
Baked, Czardas, 211
Baked Fried, Holland Style, 224-25
Baltic Stew, 234-35
Barbecued, 227-29
Bardelli's Chicken Jerusalem, 221-22
Bombay Curry in a Chafing Dish, 239-40
Bott Boi, 246-47
Breast of, Kiev, 231-32
Breast of, Smitane, 230-31
Broiled, Vermouth, 226
Celeste, 218
Charante, 218-19
Charcoal Broiled, 226-27
Chinese Almond with Rice, 243-44
Currie, à la Mori, 240-41
Curry, 237-39
Divan, 241-42
Fried, Baked in Cream, 215-16
Fritos Chicken Patties, 244-45
Hash Parmentier, 245-46
Legs, à la Drennan, 220-21
Liver Omelet, 351
Livers, Curried, 249-50
Livers, in Sour Cream, 248
Livers, Sauce Madeira, 248-49
Livers, Sauté à la Marsalla, 250

Chicken *(Continued)*
Montparnasse, 219
Old Fashioned Chicken Pie, 236-37
Orleanne, 209
Pollo al Vino, 229-30
Salad, Curried, 329
Sans Souci, 223
Sauté Sec, 225
Scalloped, Casserole, 232-34
Sherried, in a Casserole, 210
Supreme, 223-24
Trafalgar, 244
Tuna Casserole, 74
Vichyssoise, 222
With Rice, 235-36
Chilean Soup à la Mandel, 53
Chili Sauce, Carlyle Stevens', 339-40
Chilled Black Bean Soup, 62
Chinese Dishes
Butterfly Steak, Hong Kong Style, 108
Cantonese Egg Rolls, 25-27
Cantonese Egg Rolls, dough, 27-28
Chicken Almond with Rice, 243-44
Chinese Cold Roast Pork, 25
Cookery, 87
Fried Rice, 313
Fried Rice with Ham, 313-14
Kan's Asparagus Beef, 132-33
Kan's Sweet and Sour Pungent Pork, 158-59
Lobster Cantonese, 86-87
Soup, 62
Steamed Lobster with Pork, 88
Tomatoes and Green Peppers with Pork, 159
Chipped Beef in Cream à la Corcoran, 131
Chocolate Ice Box Cake, 364-65
Chops
Cooking, 139-40
Lamb, en Casserole with Red Wine, 140
Lamb, Strogonoff, 141
Lamb, Grilled, with Mayonnaise, 141-42
Pork, and Peanut Butter, 150-51
Pork, Beatrice, 149
Pork, Hawaiian Braised, 150
Pork, Vegetable Casserole with Rice, 151-52
Pork, with Anise, 149
Veal, Baked in Onion Sauce, 170
Veal, Baked in White Wine, 169-70
Choucroute Garni (Sauerkraut), 285-86
Chowder, 49